James Nogalski
Redactional Processes in the Book of the Twelve

Beihefte zur Zeitschrift für die alttestamentliche Wissenschaft

Herausgegeben von
Otto Kaiser

Band 218

Walter de Gruyter · Berlin · New York
1993

James Nogalski

Redactional Processes in the Book of the Twelve

Walter de Gruyter · Berlin · New York
1993

∞ Printed on acid-free paper which falls
within the guidelines of the ANSI to ensure
permanence and durability

Library of Congress Cataloging-in-Publication Data

Nogalski, James.
   Redactional processes in the Book of the Twelve / James Nogalski.
      p.   cm. — (Beihefte zur Zeitschrift für die alttestamentliche
Wissenschaft, ISSN 0934-2575 ; Bd. 218)
   Revision of part of thesis (Th. D.) — Universität Zurich.
   Includes bibliographical references and index.
   ISBN 3-11-013767-4 (alk. paper)
   1. Bible. O.T. Minor Prophets—Criticism, Redaction. I. Title.
II. Series: Beihefte zur Zeitschrift für die alttestamentliche
Wissenschaft ; Bd. 218.
BS410.Z5   vol. 218
[BS1560]
224′.9066 — dc20
                                          93-37633
                                           CIP

Die Deutsche Bibliothek — Cataloging in Publication Data

Nogalski, James:
Redactional processes in the Book of the Twelve / James
Nogalski. — Berlin ; New York : de Gruyter, 1993
   (Beihefte zur Zeitschrift für die alttestamentliche Wissenschaft ; Bd.
218)
   Zugl.: Zürich, Univ., Diss., 1991 zusammen mit 1 anderem Werk des
Verf.
   ISBN 3-11-013767-4
NE: Zeitschrift für die alttestamentliche Wissenschaft / Beihefte

ISSN 0934-2575

Printed in Germany
Printing: Werner Hildebrand, Berlin
Binding: Lüderitz & Bauer-GmbH, Berlin

Preface

The following study evaluates the implications of catchwords as a significant factor for understanding the development, literary movement, and theological intentions of the Book of the Twelve. For reasons of space, this volume appears independently, but it is integrally related to a previous work in this series, *Literary Precursors to the Book of the Twelve*. This previous study documented the historical evidence for treating the Book of the Twelve as a single corpus, and it discussed scholarly models which attempted to explain that unity. It challenged long-standing scholarly assumptions that the Book of the Twelve arose only via the incorporation of the final forms of the individual writings. As evidence, it demonstrated that these writings consistently end with a series of words (and phrases) which reappear at the beginning of the next writing. Such consistency demands attempts to explain these catchword associations. Attempting to divide this extensive exegetical task meaningfully, the first volume examined individual passages from six writings involved in these links. These six writings (Hosea, Amos, Micah, Zephaniah, Haggai, and Zech 1-8) were selected because evidence suggested that their initial and concluding passages received minimal adaptations, usually in the form of short redactional glosses, specifically oriented to the Book of the Twelve. Thus, the literary form of these writings was substantially fixed prior to incorporation into the Book of the Twelve. Simultaneously, observations suggested that the literary forms of these writings prior to their incorporation into the Book of the Twelve were closely associated with the transmission of two multi-volume corpora, one which contained Haggai and Zech 1-8 (the Haggai-Zechariah corpus) and one which contained Hosea, Amos, Micah, and Zephaniah (the Deuteronomistic corpus).

The current volume evaluates the initial and concluding passages of the remaining literary sections of the Book of the Twelve (Joel, Obadiah, Nahum, Habakkuk, Malachi, Jonah, and Zech 9-14). It assesses the extent of editorial and/or compositional activity manifesting awareness of the Book of the Twelve as a literary corpus. In keeping with the procedure of the previous volume, the macrostructure of each writing will be discussed, along with scholarly theories affecting date and unity. Then, a literary-critical analysis of the pertinent passages focusses on the units and sub-units of the texts with an eye toward identifying literary tensions, and evaluating those results in light of the relationship to the catchwords and to other issues impacting the understanding of the Book of the Twelve. Special attention is given to models for understanding the writing's final form by entering into dialogue with recent redactional treatments of each of the writings.

Increasingly, in the course of this investigation, it became obvious that one could not develop theories about the growth of the Book of the Twelve without constantly having to make decisions on the intertextual relationships involved in these prophetic writings. Thus, not only does this volume provide a scripture index as an aid to locating discussions of particular passages, and it also provides an appendix of allusions and citations noted in this study. This appendix lists the texts involved, and it indicates whether this study presumes a given text is the source text or the receiving text since this decision necessarily effects the understanding of the development of the corpus.

As with the first volume, the tentative nature of conclusions reached in this volume must be acknowledged. Often, a single observation could be interpreted plausibly in more than one fashion, depending upon larger subjective criteria. Some attempt has been made to illustrate this complexity by evaluating alternative explanations in the exegetical discussions. Nevertheless, so little work has been attempted previously on the question how the Book of the Twelve came into existence, that an attempt to provide a systematic treatment of the issue is warranted. Hopefully, it will provoke scholarly discussion of the issues involved.

Special thanks again go to Prof. Dr. Otto Kaiser and to the staff at De Gruyter for their assistance in the preparation of these volumes. Their gracious help and suggestions made this publication possible. The two volumes represent an edited version of my dissertation submitted to the theological faculty at the University of Zürich in 1991 under the supervision of Prof. Dr. O.H. Steck. I wish to express my sincere gratitude to him and to other mentors, friends, and colleagues who have aided my academic pilgrimage. My greatest source of strength came from my wife, Melanie, whose encouragement, support, and interaction during the long process leading to the fruition of this study motivated, sustained, and influenced its completion.

Table of Contents

Preface v

Joel

1. The Macrostructure of Joel 1
2. The Literary Units and Context of Joel 1:1-14 7
3. The Literary Function of Joel 1:1-14 13
    3.1. Backward to Hosea 13
    3.2. Connections Forward in the Book of the Twelve ... 23
4. Summary of the Hosea - Joel Transition 25
5. Joel 4:1-21: Eschatological Judgment and Promise of Salvation 26
    5.1. Joel 4:1-3: Literary Introduction 26
    5.2. Joel 4:4-8: Oracle against Tyre, Sidon, and the Philistine Regions 28
    5.3. Joel 4:9-17: Judgment in the Valley 30
    5.4. Joel 4:18-21: Eschatological Promise of Restoration . 37
6. Allusions and Quotes in Joel 4:1-21 42
7. The Date of Joel 4:1-21 48

Obadiah

1. The Macrostructure of Obadiah 58
2. The Interrelationship of Obad 1-9, Jer 49:7ff and Amos 9:1ff 61
3. The Interrelationship of Obad 15-21, Jer 49:7ff; 25:15ff and Amos 9:1ff 69
4. The Relationship of Obadiah to Isaiah and Ezekiel 74
5. The Relationship of Obadiah to Micah 78
6. The Units in Obad 15-21 79
7. Toward a Synthesis 89

Nahum

1. The Macrostructure of Nahum 93
2. Various Redactional Models 93
3. Dating the Book of Nahum 97
4. Literary Observations on Nah 1:1,2-8,9-11 99
    4.1. A Two-Layered Superscription: Nah 1:1 99
    4.2. The Acrostic Elements in Nah 1:2-8 101

viii

4.3. A Semi-Acrostic Hymn: Nah 1:2-8 103
4.4. Nah 1:9f,11-14; 2:1-3 111
5. The Role of Nah 1 in the Book of the Twelve 115
6. The Literary Units in Nah 3:1-19 117
7. The Growth of Nah 3:1-19 123
8. Dating the Layers of Nahum 127

Habakkuk

1. The Macrostructure of Habakkuk 129
2. Dating Habakkuk: Traditional Arguments and Problems ... 134
3. Literary Observations on Hab 1:1-2:5 136
4. Hab 1:1-17 and the Relationship to *Stichwörter* in Nah 3:1-
   19 146
5. Redactional Summary and Re-evaluation of the Date of Hab
   1:1-17 150
6. Cultic Transmission of Hab 3:1-19 154
7. The Literary Units in Hab 3:3-15 159
8. The Literary Frame (Hab 3:2,16-19a) 173
9. Summary of Redactional and Temporal Observations 180

Malachi

1. The Macrostructure of Malachi 182
2. The Date of Malachi 186
3. Literary Observations on Mal 1:1-14 187
4. Contrasting Motifs in Mal 1:1-14 and Zech 8:9-23 197
5. A Haggai-Zechariah-Malachi Corpus? 201
6. Further Indications of a Wider Literary Awareness in
   Malachi 204
7. Summary and Reflections on Proto-Zechariah and Malachi . 210

Zech 9-14

1. Zech 9-14 Distinct from Zech 1-8: A Brief Summary of
   Research 213
2. Preliminary Observations Concerning Zech 9-14 217
3. The Units within Zech 9:1-17 and Their Literary
   Relationships 219
4. The Position and Function of Zion in Zech 9:9-13 229
5. Zech 9-13 as Corpus 232
6. Zech 14:1-21: Positive and Negative Aspects of the Final
   Judgment 236

7. Zech 14:1-21 and Its Function in the Book of the Twelve .. 241

Jonah
  1. The Macrostructure of Jonah 248
  2. Literary Observations on Jonah 1-2 250
  3. Theories on the Transmission and Redaction History of
      Jonah 255
  4. Problems of Genre and Jonah 262
  5. Jonah 2:3-10 and the Book of the Twelve 265
  6. The Position, Function, and Date of Jonah 270

Summary
  1. Pre-existing Multi-volume Corpora 274
  2. The Joel-related Layer 275
  3. Subsequent Additions 278
  4. Provenence for the Book of the Twelve 279

Works Cited 281

Appendix of Allusions and Citations 290

Index 292

Joel

The book of Joel does not contain data in the heading (1:1) which provides explicit information about the time of the prophet. Not surprisingly, scholarly opinions for dating the components of Joel range from the ninth to the second century. Most recent works, however, argue for a post-monarchic date, either in the sixth century or in the first half of the fourth century.[1] After evaluating the arguments, this investigation will presume the later date as the starting point in discussing Joel, although observations for narrowing these parameters will be offered following discussion of Joel 4:1-21.[2]

1. The Macrostructure of Joel

Two questions of unity impact the investigation of the structure of Joel, namely the relationship of chapters 1-2 and 3-4 to one another and the relationship of 4:4-8 to its context. Earlier work spent much time and energy discussing the unity of Joel, often characterizing chapters 1-2 as "historical" over against the "eschatological" material in 3-4. By contrast, a considerable consensus of recent commentators treats Joel as a unified work.[3] Descriptions of this unity, however, offer no such consensus. Commentators describe Joel variously as the recording of a ritual, a loose

---

[1] A comprehensive study on the problems of the date of Joel is not possible. These arguments are presented in the commentaries. An excellent summary article which gives a balanced treatment of the major views and the scholars holding those positions is available in J.A. Thompson, "The Date of Joel," in *A New Light unto My Path. Old Testament Studies in Honor of Jacob M. Myers*. H.N. Bream, ed. (Philadelphia: Temple University Press, 1974), 453-464. A more detailed discussion of the date follows at the end of the discussion of Joel 4:1-21. See below, page 48.

[2] These arguments normally include the fact that the temple cult is functioning (presupposing the rebuilding of the temple), the lack of any mention of a king, late vocabulary, and the reliance of Joel upon traditions and quotes of numerous other prophets.

[3] Compare Wolff, *BK* 14/2, 5ff; Rudolph, *KAT* 13/2, 23; Allen, *Joel, etc.*, 25ff; Weiser, *ATD* 24, 89f; Keller, *CAT* 11a, 101ff. See also the older commentary of Marti, *Dodekapropheton*, 111.

collection of small oracles, a commentary on other prophetic books, an apocalyptic treatise, and a two-fold account (the call to repent following a locust plague and the results of that repentance).[4] A summary of the macro-structure will elucidate the literary content and movement within Joel in order to discuss its character.[5]

Many past treatments have sought to distinguish between the historical and eschatological perspectives of Joel, by separating chapters 1-2 from 3-4. However, more recent work centers upon explaining the order of the material as it stands. Two positions appear frequently in describing the macrostructure of Joel. The first divides Joel by its content, and the second by its form.[6] Those dividing Joel by content usually separate chapters 1-2 from 3-4 by claiming the first two chapters reflect a prophetic confrontation

---

[4] Not all of these positions are mutually exclusive, and indeed Joel is often described as a cross between a classical prophet and a typical cult prophet of salvation. The majority of commentators argue Joel was inspired (in varying degrees) by an actual locust plague: Wellhausen, *Skizzen und Vorarbeiten*, 206; Marti, *Das Dodekapropheton*, 111; Nowack, *Die Kleinen Propheten*, 82; Wolff, *BK* 14/2, 6; Rudolph, *KAT* 13/2, 25; Allen, *Joel, etc.*, 29-31; Kapelrud, *Joel Studies*, 177; Willem S. Prinsloo, *The Theology of the Book of Joel*, BZAW 163 (Berlin: DeGruyter, 1985), 14. Robinson, *HAT* 14, 55; and E. Kutsch, "Heuschreckenplage und Tag Jahwes in Joel 1 und 2," *TZ* 18 (1962): 81-94, are typical of those who argue chapters 1-2 were locust plague inspired while chapters 3-4 are apocalyptic. There is a sizable minority, however, who shy away from explanations of locust plagues. Some do so on the basis of the apocalyptic tendencies in the entire book: Merx, Hengstenberg (see Bič, *Das Buch Joel*, 6-8). Others are more concerned with the liturgical use of Joel: Graham S. Ogden, "Joel 4 and Prophetic Responses to National Laments," *JSOT* 26 (1983): 97-106; Keller, *CAT* 11a, 104ff; Bič, *Das Buch Joel*, 106. Significantly, Bo Reicke, "Joel und seine Zeit," in *Wort - Gebot - Glaube. Beiträge zur Theologie des Alten Testaments. Walther Eichrodt zum 80. Geburtstag* (Zürich: Zwingli Verlag, 1970), 133-141, argues no locusts are intended, but a political army is intended throughout chapters 1-2 which leads to judgment against the nations in chapter 4. See the more explicit discussion of the recent model put forth by Siegfried Bergler, *Joel als Schriftinterpret*, Beiträge zur Erforschung des Alten Testaments und des antiken Judentums 16 (Frankfurt: Peter Lang, 1988), as a starting point for the discussion below, page 5.

[5] This character must account of the recent work of Bergler, (see below, page 5), as well as the literary horizon of Joel (below, page 13).

[6] Examples of those who divide by content and form respectively are: Rudolph, *KAT* 13/2, 23; and Wolff, *BK* 14/2, 5ff. For a thorough comparison of the arguments see, Leslie Allen, *The Books of Joel, etc.* 39ff. Prinsloo, *The Theology of the Book of Joel*, 122-127, is somewhat of an exception in that he argues for a climaxing schema throughout the book in which one pericope builds upon another.

of the people in specific response to an actual locust plague.[7] Those dividing Joel by form note that beginning in 2:18, the oracles occur predominantly in the divine first person, and that they function as the response to the call to lament in 1:2-2:17 (and presumably its execution). The division by form offers a better perspective from which to view the entire structure of the book, but caution is required since not everything in the book conforms precisely to such a division.

Several literary markers help to distinguish the larger units in Joel.[8] An imperative style and a call to lamentation dominate 1:1-14. Different groups or entities are addressed, normally with an explicit addressee (1:2,5,8 [no addressee],11,13). This composite call to lament precedes a literary depiction of a drought (1:15-20), a description containing both prophetic and communal elements, which functions as an interpretation of the coming

---

[7] These arguments become increasingly difficult to maintain in light of recent studies on the literary expression of the locust motif in Joel. The major problem with this view hinges on the question of whether the disaster in Joel presumes a locust plague, a drought, and/or the attack of a hostile enemy. For a clear summary of the manifold problems of an actual locust plague as the background even for chapters 1-2, see Reicke, "Joel und seine Zeit," 135ff; and Bergler, *Joel als Schriftinterpret*, 259-261. For the manner in which this affects a reading of Joel in its Book of the Twelve context, see below, page 23.

[8] The extent of the individual units in Joel is relatively easy to identify, albeit the manner in which these units are viewed is disputed. The many parallels between different parts of the book are irrefutable, but attempts such as those of Bourke and Allen to impose an absolute symmetrical structure on the book must continue to be viewed skeptically. Bourke, "Le Jour Jahvé dans Joël," *RB* 66 (1959): 5-31, has argued for a symmetry of structure, but his symmetry cannot account for the integral passage of 2:18-20, and even though Bourke maintains the structural key to the book is the Day of YHWH, he ignores the first reference to the Day of YHWH (1:15) in his structural diagram. Initially more appealing is the scheme of Allen, *Joel, etc.*, 39-43, who argues for two structurally parallel parts of prophetic lament and divine response (1:2-20, parallels 2:1-17, and 2:18-3:5 parallels 4:1-21). However, his proposal raises methodological questions regarding the manner in which he isolates and labels his strophes. For example, he cites 2:6-9 as a piece which concentrates upon the city of Jerusalem, thus forming a natural parallel to the Zion lament in 1:8-10, yet he offers no explanation as to why he makes no similar claim for 2:1ff which explicitly mentions Zion as city; he also separates 1:13f from 1:2-12, in spite of the similar imperative style, with the rationale that its cultic orientation places it more in keeping with 1:16-20, yet he offers no explanation for the cultic references of earlier material (see especially 1:9); another question could well be raised in light of 1:5-7 with regard to his claim that the divine material begins in 2:18. While Allen makes many highly significant observations, one garners the distinct impression that at times he is more interested in balancing his strophic parallels than in describing the text as it stands.

of the wrathful day of YHWH. The next section begins with an imperative call to sound the alarm (2:1). It picks up on the day of YHWH motif introduced in 1:15, but depicts a military attack. YHWH commissions and leads the attacking army, portrayed as a locust swarm, against Zion (2:11).[9] Following this announcement of impending attack, Joel 2:12-17 introduces a further appeal to repent, in order to avoid the coming destruction, using both divine (2:12) and prophetic imperatives (2:13-17).

The second portion of the book begins with 2:18, and constitutes the assurance of YHWH's positive response to the people presuming they do indeed *repent*.[10] This promissory response depicts immediate (2:18-27) and long term (3:1-5; 4:1-21) results to a positive reaction to YHWH's message of repentance.[11] The response proffered in the first unit (2:18-27) promises immediate aid, and deals explicitly with the dual themes of the locust army (2:20,25) and the drought (2:19,21-24) which recur side by side throughout first two chapters.[12] Joel 3:1-5 interprets the day of YHWH motif from a perspective which is expanded chronologically (3:1 — "It will happen afterward"), and soteriologically (3:1 — "all mankind"; 3:5 — "all who call on the name of YHWH) so that it depicts YHWH coming in judgment while leaving open the possibility of deliverance for those who call on his name. From a literary perspective, it is important to note that Obad 17 is explicitly cited in 3:5.

Joel 4:1-21 contains four inter-related units: 4:1-3,4-8,9-17,18-21. As mentioned already, much has been written about the insertion of 4:4-8 into a longer unit (4:1-3,9ff). Those seeing Joel 4:4-8 as an insertion often argue that the motivation for this insertion relates to the catchword "sell" in

---

[9]   Note the *inclusio* at the beginning and end of this unit (2:1,11) which specifically mentions the "day of YHWH."

[10] Note the imperfect consecutive at the beginning of the response in 2:18, which should be translated "and then ...". It is very interesting to note a very similar technique at this point between Hosea 14 and Joel 2:18.

[11] Allen, *Joel, etc.*, 43, notes this distinction between 2:18-27, and 3:1-5, but his polarities of "immediate" and "supernatural" blessings do not convey the proper dichotomy in light of the chronological formulae in 3:1 and 4:1. It is doubtful that a natural-supernatural distinction functioned in the mind of the compiler of Joel. When everything is directly controlled by God, such distinctions have little meaning. For further discussion of the role of 3:1-5 in relation to its context, see Rudolph, *KAT* 13/2, 23ff.

[12] The interchangeable use of this imagery is strong evidence that these motifs are not to be taken literally, certainly not on the compositional level of the book. See further discussion in Bergler, *Joel als Schriftinterpret*, 259-261; and Reicke, "Joel und seine Zeit," 135ff.

4:3.[13] Several problems with this insertion model have been put forth, but proponents of the chapter's unity typically focus upon defending 4:4-8 as a parenthetical concretization of 4:1-3 that does not require separation from the remainder of the chapter.[14] However, a more adequate picture of the chapter's unity arises with the recognition that the problem should be approached from a different perspective, by seeing 4:1-3 as a literary introduction to 4:4-21. It is certainly no coincidence that 4:4-8 takes up "sell," but it is likewise no coincidence that the themes of the entire chapter appear in abbreviated form in 4:1-3. Indeed they appear in chiastic order:

> A The coming restoration of Judah and Jerusalem (4:1)
> B Judgment against the nations in the valley of Jehoshaphat (4:2)
> C Slavery of YHWH's people (4:3)
> C' Slavery of YHWH's people (4:4-8)
> B' Judgment against the nations in the valley of Jehoshaphat (4:9-17)
> A' The coming restoration of Judah and Jerusalem (4:18-21)

Truly, the chapter should be viewed in its entirety, but the unity of the chapter is on a literary or redactional level, and not on the level of a spoken or liturgical formulation.[15]

Prior to a discussion of the individual units, the work of Bergler should be brought into the discussion, because it sheds light on the question of the compilation of Joel.[16] Bergler does not question the book's unity, but he believes most commentators use the word too glibly when speaking about Joel. Bergler attempts to refine the definition of what constitutes Joel's "unity" in light of the diverse images in the book. Bergler determines that Joel presents a unity which has been fashioned out of several independent blocks of material, meaning that editorial work unites the

---

[13] See especially Wolff, *BK* 14/2, 89; Watts, *Joel, etc.*, 44.

[14] See especially Rudolph, *KAT* 13/2, 80ff; Allen, *Joel, etc.*, 111-114. Surprisingly, Bergler, *Joel als Schriftinterpret*, 102f, puts forth similar arguments.

[15] More will be said about the composition and function of this unity under the discussion of the connection between Joel and Amos. Here it need only be noted that the construction of Joel 4 appears to have the setting of Amos 1-2 in mind in much the same manner that the metaphorical description of botanical desolation in Joel 1-2 expands and reverses the botanical motifs of Hosea, particularly 14:2ff and 2:1ff.

[16] Siegfried Bergler, *Joel als Schriftinterpret*, Beiträge zur Erforschung des Alten Testaments und des antiken Judentums 16 (Frankfurt: Peter Lang, 1988). Bergler's work contains two parts. In the first part, Bergler carries out a thorough literary and form-critical analysis of the book. The second part investigates the background of Joel's use of sources.

disparate pieces. Bergler concentrates upon determining the sources of the
first two chapters. He isolates and analyzes several motifs (day of YHWH,
locust plague, drought, and portrayal of an enemy) which help determine
the current unity of the work. Bergler concludes that in the first two
chapters Joel fashions this "unity" by combining several independent (pre-
existing) pieces with his own commentary.[17] This commentary unites the
various parts in order to proclaim that only true repentance on the part of
the people will convince YHWH to change the situation from suffering to
salvation. The salvation comes in two stages, the reversal of the present
drought (2:19ff) and the reversal of the day of YHWH to a judgment which
includes the nations (3:1-5; 4:1-21). The particulars of his discussion, as
they relate to Joel 1:1ff and 4:1ff, will be discussed in more detail below,
but Bergler's model goes a long way toward explaining the function of
quotes and allusions in Joel since the citation of other texts appears in
Joel's connecting material, not in the pre-existing blocks. For Bergler, the
"unity" of Joel derives from the compositional skills of a creative prophet
who artfully constructed a literary work, extensively using both pre-existing
blocks and citations of other works for his own purpose.

---

[17]   The independent entities, according to Bergler, include two drought poems (1:5,9-13,17-
      20), an enemy poem (2:1a;1:6-8;2:2ab,ba,4f/7-8a/8b-9), and a salvation oracle (2:21-
      24*,26a), which are woven together by Joel's own connecting material.   Joel's
      combination of the drought poems with the day of YHWH motif serves as introduction
      to the description of the enemy attack on the day of YHWH. These motifs establish
      a dichotomy in which the present drought serves as precursor to the imminent day of
      YHWH. The salvation oracle serves as the foundational turning point of the book, in
      which Joel formulates the need for repentance, not just lament, if YHWH is to change
      the present situation. Bergler argues that Joel adds his own interpretive material to
      create this change by a call to repentance (2:12-14) based upon Amos 4:6ff; Jon 4:2;
      3:9a. Based on Jer 14:1-15:9 — which also includes the motifs of the present drought
      and future attack of an enemy — Bergler argues Joel follows a liturgical *schema*: a
      twice repeated lament and prayer leads to the expectation of YHWH's response, which
      comes in two movements. The first presents a salvation oracle, reworked, in part, on
      the basis of Hos 10:12. The second (3:1-4:21) is guided by an eschatological outlook.
      Unlike the first section, Bergler does not find that Joel utilizes pre-existing material
      in 3:1-4:21.

2. The Literary Units and Context of Joel 1:1-14

Joel 1:1-14 manifests three literary units.   Joel 1:1 provides the superscription to the book.[18]   Joel 1:2-4 constitutes the summons proper which presents the setting, and 1:5-14 constitutes a composite call to national repentance.

The summons proper in 1:2-4 introduces Joel by setting the scene in the imagery of a locust plague of singular dimensions.   Joel 1:2a demands the attention of the elders and the inhabitants of the land, followed by a disjunctive rhetorical question in 1:2b which presupposes a negative answer. Joel 1:3 commands the hearers to recount the message to succeeding generations. Joel 1:4 describes the present scene using graphic terms of the destruction of a plague of locusts.[19]   The mention of the elders and the inhabitants of the land as the addressees of 1:2-4 forms an *inclusio* with 1:5-14.[20]

Joel 1:5-14 presents a composite call to repentance on account of the deplorable conditions of the present situation.[21]

> 1:5-7   Address to drunkards
> 1:8-10 Address to Zion
> 1:11-12 Address to farmers
> 1:13-14 Address to priests

This composition is structured with imperatives addressed to different groups, followed by a reason for the lamentation.   Joel 1:5-7 constitutes a divine summons addressed to the drunkards who will not have wine because

---

[18] In most cases, the superscriptions will be given only cursory treatment unless the headings have significant contributions to the question of the broader corpus.

[19] Elsewhere in Joel, the imagery of the locusts intertwines with the imagery of an invading army (cf. 1:6, 2:1-10,20), so that in the end the two motifs run together.

[20] Some argue these two references indicate disunity, since the address in 1:2 assumes the presence of the elders and the inhabitants, while 1:14 assumes their absence, indicating a separate setting.   Bergler, *Joel als Schriftinterpret*, 57f, demonstrates a different function between the calls to repentance and the call to constitute a cultic assembly in 1:14.   Bergler assigns 1:14 to the hand of the compiler Joel, not to the pre-existing block which Joel uses.   Bergler therefore associates 1:14 with the same hand as 1:2-4 on the basis of the common audience they share.

[21] Wolff, *BK* 14/2, 23f, summarizes the elements involved in such a communal call to lament.   The use of the imperative, the vocative, and the reason for lament (with כי or על) provide the common characteristics.   Wolff also provides examples including, Zech 11:2 and Isa 23:1-14 which are also multi-strophe calls to the people.

of the land's destruction.[22]   Joel 1:8-10 differs in construction from the other elements of 1:5-14 because the addressees are missing in the opening line.[23]   The 2fs imperative אלי with no vocative has created debate concerning the identity of the addressee for these verses. Many have sought an unwarranted emendation or reconstruction.[24]   However, the suggestion that the verses address a personified Zion is more likely, since it is not only perfectly consonant with MT, but also with the sense of the passage.[25]   In addition, the use of 2fs for the personified Zion appears elsewhere in the Book of the Twelve at relatively frequent intervals, sometimes without an explicit introduction.[26]   In contrast to the locust motif in 1:2-4, Joel 1:8-10 uses the language of a drought. Likewise, Joel 1:11-12 employs two imperatives calling on the farmers and vinedressers to be ashamed and lament because the fruit of the tree has withered away. The predominant imagery in this sub-unit also presupposes the devastation of a drought rather than a locust plague.[27]   Joel 1:13-14 concludes the call

---

[22]   The invasion of another nation as the cause of destruction in 1:6 is distinct to 1:2-14. This is a clue that the plague described in 1:4 is understood metaphorically, not historically. A second distinctive feature is that only these verses in 1:2-14 are placed in the mouth of YHWH as seen in the references to "my land", "my vine", and "my fig-tree" in 1:6-7.   The first person voice of YHWH reappears at the beginning of significant units in the "prophetic" sections of the book in 2:1,12, and from 2:18 to the end of the writing (with the exception of certain prophetic comments upon the divine material 2:21-24; 3:5; 4:18-21).   For this reason, one cannot separate these units formally solely on the basis of the speaker, although other considerations may well point to redactional/compositional concerns in this material.   See discussion of Bergler's thesis beginning page 9.

[23]   The addressees of the call to lament are mentioned specifically in 1:2,5,11,13, but 1:8 specifies no addressees.   Only the unique form אלי is present, a feminine singular imperative with no explicit subject. Some, e.g. Wolff, BK 14/2, 21, assume an addressee other than Zion, arguing the feminine addressee in 1:8 represents a textual corruption, but see the discussion of the textual support in James D. Nogalski, Literary Precursors to the Book of the Twelve (Berlin: De Gruyter, 1993), 23.

[24]   Wolff, BK 14/2, 21; Rudolph KAT 13/2, 39; Robinsion HAT 14, 58, etc.

[25]   So Allen, Joel, etc., 52. Bergler, following Schmalohr, suggests "land" from 1:6 as the subject, a suggestion which carries merit in light of the metaphors of the trees with its branches.   Either explanation is preferable to emendation, but if "land" is understood, one should assume that land is Judah (and not all Israel).   See below, 18.

[26]   Such as Mic 7:8-20; Zeph 3:14-20; Nah 1:12f (see discussion of those verses in the context of the structure of Nahum).   Perhaps a case could be made as well for Hos 2:1ff, at least in a later reading of the material.

[27]   While the ruination of the harvest of the harvest in 1:11 could refer to either a plague or a drought, the imagery of 1:12 does not presuppose a locust plague.   It uses the verbs אמלל (languish) and יבש (wither), which imply lack of water, not locusts.

to repentance with imperatives addressed to priests and ministers of YHWH. Nothing in these verses entirely precludes a specific setting of lamentation as a response to the destruction of either a drought or a locust plague, although the use of מנע is more likely used in drought material.[28]

Bergler aptly demonstrates that this traditional presentation of Joel 1:5-14, based upon the imperatives as introductory elements, raises significant questions about its *original* unity, both in relation to 1:2-4 and within the strophes in 1:5-14. To understand Bergler's theory, one must note that he begins by looking at the "day of YHWH" speeches in chapters 1-2, and then turns to the three interrelated motifs recurring in these chapters: locusts, an enemy attack, and a drought. Bergler develops an interesting picture from the enemy portrayal in Joel 2:1-11.[29] He argues that these verses, in their present form, result from a compositional style which adapts a poem about an enemy attack by incorporating loosely related day of YHWH sayings. These sayings quote from other portions of Joel and from other day of YHWH material outside Joel.[30] Bergler believes the poem consists of the introductory call (2:1aa) and three strophes which demonstrate consistent stylistic affinity (2:1a,2ab,ba,4f/7-8a/8b-9). Bergler's literary analysis provides two significant points of departure which effect this work. First, Bergler documents the fundamental image of an author who adapts pre-existing material (in this case to relate it to the day of YHWH) as a means of shaping the book. Second, through his careful distinctions between quote and source material, Bergler establishes a pattern for the author upon which he builds to describe the character of the remainder of the book.

Bergler next turns to the question of the existence of the enemy motif in chapter one, and observes that this motif appears only in Joel 1:6-8.[31] He notes that the consensus regarding Joel 1:5-20 as a call to national lament masks some very real tensions within the chapter, two of the most significant being the problematic call to repentance to a feminine entity in Joel 1:8, and the presupposition of drought, rather than locusts, as the primary threat in 1:5-20.

---

[28] There is an affinity between this passage with other uses of מנע in contexts of the lack of rain: Ezek 31:15; Jer 3:3; Amos 4:7.

[29] Bergler, *Joel als Schriftinterpret*, 49-52.

[30] See also Bergler's discussions of the day of YHWH material, *Joel als Schriftinterpret*, 33-44.

[31] Bergler, *Joel als Schriftinterpret*, 53-56.

Bergler resolves the tension of the feminine adressee in 1:8 by demonstrating the tensions exist with 1:9ff, while with the enemy motif in 1:6-8 presents a consistent picture. Bergler argues that 1:6-8 has been inserted between 1:5 and 1:9.[32] He maintains that Joel 1:6-8 originally served as the first strophe of the enemy poem in 2:1-11, because of the common vocabulary, the divine speech style, and the function 1:6-8 would have served, form-critically, for that poem.[33]

As for the drought motif which dominates most of the chapter, Bergler disagrees with the scholarly consensus regarding the original unity of 1:5-20. He notes that scholars have divided these verses variously. Almost all separate 1:15ff in some manner, and a significant portion recognizes a change already in 1:13.[34] Bergler separates Joel 1:14 from the preceding, despite its use of a similar imperative style, because it

---

[32] Bergler, *Joel als Schriftinterpret*, 54-56. Bergler notes that the drunkards in 1:5 are called to lament over the loss of their sweet wine, while 1:6-8 presuppose an enemy destruction. In addition, he makes an excellent case for the unity of Joel 1:6-8. He understands the beginning of Joel 1:6 as a type of introduction: A nation has come up against "my land." Bergler describes the remainder of the verses as the characterization and action of this nation: he has the teeth of a lion, he makes my makes my vine and fig-tree into splinters, etc. He makes its (3fs) branches white. This last reference marks the change of subject which explains 1:8: lament (אֱלִי). He argues correctly that these verses use purely metaphorical speech. My vine and my fig-tree must refer to Judah while the phrase "its branches" also relates to these same images.

[33] Bergler, *Joel als Schriftinterpret*, 55f. Bergler notes the shared vocabulary in 1:6; 2:2 regarding the description of the enemy. Stylistically, the first chapter contains divine speech only in Joel 1:6-(7)8, while this speech form is characteristic for the enemy poem in 2:1ff. Form-critically, Bergler argues (49) that 2:1ff, when seen as an independent poem, begins with a call of alarm to Zion which contains no retrospective cause for that alarm, nor does it include a כִּי sentence which indicates a rationale. Bergler maintains Joel 1:6-8 originally followed the call to alarm in 2:1, and that, in the original poem, it served as the rationale for the alarm. Bergler's scenario portrays 1:6-8 as an announcement that Judah has been ransacked by an invading nation, and that this enemy now stands poised to attack Jerusalem. The poem calls Zion to prepare for battle in light of this threat. For discussion of the problems associated with this picture, see below, footnote 41.

[34] Bergler, *Joel als Schriftinterpret*, 53. Among others, Bergler cites Wolff's failure to account for the double use of the priest/temple offering theme, and the fact he cannot readily explain the feminine imperative in 1:8 according to the formal schema: See Hans Walter Wolff, "Der Aufruf zur Volksklage," *ZAW* 76 (1964): 48-56; and *BK* 14/2, 22f. Additionally, others distinguish between the lament in 1:5-12 and a call to fast and prayer in 1:13f: Rudolph, *KAT* 13/2, 46; Marti, *Dodekapropheton*, 118f, 122f; Sellin, *Zwölfprophetenbuch*, 116, 119.

functions with 1:2-4 as a ring composition around 1:5,9-13.[35] He argues
that 1:17-20 represents another pre-formulated element which Joel adopts
into the context.[36]

Bergler associates the locust motif with the composition level of the
book. In the first chapter, he limits the locust motif to the prologue, Joel
1:2-4, for the following reasons:[37] 1) It agrees with the larger audience of
Joel 1:14-16, which calls on the witness of the elders and inhabitants to
witness the uniqueness of the plague.   2) Joel 2:2b,3 returns to the
reference to the past in similar manner to 1:2, and refers to the generations
to come. 3) Joel 2:25 promises replacement for the years of the locusts.
4) Joel 1:2-4 places the accent upon the commission to the present
generation while 3:1f places a similar commission on future generations.
Bergler depicts the remainder of the material in the chapter as the
particular formulations of the author.[38]

Bergler's model has much to commend it in the first chapter of Joel.
His delineation of units in Joel 1:2-20 helps to distinguish between
inherently unified blocks of material and other portions which demonstrate
a clear progression of thought, but which do not, upon close examination,
reveal a consistent picture. As such, Bergler affords an excellent starting
point for the discussion of the literary tensions in Joel 1:2ff, but two
suggestions will be offered here by way of correction and/or enlargement
of perspective to Bergler's model. First, Bergler incorrectly isolates the
locust imagery in chapter one to Joel 1:2-4 alone. The locust imagery plays
a central role in the metaphorical language of 1:6-8.[39] Second, Bergler's

---

[35]   Bergler believes 1:14 presupposes the same wider (literary) audience as 1:2-4, indicated
    by the common vocabulary which serves as *inclusio* to 1:2.

[36]   Bergler, *Joel als Schriftinterpret*, 62f, treats Joel 1:17-20 as a two strophe poem. Unlike
    the first part, in which the strophes appear in *Ringkomposition*, the author intertwines
    them so that each strophe has portrayals of the situation as well as rationale (a:
    17a/18aa; b: 17b/18ab), and each has a call to prayer with a rationale (c: 19a/20a; d:
    19b/20b). He therefore sees an abcd format repeated twice: situation/rationale; prayer/
    rationale.

[37]   Bergler, *Joel als Schriftinterpret*, 107-109.

[38]   Although Joel may quote from other sources, the quotes are either short or constitute
    allusions to other texts, which Joel utilizes as parts of his own sentence structures.

[39]   Note especially Joel 1:7, where the description of the enemy's destruction clearly plays
    off the locust metaphor to refer to the nation which invaded the land: "He made my
    vine for destruction, and my fig tree for splintering; and stripping it, he stripped it and
    cast it away. Its branches become white." In order to interpret these verses, one must
    reckon not only with the enemy portrayal on the basis of 1:6 (which Bergler does well),
    but also with the metaphorical locust motif.

argument that 1:6-8 plays off the enemy portrayal in 2:1ff correctly
associates the two passages, but his argument that 1:6-8 formed the original
introduction to the enemy poem in 2:1ff is not very convincing for two
reasons. First, he fails to demonstrate effectively that the current
introduction of 2:1 requires 1:6-8.[40] Relatedly, Bergler's theory of a two-
tiered threat, which postulates that the destruction of Judah leads to the
alarm call in Zion, may be a possible hermeneutic in 1:6-8, but it does not
harmonize smoothly with the poem in 2:1ff, even in Bergler's reduced
form.[41] For these reasons, one must seek other explanations for 1:6-8.

In the larger context of Joel, the remaining chapters presuppose the
first chapter. Chapter two parallels chapter one in much of its structure,

---

[40] While Bergler correctly characterizes the independent nature of 2:1-11, one must
question whether he conclusively demonstrates the existence of a radically shortened
version of that poem. In particular, Bergler does not clearly establish that the present
rationale for the call to alarm is not original to the poem. He too quickly assumes
(49f) that the poem must be reconstructed without any reference to the day of YHWH,
since this motif represents one of the red flags of Joel's own interpretations. It makes
at least as much sense, however, to suppose that reference to the day of YHWH in the
poem might well have served to draw Joel to the poem in the first place. Apparently,
only this reason causes Bergler to eliminate the כי clause which follows the call to
alarm in 2:1.

[41] Bergler correctly notes that the similarities of the enemy image in 1:6-8 with 2:1-11
argues for a closer relationship than one might conclude from their position. He also
correctly observes, however, that the perfects in 1:6-8 do not coincide well with the
future attack described in 2:1-11. Bergler still postulates an original unity, by
differentiating between a recent attack on Judah and an impending threat to Jerusalem.
He therefore argues 1:6-8 appeared immediately after the alarm cry in 2:1 as a
rationale. He paints the scenario thus: Zion is called to alarm, because Judah has
fallen and only Zion remains. This scenario does not hold up under closer inspection,
however, since the future threat in 2:1 endangers "all the inhabitants of the land."
Stylistically, Bergler argues even 1:8 fits well with the enemy material from 2:2, on the
basis of the preposition כ, the passive construction, and the preposition על. He says
that its position was changed when it became the *Begründung* for the first lament. This
suggestion appears somewhat suspect in light of the fact that the phrases have very little
in common besides this formal character. Particularly, the last elements do not
coincide. Joel 1:8 says, "Lament *like* the virgin *because* of the Baal of her youth." Joel
2:2 has no verb, but relates to the day of YHWH sayings in the first bi-cola: *as* the
dawn is spread *over* the mountains. Bergler makes an excellent case for the
relationship of 1:6-8 and 2:1-11 to one another, but one must object to his arguments
that they reflect an original unity. It is wiser to presume that these verses literarily
anticipate the threat from the enemy 2:1ff.

and utilizes similar imagery.[42] Chapter four picks up several motifs from chapter one through citations, but reverses the picture of judgment into one of promise.[43] Having noted the composite literary character of 1:1-14, and its function in the overall unity of Joel, it is now important to turn to a discussion of the literary horizon of the passage in order to demonstrate the redactional function played by this material in the Book of the Twelve.

3. The Literary Function of Joel 1:1-14

Joel functions redactionally in the shaping of the Book of the Twelve. Arguments will be presented here that Joel was either composed, or altered to such an extent, that it must be read in its context in the Book of the Twelve in order to grasp its full implications. The connections in Joel 1:2-14 include not only references backward to Hos 14:5ff, but also to other passages in Hosea, especially 2:3ff and 4:1ff. Second, certain themes and important catchwords throughout Joel introduce concerns taken up elsewhere in the Book of the Twelve. Third, the following section will demonstrate that similar connections exist in Joel 4:1ff which tie Joel forward to Amos. Fourth, Joel plays an important function in shaping the overall structure of the Book of the Twelve to reflect the macro-structure of Isaiah.

3.1. Backward to Hosea

The *Stichwörter* in Joel 1:1-14 which point backward to Hos 14:5ff are "this" (Joel 1:2, twice), "inhabitants" (Joel 1:2,14), "wine" (Joel 1:5), "vine"

---

[42] For a more thorough discussion of the unity of Joel 1:2ff with the remainder of the book, see Allen, *Joel, etc.*, 25-27; and Willem Prinsloo, *The Theology of the Book of Joel* (Berlin: Walter de Gruyter, 1985), 2-5. This unity does not, however, presuppose a single natural calamity as the historical background of the component parts. For a summary of the tensions arguing against isolation of a single event even for chapters 1-2, see especially Wolff, *BK* 14/2, 5-7; and the arguments of the political nature of the enemy in chapters 1-2 in Reicke, "Joel und seine Zeit", 134ff, and Ogden, *JSOT* 26 (1983): 104. The observations of the political nature of the enemy lead Reicke and Ogden to entirely different positions regarding the date of the book, but are nevertheless remarkably striking in the common picture they portray.

[43] See especially Wolff, *BK* 14/2, 7; and Ogden, *JSOT* 26 (1983): 100-102.

(Joel 1:7,12), and "grain" (Joel 1:10). This array of words occurs across the major units and sub-units of 1:2-4,5-14. When one considers other significant similarities between Hos 14 and Joel 1 — the preponderance of botanical imagery and the similarity of *Gattung* (call to repentance) — these catchwords provide a ready transition from one book to the next. These words occur in both the pre-existing drought material — as described by Bergler — and in the compositional material which unites them. This overlap raises the possibility that the end of Hosea functioned as the hermeneutical backdrop from which Joel began. Previous discussion of Hos 14:5ff noted that, within the Book of the Twelve, Joel 1:2ff functions primarily as juxtaposition to the healthy picture of Israel provided in Hos 14:5ff.[44] The use of the *Stichwörter* in Joel helps to facilitate this task, but considerable evidence indicates that the compilation process of Joel deliberately created this juxtapositional function.

In light of Bergler's isolation of Joel 1:2-4 to the compilational layer of the book, these verses deserve further consideration. Under the influence of form criticism, and particularly since the commentary of Wolff, scholars normally classify Joel 1:2-4 as a *Lehreröffnungsruf*. They treat this classification as one derived from a wisdom setting which points forward to that which follows.[45] However, little work has been done which takes account of the literary function of this formula. It is by no means correct to say that the use of the formulaic expression "hear this ..." absolutely presumes an oral setting, or that it excludes a connecting function to its literary context. Indeed, this formula often plays a literary role by connecting one oracle (or collection of oracles) to another.[46]

---

[44] The chapter also functions as a link to Hos 2:3ff and a Judean actualization of Hosea on the basis of Isaiah, see Bosshard, *BN* 40 (1987): 32. See my discussion of Hos 14:2ff in *Literary Precursors to the Book of the Twelve*, BZAW (De Gruyter, 1993).

[45] See Wolff's arguments, *BK* 14/2, 22.

[46] Interestingly, the formula "hear this" appears nowhere else at the beginning of a biblical book in its present form. The phrase only once — in Ps 49:2 — introduces a psalm, but even this psalm is part of the larger Korahite corpus, where it is the final psalm in the initial collection (42-49). Similarly, Mic 3:9 utilizes the formula to introduce the *final* oracle of the complex 1-3, which contains the majority of the early material of that book (see discussion of Micah's structure in Nogalski, *Literary Precursors*). This final oracle essentially summarizes chapters 1-3. Elsewhere, the phrase appears in passages where it clearly bridges two literary pieces. The best example is the *two-fold* use of the similar phrase "hear the words of this covenant" in Jer 11:2,6. In Jer 11:2 it introduces something new and clearly refers to the following material, but 11:6 uses the identical phrase to refer back to the covenant in 11:4. In Isa 48:1 "hear this" plus the vocative introduces a passage (48:1-11) which seeks to justify the destruction of Jerusalem (cf

In light of this connective function it is legitimate to ask if the use of the phrase, "Hear this ..." in Joel 1:2 might not also serve a double function, and refer back to preceding material, in spite of the fact that this material appears in another book. If so, one must then ask if this reference to preceding material is *functional only*, assumed only when viewed from a later perspective, or whether the linkage is *deliberately created* by the author. When one considers the possibility of a literary function, one finds that it is indeed possible to "read" the phrase as a reference to the preceding promise. Significantly, such a reading offers resolution to some problems which have plagued the interpretation of Joel 1:2. To begin with, the word "this" appears twice in Joel 1:2, but these occurrences are normally treated separately. Commentators often assume the first reference is part of a general call, and that the second use of זאת should be read as though it had the preposition כ in front of it (כזאת).[47] In so

---

48:10f), even as it proclaims the destruction of Babylon on both sides (47:1-15; 48:14). In this regard, the phrase "hear this" *functions* as a reference to the destruction of Babylon in the previous chapter, in essence indicating that even though Jerusalem is justifiably punished they may take comfort in the fact that their destruction was not like the destruction of Babylon. Isa 48:16 also contains the phrase "hear this" (along with "listen to me"), and serves the double function of introducing a short saying which in turn points back to the material in 48:12-16. Hos 5:1 introduces a new unit, but "hear this priests" picks up its addressees, not germanely from the material which follows, but from the reference to the destruction of priests in 4:9. It thus applies the message of the preceding oracle to that which follows. The literary function of this example demonstrates the decision of a collector to place 5:1ff in its present location in part because of the reference to priest. Similarly, the phrase "hear this word" in Amos 3:1; 4:1; 5:1 has no direct connection to the preceding content, but the likelihood of a complex of Amos words which included these three chapters is frequently mentioned (see discussion of Amos' structure in Nogalski, *Literary Precursors*), and the use of the phrase "hear this word" as markers for the units also points to a connecting function played by the phrase within a complex of material. This overview clearly demonstrates that while the call to "hear this ..." is primarily an introductory formula, it is rarely, if ever, utterly divorced from surrounding literary material, and often has clear connections to preceding oracles. The literary function of this phrase by no means requires it was always composed in light of its literary position, but there are cases (e.g. Hos 5:1) where the composition of the phrase as a bridge from one section to another makes the most sense.

47   See particularly Wolff, *BK* 14/2, 20f. Note, however, that all of the texts he cites contain the preposition. See above text note Joel 1:2a in Nogalski, *Literary Precursors*, 23. Others simply ignore the problem of the antecedent of "this": for example, Allen, *Joel, etc.*, 46, translates זאת with "such a thing" to avoid the problem. See also Rudolph, *KAT* 13/2, 36. On the possibility of assuming the preposition כ in Hebrew, see *GK* §118r, which also implies the infrequency with which this usage occurs.

doing, they *presume* two different antecedents for the same pronoun, as though translating, "Hear *this word* ... Has (anything like) *this locust plague* happened in your days ...". A different picture arises, however, if one translates the second phrase as it stands without assuming the infrequently attested comparative construction. The question ("Has this happened in your days ...?") becomes unintelligible, if one merely presumes an oral setting. Several observations support this contention. First, the use of the two-part rhetorical question introduced with ה ... ואם expects a negative answer. Thus, when one reads the question "has this happened in your days or in the days of your fathers?," the reader should assume the answer is "no." This formulation poses difficulty for those who see in Joel an oral setting of a literal locust plague.[48] Why should Joel ask "has this happened?" in a manner which expects a listener to answer no, if his audience could see that it had happened? Second, the use of the interrogative ה with the verb היה is rare, but in the other occurrences it is used to ask a question about *previous* material.[49] Third, Bergler (and others) increasingly portray Joel as a literary work from the outset, not simply a record of prophetic sayings. The setting of this literary work requires further deliberation.

The most natural reading of Joel 1:2 would therefore expect something had preceded the verse to which "this" now refers. Hos 14:2ff provides the expected background for this question, and indeed on two related levels — the question of repentance and of promise. As Jeremias demonstrates, Hos 14:2-9 is an extended call to *true* repentance with a promise of well being which will result *in the event of this repentance*.[50] By alluding back to Hos 14:2ff, Joel 1:2ff acknowledges that the promise has

---

[48] Naturally, these difficulties caused the suggestion that one must presume the preposition in the first place.

[49] There are only three other usages of the interrogative with a form of היה in the Old Testament. In 2 Kgs 7:2, the royal officer asks "could this be?" in a clear reference to the preceding prediction of Elisha in 7:1. 2 Kgs 7:19 is essentially a verbatim recollection of 7:2 to demonstrate the fulfillment of Elisha's prediction, but again the same form is used to point to the preceding material. In Deut 4:32 the question is asked: "Indeed ask about the former days which were before you, from the day when God created man upon the earth and unto the end of the heavens, *has there been* (anything) like this great word (כדבר) or has anything like it (כמהו) been heard." Reference to "this great word" does not anticipate a speech which follows, as is clear from the following verse. Rather, it recalls the event of hearing the voice of YHWH at Horeb and the ensuing speech which began in v.12. (cf. Deut 4:33 with 4:10).

[50] Jeremias, *ATD* 24/1, 169-174.

not been fulfilled, but counters that the blame should be placed on the shoulders of an unrepentant people, not on YHWH.

Relatedly, this extended horizon of Joel offers a solution to another problem in Joel studies, namely the guilt of the people. Scholars frequently note that Joel contains little condemnation of the people.[51] He offers no reason why the locust plague/drought has come upon the people. This lack of guilt has even led to the suggestion that Joel's call to lament should be read like laments in the Psalms which presume the innocence of the people in a situation of unjust suffering.[52] However, this understanding of the people's unjust suffering creates more problems than the lack of guilt. Nothing in Joel 1:2ff explicitly states the suffering of the people is unjust.[53] If the writer of the Joel material had intended to portray an unjust suffering, it would have been necessary to bring some explicit reference to the injustice. This is no argument from silence. First, the tone of the call to repentance begins negatively in 1:5 with a confrontation of the drunkards. Second, the utilization of the locust imagery in Joel draws emotional power of guilt from an important passage, namely the temple dedication speech of Solomon in 1 Kgs 8:37-39(=2 Chr 6:28-30).

> If there is famine in the land, if there is pestilence, if there is blight, mildew, locust or grasshopper, if their enemy besieges them in the land of their cities, whatever plague, whatever sickness there is, whatever prayer or supplication is made by any man or by all your people Israel, *each knowing the affliction of his own heart*, and spreading his hands toward this house; then hear you who are in heaven your dwelling place, and forgive and act and render to each according to all his ways, and whose heart you know, for you alone know the hearts of all the sons of men.

This passage unites the motifs of a locust plague and enemy attack leading to a repentance based upon the knowledge of guilt. One may assume that this passage played a very important part as the background for Joel. Even more impressive is the fact that the preceding verses, 1 Kgs 8:35-36 (=2 Chr 6:26f), also bring in the motif of a drought caused by the sin of the people:

---

51 See Bič, *Das Buch Joel*, 106, and others.

52 Graham Ogden, "Joel 4," *JSOT* 26 (1983): 97-106.

53 Even Ogden only supports his argument with the citation of Joel 4:19 which mentions the innocent blood of Judah. However, the situation in chapter four has changed and is clearly understood as a future event following the repentance of the people presumed as the background for the assurance in the second half of Joel.

When the heavens are shut up and there is no rain, *because they have sinned against you*, and they pray toward this place and confess your name and turn from their sin when you afflict them, then hear, you who are in heaven, and forgive the sin of your servants and of your people Israel, indeed teach them the good way in which they should walk. And send rain on your land which you have given your people for an inheritance.

There is therefore good reason to suppose that Joel presumed the guilt of the people whom he called to repentance. Indeed, several indicators reveal that the need for repentance is based upon pictures of sin and guilt taken from Hosea.

The call to the "drinkers of wine" in Joel 1:5 is reminiscent several passages in Hosea in which wine of various types is pictured as being involved with improper worship. The metaphorical depiction in Hos 2:10f admonishes the bride of YHWH for using YHWH's gifts — including new wine (תירוש) — for the worship of Baal. For this reason, YHWH withdraws the harvest of these elements (2:11), precisely the situation with which Joel opens. Hos 2:24 promises a future return of the new wine and oil upon the faithful betrothal of YHWH and the bride who committed harlotry/idolatry with these elements (cf 2:22f). In 4:11 and 7:14, wine likewise appears in situations of false worship. In the former, it is responsible for the removal of understanding which leads to the worship of idols. In the latter, the people do not assemble to cry to YHWH, but "for the sake of grain and new wine they assemble themselves." In light of this passage, the cutting off of the sweet wine in Joel 1:5 exhibits a bitter sense of irony. The drinkers of wine, or those who assemble themselves for the sake of wine, are now called to come together to lament the fact that there is no wine for which to assemble (cf also Joel 1:10).

In a similar vein, the feminine addressee in 1:8 takes up Hos 2:3ff. The common explanation offered for 1:8 requires the assumption that Joel offers a comparison to a betrothed "virgin" whose husband has died.[54] This explanation distinguishes a two part concept of marriage in which the betrothed woman, who is considered the wife of the man, still lives with her family, since the marriage is not consummated. Hence, she can be both בתולה and married woman. As interesting as this phenomenon is, one must seriously question if this picture provides the background of this verse. Bič correctly notes the problems with this explanation in that while בתולה may be translated as young woman or virgin, it is not possible to translate בעל as bridegroom, which would be required to make the picture

---

[54] Wolff, *BK* 14/2, 34f; Rudolph, *KAT* 13/2, 44f; Allen, *Joel, etc.*, 52f; etc.

consistent within itself.[55]   His suggestions that the בתולה should be understood proverbially (thus, *the* virgin), and that בעל be taken as a literal reference to the god are also correct, although issue must be taken that the virgin is Anat mourning over Baal. A much simpler, and literarily more consistent picture can be drawn from Hos 2:3ff.

Hos 2:3ff presumes that the bride deserts YHWH in order to take up a life of harlotry (idolatry) in which she takes YHWH's gifts for the worship of Baal. Significantly, the text predicts the destruction of those gifts which she uses for this idolatry. These gifts constitute the very things which Joel presumes as devastated, namely the grain, new wine, oil (Hos 2:10, cf Joel 1:10); vines and fig trees (Hos 2:14, cf Joel 1:7,12). This repetition cannot be accidental. Joel delineates these elements to refer back to the example of YHWH's wife in Hos 2:3ff. Indeed, Joel inverts this picture, ironically depicting the woman girded with sackcloth, typical clothes for lamentation and mourning, rather than the fine gifts of YHWH such as silver and gold (Hos 2:10), and earrings and jewelry (Hos 2:15). However, even this irony is consistent with Hos 2:8-17. In those verses, YHWH prevents her from pursuing her lovers (2:8), until she decides to return to YHWH in 2:9: "And then she will say, I will return to my first husband (אישי הראשון), for it was better with me then than now." YHWH further elaborates on the abuses of her past (2:10), followed by the pronouncement of judgment in

---

55 Contra Wolff, *BK* 14/2, 34, who disagrees with Bič, but provides no evidence. Note that the Hebrew word חתן more typically refers to bridegroom (e.g. Jer 7:34). Milos Bič, *Das Buch Joel.* Berlin: Evangelische Verlagsanstalt, 1960, 22f. Bič strongly disagrees that בתולה in 1:8 could in anyway refer to a young woman who is betrothed yet not "officially" married. He maintains that בתולה means virgin and that בעל may mean "lord" or "husband" but not bridegroom. Bič agrees with the suggestion made by Hvidberg that this reference to virgin is made proverbially. For Bič such a proverb readily stems from the virgin Anat weeping over her brother/husband Baal as she seeks the fallen God, and then brings him back from the nether-world. Bič takes the phrase as an example of the YHWH/Baal conflict which was still raging at the time of Joel. He understands Baal to be a literal reference to the god and not a husband. G understood this reference, hence the double אלי to emphasize that YHWH is speaking and not Baal and then the translation of Baal as husband is a polemical weakening of the force of this word. Bič's own explanation of the feminine imperative is that it is speaking to the *daughter of Zion.* Bič further maintains that since there is no mention of the rejoicing over the return of the divinity (as in the Baal cycle) that we can safely assume this text was a rite of mourning over the departure of the divinity. Wolff correctly discounts Bič's explanation on the basis of date, but neither Wolff nor Bič adequately explain the phrase "of her youth." Contra Bič, the use of בעל need not necessarily imply an ongoing debate between Baal and YHWH, and therefore is not evidence for an early composition of Joel.

2:11-15 which culminates in YHWH's determination to "punish her for *the days of the Baals*." Only after this announcement of punishment does YHWH open the possibility of reconciliation (2:16f), in which he allures the wife into the wilderness in order to remind her of her true husband, thus enabling her to "sing there as in the *days of her youth*." In an addendum, YHWH, in a beautiful play on words, promises that "in that day, ... you will call me my אישי (my husband), and *no longer* בעלי (my Baal). This allegory presumes the division of time into a certain schema: the ideal time of the days of her youth when she lived in prosperity with her first husband; the present "days of the Baals" in which she lives in harlotry; and the future ideal time when repentance allows her to return to YHWH.

Returning to Joel, it is important to ask how closely the picture from Hos 2:3ff fits Joel 1:8. First, is it possible that YHWH's wife in Hos 2:3ff could be the בתולה to whose lament Joel 1:8 refers? This question may be answered affirmatively, since בתולה has another meaning, other than virgin or young woman, specifically, the word is also a title used for personified entities in the ancient near east. As such it is used in the Old Testament in connection both with Zion and with Israel, but in the Joel context בתולה must refer to Israel, another indication of the supposition of Hos 2:3ff.[56] The reason for this supposition is the presence of two

---

[56] The virgin Israel is used in Amos 5:2; Jer 31:4,21; 18:13 (significantly, Jer 18:13 also picks up Hoseanic imagery when it says that the virgin Israel has done an appalling thing by forgetting her God). Zion normally receives the additional appellation virgin "daughter" — 2 Kgs 19:21 = Isa 23:12; Lam 2:13. The phrase "virgin daughter" is also used of other geographic entities as a title: Sidon (Isa 23:12); Babylon (47:1); Judah (Lam 1:15); Egypt (Jer 46:11). Finally, virgin daughter appears in conjunction with the people of YHWH (Jer 2:32; 14:17). It is thus significant that only Israel is ever cited as "virgin" without the phrase "virgin daughter." Conversely, Israel is never called "virgin daughter." While YHWH's wife in Hos 2:3ff is never explicitly named, the context demands an understanding of Israel as the intended entity. However, care must be exercised at this point by noting that there is an inordinate amount material in Hos 2 which sounds as though it could well have been composed in Zionistic circles, keeping open the possibility that the chapter has itself been redacted by the very group(s) responsible for the tradent of the Book of the Twelve as a whole, and not merely in the tradent of Hosea alone. There is no space in this investigation of the seams of the writings in the Book of the Twelve to treat this subject thoroughly, but it is indeed plausible to suppose someone has shaped, and later read, Hos 2:3ff as a theological introduction to the Book of the Twelve, in much the same manner as the other major prophetic books have introductory blocks which serve a theological function for the book. For example, see the recent dissertation of Mark Edward Biddle, *A Redaction History of Jeremiah 2:1-4:2* (Zürich, Theologischer Verlag, 1990), 259ff, for a discussion as to how Jeremiah 2:2b-4:2 functions as a "theological prologue" to Jeremiah.

feminine entities in Joel 1:8, the one who is directly addressed (Zion) and the other who is used as an example (כבתולה, *like* the virgin).

Finally, one further observation signifies the failure of the frequent attempt to explain the picture of Joel 1:8 as that of a betrothed woman who has lost her husband, while at the same time strengthening the connection to Hos 2:3ff. The tensions created by the phrase "of her youth" make no logical sense in this interpretation of the metaphor. The phrase "of her youth" does not fit the picture as explained by Wolff and others, since it obviously refers to a previous time from the perspective of some considerable distance. The phrase is almost synonymous with "long ago."[57] In light of the early age of betrothals, the phrase "husband of her youth", or husband of long ago, would be very difficult to explain. Even if the marriage had not been consummated, it would not make sense to use the term בתולה either in the sense of virgin or young woman along with this chronological phrase. The picture of a "young woman" grieving over her husband of long ago hardly seems to fit Joel 1:8. If the picture intended the death of the husband of her youth, this situation would imply that the woman would be considerably older by now, and בתולה would be inappropriate. If her husband had been dead for a considerable time she would have been a widow, not a young woman.

Such tension is not created when בתולה is understood as a title for Israel, the wife of YHWH, as depicted in Hos 2:3ff. Indeed the tension is resolved when the phrase is seen in this light. The chronological distance implied in the phrase may be accounted for by its use in Hos 2:17 to refer to the ideal time of the past. The phrase "because of the Baal of her youth" offers a reason for repentance, not the picture of a suffering innocent.[58] In light of the connection to Hos 2:3ff which is consistently

---

[57] Cf the similar phrase, the wife of your youth, in Mal 2:14; Prov 5:18, and Isa 54:6; which implies a marriage covenant in the past, as well as a continuing relationship.

[58] Joel 1:8 deliberately plays on the איש/בעל dialectic in Hos 2:9ff to the point of establishing a double entendre. Those verses refer to the present time of idolatry as the days of Baals (2:15), but to the past, the ideal time with her first husband, as the days of her youth (2:17). Nevertheless, the text also indicates that the bride called YHWH Baal during that time: "You will *no longer* call me my master (בעלי)." The double entendre of Joel 1:8 results from its combination of Baal with the phrase "of her youth." First, Joel 1:8 can be read as an explicit reference to the wife's action in Hos 2:9, where she desires to return to YHWH — her first husband — when she realized the pursuit of other lovers brought her no gain. The sense of the verse would then be: realize, as she did, that you were better off with YHWH. Second, the phrase can be read in a more accusing tone if one presumes Joel looked back on Hosea's account as something from the past. The Baal of her youth could also be understood as a

apparent in Joel 1:8, the verse could be paraphrased as a command to Zion to repent as Israel had to repent for her idolatry and turning from YHWH.

The Hosea imagery introduced in Joel 1:1-14 goes well beyond these verses. Joel offers further evidence that the question of the unfulfilled promises of Hosea served as the springboard for the compilation of the Joel. Bergler demonstrates clearly that Joel 2:23 quotes Hos 10:12 as confirmation that YHWH's immediate blessings of rain will result from the true repentance of the people described in Joel 2:12-17.[59] This reiteration that the promise will be fulfilled after true repentance, coincides precisely with the larger context of Hos 14:2-9, which requires true repentance from the people prior to YHWH's change of heart.[60] When Joel 1:2ff calls for repentance, it does so with the presumption that the unfulfilled promises of Hosea result from a lack of dependence on YHWH on the part of the people.

Thus, the connections from Joel 1:2ff backward to Hosea demonstrate that Joel deliberately picks up where Hos 14:2ff leaves off, by literarily (hear this, has this happened) and graphically acknowledging that the promises given by Hosea remain unfulfilled in Joel's time. In addition, further connections to images of guilt from Hosea's message to Israel imply that Joel transfers this guilt to his own message to Jerusalem. The demonstration of this hermeneutic confirms the suspicion of Bosshard who suggests the function of Hosea with Joel 1:2ff is similar to that of Isaiah 1-11, namely to bring words of judgment against YHWH's people *from a Jerusalem-Southern kingdom perspective.*[61] This investigation of the connections backward to Hosea in Joel 1:2ff confirms that it is precisely this hermeneutic which combines Joel's depiction of the situation with the guilt described in Hosea. A description of the connective function of Joel 1:2ff is not complete, however, without brief reference to the introduction of themes which also point forward to other portions of the Book of the Twelve.

---

reference to the rebellious period of idolatry, providing the reason for her repentance. The sense of this reading would be: you repent like the בתולה had to repent when she chased Baal long ago. Both sides of this double entendre connote a strong tenor of guilt, since both emanate from the supposition that the wife of Hos 2:3ff forsook YHWH.

[59] Bergler, *Joel als Schriftinterpret*, 92.

[60] See especially Hos 14:3, where the allusion to true repentance takes the form of a reference to the "fruit of our lips."

[61] Bosshard, *BN* 40 (1987): 32.

3.2. Connections Forward in the Book of the Twelve

Joel exhibits numerous connections to other portions of the Book of the Twelve which serve to anchor its pivotal redactional role. With the limitation of this work to passages in the seams of the writings, it is only possible to highlight some of the connections appearing in Joel 1:1-14.[62]

The most notable of these connective devices is the depiction of the locust plague, particularly as described in Joel 1:6f, which plays a significant role in the Nahum-Habakkuk connection.[63] Nah 3:15 predicts Assyria's destruction by a metaphorical locust, while Nah 3:17 mocks the once powerful Assyrians, who, even though they had been as numerous as locust hordes, still cannot prevent their own destruction.[64] Hab 1:9 picks up locust imagery again, but this time applies it to the Babylonians, whose imminent rise is to be more feared than the Assyrians. Within the larger movement of the Book of the Twelve, Joel 1-2 prepares the literary groundwork for the expectation of a horde of destruction coming against Jerusalem. Joel's masterful description an invading army in terms of a locust plague remains vivid to anyone who reads the Book of the Twelve as a single literary work.[65] When one notes also that Joel 2-4 parallels the anti-Babylonian oracle of Isa 13, the reader can scarcely avoid perceiving Joel's locust-army metaphors in Nahum and Habakkuk in relation to the history of Judah and Jerusalem.[66] Those references, as will be shown, have been inserted into their contexts, making clear that someone utilized the locust army from Joel 1:4,6f as a paradigm for the punishment of Judah and Jerusalem at the hands of political enemies. Other motifs in Joel 1:1-14 demonstrate a similar paradigmatic function.

A second connective motif concerns the accentuation of the present situation using the botanical imagery in Joel 1:5ff. This motif appears regularly in the Book of the Twelve at significant locations. It is certainly not unknown elsewhere in the Old Testament, but its use in the Book of

---

[62] For a listing of others, see discussion below on Joel 4:1-21 and its relationship to Amos. See also Bosshard's discussion of the relationship of Joel, Obadiah and Zephaniah (Bosshard, *BN* 40 1987): 37f); Schneider, *The Unity of the Book of the Twelve*, 88f; and Bergler, *Joel als Schriftinterpret*, 21-31.

[63] For a fuller treatment of this connection see the appropriate chapters below.

[64] Nah 3:17 stems from an early form of the book, while the destruction of Assyria by locusts plays off Joel. See discussion of Nah 3:1ff in the Nahum chapter below.

[65] On the impossibility of literal locusts being able to perform the destruction as pictured in Joel 1:7, see Reicke, "Joel und seine Zeit," 135.

[66] See Bosshard, *BN* 40 (1987): 31.

the Twelve facilitates a literary consistency by returning to similar motifs. This botanical imagery may appear in depictive and in eschatological contexts. It appears in both redactional and non-redactional passages in almost every connection of the Book of the Twelve.[67] The presence of this imagery by no means necessitates that all the material stems from the same literary level, but it presents a common characteristic which will need to be analyzed in the course of this investigation.

One other connective feature of Joel deserves mention, in spite of the fact that it does not appear specifically in Joel 1:1-14. The day of YHWH, in its various manifestations, is an important concept in both Joel and the Book of the Twelve.[68] Significantly, only Isaiah contains as many references to the day of YHWH as the Book of the Twelve.[69] Again, this emphasis cannot be used to say that all of the day of YHWH material belongs to the same hand, but it adds considerable weight to the arguments of a common tradent for the two works, as well as for the Book of the Twelve as a whole.

Before concluding, a brief word should be devoted to Joel's compilation, specifically to an understanding of Joel 1:2-4. Bergler demonstrates the purely redactional and literary role played by these verses, with specific regard to the locusts. It has been argued here that the verses pick where Hos 14:2ff leaves off. It will further be demonstrated how comments inserted into other contexts reach back to Joel for a paradigm explaining historical periods. For these reasons, the character of these verses should not be divorced from their position and function in the Book of the Twelve. This observation has significant implications for understanding 1:2-4. Rather than representing the record of an oral speech delivered by the prophet, the literary character of the verses requires a broader spectrum. In light of the use of Joel throughout the Book of the Twelve, the verses read like something *approaching* an "apocalyptic" introduction. Most commentators fail to accent that the locust motif of Joel 1:4 does not evidence a single locust attack. Rather, it depicts a series of attacks, each consuming what the last one relinquished. Joel 1:6f explicates the locust metaphor as a political enemy. When one reads 1:4 in this light,

---

[67] The botanical imagery does not actually occur in the Obadiah-Jonah connection, (cf Obad 11-14), but this connection post-dates an Obadiah-Micah connection (see below).

[68] The first specific reference to the day of YHWH tradition begins immediately after the call to repentance with the description in 1:15ff.

[69] A good indication of this emphasis may be found in the phrase ביום ההוא which appears 42 times in the Book of the Twelve and 45 times in Isaiah, yet appears, by contrast, only 12 times in Jeremiah and 13 times in Ezekiel.

then its suitability as a paradigmatic introduction becomes clearer. Judah and Jerusalem have been continually beset by "locust" attacks. This aspect provides the future orientation of Joel 1:3 more significance than it normally receives. As a reference to a past locust attack, its command to relate "it" to future generations ofers little more than a command to recount the last flood or the last tornado. Given the manner in which Joel is used elsewhere in the Book of the Twelve,[70] however, 1:3 serves as a command to repeat the message of the book to succeeding generations: future salvation — in light of present devastation — depends upon the proper relationship to YHWH. This recounting takes place literarily with the incorporation of several prophetic writings into the Book of the Twelve.

4. Summary of the Hosea - Joel Transition

Joel exhibits literary connections both forward and backward. The connections backward have been treated in more depth here, but the strength of the connections forward will become clearer in the following discussions, because they often rely on Joel's introduction of these themes. A summary of the observations regarding the *Stichwort* connection between Hosea and Joel indicates several points of interest with regard to the manner by which these writings were attached.[71] In Hosea, four of the five *Stichwörter* appear in material secondary to the divine promise in Hos 14:5-10. Three of these words appear in the parenthetical insertion of 14:8a and another in the rhetorical ending of the book in 14:10. Whereas 14:10 has only the book of Hosea in its literary horizon, 14:8a deliberately picks up imagery from Hos 2:3ff from a post-exilic perspective, and serves to prepare the reader for Joel. In Joel 1:1-14, the *Stichwörter* appear more integrally involved in the units of which they are a part, but such is to be expected in light of the redactional function of Joel, which incorporates images of guilt from Hosea (Joel 1:5,8), takes up where Hos 14:2ff leaves

---

[70] The Book of the Twelve implies the larger corpus, but likely, Jonah — which in many respects argues with the attitudes of Joel — and Zech 9-14 were not incorporated into the Book of the Twelve at the point Joel and the Joel-related motifs entered. See appropriate discussions in those chapters.

[71] Elaboration of the rationale for the following statements relating to Hosea may be found in Nogalski, *Literary Precursors*, 58ff.

off (Joel 1:2), and introduces motifs which play an important role in the larger movement of the Book of the Twelve.

Direct indications of date are difficult to ascertain in this connection because of the lack of concrete events or places named. Some observations do, however, affect the date of the material. The dual function of Hos 14:8 as literary bridge presupposes the presence of Joel, but its inclusion into Hos 14:8 is best seen as part of the same process which added Joel. Nothing in Joel 1:1-14 argues strongly against an acceptance of a date between 400-350 argued by a strong contingent of exegetes, but Joel's redactional function in the Book of the Twelve strongly argues against those who argue for a sixth century date. In addition, the addressees and the situation presumed in Joel reflect an actualization and reapplication of Hosea in post-exilic Jerusalem.

5. Joel 4:1-21: Eschatological Judgment and Promise of Salvation

The fourth chapter of Joel presents a redactional unity containing four individual units: the introduction in 4:1-3; the oracle against Tyre, Sidon, and the Philistine confederation in 4:4-8; the eschatological call to judgment in 4:9-17; and the eschatological promise of restoration in 4:18-21. This chapter previously discussed the position and function of 4:1-21 in the macrostructure of Joel, and here it need only be repeated that Joel 4:1-21 depicts the long term effects (with considerable eschatological imagery) of the divine response to the prayer of the priests 2:17.[72]

5.1. Joel 4:1-3: Literary Introduction

The literary introduction (4:1-3) separates itself formally from the preceding material by a rather protracted introductory formula containing eschatological overtones (בימים ההמה ובעת ההיא). In spite of this formal separation, Joel 4:1-21 presupposes chapter three. Joel 4:1-21 expands the thoughts of that chapter, particularly 3:3-5.[73] This literary introduction extends through 4:3, after which point a new unit begins with the marker

---

[72] See discussion of the macrostructure of Joel above, page 4.

[73] See Wolff, *BK* 14/2 70f; Bergler, *Joel als Schriftinterpret*, 99; Rudolph, *KAT* 13/2, 24; Allen, *Joel, etc.*, 27.

וגם. In addition, one may assume the inner unity of this introduction on syntactical grounds. The protracted introductory formula in 4:1a,ba ("For behold in those days and at that time") is inseparably bound to both the dependant clause in 4:1b (when I return the possessions of Judah and Jerusalem), and to the pronouncement of 4:2f ("Then I will gather the nations ..."). Joel 4:2 and 4:3 are likewise closely related, based on the connecting ו, and on the common subject of the nations in the plural verbs (פזרו, חלקו, ידו, יתנו, מכרו).

As noted already, Joel 4:1-3 introduces 4:4-8,9-17,18-21 by summarizing the themes of these other units:

> A The coming restoration of Judah and Jerusalem (4:1)
>   B Judgment of the nations in the valley of Jehoshaphat (4:2)
>   C Slavery of YHWH's people (4:3)
>   C' Slavery of YHWH's people (4:4-8)
>   B' Judgment of the nations in the valley of Jehoshaphat (4:9-17)
> A' The coming restoration of Judah and Jerusalem (4:18-21)

Joel 4:1-3 presents a literary composition associated with the compilation of the book. The verses presuppose their location following chapter three, and presuppose the existence of the three remaining units of chapter four. It will be demonstrated that the current form of the remaining units presuppose material from other portions of Joel, supplying evidence that chapter four as an entity must have been composed in light of the entire book of Joel, and could not have been transmitted independently in its present form.[74] The interdependence of chapter four does not necessarily

---

[74] Logically, these observations only argue that Joel 4:1-21 is the latest block of material to enter the book. They do not prove that chapters 1-4 were compiled simultaneously. The fact that the call to repentance receives three different resolutions — the promise of rain (2:18-27), the pouring out of the spirit (3:1-5), and the judgment against the nations — could speak for more than one layer of compilation. Traditionally, scholars — such as Allen, *Joel, etc.*, 38; and particularly Prinsloo, *Theology of Joel*, 123, 126 — argue against separating these responses into separate layers, because the three responses represent a heightening of promise motifs, but these arguments need qualification. Following YHWH's universal promise to "pour out my spirit on all flesh," judgment against the nations presents a noticeably anti-climactic tone, and it is difficult to perceive climactic tendencies, without presupposing "all flesh" refers only to Judeans. This decline in tenor, at least in part, leads some to postulate different compilational layers. Plöger, *Theocracy and Eschatology*, 100-105, for example argues 3:1-5 was inserted between 2:27 and 4:1. Plöger has not found many followers, because of the strength of the recent arguments for unity by other scholars: e.g. Wolff, *BK* 14/2, 5-7; Rudolph, *KAT* 13/2, 23f; etc. They argue convincingly that Joel 4:1-21 reflects

imply that the entire chapter was composed specifically for the book. Bergler's model of the compilation of chapters 1-2 demonstrates a considerable amount of adaptation of pre-existing material, as well as the simple incorporation of pre-existing poems into the context with little change. Bergler himself does not believe chapter four exhibits this same use of pre-existing blocks,[75] but it will be argued here that the incorporation (4:4-8) and adaptation (4:9-17) of pre-existing units, together with compositional blocks (4:1-3,18-21) at the beginning and end of the unit provide the clearest explanation for the compilation of the chapter.

5.2. Joel 4:4-8: Oracle against Tyre, Sidon, and the Philistine Regions

The next unit, Joel 4:4-8, constitutes an oracle against Tyre, Sidon, and the Philistine regions. The boundaries of the unit are marked at both ends: by וגם in 4:4, and נאם־יהוה as a closing formula in 4:8. The clear connection of the content of 4:4-8 affirms the unity of these verses. The specific geo-political entities are called to attention in 4:4 for as yet unnamed actions which have provoked YHWH to retribution. The actual

---

knowledge of 3:1ff. What then accounts for the shift in the orientation of Joel 4:1ff? The introductory formula in 3:1 and 4:1 provide a certain evidence for a chronological ordering of the events: YHWH will pour out his spirit (3:1), performs wonders in the sky (3:3f), allow those calling on the name of YHWH to be delivered (3:5). Then YHWH will gather the nations (4:2). At the same time, this movement assumes deliverance takes place in Jerusalem (3:5; 4:1). The remainder of chapter four also offers little hint of salvation for "all flesh" in universal terms as it outlines the judgment against the nations. Therefore, one must either understand "all flesh" to refer only to Judah and Jerusalem, or one must postulate that the salvation for those beyond Judah and Jerusalem does not find further elaboration within Joel. Two brief observations are offered here as possible explanations for this tension, although admittedly more work is required before a decision can be reached. First, given Joel's paradigmatic quality within the Book of the Twelve, it is not inconceivable that this motif was not intended to find its resolution in Joel. Other passages within the Book of the Twelve (particularly Zech 8:20-23 and Mal 1:11-14) do offer more hope for deliverance of those outside Judah which coincide more readily with Joel 3:1f. Joel 3:1f may thus be pointing forward to later portions of the corpus. Second, and at this point more demonstrable, the shift in tenor for Joel 4:1-21 reflects the literary parameters within which Joel was compiled. Not only did Joel 1:2ff begin where Hosea left off, but the judgment against the nations in Joel 4:1-21 offers a suitable — albeit more eschatologically oriented — transition to the oracles against the nations in Amos 1-2. Compare especially Joel 4:16 and Amos 1:2.

[75] Bergler, *Joel als Schriftinterpret*, 342.

crimes committed, delineated in 4:5f, are two-fold. The oracle accuses these western neighbors of pillaging the temple (a clear reference to the destruction of 587), and of selling Judeans and Jerusalemites as slaves to the Greeks.   The punishment pronounced against these people (4:7f) precisely reverses these crimes. Joel 4:4-6 accuses Tyre, Sidon, and all the Regions of Philistia of unwarranted and unilateral acts of aggression (4:4).[76] Their punishment assures that their own deeds will come back to haunt them (4:7b) as a repayment for those actions. The reversal of the punishment is even more graphically displayed in 4:7a,8 by the promise that those Judeans who had been sold into slavery across the sea to the *northwest*, would in turn sell the population of the Mediterranean Seaboard as slaves to the Sabeans, a group traditionally known as controllers of the trade routes to the *southeast*.[77] The picture is one of poetic justice which goes full circle:

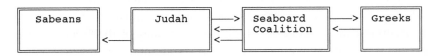

The seaboard coalition sells the Judeans and Jerusalemites across the sea to the Greeks (northwest), but the slaves return as part of a process in which they in turn sell their captors in exactly the opposite direction, toward the desert (southeast).[78]

Discussions of the origin of Joel 4:4-8 depend heavily upon the presuppositions brought to the text. Those who argue the verses were inserted later rely heavily upon the fact that these verses operate with different motifs than the remainder of the chapter, and thus tend in the direction of an independent oracle against these regions, later placed into this chapter on the basis of the catchword "sell" in 4:3.[79]   Those who

---

[76] The artistic reference to the recompense in 4:7 points back to 4:4. See discussion of the structural symmetry of 4:4-8 in Prinsloo, *Theology of Joel*, 95f; and Bergler, *Joel als Schriftinterpret*, 102f.

[77] Biblical traditions attest this view of the Sabeans: 1Kgs 10:2; Ezek 27:22f; 38:13. See further, Rudolph, *KAT* 13/2, 81; Allen, *Joel, etc.*, 111; Wolff, *BK* 14/2, 95. For discussion of the date of the passage, see below, page 50.

[78] There is no reason, contra Bič's suggestion, *Das Buch Joel*, 90, to read בני היונים as "sons of mire" rather than a reference to the Greeks.

[79] Wolff, *BK* 14/2, 89f and Watts, *Joel, etc.*, 44. Even Rudolph, *KAT* 13/2, 24,82, who believes the passage is genuine has difficulty explaining its place in the context. He suggests it originally appeared after Joel 4:21.

argue Joel 4:4-8 is not a later insertion play down the differences and
accentuate the verses as a concretization of the more general
announcement against the nations, thereby reflecting an inherent logic.[80]
In actuality, both sides of this argument make solid observations, which are
not as mutually exclusive as their proponents typically presume. When
viewed against the chiastic structure of 4:1-21, both the independent
background and the inherent logic can be taken into account, by the
application of Bergler's model of an author who was not averse to
incorporating independent blocks to shape larger literary units. It is very
difficult to accept the thesis that Joel 4:4-8 was composed specifically for
the book. It contains too many distinctive features from the remainder of
the chapter and the book. Its precise cyclic justice, together with the
opening and concluding formulas, add to the impression that it stood alone
prior to its incorporation into Joel. On the other hand, there is a logic to
its *position* in the chapter. When this logic is combined with observations
on the independence of 4:9-17*, however, one recognizes that this logic is
the imposed logic of an "author" who combines diverse material.

5.3. Joel 4:9-17: Judgment in the Valley

The third and largest unit of the chapter, Joel 4:9-17, portrays a scene
of judgment against the nations. It begins with a series of imperatives in
4:9 following the closing formula in 4:8. Formally, the unit continues
through 4:17, since the ביום ההוא formula in 4:18 signifies a new subject.
Most scholars relate 4:9 directly to 4:2 because of the judgment in the
valley of Jehoshaphat, without pausing to explain the tension between the
two portrayals. In 4:2, YHWH explicitly claims he will gather the nations
into the valley, and "bring them down" into the valley. By contrast, the
nations in 4:9ff are told to "gather yourselves" in the valley (4:11). When
viewed in light of 4:9-17 in its entirety, 4:2 does not coincide as closely as
most presume.

In order to properly understand the portrayal of the action in this
passage one must recognize the parties involved. The action is confusing
because the 2mp references in these verses refer to three different groups:

---

[80] Allen, *Joel, etc.*, 111, 114; Bergler, *Joel als Schriftinterpret*, 102f; Rudolph, *KAT* 13/2,
81f.

the congregation, the surrounding nations, and the heavenly host.[81]
Additionally, the 2ms reference in 4:11b is often emended which masks the
change of speaker inherent in MT.[82] However, when one recognizes that
the speaker alternates regularly in these verses, the structure of the passage
becomes clear:

```
4:9aa   Prophet to people:
          Proclaim this among the nations.
4:9ab-11a YHWH to the nations:
          Prepare for battle.
4:11b   Prophet to YHWH:
          Bring down your warriors.
4:12-13 YHWH to heavenly host:
          Prepare to descend for judgment.
4:14-16 Prophet to people:
          Description of the day of YHWH.
4:17    YHWH to people:
          Then you will know I am your God.
```

A frame directed to the audience (4:9aa,14-16, 17) encompasses the entire
unit. The frame announces the coming judgment upon the nations, and

---

[81] Joel 4:9aa commands a group, as noted by the plural imperative קראו, to convey the
speech that follows to the nations. Theoretically, the speaker could be either the
prophet of YHWH. The prophet is presumed here because of the liturgical character
involving the congregation. The speech which follows (4:9ab-11a) is the command
which comes from YHWH. Despite the fact that no divine "I" markers explicitly
specify YHWH as the speaker, the introduction which immediately precedes marks that
which follows as a quote from YHWH. The prophet responds (4:11b) with a petition
asking that YHWH bring down his heavenly army. One may assume that the army
refers to the heavenly host because the verb נחת implies descent. This petition
addresses YHWH directly. Theoretically, the verse could be placed in the mouth of the
congregation, but it seems wiser to presume the prophet speaks directly to YHWH
rather than the people. YHWH responds to the petition in 4:11b with a command
(4:12f) to his heavenly army to prepare for battle. Joel 4:12 contains divine "I" material
indicating YHWH as the speaker, and the plural commands are best read in light of
the prophetic reference to YHWH's heavenly army in 4:11b, and constitute YHWH's
decision to sit in judgment. The action of the scene advances with 4:14-16a by the
depiction of the nations arrayed in the valley, awaiting YHWH's judgment. The events
of the day of YHWH are also poetically described in these verses. In 4:16b,17 both the
prophet (4:16b; who affirms YHWH as refuge to Israel) and YHWH (4:17) predict a
positive outcome. Particularly, YHWH's speech demonstrates that the entire battle
scene should be viewed as proof of YHWH's power.

[82] This petition is often emended to avoid the interruption of the divine speech: so Allen,
Joel, etc., 107; Stuart, *Word* 31, 265; Wolff, *BK* 14/2, 87f. Rudolph, *KAT* 13/2, 76f,
transposes 4:11b after 4:12 to smooth the context. Wolff at least admits the image of
MT corresponds to other passages, significant among these 2 Chr 20:22. See below,
page 32.

simultaneously defines the day of judgment as one of refuge for the people of YHWH (4:16) which will be proof of YHWH's power (4:17).

The heart of the unit (4:9ab-13) relates a dramatic episode to the people in which YHWH calls all the nations to battle (4:9ab-11a), presumably because they threaten his people. This dramatic account is followed by the prophetic petition that YHWH send down his heavenly host, which in turn prompts YHWH to command that host to descend and prepare the judgment in the valley of Jehoshaphat, where he will sit as judge against the nations.

The alternation of speakers and the dramatic/liturgical quality of 4:9-17 raises the question as to whether these verses have their origin outside the book of Joel. Did these verses exist in some earlier form? There is good reason to suspect that such is the case. First, the verses are clearly separated from the other units in the chapter. The unit before (4:4-8) and after (4:18-21) each have their own introduction, and 4:4-8 has its own conclusion. The events portrayed in 4:9-17 are thus not inherently bound to the remainder of Joel 4:1ff. Second, a possible background for 4:9-17 may be noted in the legend of Jehoshaphat in 2 Chr 20:1-30.[83] The most common argument against the legend of Jehoshaphat as background material for Joel 4:9-17 claims only Joel understands the "valley of Jehoshaphat" symbolically, whereas 2 Chr 20:1ff depicts a historical battle.[84] However, in light of very real parallels which exist between the two passages, such an easy dismissal cannot be accepted without qualification. Several passages portray a tradition of eschatological judgment in a valley, but none of these passages so closely parallels the elements of Joel 4:9-17 and the non-eschatological passage in 2 Chr 20:1-30. A chart will help bear this out.[85]

---

[83] This suggestion is not entirely new. Earlier authors suggest that these two passages had something in common, but this suggestion has not received much treatment in recent commentaries. See Wolff's reference to Jensen's Danish work, *BK* 14/2, 92. Rudolph, *KAT* 13/2, 79, appears to be arguing against this idea, although he cites no specific author.

[84] See Rudolph, *KAT* 13/2, 79; Allen, *Joel, etc.*, 109.

[85] The first two passages were chosen because of the tradition of the judgment of multitudes in a valley. Ezekiel 39 and Isaiah 22 were chosen for similar affinities, and for their assignation to a "valley-tradition" by Kapelrud, *Joel Studies*, 145-47. The numbers are the verse numbers of the passage. "X" = the reversal of a particular Motif.

Element	2 Chr 20:1-30	2 Chr 14:9-17	Joel 4:9-17	Ezek 39:1-16	Isa 22:1-14
Announcement/ call of attack of multitude	1-2	9	9-11,14		
Who is attacked?	Jehosha-phat	Asa	Jerusalem	Gog	Jerusalem
Who fights for Israel?	YHWH	Asa & YHWH	YHWH	YHWH	Jerusalem
Fear of king	3				
Look to YHWH for help	3	11	16		
Gathering of Nation for prayer/fasting	4				12X
Prayer of king/prophet	6-12	11	11b		
Petition to YHWH for aid	12	11	10		
Knowledge of YHWH motif	12		17	6,7	
Judgment (שפט) motif	12		12		
Divine/prophetic response	14-17		12f		14
Affirmation that battle belongs to YHWH	15,17	11	9-17	1-16	
Battle in Valley	16 (נחל) 26 (עמק)	9 (גיא)	12 (עמק)	11-15 (burial)	5 (גיא) 7 (עמק, plural)
Judah & Jerusalem	17f	12,15	Context		
King/people give thanks	18f				

Element	2 Chr 20:1-30	2 Chr 14:9-17	Joel 4:9-17	Ezek 39:1-16	Isa 22:1-14
People as spectators at battle	20f		Liturg. frame		
Weapons used by victors	22f (confusion)	13 (YHWH's army: Judah)	11b (heavenly host)	2f (YHWH himself)	6f (Kir, Elam)
Description of losers weapons		9		3f	10f (?)
Taking of spoils	24f	13-15			
Etiology of valley	26		12	11	
Return to Judah and Jerusalem	27f	15			
Fear of YHWH by nations	29	14			
Day of YHWH/that day			14	11,13	8,12
Length of Clean-up	25 (3 days)			12 (7 mos)	

Clearly a considerable number of interrelated thematic and structural elements link all of these passages, which tends to support Kapelrud's contention of the existence of a "valley-tradition".[86] However, it does not automatically follow that all of the various manifestations of this tradition are as independent of one another as he supposes, particularly in the case of Joel 4:9-17 and 2 Chr 20:1-30.[87]

---

[86] Kapelrud, *Joel Studies*, 144ff.

[87] A detailed comparison of all these passages is not possible here. The following observations describe certain basic similarities and differences. *2 Chr 14:9-17* contains numerous similarities to 2 Chr 20:1ff, which may be attributed to their common tradent. Neither passage from Chronicles has a parallel in Kings. The use of several motifs fit well with the Chronicler's overall theology and should be understood as part of the stereotypical use of material by the Chronicler. Note the formulations of looking to YHWH for help (14:11; 20:3), the prayer of the king (14:11; 20:6-12), the affirmation

The most notable similarities between 2 Chr 20 and Joel 4:9-17 are found in the vocabulary. While "multitudes" and "valley" appear in the other traditions, only Joel 4 and 2 Chr 20:1-30 use a singular form of עמק for valley. The unusual name Jehoshaphat likewise appears in both passages. 2 Chr 20:1-30 naturally refers to the king Jehoshaphat while Joel 4:9-17 refers to a symbolic valley of Jehoshaphat, but the allusions could be intended to bring to mind those events in which YHWH miraculously repelled the attack of hostile nations.[88] The combination of the war (מלחמה) motif (2 Chr 20:1; Joel 4:9) and the judgment (שפט) motif (2 Chr 20:12; Joel 4:12) appear in only these two passages among those compared.

Several structural elements relate Joel 4:9-17 and 2 Chr 20:1-30 to one another as well. Both contain an announcement of the battle (2 Chr 20:1f; Joel 4:9) followed by a plea for help from YHWH (2 Chr 20:6-12; Joel 4:11b), which receives a divine response (2 Chr 20:14-17 [through a prophet]; Joel 4:12f). In both passages the people play a role as spectator at the battle (2 Chr 20:20f; Joel 4:17a). Both passages provide an etiology of the valley in which the action occurs (2 Chr 20:26; Joel 4:12).[89] Both

---

that the battle belongs to YHWH (14:11; 20:15,17); the taking of spoils (14:13-15; 20:24f); the return to Jerusalem (14:15; 20:27f); and the fear of YHWH on the part of the nations (14:14; 20:29). *Ezek 39:1-16* has many common threads as well, but the picture is so distinct from 2 Chr 20:1ff that it is doubtful one may speak of literary dependence. Note especially that Ezek 39:11-15 does not depict the battle of multitudes in the valley, but rather the burial of Gog and his multitudes. Less similar, but still related in several basic factors is the passage from *Isa 22:1-14*. The enigmatic "valley of vision" in 22:1,5, apparently as a reference to Jerusalem (note the 2fs material), is the place of battle in which God uses Elam and Kir as instruments of attack.

[88] It is exactly this symbolic character of the valley of Jehoshaphat in Joel 4:12 which makes the comparison of these passages so poignant. The contention, often implicit, on the part of commentators that the valley of Jehoshaphat cannot be symbolized and still refer to the legendary account of the battle is logically elusive.

[89] The difference in the names of the two valleys is significant at this point, and is intricately involved with the primary intention of the two passages. 2 Chr 20:1-30 is interested in the deliverance of the people, hence the valley (Beracah) in which the battle occurred was one of blessing (ברך), while Joel 4:9-17 concentrates on the judgment of the nations, hence the reversal of the name into the valley of Jehoshaphat (= YHWH judges) skillfully alludes to the story of Jehoshaphat and to the act of judgment.

passages utilize a knowledge of YHWH motif (2 Chr 20:12; Joel 4:17), although the motif is less stylized in 2 Chr 20:1ff.[90]

These comparisons demonstrate that Joel 4:9-17 bears a striking similarity to 2 Chr 20:1-30, but the two passages are by no means identical. How then should this relationship be understood? Two possibilities, which are not mutually exclusive, present themselves for discussion: 1) The writer of Joel 4:9-17 utilizes the Jehoshaphat story merely as a model to demonstrate how YHWH will judge the nations. This understanding allows the explanation of the differences based upon the eschatological intention of Joel 4:1-21 over against 2 Chr 20:1ff. 2) The compiler of Joel 4:9-17 adapts a previously existing liturgy which was based upon (but not slavishly so) the legend of 2 Chr 20:1ff, or at least a related tradition very close to this legend.[91] This possibility could account for the tension between 4:9-17 in its present form and the material in the remainder of the chapter. A liturgy based on 2 Chr 20:1-30 would account for the 2mp material in the frame of 4:9aa,17. It would account for the tension of Joel 4:4-8 in that one could assume the earlier liturgy would have been more related to the enemies of 2 Chr 20:1-30 (Moab, Ammon, and certain Edomites).[92]

The redactional use of pre-existing material in Joel 4:9-17 receives further support from the fact that one block of material in Joel exhibits a suspicious lack of parallel to the Jehoshaphat story, namely the prophetic day of YHWH description in 4:14b-16a. Since the other prophetic examples of the tradition likewise have day of YHWH material embedded in them, this block is in keeping with the so-called valley-tradition (see above chart), but not with the 2 Chronicles story. This block, 4:14b-16a, is likewise not bound tightly to the literary movement of 4:9-17, since this day of YHWH material in Joel 4:14b-16a begins with a כי clause which can be described as having a transitional function.[93] Even more suspicious is the

---

[90] Joel 4:17 uses the stereotypical phrase "And you will know that I am YHWH your God" which is prevalent in the Pentateuch in various formulations. Interestingly, the phrase also appears in Ezek 39:6f, only with the nations as subject. In 2 Chr 20:12, the people confess their own lack of knowledge together with their dependence upon YHWH.

[91] In the space available, it is not possible to evaluate thoroughly the relationship between these two passages. The matter becomes extremely complicated because of the uncertain state of research on the date of the accounts in Chronicles. See further discussion of the problems of dating below, page 54.

[92] For a summary of the problems of the identification of the third group, see Raymond, B. Dillard, 2 Chronicles, Word Biblical Commentary 15 (Waco, Texas: Word Publishing Company, 1987), 155f.

[93] The section begins, "for the day of YHWH is near in the valley of decision."

fact that while it introduces the day of YHWH theme on the basis of the near context 4:9-17, it is followed by two quotes, one from Joel 2:10 and one from Amos 1:2.[94] These quotes serve to anchor chapter four to the day of judgment material in Joel 2:1ff, and to anticipate the oracles against the nations in Amos 1-2. If one removes these quotes and the transition, the underlying liturgy (4:14a,16b) reads smoother than the text with the cumbersome quoted material: "Multitudes, multitudes are in the valley of verdict ... but YHWH is a refuge for his people." The picture which remains presumes the nations await judgment in the valley while YHWH protects his people. This picture conforms well to the liturgy. One final piece of evidence that this block has been inserted into a pre-existing literary context notes that both the technique and motif correspond to those of the compilator in chapters 1-2 as described by Bergler.[95]

In summary, Joel 4:9-17 takes up and eschatologizes the Jehoshaphat tradition of 2 Chr 20:1ff, although whether or not that tradition already existed in literary form remains undetermined. The perspective of 4:9-17 is more universal (geographically and cosmically) in relation to the judgment motifs found therein, but the essential message is very similar. YHWH, without human aid, will act on behalf of his people centered in Jerusalem to eliminate the threat posed by other nations. In addition, the dramatic/liturgical character of most of the unit suggests strongly that the current form of 4:9-17 is itself an adaptation of pre-existing material originally designed for use in a congregational setting. Finally, the disjunction of 4:14b-16a — both formally in comparison to 2 Chr 20:1ff and literarily in the use of quoted material and superfluousness to the surrounding text — indicates this block has been inserted into the existing literary context.

5.4. Joel 4:18-21: Eschatological Promise of Restoration

The fourth and final unit of the chapter (4:18-21) begins with its own introductory formula and continues to the end of the book. The

---

[94] Note also that the quote from Amos 1:2a ends with the completion of the quote from Joel 2:10, the trembling of the heavens and earth.

[95] Bergler, *Joel als Schriftinterpret*, 52, describes the compilator's adaptation of pre-existing literary blocks through the specific introduction of the day of YHWH motif in 2:1ff. Despite the similarities, Bergler does not see 4:14b-16a in this light, but treats the entire chapter as free composition by Joel.

introductory formula in 4:18 is no mere appendage. It has a clear antecedent in 4:14, and it coincides with the thematic structure of the chapter as outlined in 4:1-3. The form of the unit could best be described as a promise of restoration that includes four thematic elements: an eschatological depiction of weal (4:18), a specific condemnation of Egypt and Edom (4:19), a promise of continual habitation in Judah and Jerusalem (4:20,21b), and a promise of revenge (4:21a). Several tensions within these verses deserve attention. First, the thematic elements may all be classified as positive elements when seen from the perspective of Judah and Jerusalem, but they involve alternating positive and negative actions on the part of YHWH. Positively, YHWH will bring abundance to Judah and Jerusalem enabling bounteous habitation of the region with YHWH dwelling in Zion (4:18,20,21b). Negatively, YHWH will bring destruction to two particular enemies, Egypt and Edom (4:19), and YHWH will mount a campaign of revenge (4:21a). This tension should not, however, be seen as evidence of separate layers of material, since these two aspects are often portrayed as two sides of the same coin. Indeed they are present in the remainder of the chapter, and play an integral role in the structure of this unit.[96]

A second tension in 4:18-21 results, as in the previous unit, in the confusion which exists as to the intended speaker. The third person reference to YHWH in 4:18,21b indicates the speaker is the prophet, but the divine first person speech of 4:21a indicates YHWH as speaker. This oscillation implies that the vacillation of speakers from the previous unit continues in this section as well. The reference to YHWH in 4:21b should best be understood in light of the entire unit in which YHWH will act to demonstrate that he is indeed lord of Zion.

A third problem concerns the interpretation of the referents of the third person plural suffixes in 4:19b,21a. These references are most often understood as referring to a single entity, but a question must be raised as to whether the text intends the same group.[97] The question can be satisfactorily resolved with the recognition of the tight structural relationship of verses 19-21.

---

[96] Compare the judgment on Tyre, Sidon, and the Philistines in 4:4-8 on behalf of YHWH's people (4:7f); the judgment of the nations in 4:9-17 with the comfort to YHWH's people in 4:16f, and the structural parallel of 4:19-21 noted in the chart in the next paragraph.

[97] Examples include Allen, *Joel, etc.*, 125, who argues that "their land" refers to Judah as the place where the bloodshed occurred, while "they poured" refers to Egypt and Edom; and Rudolph, *KAT* 13/2, 87, who believes the atrocities occurred in the foreign lands.

———————— 4:19

מצרים לשממה תהיה ┐
ואדום למדבר שממה תהיה ┘ A   ┐ 1
מחמס בני יהודה אשר-שפכו דם-נקיא בארצם   B ┘

———————— 4:20

ויהודה לעולם תשב ┐
וירושלם לדור ודור ┘ A'   ┐ 2

———————— 4:21

ונקיתי דמם לא-נקיתי   B' ┘
ויהוה שכן בציון

19. Egypt will become a desolation,
    And Edom will become a wilderness of desolation ┐ A   ┐
    For the violence to the sons of Judah,   ┐   1
    When they poured out innocent
              blood in their land   ┘ B   ┘

20. But Judah will be inhabited forever,   ┐
    And Jerusalem for generation to generation. ┘ A' ┐
                                                        2
21. And I will pour out
        their blood that I have not poured out. ┐ B' ┘
    For YHWH dwells in Zion.

These verses comprise two interrelated thought units which are *structural parallels, but thematic contrasts.* The two sections labeled A and A' contrast the conditions of two pairs of political entities: Egypt and Edom will become uninhabitable, whereas Judah and Jerusalem will be habitable forever.[98] Taking the cue from this literary device, one asks if those sections labeled B and B' might not also be read as contrasts.[99] When viewed from this perspective the B sections contrast closely with one another in that each element of the first section has a corresponding element in the second clause:

---

[98] The utilization of the verbs שמם and ישב carry the intended polarity in these elements. The structural parallel is noted by the two-fold mention of Egypt-Edom and Judah-Jerusalem.

[99] The close relationship of these verses has occasionally been noted. See especially Rudolph, *KAT* 13/2, 76,78a, following Duhm. However, both Rudolph and Duhm have argued that 4:21a has been transposed and should have followed 4:19. This suggestion assumes a corruption to the text which is unnecessary in light of the structure and meaning of the passage. Recently, Bergler, *Joel als Schriftinterpret*, 106, diagrams this structure very similarly.

Element	4:19b	4:21
Subject of verb	Edom and Egypt	YHWH
Verb action	pour out	empty out (נקיתי)
Object	innocent blood (דם־נקיא)	their (Egypt and Edom) blood (דמם) that I have not emptied out.
Cause and place of action	because of the violence (done) to the Judeans in their land (Judah)	for YHWH dwells in Zion

The parallel elements allows the isolation of a clear train of thought. Joel 4:19b offers a rationale for the destruction by citing the provocative *action taken against YHWH's people*, whereas 4:21 contrasts the negative fate of Egypt and Edom with the positive fate of Judah and Jerusalem created by a *divine response on behalf of YHWH's people*: Egypt and Edom have poured out innocent blood in Judah, which prompts YHWH's promise to empty out the blood of the perpetrators of these acts. The parallel structure indicates that the use of the 3mp suffix is not intended to refer to the same group. "Their land" refers to Judah while "their blood" refers to Egypt and Edom.

The parallel structure and thematic contrasts in these verses offers fresh evidence for a decision on two particularly thorny questions which have plagued the interpretation of these verses. The first question concerns the place in which the innocent blood was spilled. By relying upon the parallel structure, one may state with confidence that the author is referring to bloodshed which has occurred in Judah.[100] The second question relates to the disputed derivative of a root נקה, meaning "to pour out."[101]

---

[100] The parallel element to innocent blood spilled "in their land" which reflects the rationale for YHWH's retaliation states that YHWH dwells in Zion. The fact that YHWH dwells in Zion makes a more poignant statement when it contrasts with the accusation that Egypt and Edom spilled blood in YHWH's land.

[101] The phrase וְנִקֵּיתִי דָּמָם לֹא־נִקֵּיתִי causes problems. The piel נָקָה, to leave unpunished, is inconsistent with the context. It is often argued that G assumes different roots, נקם, "to avenge," for the first verb (ἐκδικήσω), but נקה with MT for the second (ἀθωώσω). V translates both from the same root נקם, "to avenge." In spite of problems, MT is preferred. G has problems translating the verb נקה when it is used twice: Exod 34:7; Num 14:18; Jer 30:11; Nah 1:3. In addition, G elsewhere translates נקה with ἐκδικήσω (Zech 5:3 [twice]). Other suggested translations: 1) The word

Given the attestation (albeit infrequent) of such a nuance, its use here is clearly to be preferred on structural and literary grounds.

Thus, Joel 4:19-21 exhibits a discernible structure and train of thought which binds the verses together. How then does 4:18 fit into this unit? The key lies in the use of the marker "on that day" in 4:18a. It was noted that in the context of Joel 4:18, the phrase on that day has a clear antecedent. The reference to "that day" (4:18) specifically intends the "day of YHWH" mentioned in 4:14, an observation which may be clearly demonstrated. Whereas 4:14 announces the imminence of the day of YHWH, 4:15f depicts the immediate results of the coming day in terms of the fear showed by nature (the sun, moon, heavens and earth). This is followed by a word of comfort that YHWH is a refuge to his people. It is this thought, YHWH's coming as refuge, which is expanded in 4:18-21, as noted in the fact that the thematic order of 4:18-21 is precisely the same as that of 4:14-17.

4:14 Day of YHWH comes	4:18aa Results of Day of YHWH
4:15-16a Nature responds in fear	4:18 Nature a blessing for Judah
4:16b,17 YHWH is a refuge	4:19-21 YHWH's refuge demonstrated
YHWH dwells in Zion	YHWH punishes two foreign nations
and protects it from foreigners	YHWH dwells in Zion

The unit of Joel 4:18-21 thus takes up the theme of 4:17, and expands it in light of the coming day of YHWH motifs in 4:14-17. Joel 4:18-21 stresses that the day of YHWH will be a positive one for Judah and Jerusalem, but one which will have devastating effect upon Egypt and Edom in particular. Before turning to the question of possible dates for this passage, another important characteristic of these verses requires treatment, namely the use of quotes and allusions present in Joel 4:1ff, more specifically in 4:14-21 where the phenomenon occurs with regularity.

---

derives from an Akkadian root meaning to "sacrifice, offer a libation"; 2) Emending the text; 3) The word is used here in the sense of "to empty" (cf Isa 3:26; see G. Warmuth, "נקה," *ThWAT*, vol 5, 592; Rudolph, *KAT* 13/2, 78); 4) The opening phrase is translated as a question ("shall I leave their blood unpunished?") followed by a denial ("I will not"). The first option would not fit the context, and the second option lacks textual support. The latter two options are textually possible and a decision must be made on literary grounds. Based on the literary discussion below, option #3 has been chosen here.

6. Allusions and Quotes in Joel 4:1-21

Joel 4:1ff presents a unit with a considerable degree of
interrelatedness, but another phenomenon further demonstrates the artful
mastery of the person who brought these units together, namely the use of
allusions and quotes in Joel 4:1ff. However, the scholarly discussion of this
phenomenon requires some refinement, in terms of what constitutes an
allusion and its function in the context. Joel 4:18-21 deliberately takes up
several words from earlier occurrences in Joel.[102] Without exception
these words turn undesirable and disastrous circumstances from Joel 1-2
into promises of future weal. In Joel 1:5, the sweet wine (עסיס) has been
cut off from the land, but in 4:18 it will drip from the mountains on the day
of YHWH. The creek beds (אפיקי) in 1:20 have dried up, while in 4:18
they will flow with water. The house of YHWH in 1:9 has lost its grain
offering and drink offering, but in 4:18 the house of YHWH will be the
center of a spring. Joel 2:3 refers to Judah as a wilderness of desolation
(מדבר שממה) in the wake of the coming destruction, but in 4:19 the
phrase refers to the destruction of Edom, because of the shameful
treatment which Edom gave Judah. The phrase from generation to
generation (דור ודור) in 2:2 contrasts the incomparability of the destructive
force, while in 4:20 it refers to the long lasting endurance of Jerusalem.

The number of these allusions, their function as deliberate reversals
of the disaster described in the first two chapters, and the integral
involvement of the words in 4:18-21 convincingly indicate that these verses
were composed for their context in the Joel book. Joel 4:18-21 could not
have existed prior to chapters 1-2. In addition, their position at the end of
the book offers a very fitting promissory conclusion to Joel. Clearly, the
writer of 4:18-21 is well versed in the use of allusion to other material as a
means of making a specific point. Interestingly, this reversal of previous
material is the same technique utilized in the connection between Hos
14:5ff and Joel 1:2ff.[103]

---

[102] The function and existence of these words have been noted before. See especially,
Wolff, *BK* 14/2, 100, Allen, *Joel, etc.*, 123f, Rudolph, *KAT* 13/2, 86; etc.

[103] Joel 4:18-21 thus brings the hermeneutical line of thought full circle. The promises of
Hos 14:5ff were acknowledged as unfulfilled by Joel 1:2ff. Only true repentance could
reverse the present state of drought, destruction, and foreign occupation. The insertion
in Hos 14:8 bears considerable similarity to Joel 4:18-21 as well. Wine appears in both
Hos 14:8 (יין) and in Joel 4:18 (עסיס) as a positive sign of YHWH's restoration. Both
passages promise restoration (Hos 14:8a; Joel 4:18,20) using the root ישב. The larger
context of Joel reflects a more eschatological/apocalyptic orientation than Hos 14:5ff.

Allusions to individual words are not, however, the only means by which the author of this chapter creates a message. Three particular instances inside 4:14-17,18-21 exhibit the characteristics of doublets with significant passages from elsewhere:

Joel 4:15 = Joel 2:10b	The sun and the moon grow dark, and the stars withdraw their brightness.
Joel 4:16aa = Amos 1:2a	And YHWH roars from Zion, and from Jerusalem he utters his voice.
Joel 4:18a = Amos 9:13b	The mountains will drip new wine, and (all) the hills flow with milk (undulate).[104]

While these citations are often noted, the question as to how these doublets function within the Joel context receives little treatment.[105]

Joel 4:15 operates with the same hermeneutical motif as the allusions in Joel 4:18-21 mentioned above. It takes an earlier threat and turns it into something positive. Joel 2:10b lies at the apex of Joel 2:1-11 which portrays judgment *against Jerusalem and Judah* on the day of YHWH. The verse follows a description of YHWH's army from the north as a locust swarm which thunders across the land, devouring everything in its path. The prophet declares that the earth, the heavens, the sun, the moon, and the stars demonstrate their fear before the might of this army.[106] In Joel 4:15

---

[104] The parentheses show slight differences in the Amos passage. The last phrase of Amos 9:13b lacks an object, and reads "and all the hills will undulate."

[105] The vast majority of exegetes consider the Joel passages derive from Amos: Allen, *Joel, etc.*, 120; Stuart, *Word* 31, 269f; Wolff, *BK* 14/2, 98. A few claim common traditions for the two passages, or they refuse to speculate on the source (so Bič, *Das Buch Joel*, 99, in spite of the fact that he dates Joel in the 9th or 8th century, prior to Amos). Bergler, *Joel als Schriftinterpret*, 143-145, argues the dependency relates to the redactional history of Amos, perhaps within the realm of the Book of the Twelve.

[106] This depiction contains imagery which borders on full-fledged apocalyptic. The lack of a clear definition as to what distinguishes apocalyptic from eschatological makes one cautious about labeling Joel 2:1-11 as apocalyptic, yet the extraordinary nature of this army (2:4f), the fact it is on a divine mission (2:11), and the fact that this army affects the cosmos in much the same manner as YHWH (cf 2:10 and 4:15), all serves to paint a picture which comes very close to apocalyptic literature. See Paul Hanson, *Old Testament Apocalyptic: Interpreting Biblical Texts* (Nashville: Abingdon, 1987), 35-38. Hanson himself does not mention Joel 2:1-11 in his list of developing apocalyptic literature, while including 3:1-4:21. Compare also Brevard S. Childs, "The Enemy from the North and the Chaos Tradition," *JBL* 78 (1959): 187-198, as it relates to Joel 2:20.

the declaration of the darkening of the heavens forms part of the description of the day of YHWH, but 4:15 refers to the fear of the coming of YHWH, not a fear of an advancing army. The events of the day of YHWH in Joel 4:15 are directed against the nations, not against Judah and Jerusalem.[107] The change in the recipient of judgment in the citation in 4:15b corresponds well with the tendency in 4:18-21 to reverse the threat of chapters 1:2-2:11.

The citations in Joel 4:16a,18a of Amos 1:2a; 9:13b require deliberation on several fronts. On the one hand, these doublets fit *relatively* well into the Joel context.[108] On the other hand, the presence of these two doublets, effectively bracketing the entire book of Amos at a very late stage in its development, create the plausible impression that they are related in some way to the placement of Joel and Amos within the Book of the Twelve.[109] The possibile explanations of these doublets requires evaluation. They may be summarized as follows:

1. The use of common material is accidental, offering at most a rationale for the placement of Joel and Amos next to one another in the corpus.
2. Amos draws on Joel in both places.
3. Joel draws on both sayings attributed to Amos.
4. One doublet belongs to Joel and one to Amos.

Because of this widely recognized bracketing function, decisions reached on these possibilities have implications for understanding the formation of the Book of the Twelve.[110] Evidence for this decision must necessarily

---

[107] Attempts to understand these images as references to a total eclipse fails to understand the role of the language in these verses. Some even seek to date Joel by determining at what point eclipses would have occurred in the fourth century: so F.R. Stephenson, "The Date of the Book of Joel," *VT* 19 (1969): 224-229.

[108] Joel 4:16a has been incorporated into pre-existing material, but it has been done so with *explicit* reference to the Joel book. See discussion above, page 36.

[109] See the discussion of the macrostructure and growth of Amos later in this chapter for demonstration that both Amos 1:2 and 9:13 are part of later redactional work on Amos, but that they do not, in all likelihood, come from the same layer.

[110] Decisions on these verses are admittedly difficult and must wrestle with a frequently encountered dilemma in the Book of the Twelve. One must often decide questions of dependence between two passages, *both* of which belong to the redactional work of their respective books. These decisions demand a broad perspective which includes the evaluation of the redaction histories of both works, a working concept of how the Book of the Twelve received its "unity," and a considerable degree of humility, recognizing that unnoticed factors may tip the balance in the other direction.

presuppose literary decisions made in Amos as well as Joel.[111] The first
option, accidental occurrence, is unlikely because the correspondences are
too close, and the literary tensions of the respective passages indicate
redactional work.[112]   Given this presupposition of a deliberate
relationship, it is necessary to ask the question of dependence.

Does Amos draw from Joel? On the basis of the analysis of Amos
elsewhere, one may say that in the case of Amos 1:2, the answer must be
negative. While Amos 1:2 is certainly not "genuine," Amos 1:2 functions
significantly within the structure of the corpus which extended from 1:1-9:6.
In all likelihood, the date of the formation of this corpus preceded the
compilation of Joel by more than a century. By contrast, Amos 9:13
belongs to the latest stage of redaction on Amos, and is not part of this
earlier corpus. Not only does it appear within the later promissory material
of Amos, but it creates a certain amount of literary tension which points to
its insertion into a previously existing context.[113]   Thus, Amos 9:13 could
conceivably draw from Joel 4:18.

Does Joel draw from Amos? It is possible to affirm the likelihood
that Joel 4:15 draws from Amos 1:2. The date of the respective writings
would pose no difficulties. The doublet in Joel 4:15 has been incorporated
into existing material. It also ties the doublet to judgment against the
nations.[114] This motif is explainable from an awareness of Amos 1:2 at
the head of Amos oracles against the nations. Joel's use of this motif is
more eschatological/apocalyptic than the oracles in Amos, arguing that Joel
introduces a new frame of interpretation, which intends to reinterpret
judgment against the nations from this eschatological perspective.
Essentially, Joel creates his own oracles against the nations which play off
the oracles of Amos.[115] The case for Joel's dependence upon Amos 9:13
is less likely. Joel 4:18 appears more intricately involved in its literary unit
than either Amos 9:13 or Joel 4:15. The vocabulary of Joel 4:18 makes

---

[111] Elaboration of the reasons for decisions on Amos reflected in the following discussion
may be found in Nogalski, *Literary Precursors*, 74-122.

[112] Because of the use of similar phrases elsewhere (Jer 25:30), the argument for a
common tradition could be used for Joel 4:16 and Amos 1:2 more effectively than with
Joel 4:18 and Amos 9:13, but it still seems unlikely.

[113] See the literary discussion of Amos 9:13 Nogalski, *Literary Precursors*, 116-119.

[114] Compare the combination of the quote from Joel 2:10 and the context of 4:1-21 which
draw together the motif of the enemy attack and judgment of the nations.

[115] Particular attention should be given to the inclusion of Joel 4:4-8,19f, which update
Amos 1-2. The combination of these entities is also significant for who they do not
condemn. See the discussion of the date of Joel 4:4-8,18-21 beginning on page 48.

more sense when read in the context of the book.[116] By contrast, Amos 9:13 evidences tensions within its literary context which place it in the latest stage of Amos redactional work, although this stage is admittedly difficult to date. Thus, a careful evaluation of the relevant factors indicates that one cannot assume that the existence of these doublets in Joel requires they be treated identically. This evaluation indicates that Joel 4:15 takes up Amos 1:2 while Amos 9:13 draws from Joel 4:18.

In addition to the self-quotes of Joel and the doublets with Amos, Bergler cites a series of fourteen allusions to the book of Obadiah.[117] While Bergler admits not all of these "connections" are of equal value, he nevertheless asserts these allusions constitute deliberate attempts to transfer the hatred of Edom as an enemy-type into a wider context.[118] Bergler demonstrates a considerable similarity of vocabulary between Joel 4:1ff and Obadiah, but his primary contention that the entire chapter deliberately takes up Obadiah as a typological description of enemies is unconvincing.

---

[116] Note the meaningful reversal of images discussed above, page 42.

[117] Siegfried Bergler, *Joel als Schriftinterpret*, 301-319. Bergler lists the following relationships between Joel 3-4 and Obadiah: Joel 3:5b (2:3b) quotes Obad 17a,18ba; Joel 4:17 quotes Obad 17a,11ab; Joel 4:3a actualizes Obad 11ba; Joel 4:4,7b transfers the accusation imagery of Obad 11b,15b from Edom to the Philistines and Phoenicians; Joel 4:3 and Obad 16a mention the drinking of the nations; Joel 4:6 belies the same historical situation as Obad 9b,7 (Bergler, 308, believes these verses reflect the Nabatean incursion that instigated the composition of Obadiah since this part is missing from the Jeremiah parallel); Joel 4:8 and Obad 18 have the same closing formula; Joel 4:19 mentions the violence along with Obad 10a; Joel 4:21 takes up Jer 49:12 (innocent blood); Joel 4:9 takes up Obad 1b; Joel 4:11b takes up Obad 9; Joel 4:14b takes up Obad 15a; Joel 4:6,7 takes up Obad 19,20; Joel 4:12,17 and Obad 21 have similar themes.

[118] It is impossible here to thoroughly evaluate every "allusion" cited by Bergler. The connections run the gamut of qualitative use of Obadiah material from the very obvious to the very weak. Two examples will illustrate the extremes within which he works. When he cites Joel 3:5 he is on solid ground because of the very clear and specific reference ("just as YHWH said") indicating a quote, as well as the similarity of language. However, when Bergler mentions the use of the verb "to drink" in Joel 4:3 and Obad 16a, he uses more questionable methodology. In the Obadiah passage the drinking refers to the drinking of the nations as punishment in the sense of the cup of reeling, (cf Jer 25:15-17). In Joel 4:3, the drinking connotes the frivolous utilization of the proceeds gained from the sale of Judean slaves. A direct connection, much less a deliberate expansion of the Obadiah passage is difficult to ascertain. In addition, many of Bergler's allusions appear general enough that they could derive from Jer 49:7ff rather than directly from Obadiah. However, even the likely quote in Joel 3:4, despite its closer similarity to Obad 17, could also refer to 2 Kgs 19:32f (=Isa 37:31f).

These similarities are better understood as indicators of a common tradent, and perhaps even a common historical background, but not the literary dependence of Joel upon Obadiah in the fashion he describes.[119]

One further allusion requires mention here as demonstration of a phenomenon not often noted, namely the use of Joel by other writings within the Book of the Twelve. These allusions demonstrate a literary awareness within the larger corpus which incorporates Joel. The protracted introduction in Joel 4:1 manifests several points of contact with Zeph 3:20. This may be shown in the following:

Joel 4:1   Zeph 3:20

כי הנה בימים ההמה ובעת ההיא   בעת ההיא אביא אתכם

אשר אשוב את־שבות יהודה וירושלם   ובעת קבצי אתכם

כי־אתן אתכם לשם

ולתהלה בכל עמי הארץ

בשובי את־שבותיכם לעיניכם

Both verses contain the phrase "at that time" and the reference to the returning of the possessions. The question as to which verse (if either) depends upon the other can be determined with some degree of certainty in this case. Joel 4:1 is inseparably bound to 4:1-21 as a redactional unity. Zeph 3:20 constitutess part of a redactional unit as well, Zeph 3:18-20, the function of which relates to the portrayal of historical periods incorporated into the Book of the Twelve. The fact that Zeph 3:19 quotes Mic 4:6f with slight, but meaningful literary changes, means that these verses are already operating from a perspective which includes more than the neighboring writing in the Book of the Twelve. It is thus not surprising that Zeph 3:18 would cite Joel 4:1 as well.[120] These verses introduce the shift into the post-exilic section of the Book of the Twelve. Zeph 3:20 helps to raise the expectation that a significant change is about to occur, since it reformulates the promise of Joel 4:1 to portray its imminent fulfillment. Joel 4:1

---

[119] The compilation of Obadiah, like Joel, demonstrates considerable awareness of its position within the Book of the Twelve, particularly with the writings on either side. It seems fairly certain that these two writings entered the Book of the Twelve together, so the common vocabulary and themes are not surprising. See also the discussion of Bosshard, *BN* 40 (1987): 37-49, who believes Joel and Obadiah are both redactional texts within the Book of the Twelve.

[120] The dependance of Zeph 3:20 upon Joel 4:1 is further supported by the tensions of Zeph 3:20 (with its 2mp reference) even within its context. See the literary discussion of Zeph 3:20 in the chapter on the Zephaniah/Haggai connection.

anticipates events whose realization lies in the distant future (in those days and at that time) whereas Zeph 3:18-20 implies that the time of (partial) fulfillment is much closer. The use of הנני plus the participle in 3:19, and the use of "before your eyes" in Zeph 3:20 both indicate an expectation of nearness which is not present in Joel.[121]

This brief evaluation of several quotes and allusions in Joel 4:1-21 indicates that their treatment requires a considerable degree of caution. The assumption that Joel's penchant for citation requires all these allusions to be ascribed to his use of other material does not stand up under close scrutiny. To be sure, Joel does make ample use of allusion and citation, but, particularly within the Book of the Twelve, other writings are also prone to draw from Joel. The literary context of the Book of the Twelve must therefore be borne in mind when evaluating allusions and citation in Joel and other writings.

Joel 4:1-21 serves at least three functions. First, it functions primarily as the conclusion to Joel (hence the references to Joel 1-2), but, second, it also serves as an introduction to Amos (Joel 4:4-8,15). Joel 4:1ff actualizes and eschatologizes Amos' oracles against the nations. Third, the chapter serves as a foundation from which other passages draw (e.g. Amos 9:13; Zeph 3:20). Before turning to a discussion of Amos's oracles against the nations, it is necessary to consider the question of the date of Joel 4:1ff in more detail.

7. The Date of Joel 4:1-21

Several indicators affect the determination of the date of composition of Joel 4:1-21: the mention of specific nations, the "scattering" of YHWH's people, and the early apocalyptic nature of the chapter. In addition, despite the redactional unity of the chapter one cannot decide *apriori* that the individual units themselves (1-3,4-8,9-17,18-21) all come from the same time. For this reason, the question of date will be approached for each of the individual units.

Joel 4:1-3, because of its function as a redactional frame, necessarily presupposes the remainder of the chapter and thus represents the latest possible date for the compilation of the chapter. Unfortunately, the verses contain no specific mention of persons or geographical entities which offer

---

[121] See further discussion of Zeph 3:20 in Nogalski, *Literary Precursors*, 214-215.

precise dating criteria, but certain indicators do allow some narrowing of
the parameters. Joel 4:1-3 presupposes a devastated Judah and Jerusalem
to whom YHWH promises restoration of possessions.[122] The verses
claim the cause of this devastation results from the fact that "the nations"
have divided the land and scattered YHWH's people (4:2). This situation
causes severe problems to those who argue for a pre-exilic date. The
picture presupposes the destruction of Jerusalem, and the Babylonian
exile.[123] What is not immediately clear is the question as to how far in
the past these events occurred. Is the passage concerned with the specific
events surrounding Jerusalem's destruction, with the diaspora, or both?
Material from other portions of Joel clarifies the picture considerably.
Given the existence of the temple and the functioning of the cult in Joel 1-
2, and the fact that Joel 4 presupposes these chapters, it is necessary to
assume a date well into the Persian period. Likewise, the casual mention
of the wall in 2:9, a passage whose Zion orientation clearly refers to the

---

[122] See Joel 4:1, which makes explicit reference to the restoration of Judah and Jerusalem.

[123] Contra Rudolph, *KAT* 13/2, 25ff, who believes Joel was written in the time between
597-587, that is, between the two Babylonian deportations. He attempts to overcome
this problem by arguing that Joel reflects the situation following the first Babylonian
deportation, but not the destruction of Jerusalem. As evidence he claims that this first
deportation involved neighboring countries. He believes Babylon is not mentioned
because as the occupying power, they could not be openly condemned. Problems with
this view are manifold. First, the early apocalyptic character of the chapter parallels
or supersedes other apocalyptic literature which arose no earlier than the post-exilic
period (Hanson, *The Dawn of Apocalyptic*, 1-31, especially 23-28; cf Plöger, *Theocracy
and Eschatology*, 96-105). Second, the failure of the mention of Babylon out of fear
raises significant questions, namely: why would it be any more permissible to declare
divine judgment upon "all the nations" (4:2) than to announce the power itself? And
second (as Rudolph himself points out), 4:17b has in mind an occupying power (as
opposed to an occasional passerby from another land). Would such a negative
statement be any more permissible to the Babylonians than calling them by name? Or
to put this question in other words: would a prophet who was presumably afraid to
mention Babylon have the courage to proclaim the "strangers" would not continue to
rule Jerusalem? Joel 4:1-21 does not reflect the words of a fearful or prudent author.
These words portray divine retaliation and restoration. Finally, the term "scattered" in
4:2 portrays a picture in which YHWH's people have been scattered among several
nations. In all likelihood, this picture includes more than the first Babylonian
deportation. It includes the aftermath of the destruction of Jerusalem, in which Judah
lost territory and inhabitants to its surrounding neighbors, particularly Edom (Obad 11-
14) and later some of the Philistines (Neh 4:7; 13:23f) appear to have taken advantage
of Judah's devastated state. See Wolff *BK* 14/3, 35f for a summary of Edom's role
following the destruction. For discussion of attitudes toward Tyre immediately after
Jerusalem's destruction, see Zimmerli, *BK* 13/1, 93*-95*.

wall of Jerusalem, presupposes the rebuilding of the wall by Nehemiah circa 445.[124] Thus, one may say with relative certainty, that Joel 4:1-3 was composed at some time after 445, and in all likelihood some considerable time afterwards, since neither the *existence* of the temple nor the city wall are at issue anywhere in Joel.

The second unit, Joel 4:4-8, contains a strong condemnation of three entities: Tyre, Sidon, and the Regions of Philistia. Tyre and Sidon are frequently mentioned in connection with one another as the chief cities of Phoenicia. That the author intends the entire coastal region is clear from the inclusion of the phrase "all the regions of Philistia," a term for the Philistine pentapolis.[125] Scholars normally take one of three positions in dating these verses.[126] The first group accents the mention of Tyre, Sidon, and the Greeks and conclude that the passage must come from the late Persian or Greek period.[127] A second group argues that the mention of the Sabeans in the context of trade indicates a time prior to the end of the 6th century, after which time they "lost control" of the trade routes.[128]

---

[124] Several scholars attempt to deny the validity of this argument. So, for example, G.W. Ahlström, *Joel and the Temple cult of Jerusalem*, VT.S 21 (Leiden: E.J. Brill, 1971), 18; Reicke, "Joel und seine Zeit," 137. Their evidence is not convincing. Reicke believes the reference to the city wall could refer to any city, despite the clear Zion context of 2:1ff. Ahlström argues the context does not demand that the wall be standing. However, the context of 2:9 includes the wall within a series of statements about the attack on the city, the houses, and the windows. There is no hint that any of these items were in a devastated state (prior to the coming of the locust army). There is no mention of ruins, and the wall is in no manner set apart to indicate that it is not standing. The wall may thus be said to be standing in the mind of the author of these verses. Most scholars date the mission of Nehemiah in 445 under Artaxerxes I. The rebuilding of the wall appears to have motivated his mission to Jerusalem (Neh 1:3), and he began immediately to make plans to rebuild it (Neh 2:11ff). Nehemiah reports the rebuilding took 52 days (Neh 6:15), but this reckoning may only refer to the actual construction time. Josephus claims it took two years and four months to rebuild. See Antonius H.J. Gunneweg, *Geschichte Israels bis Bar Kochba* (Stuttgart: Kohlhammer, [5]1984), 143f; Miller/Hayes, *A History of Ancient Israel and Judah*, 469f.

[125] The only other occurrence of the phrase appears in Josh 13:2f, where it is clear that the area includes Gaza, Ashdod, Ashkelon, Gath and Ekron.

[126] The elimination of an early pre-exilic date was discussed above on the basis of scholarly consensus. See the summary article by Thompson, "The Date of Joel," 453-464.

[127] See especially Wolff, *BK* 14/2, 93f; and most recently, the discussion of Bergler, *Joel als Schriftinterpret*, 563-565.

[128] Allen, *Joel, etc*, 111; Jacob Myers, "Some Considerations Bearing on the Date of Joel" (*ZAW* 74 (1962): 177-195), and others. The arguments of Allen are based in large part upon reference to the article by Myers, 186-190. Several problems exist with this

A third group argues that the background of this oracle reflects the time between the two deportations, and refers to exploitation of Judah following the removal of its leading citizens.[129]

Beginning with the arguments of the third group, it is highly unlikely that 4:4-8 stems from the years between 597-587. During this period Tyre and Sidon were intricately involved in anti-Babylonian intrigue.[130] Egypt essentially dominated Sidon until 593, and Tyre's strong anti-Babylonian feelings are attested by the fact that it was besieged by Nebuchadrezzar for thirteen years beginning in 585, within two years of the destruction of Jerusalem. Incringement upon a potential ally by Tyre and/or Sidon between 597-587, when so much hung in the balance would make very poor politics indeed.[131] Just as damaging to this argument is the fact that those nations mentioned as taking part in raids on Judah following the rebellion of Jehoiakim are *precisely those nations that are not mentioned in Joel*, namely: bands of Chaldeans, Syrians, Moabites, and Ammonites.[132] Not one of these groups are cited in Joel, which is highly problematic, especially when coupled with the fact that Babylon is not mentioned.[133]

---

article, not the least of which is that while Myers treats several aspects of dating, he nowhere treats the problem of the existence of the temple in Joel. The temple itself is not at issue, indicating that it had been built some time previously. Myers himself assumes a date in the time of Haggai-Zechariah. Problems with this date are recognized implicitly by Wilhelm Rudolph, "Wann wirkte Joel," in *Das ferne und nahe Worte. Festschrift L. Rost*. F. Maass, ed., BZAW 105 (Berlin: Töpelmann, 1967), 193-198, particularly in relationship to the unquestioned existence of the temple, and its fully functioning cultic apparatus.

[129] Rudolph, *KAT* 14/2 24-29. Schneider, *The Unity of the Book of the Twelve*, 74-89, follows Rudolph in several arguments, but argues Joel comes from the late pre-exilic period, contemporary with Jeremiah. This date is highly unlikely, since even Rudolph acknowledges some major destruction to Jerusalem had already occurred.

[130] Note especially the meeting in Jerusalem in 593 at the instigation of Egypt which was attended by Ammon, Moab, Edom, Tyre and Sidon which sought means to thwart the activity of Babylon. See Jer 27:3. See also the discussion above, footnote 123.

[131] It is true that Ezekiel has a substantial oracle against Tyre delivered *after* the Jerusalem's destruction (Ezek 27-28). However, Tyre's crime, according to that passage, is one of pride, not the taking of slaves. This boasting presumably ceased, however, when Nebuchadrezzar began the siege of Tyre in 585. This attitude toward by Tyre (as well as Edom) does not affect the date of the Joel passage, because Joel was written at a point when the temple was functioning, which it was clearly not doing at the time of the Tyre activity mentioned by Ezekiel.

[132] See 2 Kings 24:2f.

[133] Contra Rudolph, *KAT* 13/2, 26, and others, who say it is just a sign of caution or prudence on the part of Joel.

The arguments of the second group may likewise be eliminated from two angles, historical and literary. *Historically*, this group argues that the decline of the Sabeans as a trading power argues for an early post-exilic date of Joel This argument has gone virtually uncontested in exegetical literature.[134] Whereas one cannot deny there was a lessening of the Sabean influence in the South Arabic trade routes, it is simply erroneous to imply from this decline that all contact between Palestine and the Sabeans ceased by 500. Indeed, there are indications that in spite of a gradual decline, occasional flashes of major political and/or economic activity appeared in the region.[135] From a *literary* perspective, this group overlooks the function of the Sabeans in Joel 4:8. The Sabeans do not function primarily as slave traders. The Sabeans are mentioned because they are a distant nation which lay in the opposite direction of the place where the Phoenicians and Philistines had sold the Judeans.[136] Too much emphasis has been placed upon an active participation of the Sabeans in the picture of Joel 4:4-8. The Sabeans in 4:4-8, like the Greeks, are merely the receivers of the slaves, not the instrument by which they are sold.[137] One may not say that the mention of the Sabeans presupposes a time prior to the end of the sixth century.

The third group offers the strongest argument when they accent the mention of Tyre, Sidon and the Philistines in common cause against the Judeans. The grouping of these political entities together need not, of course, imply that they had any kind of official alliance, but the fact remains that their grouping together accords well with the period between 400-351. At this time, Sidon and Tyre, together with Arvad, had formed a coalition and met together annually (in the presence of Persian authorities). By 351 this group considered itself strong enough to rebel against Persia. However the Persians devastated the city of Sidon in 351 after which time the others quickly recapitulated, providing a *terminus ad quem* for the dating of this passage. Second, the accentuation of "all the regions of Philistia" would

---

[134] Allen, *Joel, etc.*, 111; Meyers, *ZAW* 74 (1962): 186-188.

[135] Note particularly the major building campaigns of the Sabean kings after 450. IDB, vol 4, 145f. These campaigns would hardly have been possible for the Sabeans under totally failed economic conditions. Some form of substantial commerce must have been maintained, at least periodically.

[136] See above discussion, page 29.

[137] Rudolph, *KAT* 13/2, 77, and others place too much emphasis on the change of preposition from ל to אל in 4:8. The expression should better be understood as a parallel statement to stress their geographical location. The Sabeans are mentioned because they are a distant nation, not because they were famous as slave traders.

make sense during this period since some of the regions were relatively independent (Ashdod, Gaza), but others were controlled by Tyre (Ashkelon), meaning that apart from this designation it would not necessarily be assumed the Philistines would have acted together. A third support for a Persian date of 4:4-8 is the concentration upon the nations west of Jerusalem, while the Trans-jordan region to the east is totally neglected.[138] The destruction of sedentary life in Ammon and Moab, apparently by the Babylonians, makes this lack of mention understandable, whereas a date from the late pre-exilic period would fail to account for the mention of Tyre and Sidon, when these countries were more actively involved in subterfuge against Judah.[139] Finally, the destruction described for Tyre makes no mention of Nebuchadrezzar's siege against that city. Tyre, as pictured in Joel 4:4-8, is capable of aggressive action and/or maintains a considerable degree of economic stability. This observation leads to the conclusion that one must suppose a period well after the Babylonian siege of Tyre. Indeed, the Babylonian siege of Tyre as a means of punishment would have offered an excellent point of contact for the announcement of punishment on Tyre had the writer of Joel 4:4-8 had the events of 587 in mind.[140] By the same token, the context mentions the Greeks as the recipients of *Judean* slaves, but makes no allusion to the overthrow of Tyre by Alexander in 332. The author of these verses has events in mind other than the events immediately following the destruction of Jerusalem. Indeed, one may expand this argument. Sidon was captured by Babylon in 593. Ashkelon was destroyed by Nebuchadrezzar in 604 for refusing to pay tribute. Ashdod likewise experienced deportations under the Babylonians.[141] It would thus not make sense that any of these would

---

[138] Edom is of course mentioned in 4:19, but not in this unit. In addition, Edom is the only one of the three which appears to have survived the Babylonian period sufficiently to pose any real threat.

[139] Note the role of Ammon prior to Josiah when it began encroaching upon former Northern territories. Closer to the time suggested by Rudolph, Ammon was also (like Tyre and Jerusalem) involved in Anti-Babylonian activities. See "Ammon" in *IDB*, vol. 1, 112. See also Zeph 2:8-11; Jer 49:1-6.

[140] Compare Ezek 28; 29:12 for an example of a Tyre oracle which portrays the Babylonian siege as punishment for taking advantage of the Judean situation following the destruction of Jerusalem. The same arguments also indicate the date of the passage is not as late as the Alexandrian campaign of 332 in which Tyre was also besieged. A date after Alexander is also unlikely since Sidon was devastated in 351, and was not a strong power thereafter.

[141] These deportations likely took place around the time of the destruction of Jerusalem and included the king of Ashdod, as noted by his inclusion in a list of those in Babylon.

be included in a reference to events between 597-587. Again, it must be underscored that whatever events the author refers to in Joel 4:4-8, the combination of political entities mentioned in these verses makes it unlikely that the author intends events around the time of the Babylonian conquest of the region.[142]

In addition to the specific nations, Joel 4 uses the title יון for Greece, a title attested in the later Persian period. This title has several biblical parallels, but their date is often disputed.[143] There is, however, one clear piece of evidence that the title was in common use in the latter Persian period. Among the correspondence of the Elephantine colony from the fourth year of Artaxerxes II (402) a bill of sale for a house appears which quotes the price in both Persian (karsh) and Greek (stater) currency. The Greek currency is identified as the כסף יון.[144] All of this evidence strongly suggests a late Persian period date before Sidon's destruction.

Joel 4:9-17 affords no concrete reference points from which to date the passage. 2 Chr 20:1-30 as a tradition offers little help for dating Joel 4:9-17. The date of the Chronicler has itself created considerable scholarly debate of late, although it appears that a consensus is emerging that 1 and 2 Chronicles exhibit protracted redaction histories, which predate the attachment to Ezra and Nehemiah. If this opinion stands, the earliest version appears around the end of the sixth century.[145] The possibility

---

See W.F. Stinespring, "Ashdod," in *IDB*, vol. 1, 249.

[142] A discussion of the possible meanings of these verses will follow the discussion of the date of the entire chapter.

[143] The biblical attestations appear in genealogical material (Gen 10:2,4; 1 Chr 1:5,7); and in prophetic material (Ezek 27:13,19; Zech 9:13; Dan 8:21; 10:20; 11:2; Isa 66:19).

[144] Papyrus 12, lines 5,14. See Emil G. Kraeling, *The Brooklyn Museum Aramaic Papyri: New Documents of the Fifth Century B.C. from the Jewish Colony at Elephantine* (New Haven: Yale University Press, 1953), 270f, 275.

[145] The catalyst for this theory is due in large part to the article by Frank Moore Cross, "A Reconstruction of the Judean Restoration," *JBL* 94 (1975): 4-18 (esp. 11-14), in which he argues for three versions of Chronicles. The initial composition according to Cross dates to a time shortly after 520, and contained 2 Chr 20:1-30. The second redaction would have occurred following Ezra's mission around 458, and the third would have appeared around 400. While some disagreement may still be noted, most recent commentators seem to accept the basic thrust of his arguments for a relatively early and separate version of the Chronicler's history. See discussions in Roddy Braun, *1 Chronicles*, Word Biblical Commentary 14 (Waco, Texas: Word Books, 1986), xxv-xxix; David L. Petersen, *Late Israelite Prophecy: Studies in Deutero-Prophetic Literature and in Chronicles*, SBLMS 23 (Missoula, Montana: Scholars Press, 1977), 68-77, 100-102; Magne Saebø, "Chronistische Theologie/Chronistisches Geschichtswerk," in *Theologische Realenzyklopädie* 8 (Berlin: De Gruyter, 1981), 74-87 (esp. 79f).

exists, therefore, that versions of the Chronicler's history were in use from early post-exilic periods. If so, 2 Chr 20:1-30 would have formed a part of this version, since the battle scene carries so many distinctive features of the Chronicler. The existence of a Chronicles corpus from this early date implies that 2 Chr 20:1-30 would have existed in literary form, and thus would have been available to the writer/compiler of Joel 4:9-17. It would also allow ample time for congregational use of these motifs to have developed. If the theories of a protracted redaction history do not withstand critical scrutiny in the coming years, then more traditional dates for Chronicles come into play, but even these range between 400-200.[146] Given other factors in Joel, it does not seem wise to date 4:9-17 to the Greek period. In this case, Joel 4:9-17 more likely would be related to a common legend about Jehoshaphat, rather than its literary expression in 2 Chr 20:1ff.

When one asks about the situation presumed by Joel 4:9-17, a late Persian period again appears likely. The apocalyptic nature of the material argues for post-exilic origins.[147] The mention of "strangers" in 4:17 also demonstrates a situation in which a foreign power occupies Jerusalem.[148] The compiler of 4:9-17 offers no hint of the Davidic-messianic convictions or hopes which played such a strong role during the period of Haggai and Zechariah.[149] The nations will be brought into the valley by the heavenly host, and judged there by God. Joel pictures no military liberation, but a divine intervention by which Jerusalem will be delivered, and by which YHWH will show his power. These observations, taken together, coincide well with the dates of the previous sections in the latter Persian period.

Joel 4:18-21 provides an eschatological image of weal, but also returns to the political realm with the condemnation of Edom and Egypt. The mention of these two entities in this section initially complicates the picture of the remainder of the chapter, in large part because of the   political

---

[146] Eissfeldt, *Introduction*, 540, also argues for different redactional editions of Chronicles, with the first one coming shortly after 398. So also Rudolph, *HAT* 21, X. Kaiser, *Introduction*, 185, dates the first layer of the book between 300-200. Smend, *Entstehung*, 228, leans toward the third century date, but leaves open the possibility of a date in the fourth century.

[147] While some might place the origin of such apocalyptic material in the exilic period, its use in Joel presupposes a post-exilic date because of the existence of the temple and the presence of the wall already discussed above.

[148] Rudolph, *KAT* 13/2, 85f, contra Wolff.

[149] See Hag 2:23.

impotence of Edom during the late Persian period.[150] It is possible that the verse refers to some military incursion by Edom against Judah. Since Edom was being forced into an ever-shrinking territory by the Nabateans, and did take Judean territory, the possibility cannot be ruled out.[151] The mention of Egypt likewise is problematic. During most of the Persian period Egypt lived under Persian rule, although they revolted numerous times during this period. Indeed, for a time the Egyptians were able to throw off Persian rule long enough to sustain three native Egyptian dynasties from 404-343. However, there is also no record of Egyptian incursion into Judah during this period.[152] Is it thus necessary to move the date into the Ptolemaic period for this oracle? This is an option which would perhaps help explain this enigmatic reference to Egypt, but would complicate the reference to Edom even more. The parallelism of Edom and Egypt in 4:19 make it clear that the author sees the two countries as very closely related.

Prophetic tradition, particularly Ezekiel, more plausibly explains the references to Egypt and Edom.[153] Whereas the nations cited in Joel 4:4-8 were singled out for recent activities, Edom and Egypt are probably cited for the respective roles they played in the fall of Jerusalem.[154]

---

[150] By the end of the Persian period Edom was under considerable pressure from the Nabatean infiltration of their land.

[151] J.R. Bartlett, "The Rise and Fall of the Kingdom of Edom," *Palestine Exploration Quarterly* 104 (1972): 26-37.

[152] See summary of the period in question in Erik Hornung, *Grundzüge der ägyptischen Geschichte* (Darmstadt: Wissenschaftliche Buchgesellschaft, 1978), 130-133.

[153] See Wolff, *BK* 14/2, 101f; Allen, *Joel, etc.*, 125. Rudolph, *KAT* 13/2, 87, in large part due to his early dating, argues that the word "tradition" is misleading, since the wickedness was still a living reality, not merely the recollection of a past event. He also believes the mention of Egypt was triggered by thoughts of fruitfulness from Joel 4:18.

[154] The use of the two nations in parallel is very important. Since both Edom and Egypt are located essentially south of Judah, it might be argued that Joel is working with a geographical rubric. This argument is more plausible in light of 4:4-8 which dealt with the sea coast area. However, geography alone does not account for the parallel mention of these two entities. Reference need only be made to the nations which are not mentioned in Joel to note he had particular aims when mentioning these entities. Some action in the mind of the writer ties these two together. Egypt and Edom are cited for pouring out blood in Judah. While the phrase could have been used for any conflict, it is likely that its use in Joel 4:19 reflects back on the events surrounding the destruction of Jerusalem. Another factor behind the nations mentioned in Joel 4:1ff is their affinity to the oracles against the nations in Ezekiel. Joel 4:4-8,19f conflate the oracles of Amos and Ezekiel from the perspective of the Persian period, which betrays

Appropriately, Joel thus mentions Egypt and Edom together. Egypt's promise of aid helped incite rebellion against Babylon. When Jerusalem was attacked, Egypt sent an army against Nebuchadrezzar, resulting in a temporary lifting of the siege.[155] However, later tradition by no means viewed this act positively, since the Egyptians withdrew quickly, and did not press the attack.[156] Edom took a more active role against Jerusalem during the destruction or in the period immediately thereafter, either in preventing retreat from Babylon or perhaps even entering the city itself.[157] One may thus conclude, that the Edom and Egypt appear in Joel 4:19, not not because of recent events, but because prophetic tradition continued to accent their role in the destruction of Jerusalem.[158]

In summation, observations concerning the data pertinent ro the date of Joel 4:1-21 reveal strongest support for a date in the late Persian period. The evidence is particularly strong in 4:4-8, but is not contradicted by any of the other material. The remaining material is much less historically oriented, but the apocalyptic nature would fit well with this time period.

---

a Jerusalemite and apocalyptic orientation. The sequence of the Joel oracles which are also present in Ezekiel follows the same general order (Tyre, Sidon, Egpyt, Edom). In addition to the agreement of the order, the description of Joel 4:19 takes up the vocabulary of the exilic prophet Ezekiel when it says Egypt and Edom will become a desolation (see Ezek 29:9,12 for Egypt; 35:3 for Edom). The Edom oracle of Ezekiel 35 is particularly oriented around Edom's role following the Babylonian destruction.

[155] Miller/Hayes, *A History of Israel and Judah*, 413f; Gunneweg, *Geschichte Israels*, 124. See Jer 34:21; 37:5-11; Ezek 17:17.

[156] Jeremiah (46) and Ezekiel (29-32) traditions are particularly negative toward Egypt, having recognized from the beginning Egypt's role as instigator against Babylon was designed from its interest in self-preservation, not out of comradery against a common foe.

[157] Obadiah 12-14; Wolff, *BK* 14/3, 35f. To throw further light on the possibility of some Edom/Babylon collaboration, it should be noted that Edom was the only one of the three Trans-jordanian states which was relatively unaffected by the Babylonian conquest. For a more thorough discussion, see below under Obadiah.

[158] The role of Edom within the literary movement of the Book of the Twelve buttress this idea. See the chapter on Obadiah and the discussion of Mal 1:2-5.

Obadiah

1. The Macrostructure of Obadiah

The macrostructure of Obadiah defies a simple explanation. Scholarship generally agrees that Obadiah displays a three-fold movement: 1) condemnation of Edom (1-9), 2) the reason for the accusation (10-14), and 3) the placement of Edom's judgment in a framework of judgment upon all nations (15-21). In addition, most scholars concur that Obadiah does not represent an "original" unity. This scholarly unanimity breaks down quickly, however, when the question arises as to the delineation of the units and the models used to explain the compilation of this short book.[1]

---

[1]   See Georg Fohrer, "Die Sprüche Obadjas," in *Studien zu alttestamentlichen Texten und Themen (1966-1972)*. BZAW 155 (Berlin: Gruyter, 1981), 69-72. Fohrer provides a thorough (albeit incomplete) summary of the multitude of opinions on the delineation of the units in Obadiah. Fohrer notes several who have seen the writing as a unity and who believe it represents a *single prophetic speech*: Condamin; von Orelli; Isopescul; Theis; Edelkoort; Aalders; Bič. Others modify the idea of unity somewhat: Thompson; Haller; Olávarri. Olávarri sees a single speech which has an insertion (10-14) which is dependent upon Ezek 35. Still others see essentially *two speeches*: Wildeboer understands 1-9 as a pre-exilic prophetic speech and divides it from the post-exilic expansion; Wellhausen propounded the most accepted theory which saw 1-14 as the genuine speech of Obadiah and 15-21 as a later addition. Many simply follow Wellhausen, or modify his ideas only slightly, especially through the excision of Obad 8f: Nowack; Marti; McFadyen; S.R. Driver; C.H. Cornill; Duhm; Bewer; Augé; Robert; Feuillet; Weiser (*Einleitung*); Pfeiffer; Wolff. There are likewise those who argue for a *three-fold division*: Steuernagel; Rudolph; Vellas; Eissfeldt; Weiser (*ATD* 24); Deden. Sellin finds *four units*. Oesterley and Robinson find *seven or more units*. Fohrer himself believes Obadiah represents a collection of *six speeches*. Recently Weimar and Wehrle undertake thoroughgoing analyses of Obadiah from redactional and compositional perspectives. See Peter Weimar, "Obadja. Eine redaktionskritische Analyse." *BN* 27 (1985): 35-99, who argues the short booklet manifests the interests of six different redactional layers; and Josef Wehrle, *Prophetie und Textanalyse. Die Komposition Obadja 1-21 interpretiert auf der Basis textlinguistischer und semiotischer Konzeptionen*, Arbeiten zu Text und Sprache im Alten Testament 28 (St. Ottilien: EOS Verlag, 1987), who argues the text must be viewed from the perspective of the combination of seven different compositional blocks, and partial texts whose incorporation into Obadiah often obliterates meaningful divisions between the units. Wehrle (25-38) prefers to speak in terms of four communication levels, whose determination reflects the question of the constellation of parties involved, or the

Several factors demand consideration in order to appreciate the complexity of Obadiah's macrostructure and its relationship to the compilation of the book. These factors require some explanation. These interrelated factors are: 1) the sparsity of strong text markers and their current role delimiting the units; 2) the relationship of Obad 1ff to Jer 49:7ff; 3) the relationship of Obad 1ff to Amos 9:1ff; 4) the relationship of Obadiah to other prophetic books.

Obadiah contains relatively few markers which function absolutely as the beginning or end of text units, and those markers which do exist often demonstrate that their marking function has been superseded through incorporation into Obadiah. Obadiah contains four markers which typically introduce text units, but three of these appear in the first two verses. Two introductory phrases in Obad 1 ("the vision of Obadiah"; "thus says Adonai YHWH concerning Edom") follow directly upon one another with no oracular material between them. Explanations for this tension recognize the function of the first element as the superscription to the book, while treating the second element as a messenger formula introducing a smaller unit within the book. Obad 2 exhibits a third introductory element, since it begins with הנה, which can also introduce a new unit. The fourth introductory text marker occurs at the beginning of verse 8, where the tri-fold combination of הלוֹא ההוּא, ביוֹם, and נאם־יהוה signal a significant change in thought and theme. No other objective text marker signals the existence of an independent unit, which is not to say that the remaining material in 8-21 comes from the same hand.

Even fewer elements function as closing markers for text units. The phrase נאם־יהוה in Obad 4 at one point served this function for verses 2-4, but subtle changes in the redaction of Obadiah have all but obliterated this function.[2] Obad 18 concludes with the phrase כי יהוה דבר (for YHWH has spoken). Obad 21b concludes the book with a summary formula, which provides a suitable conclusion to the booklet. Even those who argue for several redactional layers often treat this verse as the conclusion to earlier editions of Obadiah, which retained its position because of its suitability as a conclusion.[3]

---

literary function of a given portion.

[2] See literary discussion below, page 62, which demonstrates that Obad 1-5 adapts Jer 49:7ff. The נאם יהוה formula concludes a unit in Jer 49:16, but Obad 5 immediately combines this saying with another saying from the Jeremiah context (49:9).

[3] See Wolff, *BK* 14/3, 6. Rudolph, *KAT* 13/2, 317f, does not speak of redactional layers, but sees Obad 19f as an insertion which respected the function of Obad 21 as a conclusion to the writing. Weimar, *BN* 27 (1985): 70f,73f believes the verse served both

These text markers at the beginning and end of units in Obadiah only begin to explain Obadiah as it now stands. Many questions remain unsolved if one only considers these elements. For instance, none of these markers accounts for the most dramatic shift in the movement of the book, the change from a direct singular address form to the treatment of Edom in the third person. This change occurs between verses 15 and 16, and represents a clear shift in situation, interests, and theology. This observation forces one to conclude that the demarcation of Obadiah must utilize more than simply traditional formulaic markers at the beginning and end of units, and must include other criteria such as addressee, style, and theological tendencies. The interpretation of these observations involves somewhat more subjectivity, but this admission does not relegate the attempt into the realm of unadulterated speculation. The attempt to determine the compilations of any biblical book requires caution, and this statement rings particularly true in Obadiah because of its complexity. The "inconsistencies" within Obadiah are manifold and one must seek to explain them in a manner which gives some degree of plausibility without falling prey to an atomistic approach which perceives every incongruity as evidence of a separate hand.

The process by which this structure came to being is not easy to describe, but an outline of the constitutive elements will be provided in the following pages. Each of the major movements in Obadiah depends heavily upon other prophetic formulations. In at least one case, verses 1-5, Obadiah quotes pre-existing material (Jer 49:9,14-16), while simultanously reshaping the formulation to fit the context in the Book of the Twelve. The second movement provides clear allusions to Ezek 35 and Amos 1:11f, but does not quote blocks of material as extensively as Obad 1-5. The third section takes it point of departure from Jer 25, and presents a programmatic picture of Davidic restoration through political domination. This section also owes portions of its formulation to Mic 1:2ff, and raises the distinct possibility that it also utilizes preformulated material.

---

as an earlier redactional conclusion to the book, and that it received an addition in conjunction with the final redaction.

2. The Interrelationship of Obad 1-9, Jer 49:7ff and Amos 9:1ff

The fact that a relationship exists between Obadiah and Jer 49:7ff requires little explanation, but the priority of that relationship creates dissension. Recent discussions avoid the question whether Obadiah borrows from Jeremiah or vice versa by the postulation of a "common source" for both, from which both deviate for their own particular purposes.[4] However, evidence will be presented which plausibly demonstrates that Obad 1-5 borrowed from Jer 49:7ff.[5] The differences between Obadiah and Jeremiah are admittedly slight, but these differences take on considerable significance when read in light of Amos 9. The intricate relationship between the three texts requires their common treatment. Many of the changes are explainable as Obadiah's redactional attempt to restructure the Jeremiah material so that it corresponds to the structure of

---

[4]   Wolff, *BK* 14/3, 20-22, offers typical explanations for this position. Wehrle, *Prophetie und Textanalyse*, 12f, provides an exhaustive list of those holding all three positions, but adds his own note of skepticism (14f) that these observations offer any real value. Wehrle therefore deliberately avoids the question by concentrating on the poetic expression of the final form. In a recent commentary, Stuart, *Word*, 31, 414-416, also argues for a common poetic source. Rudolph, *KAT* 13/2, 297, correctly argues that the differences between the two passages are of a kind which demand a literary relationship, but his insistence that the Jeremiah passage draws from Obadiah runs into tremendous difficulties in light of the several inconsistencies in Obadiah which make perfect sense in Jeremiah. See discussion below, page 63.

[5]   This statement is made with the recognition that the Edom material in Jeremiah is itself a compilation of Edom speeches, not made at the same time. See William L. Holladay, *Jeremiah 2: A Commentary on the Book of the Prophet Jeremiah Chapters 26-52*, Hermeneia (Minneapolis: Fortress, 1989), 372f. Robert Carroll, *The Book of Jeremiah: A Commentary*, OTL (London: SCM, 1986), 802,805f. Both of these authors, with others, believe the Edom oracle to be redactionally expanded to reflect later events, with both treating 49:12 and the parallel to the Obadiah material as redactional expansions of an earlier Edom oracular collection. While not doubting the validity of their arguments that 49:12f,14-16 bring redactional work into the Edom collection (note particularly that both authors relate Jer 49:12 to Jer 25:15ff), observations below, page 62, demonstrate a far greater likelihood that Obad 1ff draws from Jeremiah. Obadiah contains tensions that can only be explained from Jeremiah. The fact that Obadiah draws from both older (Jer 49:9, according to Carroll) and redactional passages in Jeremiah further cements these observations. See particularly Obadiah's awareness of the relationship between Jer 49:12 and 25:15ff, explained below, page 69. One may draw certain conclusions from these observations, namely that Obadiah was aware of Jeremiah in a book form which had already incorporated the oracles against the nations. Also, Obadiah likely utilized the earlier proto-masoretic version of Jeremiah reflected in the LXX.

Amos 9. While it will be necessary to demonstrate that these changes were consciously made, requiring detailed observation of the MT, it must also be noted that this restructuring was no mere scribal exercise. The compiler had a specific purpose in making these changes.

Jer 49:7-23 brings together several oracles of diverse background into a collection of anti-Edom speeches. The variety of addressees in this passage indicates these verses are compilations of several different oracles which have been shaped redactionally as part of the Jeremiah context.[6] The clearest parallels between Obadiah and Jer 49:7ff appear in the common material in Obad 1-5 and Jer 49:14-16,9. It will be helpful to begin with these verses in order to establish the relationship between Jer 49:7ff, Obadiah and Amos 9.

Jer 49:14-16,9	Obad 1-5	Amos 9:1-4
שְׁמוּעָה שָׁמַעְתִּי (14	שְׁמוּעָה שָׁמַעְנוּ (1	רָאִיתִי אֶת-אֲדֹנָי (1
מֵאֵת יהוה	מֵאֵת יהוה	נִצָּב עַל-הַמִּזְבֵּחַ וַיֹּאמֶר
וְצִיר בַּגִּים שָׁלוּחַ	וְצִיר בַּגּוֹיִם שָׁלַח	הַךְ הַכַּפְתּוֹר
הִתְקַבְּצוּ וּבֹאוּ עָלֶיהָ	קוּמוּ וְנָקוּמָה עָלֶיהָ	וְיִרְעֲשׁוּ הַסִּפִּים
וְקוּמוּ לַמִּלְחָמָה	לַמִּלְחָמָה	וּבְצַעַם בְּרֹאשׁ כֻּלָּם
כִּי-הִנֵּה (15	הִנֵּה (2	וְאַחֲרִיתָם בַּחֶרֶב אֶהֱרֹג
קָטֹן נְתַתִּיךָ בַּגּוֹיִם	קָטֹן נְתַתִּיךָ בַּגּוֹיִם	לֹא-יָנוּם לָהֶם נָם
בָּזוּי בָּאָדָם	בָּזוּי אַתָּה מְאֹד	וְלֹא-יִמָּלֵט לָהֶם פָּלִיט
תִּפְלַצְתְּךָ הִשִּׁיא אֹתָךְ (16	הִשִּׁיאֶךָ (3	אִם-יַחְתְּרוּ בִשְׁאוֹל (2
זְדוֹן לִבֶּךָ	זְדוֹן לִבֶּךָ	מִשָּׁם יָדִי תִקָּחֵם
שֹׁכְנִי בְּחַגְוֵי הַסֶּלַע	שֹׁכְנִי בְחַגְוֵי-סֶלַע	וְאִם-יַעֲלוּ הַשָּׁמַיִם
תֹּפְשִׂי מְרוֹם גִּבְעָה	מְרוֹם שִׁבְתּוֹ	מִשָּׁם אוֹרִידֵם
	אָמַר בְּלִבּוֹ	וְאִם-יֵחָבְאוּ (3
	מִי יוֹרִדֵנִי אָרֶץ	בְּרֹאשׁ הַכַּרְמֶל
כִּי-תַגְבִּיהַּ כַּנֶּשֶׁר	אִם-תַּגְבִּיהַּ כַּנֶּשֶׁר (4	מִשָּׁם אֲחַפֵּשׂ וּלְקַחְתִּים
	וְאִם-בֵּין כּוֹכָבִים שִׂים	וְאִם-יִסָּתְרוּ מִנֶּגֶד עֵינַי
קִנֶּךָ מִשָּׁם אוֹרִידְךָ	קִנֶּךָ מִשָּׁם אוֹרִידְךָ	בְּקַרְקַע הַיָּם
נְאֻם יהוה	נְאֻם-יהוה	מִשָּׁם אֲצַוֶּה
אִם-גַּנָּבִים בַּלַּיְלָה (9b	אִם-גַּנָּבִים בָּאוּ-לְךָ (5	אֶת-הַנָּחָשׁ וּנְשָׁכָם
	אִם-שׁוֹדְדֵי לַיְלָה	וְאִם-יֵלְכוּ בַשְּׁבִי (4
	אֵיךְ נִדְמֵיתָה	לִפְנֵי אֹיְבֵיהֶם
הִשְׁחִיתוּ דַיָּם	הֲלוֹא יִגְנְבוּ דַיָּם	מִשָּׁם אֲצַוֶּה
אִם-בֹּצְרִים בָּאוּ לָךְ (9a	אִם-בֹּצְרִים בָּאוּ לָךְ	אֶת-הַחֶרֶב וַהֲרָגָתַם
לֹא יַשְׁאִרוּ עֹלֵלוֹת	הֲלוֹא יַשְׁאִירוּ עֹלֵלוֹת	וְשַׂמְתִּי עֵינִי עֲלֵיהֶם
		לְרָעָה וְלֹא לְטוֹבָה

---

6   So Holladay, *Jeremiah 2*, 373, for example, argues 49:12f and 49:14-16 represent later, but not simultaneous, insertions at the hands of redactors, which interrupt the context of 49:11 and 49:18. Because of similarities of vocabulary and motifs, it is possible to suggest that 49:12 was no mere insertion, but exhibits a literary awareness of Jer 25:15. See discussion of Jer 49:12 and Jer 25:15ff, below page 69.

The changes made by Obadiah to Jeremiah may be classified to aid in their discussion. Two changes are orthographic in character and have little bearing upon either the meaning of the text or the intention of the redactor.[7] Several words in Obadiah are unexplainable in the Obadiah passage, but are consistent within the Jeremiah context.[8] Several minor changes afford a change of viewpoint from Jeremiah to Obadiah, some of which demonstrate a later perspective when read beside Jeremiah.[9] Two

---

[7] Jer 49:9a uses the full *holem* with "gleanings" (עוֹלֵלוֹת), but Obad 5 spells the same word with a defective *holem* (עֹלֵלוֹת). Jer 49:9a contains no *yodh* in the hiphil form יִשְׁאָרוּ, whereas Obad 5 does (יַשְׁאִירוּ). The most likely solution to this difference is the orthographical preference of the redactor, but another possibility should be mentioned. When one recognizes that the consonantal form of יִשְׁאָרוּ in Jer 49:9a could as well have been niphal, one could argue that the author/redactor understood the subject as gleanings, which would translate: "and no gleanings would remain." This option, while possible, is less likely because of the parallelism of the verse, and would still not explain the full *holem* in "gleanings."

[8] Note especially the 3fs reference "against her" on Obad 1. In Jer 49:14 the antecedent is the city Bozrah, and the feminine suffix is thus appropriate. In addition, other feminine references to Edom appear in Jer 49:17,18,19. Nowhere else does Obadiah mention Edom as a feminine entity. These observations create grave difficulties for those, such as Rudolph, *KAT* 13/2, 297, who wish to argue that Jeremiah draws from Obadiah. See also the discussion below, page 65, regarding the insertions in Obadiah which disrupt the simpler syntax of the Jeremiah context.

[9] None of these changes provides overwhelming evidence of a later perspective, but when taken together they do give an impression of later reflection upon the Jeremiah text. The most significant shift in temporal perspective appears in Obadiah's use of the pual perfect form of the root שׁלח (v.1) over against the passive participle in Jer 49:14. The use of the perfect stresses the completed action. A less objective shift is noted in Obad 3 in the phrase "the height of his dwelling". When compared with the parallel phrase in Jer 49:16 ("the one who *occupies* the height of the hill"), Obad 3 is readily explained by the assumption that the Nabatean infiltration of Edom had already begun. Note should be made that mention of "the cliff" in the same verse as the dwelling place of the Edomites is also less concrete in Obadiah. Jer 49:16 has הסלע ("the cliff"), while Obad 3 omits the article. Given the existence of other indexes in Obadiah which indicate a later perspective, this omission of the article may not be accidental. Note that Obadiah also deconcretizes reference to the occupation of the hill in the same verse. Jer 49:16 specifically mentions the "height of the hill" while Obad uses a more diffuse phrase, "the height of his dwelling." One may draw two conclusions. First, the redactor of the Obadiah material concentrates less on the physical aspects of the Edomite settlement. Second, this deconcretization, while perhaps a stylistic change, likely reflects the change in the status of Edom itself. One other distinction has similar tendencies, namely the omission of the fear of Edom in Jer 49:16. The terror of Edom would have been a relevant topic at the time shortly after the destruction of Jerusalem when they aided the Babylonians, but not after Edom itself was in a weakened state.

of these changes need only be mentioned   here, but one of these
significantly exchanges the 1cs "I" in Jer 49:14 for the 1cp "we" in Obad
1.[10] This change from the singular to the plural expands the addressee to
reflect a communal setting which incorporates the congregation in the
framework of the oracle.[11]   This expansion of the audience takes on
significance again in Obad 16.[12]

A substantial number of changes in Obadiah are classified best as
structural alterations on the basis of Amos 9:1ff. These changes do not
alter the content of the parallel passage so much as they adapt the
framework of the booklet to correspond more closely to Amos 9:1ff. These
changes announce judgment upon Edom in terms which parallel the
judgment upon Israel in Amos 9:1ff. Obadiah strengthens this description,
since the promises of Amos 9:11-15 militate the judgment of Amos 9:1-4
against Israel, while Edom receives no such reprieve in Obadiah.

The restructuring begins in Obad 1 with the superscription of the
book (the vision of Obadiah). Given the fact that so little of Obadiah
corresponds to the classification "vision," this title provokes questions
regarding its enigmatic relationship to the content of the book. Two
possible explanations present themselves. The first explanation simply
notes that other places use the title "vision" as a superscriptive element, not
always with visionary material.[13]   The second explanation argues that
someone deliberately selects חזון as a superscriptive element as part of an
attempt to correlate Amos 9:1ff and Obadiah. Were the use of חזון the
only touchstone with Amos 9:1ff, this option would seem less likely, but
given other structural parallels between the two sections, this option must
be held open.

The most concrete example of the connection to Amos 9 appears in
Obad 4 with the phrase "from there I will bring you down". The phrase is
part of the quoted material from Jer 49:16. The same phrase appears in
Amos 9:2, with the 3mp suffix (I will bring them down) rather than 2ms.
These משם ... אם phrases use hyperbolic polarities to demonstrate the

---

[10] A listing of other minor changes in these verses will suffice: the call to battle is
      reformulated in Obad 1 explicitly to include the congregation (let us rise up), whereas
      in Jeremiah the call is addressed to the nations alone (gather yourselves); the word play
      in Jer 49:15 on אדם is kept (despised among men [אדם]), but Obad 2 changes the
      accent to increase the hostility shown to Edom (despised are you exceedingly [מאד]).

[11] See further Wolff, *BK* 14/3, 27f; Wehrle, *Prophetie und Textanalyse*, 25; Rudolph, *KAT*
      13/2, 301.

[12] See the discussion of Obad 16 below, beginning on page 80.

[13] Cf Nah 1:1; Isa 1:1; 2 Chr 9:29; 32:32.

futility of trying to escape from YHWH's wrath.[14]   Since this phrase
existed in the Jeremiah material, some might argue that the recurrence of
the phrase appears accidentally or at most offers a reason why a collector
placed Obadiah next to Amos. Several observations argue strongly against
this possibility. First, the rarity of the verb form makes it highly unlikely
that the two would "accidentally" appear so close to one another.[15]
Further, when one notes the other alterations made in the surrounding text
in Obadiah, it becomes unlikely that someone simply placed the texts next
to one another in a form which already existed.

Several differences between Jer 49:9,14-16 and Obad 1-4 occur as a
direct result of the five אם clauses in Amos 9:2-4. These five clauses
appear in Amos 9:2-4 within the larger stylistic framework in which
אם ... מִשָּׁם (if ... from there) functions as the refrain of futility in Amos.
Only one אם ... מִשָּׁם clause appears in Obad 2-4 (and Jer 49:9,14-16). This
observation must be expanded, however, since it leads to the related
observation that Obad 2-4 does contain a total of *five* אם clauses, whereas
Jer 49:14-16,9 contains only two. Of the three extra אם clauses in Obad 2-
4, one (Obad 4aa) was created by transforming a כי clause in Jeremiah into
an אם clause in Obadiah. The remaining two אם clauses (4ab*,5aa*)
appear in the Obadiah material which has no Jeremiah parallel. One may
best characterize these two אם clauses in Obadiah as insertions, a
characterization made particularly evident in Obad 4ab*. The Obadiah
clause interrupts the much simpler syntax of Jeremiah, thereby creating a
more cumbersome sentence structure. A literal translation of this syntax
appears as follows:

Jer 49:16   Though (כי) you build like the eagle   your nest

Obad 4   Though (אם) you build like the eagle —
             and though (אם) is placed between the stars —   your nest

Clearly a redactor has inserted the phrase "and though is placed between
the stars" into the context. It not only interrupts the syntax, it also

---

[14]   The sentence in Amos 9:2 says, "though they ascend to the heavens, from there I will
bring them down." Obad 4 says, "though you build like the eagle or place your nest
among the stars, from there I will bring you down."

[15]   In addition to those verses in question (Jer 49:16; Obad 4; Amos 9:2), the verb ירד in
the hiphil imperfect appears with a suffix only three other times (1 Sam 30:15; Jer
51:40; Hos 7:12) in Old Testament literature. Only Jer 51:40 and Hos 7:12 are also
spoken by YHWH.

exaggerates the metaphor of the building of the eagle's nest, by placing the nest among the stars.

The second inserted אם clause in Obad 5a similarly adds a parallel subject to an existing clause which reads smoother without this insertion:

Jer 49:9b	... or (אם)	thieves	at night,	they would destroy	their sufficiency
Obad 5a	Though (אם)	thieves come to you — destroyers	at night —	how you would be ruined.	Would they not steal their sufficiency?

This insertion is more complicated than the first one. When compared to the Jeremiah parallel several phenomena must be explained. The first line in Obad 5 contains a verb which is not present in Jer 49:9b. The transposition of Jer 49:9a and 49:9b can explain this verb. Obad 5a quotes 49:9b before 49:9a, but for syntactical reasons must supply the verb, since Jer 49:9b relies on the verb from 49:9a. Obad 5a therefore takes the verb and indirect object (בָּאוּ־לְךָ) from Jer 49:9a which introduces the Jeremiah sentence. This inversion raises two questions. First, if Obadiah uses Jeremiah, why does it essentially quote Jer 49:14-16 and then return with no transition to Jer 49:9? Second, when Obadiah does go back and pick up Jer 49:9 why does it invert the order? The answer to both questions lies in the redactional structuring of the Jeremiah material to parallel Amos 9. Obad 5 functions as the thematic summary of Amos 9:7-10, where the themes of destruction and remnant appear. Amos 9:7-8a announces destruction upon the house of Jacob, but 9:8b-10 allows a remnant for this group.[16] The Obadiah redactor recalls both of these themes from the perspective of YHWH's word to Edom. This Obadiah redactor finds Jer 49:9 well suited to present these themes, but does not simply incorporate Obad 5 mechanically. The redactor inverts 49:9 so that the themes of destruction and remnant appear in the same order as Amos 9:8-10. One major difference demonstrates the hermeneutical shift which the Obadiah redactor creates. In Amos 9:8b-10 the sieve motif functions as a theological correction to the message of total destruction in 9:1-6,7-8a. It serves as the vehicle to sift out the remnant of YHWH's people. Obadiah, however,

---

[16] See the discussion of Amos 9:7-8a,8b-10 in Nogalski, *Literary Precursors*, 99-104.

goes to great lengths to deny Edom a similar reprieve. Edom's punishment is total. Even the gleanings, the leftovers of the harvest, will be destroyed.

A minor but significant formulation in Obad 5 comes into focus in light of the summary function this verse plays. Obad 5 contains two rhetorical questions which each begin with the particle הלוֹא, but the Jeremiah parallel contains no such particle. Amos 9:7, however, opens with two rhetorical questions, both of which begin with הלוֹא. Again the Obadiah changes may be explained in relationship to the structural elements in Amos 9.

The interplay between Jer 49:7ff, Obad 1ff, and Amos 9:1ff does not cease with Obad 5. Although the similarities of Obad 1-4 with Jer 49:14-16,9 make comparison of the three texts easier to document, much of the remaining material in Obadiah may be explained through Obadiah's adaptation of the content in Jeremiah on the basis of Amos 9. As noted above, several incongruities in Obadiah correspond to the context of Jer 49:7ff. Similarly, other references in Obad 8f take up Jer 49:7ff, although the source material is not quoted as extensively as in Obad 1-5. Obad 8f takes up two motifs from Jer 49:7,22: the wise men of Edom (Obad 8), and the annihilation of the strong men of Teman (Obad 9). Again, as with Obad 5, the order is somewhat inverted since Jer 49:7 explicitly mentions the wisdom of Teman, and Jer 49:22 mentions the strong men of Edom. In spite of the inversion, it is significant that these references appear at the beginning and end of the oracles against Edom in Jer 49:7-22, and thereby function as an *inclusio* to the entire anti-Edom oracle in Jer 49:7ff.[17]

In addition to the references to Jer 49:7,22, Obad 8 also continues the interplay with Amos by using structural elements from Amos 9. The extended introductory formula in Obad 8 contains three elements, all of which play a formative role in the shaping of Amos 9. The formula in Obad 8 begins: הלוֹא ביום ההוא נאם־יהוה (Surely, on that day, utterance of YHWH). הלוֹא appears twice in Amos 9:7; Amos 9:11 begins a new unit with ביום ההוא; and נאם־יהוה appears in 9:7a,8b,13.[18] Obad 8 follows the introductory formula immediately with a verb in the divine first person, as does Amos 9:11. Obad 8 thus stylistically parallels both Amos 9:11 and 9:13aa,14f. In addition, the verb in Obad 8 (אבד = destroy) is

---

[17] Jer 49:1-6 presents an oracle against Ammon, while the oracle against Damascus begins in Jer 49:23.

[18] The use of the phrase נאם־יהוה in Obad 8 more closely approximates Amos 9:13 because of the combination of the phrase with the יום formula. Amos 9:13 uses "utterance of YHWH" together with הנה ימים באים (behold the days are coming).

the precise antonym of the verbs (קוּם = raise up, בנה = build) in Amos 9:11,14. Taken together, these similarities mark a continuation of the same hermeneutic noted in Obad 5. Amos 9:11,13 promise restoration to the kingdom and to the people of YHWH, but Obadiah ironically interprets "that day" as a day of destruction for Edom.[19]

The ביום ההוא formula in Obad 8 introduces an eschatological dimension, as well as a thematic shift, both of which stem from Obadiah's interaction with Amos 9:1ff and Jer 49:7ff. The theme of the day of judgment upon Edom appears in Jeremiah's oracles against the nations, but the formulation in Obad 8 is relates more closely to the structural imitation of Amos 9.[20]

The thematic shift begun in Obad 8f continues through the remainder of the book, although the material in Obad 8-21 is not an original unity. The catchword "day" plays a central role in both the historical accusation in 10-14, and in the "day of YHWH" material in 15ff. Parallels with Jer 49:7ff and/or Amos 9:1ff cease in Obad 10-14, but they resume again in Obad 15ff.[21]

---

[19] Watts, *Vision and Prophecy in Amos* (Leiden: E.J. Brill, 1958), 45, observes that Obadiah is structurally parallel to Amos 8:1ff, but does not note the closer parallels to Amos 9:1ff. The similarity which he demonstrates may be explained by the fact, already demonstrated, that Amos 9:1ff makes efforts to align itself with Amos 8:1ff. See the previous discussion of Amos 9:1ff.

[20] References to "that day" (ביום ההוא) in Jeremianic oracles against the nations appear as stylized, non-introductory redactional formulations, which connect the oracles against Moab (48:41) with Edom (49:22) and the oracles against Damascus (49:26) with Babylon (50:30). Jer 48:41 and 49:22 end "... and the hearts of the mighty men of Moab/ Edom *in that day* will be like the heart of a woman in labor." Jer 49:26 and 50:30 say "... therefore her young men will fall in her streets, and all the men of war will be silenced *in that day*, declares YHHW (Sebaoth)." Other instances of יום as the day of punishment in Jeremiah's oracles against the nations do not use the formula ההוא ביום. Cf. Jer 46:10,26; 47:4; 48:47; 49:39; 50:4,20,30; 51:2,11,33,34.

[21] Emilio Olávarri, "Cronológia y Estructura Literaria del Oráculo de Abdias," *Estudios Biblicos* 22 (1963): 308f, presents interesting arguments regarding Obad 10-14. Olávarri claims these verses are a gloss, dependent upon the oracle against Edom in Ezekiel 35. His evidence is rather limited, and his suggestion that the verses are a gloss do not withstand critical scrutiny. He is on much firmer ground, however, with his observations on Ezek 35:1ff. See a more thorough discussion of Olávarri's work below, page 75.

3. The Interrelationship of Obad 15-21, Jer 49:7ff; 25:15ff and Amos 9:1ff

Obad 15a,16-21 significantly parallels Amos 9:11-15, and it also continues to demonstrate an interplay with Jer 49:7ff, specifically with Jer 49:12.[22] However, the relationship changes somewhat. In order to appreciate the change, one must take note of the textual history of Jeremiah.

Excursus: The Position of the Oracles Against the Nations in Jeremiah.

Scholarship has drawn several conclusions regarding the textual transmission of Jeremiah which bear upon the study of the Obadiah/Jeremiah relationship. The LXX recension of Jeremiah is considerably (roughly ⅛) shorter than its Masoretic counterpart. The discovery of parts of both versions in Hebrew in Qumran confirms the earlier suspicion that two separate Hebrew versions of Jeremiah existed. The LXX reflects the shorter version, and the MT represents the longer version. Scholars universally agree that the shorter version is also the older version.[23] One of the more noticeable differences between the two versions relates to the order and position of the oracles against the nations. In the LXX version these oracles occur approximately in the middle of the book (25:14-31:44), whereas the MT places these same oracles at the end of the writing (chapters 46-51). In addition to their respective positions, the oracles appear in different order, as may be noted here:

LXX	MT
Elam (25:14-20)	Egypt (46:2-28)
Egypt (26:1-28)	Philistia (47:1-7)
Babylon (27-28)	Moab (48)
Philistia (29)	Ammon (49:1-6)
Edom (30:1-16)	Edom (49:7-22)
Ammon (30:17-22)	Damascus (49:23-27)
Kedar (30:23-28)	Kedar (49:28-33)
Damascus (30:29-33)	Elam (49:34-39)
Moab (31)	Babylon (50-51)

More significant for this context than the reordering of the individual oracles, is the repositioning of the entire block. The reason this repositioning impacts the understanding of Obadiah's relationship to Jer 49:7ff concerns the redactional role of the cup of wrath material in Jer 25:15-29 (MT). While the later (MT) version separates Jer 25:15ff from the oracles against the nations, the earlier (LXX) version contains this passage precisely at the conclusion of the oracles against the nations.

---

[22] Obad 15a,16-21 will receive more detailed literary treatment in relationship to the connection forward to Mic 1:2ff later in this chapter (see page 82).

[23] See Carroll, *Jeremiah*, 50-55.

Moreover, the oracles against the nations which originally preceded this passage anticipate Jer 25:15ff in two places. Jer 51:7 likens Babylon to a golden cup in the hand of YHWH, from which the nations drank and became drunk. The result of this drinking was that the nations went mad. Jer 49:12 says *to Edom*: "Behold those who were not sentenced to drink the cup will certainly drink it, and are you the one who will be completely acquitted? You will not be acquitted, and you will certainly drink." The reference to the cup in the Edom oracle supposes the cup as a cup of punishment. Jer 25:15f expounds this theme. In 25:15f, YHWH tells the prophet to "take this cup of the wine of wrath ... and cause all the nations, to whom I send you, to drink it. They shall drink and stagger and go mad because of the sword that I will send among them." The entities which are to receive this cup are then listed in 25:17-26. Among others, this list mentions Jerusalem, the cities of Judah (25:18), and Edom (25:21). Jer 25:27f specifically states that if any nations refuse to drink they will be told that they will surely drink. Jer 25:15ff serves as the backdrop for understanding the strong affirmation in Jer 49:12 that says Edom will not escape the destiny of having to partake of the cup from which the other nations have been forced to drink. The fact that Edom, from all appearances, survived the Babylonian invasions of Palestine much better than its neighbors only serves to strengthen the emotional impact of these verses.

When one understands the position and function of Jer 25:15ff as the conclusion of the oracles against the nations in the earlier version of Jeremiah, it is possible to say that Jer 49:12 never existed without Jer 25:15ff. Jer 25:15ff explains the significance of "the cup" as it appears in Jer 49:12.

The Jeremianic imagery of the cup of wrath as YHWH's punishment underlies the reference to "drinking" in Obad 16. Obad 16 says: "For just as you (2mp) drank on my holy mountain, all the nations will drink continually, they will drink and swallow, and become as if they had never existed." Whereas Jer 49:12 addressed Edom, the addressee of Obad 16 changes to the inhabitants of Jerusalem.[24] This transition was accomplished through verse 15a.[25] The writer deliberately takes up the

---

[24] The "you" of Obad 16 must refer to YHWH's people, not to Edom, on the basis of the tradition background of the "cup." Wolff, *BK* 14/3, 44; Rudolph, *KAT* 13/2, 311f; Wehrle, *Prophetie und Textanalyse*, 34f; Weiser, *ATD* 24, 213; Horst, *HAT* 14, 115. Stuart, *Word* 31, 420, is one of the few recent commentators to presume the addressee is Edom.

[25] Obad 15 is most often assigned to two separate literary units, with 15a seen as the introduction to Obad 16ff and Obad 15b as the conclusion to Obad 1-14. So Wolff, *BK* 14/3, 19; Rudolph, *KAT* 13/2, 296; Wehrle, *Prophetie und Textanalyse*, 86f,185, although these authors differ somewhat in the extent of the unit which Obad 15a begins. See more thorough discussion in Allen, *Joel, etc.*, 133-135. Stuart, *Word* 31, 407, argues unconvincingly that this transition belongs to a single hand, because "it shares in the

theme of YHWH's cup of wrath from Jer 49:12, but in full awareness of the broader context of Jer 25:15-29, where the theme is related to all the nations, not just to Edom (as in Jer 49:12).[26] Obad 16 presupposes a degree of uncertainty on the part of the Jerusalemites that the promise of punishment in Jer 25:15ff against all the nations would be realized. Hence the writer of Obad 16 recognizes that Jerusalem, or YHWH's people in general, has indeed drunk from the cup of wrath ("just as you drank"). However, the writer continues with an affirmation that the punishment will certainly befall all the nations (cf Jer 25:15).

Obad 17-21 presumes Obad 16, but proceeds to reinterpret the meaning of the drinking of the cup of wrath in a manner which departs significantly from Jer 25:15-28. Obad 17-21 (with Obad 16) understands that Jerusalem has received its punishment, but it goes further by transforming YHWH's people centered in Jerusalem into the means by which the nations will be punished. Stated simply, YHWH's remnant becomes YHWH's tool for punishing the nations. Edom still plays the dominant role as enemy, but the surrounding nations are now included as well.[27]

As with the other Jeremiah parallels, Obad 16,17-21 also manifests a relationship to Amos 9. The parallel nature of so many of the themes of Amos 9:11-15 in virtually the same order in Obadiah argues strongly that a dependence exists on the part of Obadiah.[28] The following chart demonstrates the degree to which Obad 15a,16-21 patterns itself after the promise of salvation in Amos 9:11-15, both thematically and structurally.

---

ironic reversal theme central to the final section (15-21), and since the entire final section provides a fully adequate response to the crimes of Edom enumerated through v 14." Any sense of irony in Obad 15b does not overcome the drastic change of theme, addressee, and subject which have long been noted.

[26] This passage appeared at the end of the oracles against the nations in the earlier LXX version. Cf Jer 25:15: "Take this cup of the wine of wrath from my hand, and cause *all the nations* to drink." This command is summarily executed in 25:17.

[27] Caution is needed at this point since the material in 16,17-21 does not come from a single hand. See the literary discussion of Obad 15-21 below, page 79.

[28] For a suggestion as to why the theme of eschatological abundance is lacking, see the discussion of Amos 9:13 in Nogalski, *Literary Precursors*, 119-121, where it is noted that in the Book of the Twelve, this motif applies only to YHWH's people, and does not occur in passages of judgment against the nations. Additionally, Obadiah 15a,16-21 has likely adapted pre-existing material (see the discussion of Obad 17-21 below, page 91). This recognition helps to account for the fact that these parallels are thematic in nature, and do not quote verbally.

Element	Amos	Obadiah
Introduction with eschatological "day"	9:11	15a
Allusion to destruction of Jerusalem	9:11	16
Restoration of Davidic kingdom	9:11	19f
Possession of Edom and other nations	9:12	17f,19f
Eschatological/Agricultural abundance	9:13	x
Restoration of captivity/exiles	9:14	19f
Restoration/reclamation of cities	9:14	20
Concluding promise		
for the restoration of land/Kingdom	9:15	21

It is possible to say that Obadiah depends upon Amos, in part because of the similar phenomenon noted in Obad 1-14, and in part because of the situation presumed by Obadiah. The early layer of Amos 9:11-15 concentrated thematically upon restoration, whereas Obadiah 15a,16-21 displays a more advanced restoration by emphasizing aspects of conquest and domination.[29]

The theological perspective of Obad 16,17-21 appears in the insertion of Amos 9:12a. In both instances a post-exilic political entity, centered in Jerusalem, serves as YHWH's tool to repossess the nations of the former Davidic kingdom. Both passages utilize the verb ירשׁ (Amos 9:12; Obad 17,19f). Both passages also attach this judgment to the day of YHWH: Obadiah by means of the transitional introduction in 15a (for the day of YHWH draws near on all the nations), and Amos 9:12a by means of the context of Amos 9:11. Both passages emphasize Edom, but also incorporate other political entities. Precisely this incorporation brings another point of contact between Amos 9, Obadiah, and Jeremiah. Specifically, the formulation of Amos 9:12a, like Obad 16, appears to be cognizant of Jer 25:29, the verse which comes at the end of the cup of wrath material. Whereas Jer 25:29 emphasizes that Jerusalem (the city which is called by my name) will not escape punishment, Amos 9:12a assumes the promise of restoration for Jerusalem in 9:11, but adds a promise of political domination over YHWH's kingdom (the remnant of Edom and the nations who are called by my name).[30] As with Obad 16,

---

[29] See my discussion of Amos 9:11-15 in *Literary Precursors*, pages 104-122.

[30] Here some explanation is needed since the phrase "over whom/which my name is called," appears several times as a formulaic expression. Primarily, this phrase occurs in reference to the temple (the house over which my name is called), and it appears mostly in Jer (7:10,11,14,30; 32:34; 34:15). Outside Jeremiah, the phrase is used for the temple only in Solomon's temple dedication speech (1 Kgs 8:43; 2 Chr 6:33) The phrase carries cultic significance as well in 2 Sam 6:2 (=1 Chr 13:6), where it appears

Amos 9:12a significantly alters the message in Jer 25:15ff, by changing the announcement of judgment against Jerusalem in those verses into a promise of political restoration.

Thus, the same theological motifs found in Obad 16,17-21 appear in Amos 9:12a, and both passages depend upon the cup of wrath material in Jer 25:15ff for their formulation of this message. The theological motif shared by both Amos 9:12 and Obadiah portrays the restoration of the Davidic kingdom from a Jerusalem perspective. The common theology, the subtle assumption of Jer 25:15ff (particularly in Obad 16 and Amos 9:12a), and the other examples of the interrelationship between the Edom oracle in Jer 49:7ff, Obad 1-9, and Amos 9:1-10, all point in the direction that the compiler of Obad 16,17-21* was the same person who inserted Amos 9:12a. Additionally, these observations raise serious questions as to whether the book of Obadiah ever existed outside its position in the Book of the Twelve. The intricate structural and thematic imitations of Amos 9:1ff extend from the beginning to the end of Obadiah. These imitations serve two functions. First, they provide a judgment against Edom which both parallels and heightens the judgment against Israel in Amos 9:1-10. Second, they introduce the motif of a Jerusalem-centered repossession of the Davidic monarchy. The picture of Obadiah which develops from these observations truly places Obadiah into the realm of "Scripture Prophecy," the process by which the compilation of selected texts, together with the author's own composition, combine to bring YHWH's prophetic message.[31] Pending a more detailed analysis of Obad 15-21, it is not yet

---

in connection with the ark of the covenant. The phrase is used in relation to people five times (Deut 28:10; Isa 63:19; Jer 14:9; 15:16; 2 Chr 7:14). It is used with geo-political entities only three times: twice with reference to Jerusalem (Jer 25:29; Dan 9:18f); and once with nations (Amos 9:12). The reference in Daniel 9 is considerably later than Jer 25:29 and Amos 9:12, but it serves to show how long the traditional formulation stayed alive in the religious language of the people. The phrase as a whole has it roots in "name theology," as the heavy attestation in Deuteronomistically related passages demonstrates.

[31] The term "Scripture Prophecy" attempts to approximate terms which have begun to be used in German language literature, for which I have not encountered an English equivalent. The terms *Schriftprophetie* and *Schriftinterpret* are introduced elsewhere. See Helmut Utzschneider, *Künder oder Schreiber? Eine These zum Problem der »Schriftprophetie« auf Grund von Maleachi 1,6-2,9*, Beiträge zur Erforschung des Alten Testaments und des Antiken Judentums 19 (Frankfurt: Peter Lang, 1989), 9-22; and Siegfried Bergler, *Joel als Schriftinterpret*, Beiträge zur Erforschung des Alten Testaments und des antiken Judentums 16 (Frankfurt: Peter Lang, 1988), 32. The phenomenon comes close to the term "inner-biblical exegesis," used by Michael

prudent to postulate a date for this compilational activity, but before turning to a discussion of other passages, it will be helpful to point to further evidence of Obadiah's awareness of other Edom texts.

4. The Relationship of Obadiah to Isaiah and Ezekiel

The relationship of Obadiah to Jeremiah is not the only connection between Obadiah and other prophetic literature. To complete the picture of the dependence of Obadiah upon other prophetic oracles against Edom, works by Bosshard and Olávarri must be discussed briefly. Bosshard, as noted in the introductory chapter, argues that the macrostructure of the Book of the Twelve bears striking resemblance to the macrostructure of Isaiah. For Bosshard, Obadiah is one of the key texts in this relationship. Specifically, he notes parallels between Obadiah and Isaiah on two levels.[32] The language of Obad 5-6 is influenced by the Edom oracle in Isa 21:11f, and theological motifs in Obad 15-21 appear in Isa 24-27. In the first case he notes three words which Obad 5-6 shares with the Edom oracle in Isa 21:11f: a play on דום and דומה (Obad 5; Isa 21:11); the recurrence of לילה (Obad 5; Isa 21:11); the unusual root בעה (Obad 6; Isa 21:12). Given the fact that two of these words are very uncommon, and that both of these words appear in material which falls outside the parallel to Jer 49, Bosshard's arguments carry considerable weight.[33] Bosshard lists the following theological motifs which recur in the Isaiah Apocalypse (chapters 24-27) and in Obad 15-21: judgment against all nations/people (Obad 15a.16; Isa 24; 26:7ff); holiness of Zion (Obad 17a; Isa 27:13); YHWH as king of Zion (Obad 21b; Isa 24:23b); the old Davidic-Solomonic kingdom (Obad 19f; Isa 27:12); return from exile, relatedly the Diaspora (Obad 18,

---

Fishbane, *Biblical Interpretation in Ancient Israel* (Oxford: Clarendon Press, 1985), but his descriptions center on the broader phenomenon. His term for the prophetic manifestation of this exegetical phenomenon, "mantological exegesis," is rather misleading, implying a spontananeity which does not befit the practice. Nevertheless, his discussion of the phenomenon, 443-524, provides valuable insights.

[32] Bosshard, *BN* 40 (1987): 32f.

[33] The recurrence of לילה in the *Vorlage* of Jer 49:9 argues more strongly that its presence in Obad 5 is literarily dependent on that context rather than Isaiah. However, a clear division cannot be made because the hermeneutical line from the nightwatchman in Isa 21 to the thieves who come by night relates the two contexts rather closely, and may well represent the trigger to the association of the two passages.

20; Isa 27:13). The weight of these observations is more difficult to judge. One cannot deny that these similarities exist, but neither are they so strong that one can say without qualification that awareness of Isa 24-27 played a formative role for Obad 15-21, especially in light of the stronger connections to Jer 49:12; 25:15ff; and Amos 9:1ff. Some of these motifs are general in nature (such as the holiness of Zion), while others represent different perspectives.[34] Still, the very existence of these motifs in a corresponding position in the Book of the Twelve is striking, particularly in light of the influence of Isa 21:11f upon the formulations of Obad 5f.

The work of Olávarri brings the discussion to the accusation in Obad 10-14,15b, a passage which did not play a role in the structural and thematic parallels mentioned above. These verses are normally cited as the verses which provide the most concrete indication of the date of Obadiah. While some occasionally argue for an early pre-exilic date for Obadiah,[35] the vast majority of commentators understand these verses as a *reflection* on the events surrounding Jerusalem's destruction. These arguments are very strong. The entry of strangers into Jerusalem (Obad 11,13), the graphic portrayal of the descriptions, and the association of Edom with this tradition, all point toward the Babylonian destruction of Jerusalem as the event which the author of 10-14 describes. Little serious doubt remains that Obad 10-14 were composed after the events of 587. The question of how long after the destruction of Jerusalem these verses were written is more problematic.

Normally, the emotional power of the words themselves lead scholars to claim that 10-14 were composed rather near the destruction of Jerusalem, or at least by an eyewitness to the events.[36] Olávarri argues that while the verses presuppose the destruction of Jerusalem, there is no reason to assume they were written by an eyewitness or in the time immediately after the destruction of Jerusalem. Olávarri claims Obad 10-14 is a later gloss inserted into the context, and that it is literarily dependent

---

[34] The extent of the restoration of the Davidic kingdom appears much broader in Isaiah than in Obadiah. Isa 27:12 implies a kingdom extending from the Euphrates to the border of Egypt, while Obadiah limits the restoration to a much smaller area.

[35] Miloš Bič, "Zur Problematik des Buches Obadjah," in *VT.S* 1 (1953): 11-25, is one of the few in the last forty years to suggest this date.

[36] See, for example, Allen, *Joel etc.*, 130, who is typical of proponents of this argument when he says, "The historical passage with its passionate tone and vivid detail has seemed to many to indicate that its author was an eyewitness of the 587 B.C. tragedy." Similarly, Wolff, *BK* 14/3, 2; Rudolph, *KAT* 13/2, 297f.

upon Ezek 35 and Amos 1:11f.[37] These two arguments need to be treated separately

Olávarri's argument that Obad 10-14 is added later, as a gloss, is unconvincing. First, the verses associate themselves too tightly to their context to be understood as a gloss. Verse 10 continues verse 9 with no clear break. More importantly, Obad 9 does not make sense when read directly with verse 15.[38] This syntactical affinity leads to the second crucial flaw in Olávarri's reasoning, namely the structure of Obadiah requires 10-14 because these verses function as the accusation. Without 10-14, Obadiah would lack motivation for the bitter condemnation of Edom. Only Obad 10-14 depicts the real crime of Edom.[39] Third, verses 10-14 are already presupposed by Obad 7. This verse hints at a political alliance made by Edom which will come back to haunt them. According to verse 7, Edom's allies only use this covenant to buy time before they turn on them. Traces of this political alliance are likewise noted in verses 10-14, where Edom appears as an ally of the Babylonians. Edom is denounced because they stood by while strangers entered Jerusalem (11), and then killed and imprisoned the fugitives as they tried to escape (14).[40] For all of these reasons, Olávarri's argument that Obad 10-14 is an insertion does not carry much weight.

Olávarri's second argument, however, is considerably stronger. Given the fact that the remainder of Obadiah depends heavily upon Jeremiah, that it exhibits a structural imitation of Amos 9, and that it shows traces of Isaiah's oracle against Edom, one must carefully evaluate Olávarri's

---

[37] Olávarri, *Estudios Biblicos* 22 (1963): 308f.

[38] While Obad 15a begins a new theme the 2ms references in Obad 15b clearly tie it to the preceding verses: "As you have done it will be done to you..." If one attempts to read directly from verse 9, one is confronted by the problem that without 10-14 Edom has not done anything.

[39] The only material in Obad 1-9 (or 15-21) which might possibly be described as accusatory appears in verse 3, where Edom is said to be prideful. However, the nature of this material is more depictive than accusatory, and would not explain the harshness of the punishment announced in verse 9 (that everyone will be cut off from the mountain of Esau).

[40] Whether or not the Edomites were actually present during the Babylonian raid is difficult to say. This language could be figurative in the sense that some of those fleeing the Babylonians would naturally have fled toward Edom. The reference to the "crossroad" (14) and the phrase "*like* one of them" (11; rather than "among them") appear to portray Edom's role only as secondary. On the other hand, Obad 13 appears to portray a more active role for Edom (you should not loot his wealth on the day of his disaster).

suggestion that Obad 10-14 demonstrates dependance upon Ezek 35:1ff and Amos 1:11f. Olávarri claims Obad 10-14 derives its background and form from Ezek 35:1ff. He notes the following motifs: 1) The merriment of Edom over the downfall of Jerusalem (Obad 12; Ezek 35:15); 2) injuries and arrogance against Judah (Obad 14; Ezek 35:5-6); 3) both Obad 10-14 and Ezek 35 share literary influence from Amos 1:11-12, depicting the wrongs committed by Edom as a reenactment of the persecution Jacob suffered by Esau.[41]   From these motifs, Olávarri derives literary dependance on the part of Obadiah.

One does not gather the full extent of the similarities between Obad 10-14 and Ezek 35 merely from Olávarri's brief remarks. The general themes he cites contain numerous additional contact points in terms of common vocabulary and formulations, but these similarities do not limit themselves to Obad 10-14. One may note the following: references to the destruction of Jerusalem as the "day of their calamity" (Obad 13) and the "time of their calamity" (Ezek 35:5) both of which use אידם for the play on words with Edom; the phrase "to be cut off from the mountain of ..." Esau/Seir (Obad 9; Ezek 35:7); the use of עשה to formulate retribution (Obad 15b; Ezek 35:11); the boasting of Edom with the phrase "to make great your mouth" (Obad 12; Ezek 35:13); the use of "judge" (שפט in Obad 21; Ezek 35:11); the verb "possess" (ירש in Obad 17,19,20); Ezek 35:10); the use of the root אכל connoting the taking of land (Obad 18; Ezek 35:12); Edom's "rejoicing" (Obad 12; Ezek 35:14,15); the desolation of the "house of Israel" (Ezek 35:15) and the devastation which the "house of Jacob" and the "house of Joseph" (Obad 17,18) will apply to Edom; the themes of violence/bloodshed/slaughter of the Edomites against the Judeans (Obad 10; Ezek 35:5,6); the theme of no survivors for Edom (Obad 18; Ezek 35:7f); and the use of עבר (Ezek 35:7; Obad 17).

These formulations greatly strengthen Olávarri's observations that a relationship exists between Obadiah and Ezek 35:1ff. However, the fact that many of the formulations go beyond Obad 10-14 further weakens his first argument that these verses were inserted. One may, with relative certainty, conclude with Olávarri that the Obadiah references assume knowledge of Ezekiel, and not the other way around. In several respects

---

[41] Olávarri, *Estudios Biblicos* 22 (1963): 309, argues this motif underlies the phraseology of Amos 1:11f, and is reflected again in the formulation of Ezek 35 and Obad 10-14. Further, he cites the theme of anger from Amos 1:11 taken up in Ezek 35:5-11, and the theme of the killing of fugitives by the Edomites in Amos' oracle with Obad 10,14.

Obad 10-14, 15-21 expand upon the motifs of Ezek 35:1ff.[42] The verses
take the situation of Ezek 35:1ff, which depicts Edom's incursion upon a
devastated Judah, and turn it into a promise for Judah and Jerusalem at
Edom's expense. This reversal represents the same hermeneutic of the use
of the cup of wrath material from Jer 49:12; 25:15ff.

5. The Relationship of Obadiah to Micah

One other piece of the puzzle must be introduced here. Translation
of the two passages, demonstrates that a number of words appear in Obad
15a,16-21 which reappear in Mic 1:1-7.[43]   The existence of these
catchwords indicates a redactional connection between these writings, which
pre-dated the incorporation of the book of Jonah into the larger corpus.
A more detailed analysis of the connection appears later, but the results of
that investigation are mentioned here because they play a role in
understanding the present shape and purpose of Obadiah. The words
which tie the end of Obadiah with the beginning of Micah appear both in
the material which is germane to the majority of the unit 16-21 (the pre-
existing block) and in sections best labeled as insertions. These insertions
carry a distinctive anti-Northern perspective which is not present in the
basic material of Obad 16-21. These observations on Mic 1:1-7 complicate
any easy explanation, since they demand a choice between two possibilities.
Either they were added later to Obadiah, or they were incorporated
simultaneously with the structural imitation of Amos 9:1ff, indicating a
compilation process quite cognizant of its position in the Book of the
Twelve. If one opts for the latter option, then one must presume that the

---

[42] Note particularly the formulation of Ezek 35:10,12. Ezek 35:10 quotes the Edomites
as saying, "We will possess them" (meaning Judah). This puts the saying in Obad 17
in much stronger light: "and the house of Jacob will possess their possessions." Obad
18 likewise reverses the quote of Ezek 35:12, where the Edomites say "they (the
Judeans) are given to us for food" (אכלה). Obad 18 claims the house of Jacob and
Joseph will "devour them" (אכלום). These reversals argue strongly against Wehrle,
Prophetie und Textanalyse, 365, who concurs a literary relationship, but argues Ezek
35:1ff drew upon Obadiah. It would make no sense for an author to reverse the images
from Obadiah to Ezekiel. Ezekiel's Edom material portrays events in much more
realistic terms, as though in response to a specific event (cf especially 35:10f), while
Obadiah's oracles are less concretely phrased (cf Obad 18).

[43] See Nogalski, *Literary Precursors*, 31-32.

compilator worked with pre-existing material to some degree. In favor of this argument, one can make several preliminary observations. First, Obadiah began with the adaptation of a pre-existing block. Second, the intertwining of the two halves of Obad 15a and 15b argues that the two sections of which these verses were a part, already existed in fixed form. Third, Obad 17-21 has an inner consistency which is much stronger than often admitted.[44]

6. The Units in Obad 15-21

The complicated structural and thematic interplay between Obadiah, Amos 9:1ff, Jer 49:7ff, and Ezek 35:1ff has already been discussed. This section will make several literary observations on Obad 15-21, paying attention to the manner in which these verses have been composed. This task requires an understanding of the message of these verses in light of structural observations on Obadiah as a whole, and of its position in the larger corpus.

Traditionally, scholars clearly distinguish Obad 15a from 15b.[45] The 2ms reference to Edom in 15b coincides with the vast majority of 2ms references in 1-14. Obad 15b also demonstrates the character of a concluding speech ("Even as you have done it will be done to you."). Obad 15a, on the other hand, presents an unexpected theme: eschatological judgment on all the nations. This theme underlies verses 16-21, and 15a correspondingly demonstrates the character of an introduction to these verses. Explanations for this tension have ranged from the accidental displacement of 15b and 15a to a redactional connecting technique which

---

[44] See literary discussion in the following chapter.

[45] This distinction is almost universal. Even those authors, such as Rudolph, *KAT* 14/2, 296, who argue for a single author often describe Obad 15a,16-21 as a separate speech or poem delivered at another time, which has been woven into the present context. Allen, *Joel, etc*, 133-142, presents a confusing model in which he clearly places Obad 15a with 16 and Obad 15b with 14, thus dividing the verse, while at the same time referring to Obadiah as "a poem" with four strophes. The confusing aspect of his model revolves around the relationship of the smaller "strophes" to the whole. He describes several strophes of this poem which do not appear in consecutive verses, but he offers no real explanation as to whether he considers the gaps a sign of redactional displacement or a very peculiar writing style. Allen considers Obad 15b with 14 as a strophe, as well as 15a,16. In addition, he treats Obad 17 and 21 as a single strophe.

joined the two sections (1-14,15b; 15a,16-21) together.[46] The latter option boasts far more adherents.

Obad 16 begins an independent unit, but a unit which plays an integral role in the book's structure. The extent of the unit is clearly defined by the concluding phrase of verse 18: כי יהוה דבר. However, as in the quote of Jer 49:9,14-16 found in Obad 1-5, one notes how the function of this concluding formula has been superseded by verses 19-21, which explicate verses 16-18 from the twin aspects of the centrality of Zion and the possession (ירש) of the surrounding nations. These two aspects combine under the hermeneutical rubric of the restoration of the Davidic kingdom.

Obad 16 continues the theme of the יום יהוה upon all the nations (from 15a), relying upon the images of Jer 49:12; 25:15ff. The verse recalls the drinking of the cup as a symbolic reference to the destruction of Jerusalem. The use of the 2mp reference refers to the congregation in much the same manner as the change to plural in Obad 1 (We have heard a report; cf "I" in Jer 49:14).[47] The prophet presents this message in the form of comfort: the destruction of Jerusalem is past; now all nations will experience YHWH's judgment, only much more severely than Jerusalem. The verse draws a clear distinction in time between the judgment upon YHWH's people who have already experienced (perfect of "to drink") and the future judgment of the nations (imperfect of "to drink").[48]

Obad 16 demonstrates close affinities to 15a. Both presume a day of judgment, and both explicitly direct this judgment against "all the nations". Obad 16 also serves as the transition element to the promises for YHWH's people in the remainder of the book. Obad 16 alludes briefly to Jerusalem's past destruction as a paradigm for the devastation which the nations will experience. Obad 17ff dwells on the future well-being of Zion and the people of YHWH in which they will overcome the surrounding nations to reunify the kingdom. The 2mp reference to the congregation in

---

[46] Wolff, *BK* 14/3, 5, argues for accidental transposition. Wehrle, *Prophetie und Textanalyse*, 350, notes Obad 16 makes an effort to unite itself with both 15a and 15b (כי/כאשר), pointing toward a deliberate incorporation of the disparate parts. Rudolph, *KAT* 13/2, 311, argues for a redactional attachment, but only via the introductory כי in 15a. He does not say, however, whether the transposition of the two half-verses is an intentional or accidental device.

[47] See discussion above, page 70, of the relationship of these verses to Jer 25:15ff for an explanation of why "you" does not refer to Edom, but to Jerusalem and Judah.

[48] Wolff, *BK* 14/3, 45; Rudolph, *KAT* 13/2, 312; Wehrle, *Prophetie und Textanalyse*, 186; Allen, *Joel, etc.*, 162.

Obad 16 suggests this verse was not originally part of 17ff, where both YHWH's people and the enemies appear in the third person plural. Both of the two main sections of Obadiah begin with introductory material incorporating direct references to the audience through plural formulations. Verse 1 is a prophetic speech and uses the first person plural (we). Verse 16, on the other hand is a divine speech and appropriately utilizes the second person plural (you).

Obad 17a presents the theme of the remainder of the booklet: the reunification of YHWH's kingdom with Jerusalem as its center. The portrayal of the entities involved in this reunification lead to a somewhat confusing picture. Obad 17 parallels the mountain of Zion with the house of Jacob, which must here be understood as a reference to Judah.[49] Obad 18 expands the field of vision to include both the areas to the north (house of Joseph) and the south (house of Esau). With this expansion comes affirmation that YHWH's message is one of promise for both the house of Joseph and the house of Jacob, but not for the house of Esau. Together, Jacob and Joseph will conquer Esau. Thus verses 17-18 present a picture in which symbolic names for the Northern and Southern kingdoms represent equals in common cause against the Edomites.

The confusion stems from Obad 19-21. Syntactical tensions lead scholars to view these verses in varying manners.[50] It is possible, however, to offer a plausible explanation of the text as it now stands without resorting to emendations. Several indices argue that the source of confusion in one case results from the literary growth of Obad 19, while in another case (Obad 20) the failure to interpret a metaphor leads to suppositions of a corrupt text which prove unnecessary. First, beginning with Obad 19, the syntax of 19aα,b follows a single grammatical style,

---

[49] Jacob appears elsewhere as a reference to Judah: See H.J. Zobel, "יעקק(ו)ב," in *TWAT*, vol. 3, 752-777, especially §V.2., columns 771-773.

[50] For example, Wolff, *BK* 14/3, 46f; and Allen, *Joel, etc.*, 168-170. These authors see "Negev" as object rather than subject. Others, such as Stuart, *Word* 31, 412,420f, correctly distinguish between the direct object markers following mountain of Esau, Philistines, field of Ephraim, field of Samaria; and Gilead. The place names for Negev, Shephelah, and Benjamin function as subjects governed by the verb ירשו. Watts, *Obadiah*, 62f, does the same, but omits the Philistines because the line is metrically disturbed. Rudolph, *KAT* 13/2, 314f, believes the text corrupt, and argues that the second occurrence of the verb וירשו constitutes a transposed abbreviation for Jerusalem. His explanation is complicated by an apparent typographical error which exchanges Ephraim for Edom with no explanation. His exegetical discussion of the verse (316), however, assumes Ephraim.

whereas the syntax of 19ab interrupts this continuity.[51]   Second, the intervening sentence incorporates a distinctive viewpoint, namely, the possession of Ephraim and Samaria.   Third, the intervening sentence formulates this possession based upon clear references to Mic 1:6. Visually, the continuity of the syntactical formulation may be demonstrated as follows:

Obad 19aa,b	Obad 19ab
ירשו הנגב את־הר עשו	
והשפלה את־פלשתים	
	וירשו את־שדה אפרים ואת שדה שמרון
ובנימן את־הגלעד	

The consistent formulation on the left reads simply: "The Negev will possess the mountain of Esau, and the Shephelah the Philistines, and Benjamin Gilead."   The image portrays the reunification of the Davidic/Solomonic monarchy under Judean control.   The column on the right, which complicates the picture grammatically, adds "and they will possess the field of Ephraim and the field of Samaria."   This insertion states no subject explicitly, unlike the earlier formulations.   Given the context, the intended subject must be both the Negev and the Shephelah.

The idea of Southern regions "possessing" Ephraim and Samaria requires consideration.   ירש is a term of conquest, and as such indicates considerable antagonism against the objects with which it is used.   It is no term of alliance but one of subjugation.[52]   No other passage uses the term

---

51   The verb ירשו comes at the beginning of the verse and governs the following phrases, resulting in a normal syntactical pattern: verb + subject + object marker + object.

52   Above all, ירש appears in Deuteronomy more than 70 times, almost always in connection with YHWH's formulaic promise of the land.   In this context, the verb becomes the key means of expressing this promise in terms of the conquest.   In the conquest narratives in Joshua and Judges, the verb also plays an important part, albeit not so frequently as in Deuteronomy.   Still ירש appears in Joshua and Judges more than 25 times each.   Elsewhere in the Pentateuch, the verb occasionally appears in Genesis, in promises to the patriarchs that they will possess the land   (Gen 15:3-8; 22:17; 24:60; 28:4).   The verb is essentially lacking in Exodus, where it appears only twice in the hiphil (Exod 15:9; 34:24).   Neither one of these examples are directly related to the "promise of land" tradition.   The verb appears only twice in Leviticus (20:24; 25:46), but both appear cognizant of the promise of the land.   In 1-2 Kings the verb appears in the hiphil when it is related to the conquest motifs (1 Kgs 14:24; 21:26; 2 Kgs 16:3; 17:8; 21:2).   The verb likewise appears in Ezra (9:11,12) and Nehemiah (9:15,22-25) as reference to the conquest of the land given by YHWH.   The Chronicler (2 Chr 28:3; 33:2) takes over the hiphil formula from Kings, including it twice in the

so explicitly for Judean domination of a reunified kingdom which subordinates the strongholds of the Northern territory — Ephraim and Samaria. The choice of these terms for this context is made with deliberation, and reflects an understanding of the position of Obadiah in the context of the Book of the Twelve.

Hosea, Amos, and Micah also mention Ephraim and Samaria, but then the terms essentially disappear from the Book of the Twelve.[53] The terms play a central role in the corpus which formed the basis of the Book of the Twelve (Hos-Amos-Mic-Zeph). This earlier corpus employed Samaria and Ephraim as key terms for the paradigmatic portrayal of the fate of Northern kingdom as a warning to Jerusalem.[54] Obad 19 was not

---

Jehoshaphat material which has no parallel in Kings (2 Chr 20:7,11). As a rule ירש in the Psalms appears in close connection with the conquest tradition, although the references to the possession of the land are often couched in more cultic formulations: he who fears YHWH will possess the land (25:13); those waiting for YHWH will possess the land (37:9), etc. (cf. 37:11,22,29,34). Ps 44:4 offers a corrective emphasis: "For by their own sword they did not possess the land; ... but your right hand ... favored them." Three passages (Ps 69:36; Isa 65:9; Amos 9:12) parallel Obad 19 in terms of the view of the possession which they propose. Ps 69:36 relates Zion and Judah to the promise of possession (For God will save Zion and build the cities of Judah that they may dwell there and possess it). In Isa 65:9 YHWH proclaims, "I will bring forth offspring from Jacob, and an heir (יורש) of my mountains from Judah; even my chosen ones shall possess it, and my servants shall dwell there." Both these passages relate the possession promise to Zion and Judah similarly to Obad 16ff. The same must be said for Amos 9:12, which states, "They will possess the remnant of Edom and all the nations who are called by my name." While some confusion exists as to the exact identity of the "fallen booth of David", the Judean and Jerusalem context of 9:11-15 of this passage clearly provides a common ideological viewpoint. Further, see H.H. Schmid, "ירש," in *ThAT*, vol. 1, 778-781, and Wehrle, *Prophetie und Textanalyse*, 287.

53 The last reference to *Samaria* in the Book of the Twelve appears in Mic 1:1-7, to which Obad 19 is related on a redactional level (see discussion in the following paragraph). Samaria appears several times in Amos and Hosea, exclusively in judgment contexts: Hos 7:1; 8:5,6; 10:5,7; 14:1; Amos 3:9; 4:1; 6:1; 8:14. *Ephraim* appears more frequently in Hosea than any other book (34 times, only in chapters 4-14). Only Joshua (17 times) and Judges (23 times) come close. Within the Book of the Twelve, Ephraim almost disappears from view after this mention, appearing only in Zech 9:10,13; 10:7. However, other considerations place the incorporation of Zech 9-14 after the incorporation of Obad 19, indicating that at the point of incorporation, the reference to the possession of Ephraim was also the last reference to that entity within the larger corpus. See the chapter on Zech 9-14 near the end of this work.

54 Compare the discussion of Samaria in Mic 1:1-7 in Nogalski, *Literary Precursors*, 132-137, and the treatment of Deuteronomistic superscriptions in the discussion of Amos 1:1 (*Literary Precursors*, 84-89). Ephraim appears only in Hosea, where it plays a

an integral part of this earlier corpus, rather it comments upon Ephraim and Samaria as they appeared there.[55] Above all, the phraseology of the insertion in Obad 19 betrays this hermeneutical awareness on the part of the redactor. Given the fact that the region in question is part of the hill country of central Palestine, the terms "field of Ephraim" and "field of Samaria" appear rather strange. The Hebrew term שדה means "field", and normally refers to a relatively level area. Occasionally, the term can be used to connote a wider geographical area in the sense of "territory", a usage which obscures the pointed nature of this verse.[56] In essence, Obad 19 comments upon the judgment against Samaria in Mic 1:6 and perhaps Hosea's denunciation of Ephraim.

Mic 1:6 appears as part of the opening unit of the book of Micah, a unit which demonstrates Deuteronomistic influence.[57] The unit assumes the destruction of Samaria, and interprets this destruction as a warning to Jerusalem. The announcement of judgment against Samaria reads literally: "I have made Samaria a heap of ruins of the field, planting places for the vineyard." Based on this reference, it is possible to understand how one could afterwards refer to the "field" of Samaria, intending a negative connotation of a destroyed region. The use of the phrase "field of Ephraim" is also unattested elsewhere, but the preponderance of Ephraim in Hosea, especially in agricultural metaphors, lends itself to a similar interpretation of Ephraim as a field that has been destroyed.[58] Thus,

---

dominant role, while Samaria occurs in Hosea, Amos, and Micah. Zephaniah does not mention either of these entities, but this omission relates to its literary role as the climax of the threat and the judgment against Jerusalem in the Deuteronomistic corpus, precisely because they did not respond to the earlier example of the destruction of the Northern kingdom (cf especially Mic 1:5; Zeph 1:4).

[55] This statement presupposes the insertion of the book of Jonah into the corpus after the Obadiah-Micah connection was made. See the chapter on Jonah in this volume.

[56] See the "territory of Moab" in Num 21:20; Ruth 1:2,6; Gen 36:35; 1 Chr 1:46; 8:8; "territory of Philistia" in 1 Sam 6:1; 27:7,11; "territory of Edom" in Gen 32:4; Judg 5:4; "the territory of Israel's inheritance" in Judg 20:6; "the territory of the Amelekites" in Gen 14:7.

[57] See literary discussion of Mic 1:2-9 in Nogalski, *Literary Precursors*, 123ff.

[58] Several passages in Hosea use Ephraim in agricultural metaphors, which might also have had some influence upon the idea of Ephraim as a field: The MT of Hos 9:13 compares Ephraim to something (Tyre, rock, etc) in a meadow, but the textual problems of the passage make it difficult to explain. Hos 10:11 portrays Ephraim as a heifer harnessed to plow a field. Hos 11:8 compares Ephraim to the city "Admah", whose Hebrew spelling (אדמה), makes it ripe for a play on words with שדה. In Hos 13:8, Ephraim (cf 13:1) will be devoured by the beasts of the field.

Obad 19 demonstrates two distinct layers, both using the motif of the restoration of YHWH's kingdom, but the second layer betraying a decidedly more negative attitude toward Ephraim and Samaria than any of the surrounding verses.

Obad 20 has been the focus of much discussion. The last decades have brought relative agreement concerning the location of the regions mentioned in this verse, but not upon the text as it stands.[59] The major textual problem has been the understanding of החל הזה (this rampart). Most commentators have preferred to emend the text because the context made it difficult to explain the presence of a rampart. The confusion of the other versions increased the impression of textual corruption.[60] However, one need not resort to emendation to make this sentence meaningful. In Obad 20 "rampart" exhibits a metaphorical nuance much like Nah 3:8, which asks Nineveh: "Are you better than Thebes ... whose *rampart* was the sea, whose wall was the sea?" In light of the fact that Thebes is at least 100 miles west of the Red Sea and over 400 miles south of the Mediterranean, "rampart" is not limited to a physical structure surrounding the city. Rather, the picture is one of a geographical obstacle which served to protect the entire region from outside interference. This metaphorical understanding illuminates the use of "rampart" in Obad 20. The literary context of the verse must be taken into account. As such, the verse presupposes the existence of Obad 19 and the Jerusalem orientation of 16-21. In light of this context, one notes that the areas in Obad 18 effectively encircle Jerusalem on every side: the Shephelah to the south and west, the Negev to the south (and to the southeast with the occupation of Edom), the Benjamite expansion to the northeast, and the occupation of Ephraim to the north. Pictorially, this reunified region can well be described as a geographical buffer or "rampart" for Jerusalem. The fact that the MT specifically mentions "this" rampart adds further weight to the argument that the verse has its surrounding context in mind. "This rampart" thus

---

[59] Zarephath is a city along the Mediterranean coast between Tyre and Sidon. ספרד was apparently the Aramaic designation for Sardis. A Jewish colony existed there during the Persian period. The colony apparently came from Babylon, and was in all likelihood settled there following the Persian overthrow of that kingdom. See Allen, *Joel, etc.*, 171; Watts, *Obadiah*, 64; Rudolph, *KAT* 13/2, 315; Wolff, *BK* 14/2, 47. John Gray, "The Diaspora of Israel and Judah in Obadiah v. 20," *ZAW* 65 (1953): 53-59, disagrees, saying this location would destroy the parallelism, and suggests Hesperides in North Africa.

[60] See text note "a" in Obad 20 in Nogalski, *Literary Precursors*, 32.

refers metaphorically to the reunified region described in Obad 19 which surrounds and "protects" Jerusalem.

The metaphorical understanding of "this rampart" helps to clarify the problems of the remainder of the verse. Not only will the territorial reunification of the region occur, but the displaced citizens (the exiles of this rampart belonging to the sons of Israel, and the exiles of Jerusalem) will also be brought into this reunification process. Many commentators interpret the nominal clause אשר־כנענים עד־צרפת such that it needs the verb ירש (possess).[61] A better solution appears when one examines the structure of the verse itself. The structure parallels the exiles of this rampart and the exiles of Jerusalem with their modifying clauses as the subjects of ירשו in 20b. The text thus reads:

20aa:	And the exiles of this rampart belonging to the sons of Israel	who (are among) the Canaanites to Zarephath,
20ab:	And the exiles of Jerusalem	who are in Sepharad —
20b:	They will possess the cities of the Negev.	

The crux of the interpretation revolves around which verb must be assumed in 20aa in order to translate the nominal phrase. The choices are clear: 1) the verb "are"; 2) the verb "possess"; 3) the verb "are" plus the preposition ב. Grammatically, the first option appears most frequently, but the resulting phrase would make no sense if it were translated "the exiles ... belonging to the sons of Israel who are Canaanites unto Zarephath".[62] Option number two, the assumption of the verb "possess", takes two forms, based upon where the verb is placed. The most frequently suggested form essentially excises the relative pronoun אשר.[63] This alternative appears

---

61 So Allen, *Joel, etc*, 170f; Weiser, *ATD* 24, 209; Stuart, *Word* 31, 421; Wolff, *BK* 14/3, 41f.

62 This translation would have to understand "Canaanites" in a geo-political sense, meaning that these people lived in the region which made them Canaanites politically, but ethnically they were considered Israelites. Modern parallels exist for such distinctions between political and ethnic identities — such as Germans living in Poland, or Italian-Americans — but such a distinction is highly unlikely in Obad 20, because it is doubtful ideologically that the Sons of Israel would ever be called Canaanites in any sense, but particularly not in a poem which formulates a reconstitution of the Davidic monarchy as in Obad 17-21.

63 Most proponents of this option either delete or ignore אשר in their translations. They read "the exiles [...] belonging to the sons of Israel will possess the Canaanites unto Zarapheth". They understand "the sons of Israel" as a reference to the exiles of the

dubious from a text-critical perspective. A grammatically more appealing possibility understands אֲשֶׁר as the introduction to a relative clause (GK §138e,f) which functions as the object of the main clause. The resulting translation would be: "And the exiles ... belonging to the sons of Israel (will possess) those who are Canaanites unto Zarephath." However, this option also raises more problems than it solves. Although the use of אֲשֶׁר to introduce an object clause is attested,[64] it never appears as part of a nominal sentence, nor is it separated from the verb. In addition, the other examples of this usage typically refer back to an antecedent.[65]

The third option — to presuppose "are among" — provides the simplest explanation of the sentence, but results in a different picture of the identity of the "sons of Israel" than is normally assumed in the exegetical literature.[66] Most commentators understand "the sons of Israel" as the Northern kingdom, but this is not the only way in which the phrase is used in the Old Testament. Indeed, the term may also designate the entire undivided kingdom or only Judah.[67] The context of Obad 20 concerns the

---

Northern Kingdom. Wolff, *BK* 14/2, 42, notes the problems created by the אֲשֶׁר clause, and assumes the verb יָרַשׁ. So also, Allen, *Joel, etc.*, 170f, distrusts attempted reconstructions from other versions, because he argues that the plethora of translations found therein more likely manifests earlier attempts "to get sense out of an already corrupt text." Rudolph, *KAT* 13/2, 315, changes אֲשֶׁר to אֶרֶץ (land) on the basis of LXX, but LXX often adds בָּהּ where it does not appear in the MT.

[64] See constructions in Gen 44:1; 49:1; 1 Sam 16:3; Mic 6:1; Isa 52:15; Ps 69:5.

[65] Isa 52:15 and Ps 69:5 are exceptions, but in both instances the verb follows immediately after אֲשֶׁר.

[66] It is possible in poetic texts to assume a preposition (here בְּ), but it is also within the realm of possibility that the preposition בְּ was lost through haplography, because it would have been part of a word whose first letter was כ, whose similarity to ב could account for the oversight of a single letter.

[67] The phrase "Sons of Israel" demonstrates a marked tendency to be understood as a *Pan-Israelite* or inclusive term, encompassing more than merely the Northern kingdom. It appears frequently in the exodus and conquest traditions to describe the entire people. The term appears over 100 times in Exodus alone and is well attested in the remainder of the Pentateuch. In the conquest traditions, the term continues to be used as the collective term for the Israelites (over 80 times in Joshua and over 60 times in Judges). The "sons of Israel" appear much less frequently in Samuel-Kings: 1 Samuel (11 times); 2 Samuel (4 times); 1 Kings (21 times); 2 Kings (11 times). This drop in frequency may be attributed in large part to the content of these books, which documents the history of the unification and division of the kingdom. Above all, note that after the death of Solomon (1 Kgs 11) and the division of the monarchy (1 Kgs 12), the phrase often recurs in the form of a reminiscence of exodus or conquest traditions of Israel prior to the monarchy: 1 Kgs 14:24; 21:26; 2 Kgs 16:3; 18:4; 21:2,9. Compare

question of the reunification of the Davidic kingdom. The use of "the sons of Israel" makes more sense in its Pan-Israelite connotation than solely as a reference to the North. Several observations support this assertion. First, Ephraim is not viewed part of the kingdom in v. 19, but as a region to be possessed. Second, the distinction between the sons of Israel and the Canaanites as far as Zarephath puts the emphasis upon those people who should be considered part of the unified kingdom, not upon the Northern political entity. Third, numerous other references more clearly demonstrate the entire people as the normal frame of reference for the "sons of Israel" in the context of reunification.[68] Fourth, reference to the Sons of Israel presuming a pan-Israelite group helps clarify the reference to "this rampart" in the context of Obad 19f. Obad 20 thus continues the portrait of the reunification of the Davidic kingdom from a Judean perspective, begun in verse 19, by incorporating the exiles in Phoenicia and Asia Minor.[69]

Obad 21 functions as the conclusion to the book, reiterating themes recurring earlier: salvation for Zion (21aa, see 16f); judgment upon Edom (21ab, see 1-14,15b,18); and unification of the kingdom (21b, see 19f). In the context, the "deliverers" who ascend Mount Zion" must be seen as the triumphant army which has succeeded in "possessing" or reunifying the

---

also the account of the destruction of Samaria in 2 Kings 17. Although ostensibly discussing Samaria, the term appears in a context (17:7-9) where the message has been expanded to include Judah (17:13). The Chronicler sometimes considers the "sons of Israel" as the army of the Northern kingdom (2 Chron 13:12,16,18; 28:8). However, the term is much more frequently used for both Judah and Israel: 1 Chr 1:43; 2:1; 6:49; 27:1; 2 Chr 5:2,10; 6:11; 7:3; 8:2,8,9; 16:3; 30:6,21; 31:1; 31:5,6; 33:2,9; 34:33; 35:17. The tendency to use the "sons of Israel" with a Pan-Israelite connotation is particularly noticeable in the Chronicler's accounts of the reforms of Hezekiah and Josiah (30:6,21; 31:1; 31:5,6; 34:33; 35:17). These Judean kings, in the account of the Chronicler, institute reforms in which "the sons of Israel" (both North and South) participate. Several texts also clearly demonstrate that "sons of Israel" could be used *explicitly for Judeans*: 1 Kgs 12:17 = 2 Chr 10:17; Ezek 37:16. This latter reference is particularly clear since it speaks of two groups to be reunited: "Judah and the sons of Israel" and "Ephraim and the house of Israel."

[68] For example: Jer 3:21; 23:7; Ezek 2:3; 4:13; 35:3; 37:16,21; 43:7; 44:9,15; 47:22; 48:11; Joel 4:16; Mic 5:2.

[69] The picture of these exiles returning to repossess the cities of the Negev fits well with the assumption that Edomite incursion into Judean territory had already begun. By the time of the Maccabbees, Edomites possessed towns well into the regions once strictly considered Judean territory. Probably already during the fifth century, Edomites were moving into southern Judah, forced in part by the (gradual) takeover of Edomite territory by the Nabateans. See John R. Bartlett, *Edom and the Edomites*, JSOTS 77 (Sheffield: JSOT, 1989), 164f, and S. Cohen, "Nabateans," *IDB*, vol. 4, 491f.

kingdom. The action of the verse sets Edom apart for judgment in spite of the fact that they are not the only region which must be possessed. This distinction causes several commentators to regard the verse as part of an earlier layer concerned only with Edom.[70] However, this suggestion fails to note the use of שׁפט (to judge) rather than ירשׁ (to possess). The change is subtle, but while other regions must be repossessed in order to reconstitute the united kingdom, Edom has been accused of crimes (1-14) against Jacob, for which judgment is the appropriate response.

7. Toward a Synthesis

The literary observations allow a summary of the entire unit. Obad 15a,16-21 may be designated an extended prophecy of salvation, comprised of different compositional elements, which, when considered with Obad 1-14,15b, help to characterize Obadiah as a mosaic of anti-Edom sayings. Obad 15a functions as the literary transition from the oracle against Edom in 1-14,15b. Obad 16a provides the addressee with the 2mp references referring to the congregation. Obad 16aα alludes to the lament of YHWH's people over their drinking of the cup of wrath (the destruction of Jerusalem). Obad 16aβ-17 proclaims salvation for a remnant on Zion, and full restoration for Jacob. The salvation takes the form of restored possessions and the destruction of Edom (17,18a). The proclamation culminates in the announcement of its purpose, namely the decimation of the Edomites (18bα). The concluding formula marks the end of this prophecy (18bβ). Obad 19f repeats these same two elements, but reverses the emphasis. Obad 19f presents a second proclamation of salvation, this time emphasizing the restoration of the unified kingdom, while the destruction of Edom recedes into the background. Obad 21 combines these two motifs for a third time, by assuming the restoration of the kingdom of YHWH from a Zion perspective, and the judgment upon Edom.

Several observations help to narrow the focus for the *Sitz im Leben* of this text. First and foremost, the text as a whole belongs to the post-exilic Jerusalem cult. The allusions to the destruction of Jerusalem (16,20) and the centrality of Zion (16,21) leave little serious doubt to this assignation of time and place. The cultic background appears in the reference to the day of YHWH and in the proclamation of salvation

---

[70]   See discussion of Obad 21 and the macrostructure of Obadiah, above page 59.

attached to the oracle against Edom, which is formulated as an address in a congregational setting (Obad 16).

Second, closer evaluation of the component parts reveals different intentions motivating 15a,16, 17-18 and 19-21. Obad 17-18 relates much more closely to the theme of 1-14,15b since it portrays a unified strike against Edom alone by the house of Jacob and the house of Joseph. Obad 19-21, on the other hand, expands the interest to include the repossession of the entire region, not just Edom. As such 19-21 has more in common with the transitional material which speaks of judgment on the nations in 15a,16. However, one must also note the manner in which 19f explicates the "possession" mentioned in verse 17. The interrelationship of these parts makes it difficult to postulate a long process of the growth of the text. It is more plausible that 15a,16-21 entered Obadiah as part of a single compositional process, which sought to place the Edom oracle (1-14,15b) within a broader eschatological context of judgment against the nations for crimes against Jerusalem and Judah. However, the insertion of the phrase "and they will possess the field of Ephraim and the field of Samaria" in Obad 19 indicates that this compositional process has adapted pre-formulated material.[71]

Third, cultic and political emphases intertwine in these verses which display a nationalistic fervor and a confidence for the reunification of the kingdom. The holiness of Zion (16) and the dedication of the kingdom to YHWH (21) frame a political message of conquest/reunification. The verses portray a reunification deriving from the actions of an army, not by direct divine intervention as in later apocalyptic imagery, such as Joel 4.

Fourth, when viewed as a whole, Obadiah does not present a picture of the destruction of Edom in a stage as advanced as Mal 1:2ff. The promise of Obad 17f portrays YHWH's tool of punishment as Jacob and Joseph, and 19f portrays the Negev as the particular instrument of vengeance against Edom. These images would not be necessary if Edom were already overrun, but they seem to have been composed as YHWH's judgment response to Edom's annexation of parts of Southern Judah.

The weight of these observations points to a date between Haggai (520) and Malachi for the component parts of Obad 15-21. Haggai initiated the temple construction, but the confidence of the strength for reunification exhibited in Obad 17-21 does not fit the picture of the situation presented in Hag 1. Hag 1 portrays a people which has little hope or fervor. Telltale indications of the hope for restoration of the Davidic

---

[71] The same technique was observed in Obad 1-5, which adapts Jer 49:14-16,9.

monarchy do appear by the end of Haggai (2:20-23), but Haggai ties this hope to a specific person, an attitude which Obadiah does not evidence. The situation in Mal 1:2-5 presupposes Edom in a much weakened state. In fact, the portrayal of Edom precisely reverses that which appears in Obadiah. Obadiah quotes Edom as a high and exalted country which does not believe it will be pulled down (Obad 3). Malachi depicts Edom as a devastated country which thinks it will pull itself back up (1:2-5).[72] On the other hand, Obad 15a,16-21 intimates a decline in Edom's fortunes, which likely points to a time closer to Malachi.

More difficult, of course, is the question of the date of the attachment of these verses to Obad 1-14,15b. Assumptions that the verses were composed for this purpose do not appear entirely warranted. To be sure, the motifs from Jer 25:15ff and Ezek 35:1ff which appear in these verses tally with the interests of 1-14,15b, but other factors indicate Obad 17-21 had its own pre-history prior to this attachment. The transposition of Obad 15a and 15b points toward the attachment of a literarily established piece rather than free composition. The reworking of the particles introducing 15a,15b,16 also argues for redactional incorporation in an unusual manner reminiscent of the reshaping of the particles in Obad 1-5. The adaptation of the pre-existing material in Obad 1-5 demonstrates a marked tendency to parallel the fate of Edom with Samaria via Amos 9:1ff. Similarly, the inserted material in Obad 19 manifests an equally obvious intention to parallel the fate of Samaria with Edom via Mic 1:6. Some question remains whether to view Obad 19f as an integral part of a larger poem — hence the three-fold repetition of the twin motifs of the destruction of Edom and the restoration of a Jerusalem-centered kingdom — or whether these verses represent a later explication of Obad 15a,16-18,21 — hence the tension regarding who will conquer Edom.[73] At any rate, Obad 19 contains the Micah-related insertion indicating that it was expanded when Obadiah was

---

[72] For a treatment of the complicated question of dependence, see the treatment of Mal 1:2-5 later in this work.

[73] Obad 18 portrays the action against Edom as the work of the House of Jacob and the House of Joseph while Obad 19 portrays the Negev as the agent. Several options could explain the attachment of 15a,16-21. 1) The frame (16,21) surrounded a two strophe poem (17f,19f) composed for another occasion. 2) Two independent pieces (16-18,19f) were combined and a conclusion was added for the book. 3) Prior to incorporation into Obadiah, an earlier poem (16-18,21) was expanded which more explicitly clarified the extent of the restoration. The third option appears the most likely, although it is admittedly quite plausible that the first option could be correct. The second option does not appear very likely since Obad 19f functions so well as an explication of 17f.

compiled for its position between Amos and Micah. Dating the redactional adaptations of the pre-existing blocks in Obadiah can only be done in rather general terms, since so much of this material reflects relatively minor adaptations of earlier material, and since Obadiah exhibits considerable interest reflecting back on the events surrounding Jerusalem's destruction. Still, one can say that this compositional activity, in all *probability*, did not take place prior to the fourth century. The compilation of Obadiah utilizes texts which belong to other parts of the prophetic corpus, and it displays a relatively advanced form of "scripture prophecy" in so doing. Relatedly, Obadiah adapts its material on the basis of Amos 9:1ff at a stage which also presupposes post-exilic additions to the book. Finally, the vocabulary and situation of the latter parts of Obadiah share much in common with Joel 4:1ff, despite the more advanced apocalyptic images in Joel. This tension reflects the age of the respective pre-formulated material utilized by the two works.[74]

---

[74] See Bergler, *Joel als Schriftinterpret*, 295-333.

Nahum

1. The Macrostructure of Nahum

Several larger units in the book of Nahum stand out clearly on the basis of their opening markers, although the unity of the sections often raises questions. Nah 1:1 presents a two-layered superscription. Nah 1:2-8 contains a semi-acrostic hymn with theophanic elements. Nah 1:9-11 serves as a transition from the theophany to the Nineveh material. The messenger formula in Nah 1:12 (כה אמר יהוה) introduces a promise of deliverance for Jerusalem combined with a judgment oracle against Nineveh and the king of Assyria. Nah 2:1 begins a new section with the announcement of good tidings to Judah and defeat to Nineveh. Nah 2:4-13 brings a victory song over the defeat of Nineveh. Nah 3:1 begins typically for a woe oracle, although the later verses contain material more appropriately described as a mock or a taunt.[1] A certain logic underlies this arrangement when viewed *en toto*. The theophany portrays YHWH's arrival in judgment; the herald brings the news of Nineveh's demise and a description of the destruction; the woe and taunt in chapter three respond to the news of this destruction and (at least in part) treat the events as having already occurred.

2. Various Redactional Models

In spite of the structural movement present in Nahum, many difficulties prevent the assumption of the book of Nahum as a single speech written for a single occasion. The constitutive parts of the sections have different backgrounds, causing several distinct models to be proposed to account for the origin of Nahum. These models see Nahum either as a liturgical work, as a compositional collection utilizing various speeches of the prophet, or as the result of a two-layered redactional process. The liturgical model, as propounded by Humbert, enjoyed considerable

---

[1]   A discussion of the sub-units of chapter three follows below, beginning page 117ff.

popularity for some time.[2]   Humbert argued Nahum was a cult liturgy performed shortly after the destruction of Nineveh in 612.   The future elements of prediction were, for Humbert, cultic reenactments of that destruction.   However, Humbert's views have not withstood critical scrutiny because the liturgical character of Nahum does not simply mirror a cultic celebration.[3]   Rudolph is typical of those who see Nahum primarily as a collection of prophetic utterances that has been arranged according to a single viewpoint, the destruction of Nineveh.   Rudolph sees the work as an essential unity which has received only isolated additions.[4]

Three redactional approaches attempt to come to terms with the diverse elements inside Nahum.   Jeremias sees the booklet as a compilation of three different transmission blocks.[5]   Jeremias argues that two of these transmission layers originate with the late pre-exilic prophet Nahum, while the third is a late exilic or early post-exilic interpretive layer which provides the liturgical elements to the writing, and which relates the entire message to the downfall of Babylon.   Jeremias has been heavily critiqued for his conclusions that many of the judgment speeches in the earlier layers were originally judgment speeches against Israel and its king, which received a new interpretation as the result of the interpretive work of the final layer. Too often this critique has merely served as a dismissal of the entire work, a mistake which ignores several important insights Jeremias makes.

Schulz argues Nahum is the literary treatise of a single author utilizing his own composition as well as pre-existing material to present an

---

[2]   Paul Humbert, "Essai d'Analyse de Nahoum 1:2-2:3," *ZAW* 44 (1926): 266-280. Later, J. De Vries sought to revitalize this view: "The Acrostic of Nahum in the Jerusalem Liturgy," *VT* 16 (1966): 476-481. See also the second edition of Sellin's commentary: Ernst Sellin, *Das Zwölfprophetenbuch*, vol 2, KAT (Leipzig: Deichert, 1929-1930), 357.

[3]   Note the critiques of Jörg Jeremias, *Kultprophetie und Gerichtsverkündigung in der späten Königszeit Israels*, WMANT 35 (Neukirchen: Neukirchener Verlag, 1970), 11f; and Rudolph, *KAT* 13/3, 145. See also the extended description of the liturgical character in Schulz, *Nahum*, 111-132.

[4]   Rudolph, *KAT* 13/3, 144. In many respects, Rudolph's work parallels the conservative commentary of Maier, who also sees the book as a collection of prophetic speeches from the middle of the 7th century. Walter Maier, *The Book of Nahum: A Commentary* (St. Louis, Mo.: Concordia, 1959).

[5]   Jeremias, *Kultprophetie*, 11-55. Other scholars have also propounded similar views regarding the placement of the hymn, but have not explained these views with the detail of Jeremias. For example, see Johannes Lindblom, *Prophecy in Ancient Israel* (Oxford: Blackwell, 1962), 253.

eschatological message.[6] Schulz believes this author wrote 2:12-3:6 as a free composition while fashioning the remainder of the book from larger blocks of material. He summarizes:[7]

> Das Nahumbuch ist also das Werk eines Verfassers, der einen Gasang über die Schlacht in Ninive und eine Spottqina auf Ninive, in differenzierter Komposition, mit einem Theophanie-hymnus und einem Heilswort auf Juda zu einem Prophetenbuch verband. Seine Kompositionsmethode ist einfach. Er bediente sich grösserer, z.T. vorgegebener Einheiten, die er durch neue Rahmungen und Umstellungen zu eigentlichen Prophetenworten formte. Sukzessive Wachstumsprozesse sind also nicht anzunehmen.

Schulz thus argues for a unified composition, while at the same time recognizing that much of the material in Nahum *predates* the formation of the book. Schulz takes exception, however, to Jeremias' contention that a pre-exilic Nahum corpus existed.[8] Paradoxically, while Schulz objects to the idea of a pre-exilic corpus which has been reworked, his own theory rests upon the use of pre-existing material, but fails to bring a satisfactory explanation for either the selection of Assyria or for the question of the identity of "Nahum the Elkoshite."[9]

---

6   Hermann Schulz, *Das Buch Nahum. Eine redaktionskritische Untersuchung*, BZAW 129 (Berlin: DeGruyter, 1973), 104-110.

7   Schulz, *Nahum*, 105.

8   Schulz, *Nahum*, 135-153, goes into great detail in his dialogue regarding his methodological differences with Jeremias. See especially, 139f, where Schulz argues against a pre-exilic Nahum corpus.

9   Schulz, *Nahum*, 106f, follows Alfred Haldar, *Studies in the Book of Nahum*, Uppsala Universitets Arsskrift 7 (Uppsala: Almqvist & Wiksells, 1947), 148, in arguing that the name Nahum (נחום) reflects an allusion to passages such as 3:7 (and according to Schulz also the frame of his core poem — 1:2b,6b,7b,9 — whose first letters spell נחום). Schulz believes the name was constructed as a play on words by the post-exilic author who, by virtue of the fact that Nineveh was long since destroyed, could not use his own name or the name of a contemporary. This argument carries little weight, even with the additional observations — which Schulz does not note — that the semi-acrostic poem begins with אל and the word "stubble" (קש) appears in 1:10. By the same arguments, these words could also be an allusion to the town Elkosh. However, it appears much less straining to the imagination to simply accept the existence of a prophet Nahum from the town Elkosh. The ascription of a town of origin to the prophet makes the suggestion of an interpretive name improbable. Other disputed prophetic names, such as Obadiah and Malachi, do not go to such lengths.

Most recently, Seybold describes the growth of the Nahum corpus in a model very similar to that of Jeremias.[10] Seybold, like Jeremias, finds a pre-exilic core of prophetic sayings which have been expanded by exilic and post-exilic expansions. He differs with Jeremias in that he dates the majority of the pre-exilic material much earlier than Jeremias.[11] These dates lead Seybold to the conclusion that Nahum, unlike other prophetic books did not receive additions to the end of the writing, but to the beginning.[12] The specificity of the dates Seybold assigns to the smaller texts raises questions which will be addressed in the next section of this chapter. Nevertheless, Seybold's analysis adds weight to the impression that the Nahum exhibits a more complex and extended transmission history than is normally presumed.

Despite many differences, the works of Jeremias, Schulz, and Seybold agree upon one essential aspect of the redaction history of Nahum: the book received its final form and structure by reworking blocks of pre-existing material long after Nineveh was destroyed.[13] These views contrast sharply with those of Rudolph and others who see the collection of the prophetic words much more closely tied to the historical entity of Nineveh as the center of Assyrian hegemony. An evaluation of the possible dates for the composition of Nahum must begin with the arguments from the text used by the respective proponents.

---

[10]   Klaus Seybold, *Profane Prophetie. Studien zum Buch Nahum*, Stuttgarter Bibelstudien 135 (Stuttgart: Verlag Katholisches Bibelwerk, 1989), 19-34.

[11]   Seybold, *Profane Prophetie*, 32-34, dates the eldest layers closer to the destruction of Thebes arguing for the period around 660-650. He dates the portions of Nahum as follows: Nah 3:8-19a (660); Nah 3:2f; 2:2,4-13; 3:1,4a (650); Nah 2:14; 3:5-7 (615); Nah 1:12f; 2:1,3 (550); Nah 1:11,14; 1:2ff (400).

[12]   Seybold, *Profane Prophetie*, 32f.

[13]   Jeremias, *Kultprophetie*, 50f, dates the formative redactional work in the late exilic or early pre-exilic period, while Schulz, *Nahum*, 106,134, believes the work is post-exilic, but he does not specify an exact date beyond the fact that it was after the rebuilding of the temple. He implies that the composition originated well after the reconstruction of the temple on the basis of other parallels, particularly with other liturgical material in the prophetic writings.

3. Dating the Book of Nahum

At first glance, the date of Nahum does not appear to pose major difficulties given the specificity of the role of Nineveh as the chief antagonist in the book. Critical inspection of the book, however, reveals several features relating to the date of the book which lead in opposite directions. The graphic detail of the destruction of Nineveh in chapter two causes many scholars to argue that these events have already occurred or that they are immediately imminent.[14] Others place more emphasis upon the destruction of Thebes (663) mentioned in 3:8.[15] They argue that this event would not have been recalled 50 years later with enough force to function as vindictively as it does in Nah 3:8. Still others question the relationship of Nahum to Deutero-Isaiah, specifically Nah 2:1 and Isa 52:7:

Isa 52:7

How lovely on the mountains are the feet of him who brings good news, who announces peace, and brings good news of happiness, who announces salvation, and says to Zion, "Your god reigns."

Nah 2:1

Behold on the mountains the feet of him who brings good news, who announces peace! Celebrate your feasts, o Judah: pay your vows, for never again will the wicked one pass through you; He is cut off completely.

Some maintain that both passages merely use a stereotypical phrase, but the common formulation of these two verses is unique in the Old Testament, indicating a very high probability that one borrows from the other.[16] Often scholars acknowledge the priority of the passage in Deutero-Isaiah, but very seldom have the implications of this argument been explored.[17] Simply stated, if Nah 2:1 borrows from Deutero-Isaiah,

---

[14]   So for example, Robertson, *HAT* 14, 153; Richard J. Coggins and S. Paul Re'emi, *Israel among the Nations: Nahum, Obadiah, Esther*, International Theological Commentary (Grand Rapids: Eerdmans, 1985), 52; Smith, *Word* 32, 64.

[15]   Such as Rudolph, *KAT* 13/3, 143,145; Maier, *Nahum*, 36. Nah 3:8 is addressed to Nineveh and asks the pointed rhetorical question: "Are you better than Thebes?" The question implies that it was well known that Thebes was devastated.

[16]   Smith, *Word* 32, for example, never mentions the parallel. The phrase "who announces peace" (משמיע שלום) appears only in Nah 2:1 and Isa 52:7. The phrase the "feet of the messenger" (רגלי מבשר) likewise appears only in these two places. See further elaboration in Jeremias, *Kultprophetie*, 13-15.

[17]   See the discussion in Richard Coggins, "An Alternative Prophetic Tradition?," in *Israel's Prophetic Tradition: Essays in Honour of Peter Ackroyd*, Richard Coggins, et al, eds, (London: Cambridge University Press, 1982), 81. Coggins cites other examples of a relationship between Isaiah and Nahum: Nah 1:4 and Isa 33:9; 50:2; Nah 1:15b and Isa 52:1b. Jeremias, *Kultprophetie*, 13-15, brings strong statistical evidence in support

then a post-exilic date of Nah 2:1 must be accepted as well. The question
of importance then becomes, how intricately is Nah 2:1 involved with the
structure and message of the book as a whole? Is it merely an isolated
gloss or does it function significantly within the existing structure? As
already indicated, this verse does indeed play a significant role in the
macro-structure of the book.[18]

How does one evaluate this evidence in light of other evidence in
Nahum which points to earlier dates? The work of Jeremias provides the
strongest model when he postulates a collection of Nahum words that has
been reworked. Nah 3:8, for example, appears more understandable
between 663 and 612. Many argue that logic dictates this phrase has
greater impact if one places Nahum closer to the destruction of Thebes
(663), but these arguments are not absolutely determinative.[19] Already
Wellhausen argues that the date for Nah 3:8 is not in the immediate
chronological vicinity of the destruction of Thebes, around 660.[20] First,
a date during this period would have made it very easy for the Assyrians to
answer "yes" (since they were the ones who overthrew Thebes). Second, in
the period around 660, there is no impending threat against Nineveh, as the
passage appears to presuppose. This second argument is particularly
convincing, since those who date Nahum this early are forced to postulate
a long period of oral transmission during which time Nahum was kept alive
as an *underground* work.[21] Alternative suggestions to the early date
suggest Thebes' defeat became symbolic of Assyrian might, in spite of the
relatively quick resurgence of the city, or that the Thebes poem was an
independent unit of early origin which was later incorporated into the

---

of the priority of Deutero-Isaiah. Rudolph, *KAT* 13/3, 163, argues weakly against using
the statistical evidence in this instance over against the pure chronological
considerations elsewhere in the book.

[18] See above discussion, page 93, and the observations of Schulz, *Nahum*, 15-20.

[19] Jeremias, Rudolph, Maier, and others, believe that the closer to 663 one can place Nah
3:8, the more understandable the reference would be. Jeremias, *Kultprophetie*, 38f, also
believes the speech to which 3:8 belongs was originally directed against Jerusalem, for
which he has been properly critiqued. These authors underestimate both the longevity
of the reminiscence of Thebes' destruction as well as the irony with which it is used.
The fact that the verses are directed against Assyria, the power who destroyed Thebes,
makes the reference all the more pointed. See also the discussion in Schulz, *Nahum*,
44f, although his own suggestion of a post-exilic date pushes the date too far. The
choice of Thebes following the destruction of Jerusalem is difficult to comprehend.

[20] Julius Wellhausen, *Die kleinen Propheten übersetzt und erklärt*, Skizzen und Vorarbeiten
5 (Berlin: Reimer, 1892), 159.

[21] Rudolph, *KAT* 13/3, 144f.

Nahum corpus.[22] In short, the reference in Nah 3:8 can only be used with certainty to fix the *terminus ab quo* of the work.

The descriptive elements, especially in chapter two, also vividly portray Nineveh's destruction. Saggs, in an attempt to lend credence to the historicity of 2:7 (and 1:8), mentions "Greek traditions" that a flood wiped out part of the defenses of Nineveh.[23] However, Nahum's poetic nature could as easily explain the reference to the flood, since archaeological evidence indicates destruction by fire, not by water.[24] In addition, the description of the warriors is often ascribed to the dress and practice of the time, although others claim these images are traditional elements which do not allow an absolute conclusion.[25] As with other so-called concrete evidence for dating, the value of chapter two is relativized when viewed from a larger perspective. Modern scholarship has reached no consensus upon the date of the prophet Nahum. There is almost unanimity in dating the prophet between the fall of Thebes (663) and the fall of Nineveh (612), but a more definite date has yet to find unqualified acceptance.[26]

4. Literary Observations on Nah 1:1,2-8,9-11

4.1. A Two-Layered Superscription: Nah 1:1

The superscription of Nahum in **1:1** manifests two distinct titles ("the oracle of Nineveh" and "the book of the vision of Nahum the Elkoshite") indicating the growth of the work.[27] Most argue that the oldest of the two

---

[22] See respectively: Duane L. Christensen, "The Acrostic of Nahum Reconsidered," *ZAW* 87 (1975): 17-30; and Keller, *CAT* 11b, 105.

[23] H.W.F. Saggs, *The Might that Was Assyria.* Sidgwick & Jackson Great Civilizations Series. London: Sidgwick & Jackson, 1984), 120; see also H.W.F. Saggs, "Nahum and the Fall of Nineveh." *JTS* 20 (1969): 220-225. In this article, Saggs cites the references in C.J. Gadd, The Fall of Nineveh (1923), 17-19. Gadd, however, is more postively disposed toward harmonizing the accounts of Diodorus and Xenophon than subsequent scholarship warrants. These descriptions do not tally with archaeological evidence or with the account preserved in the Babylonian Chronicles. See Pritchard, *ANET*, 304.

[24] See Coggins and Re'emi, *Israel among the Nations*, 40f.

[25] Cf Watts, *Joel, etc.*, 112; and Coggins and Re'emi, *Israel among the Nations*, 37.

[26] Schulz is the primary exception since he dates Nahum as post-exilic.

[27] The two-fold character of this superscription has long been noted. Already Ewald, *Propheten*, vol 1, 74,80; vol 2, 5, notes the distinctions and claims Nah 1:1a as secondary. This opinion has dominated: Horst, *HAT* 14, 156; Sellin, *KAT* 12, 312;

is probably some form of the second. Proponents of this opinion argue that the attachment of a name to a collection, specifically with biographical information that cannot be derived from the content of the book, indicates that this title appeared at a relatively early stage of the collection.[28] The question of what constituted this "book of the vision" is more complicated since this title incorporates two different *Gattungen*, a book (ספר) and a vision (חזון). The use of "book" implies a literary awareness on the part of the collector. In addition, Nahum lacks a distinctive use of the verb ראה that would enable its classification as a "vision" in the sense of other prophetic visions.[29] An alternative explanation, which could account for many of the problems, is to postulate the oldest form of the superscription is not 1:1b, but 1:1a. To be sure the title in 1:1a, "the oracle of Nineveh," also causes problems since apart from this title, Nineveh is not mentioned specifically until 2:9, but other considerations indicate the problems are less significant than with 1:1b. First, the latter portions of chapter one appear consistent with an understanding of Nineveh/Assyria as the intended enemy.[30] Second, the three recent redactional studies discussed above have contested the reasoning of this majority opinion.[31] Third, Nah 1:1 manifests similarity to the superscription of Hab 1:1, which does not exhibit signs of growth.[32] Finally, and most significantly, literary considerations within 1:9ff enable the detection of an earlier structure of the book, which ultimately depends upon the mention of Nineveh in Nah 1:1a.[33]

---

[28] Elliger, *ATD* 25, 3; Rudolph, *KAT* 13/3, 148.
By way of contrast, note the superscriptions in Obadiah and Malachi which have no biographical material, and Amos, whose "biographical" material can all be derived from within the book. For an opposing viewpoint, See Schulz, *Nahum*, 108.

[29] Note Amos 7:1,4,7; 8:1; 9:1; Zech 1:8,18; 2:1; 3:1; 4:2; 5:1,5; 6:1; Hab 3:7. The verb ראה appears only twice in Nahum (3:5,7), but neither time is it part of a "vision" as such.

[30] Note specifically the 2fs suffix in 1:11, which assumes Nineveh as the enemy.

[31] Jeremias, *Kultprophetie*, 50f, and Seybold, *Profane Prophetie*, 30, argue that the expression "oracle of Nineveh" coincides better with the earlier portions of chapters two and three. Schulz, *Nahum*, 106-108, argues against the "originality" of either 1:1a or 1:1b. He argues that 1:1b is post-exilic, but holds open the possibility (footnote 292) that 1:1a introduced one of the pre-existing poems.

[32] The obvious implication would be that someone patterned Nah 1:1 after Hab 1:1.

[33] The 2fs suffix in Nah 1:11a must refer to Nineveh, and the only antecedent appears in 1:1a. When one recognizes with Seybold and Jeremias, however, that the acrostic poem (1:2-8) was placed into an existing corpus, together with a transition (1:9f), it is not difficult to imagine how the suffix got separated from its antecedent. See discussions below, page 111, and in the discussion of the context of Nah 3:1ff, page 123.

4.2. The Acrostic Elements in Nah 1:2-8

Observations and explanations of the semi-acrostic nature of **1:2-8** have a long history.[34] Recent studies tend to view the hymn as *loosely semi-acrostic*. This trend has developed, in part, from the acceptance of Humbert's arguments that the hymn never extended through the entire alphabet, and in part from negative reactions to unsatisfactory attempts to reconstruct the entire hymn.[35] Doubtless, the hymn *in its current form* does not represent a complete acrostic, but the question remains how to account for the near-acrostic form of the poem. Three models have shaped the way that scholars portray the psalm as it stands in 1:2-8: textual corruption, relativization of the acrostic elements, and signs of redactional shaping. A brief look at the underlying assumptions of these models will serve as the springboard into a more thorough analysis of the poem. 1) The textual corruption model dominated discussions of Nahum in the latter 19th and early 20th centuries. More realistic appraisals of the state of preservation of Old Testament texts in general, and several sharp attacks against radical emendations of Nahum in particular have greatly

---

[34] The acrostic nature of these verses was first mentioned by Franz Delitzsch, *Biblical Commentary on the Psalms*, vol. 1, 161, based on the observations of Frohmeyer. Delitzsch observed the acrostic only through 1:7. Since then numerous attempts have sought to "reconstruct" the acrostic in its entirety. Such reconstructions operated from the assumption that textual corruptions were responsible for the verses not being in alphabetic order. The resulting emendations necessitated by these attempts have ranged from those who argued for the continuation through the *samekh* line (Bickell, Gunkel, Happel) to those who tried to extend it through the entire alphabet (Arnold, Marti, Duhm). Sellin attempted to trace the remnants through the *ayin* line in 1:12: Sellin, *KAT* 12, 313-315. Attention to these reconstructions abated following the article of Humbert, *ZAW* 44 (1926): 266-280, who conclusively demonstrated the hymn was semi-acrostic in character, and never continued through the entire alphabet. The entire character of the hymn, as well as the form of address, changes in 1:9. Many have still attempted emendations on the interruptions of the acrostic, most notably in 1:4. Compare Rudolph, *KAT* 13/3, 151. Haldar, *Studies in the Book of Nahum*, 15-28, incorrectly argued against understanding this hymn as an acrostic, but his views have not been accepted. Schulz, *Nahum*, 9-11, 93-94, argues redaction-critically that the hymn contains a core (1:2a,3b-6) to which a frame (1:2b,3a,7-8) has been added. For Schulz, the near acrostic character of the hymn arose only secondarily.

[35] Examples: J. De Vries, *VT* 16 (1966): 476-481; and Ralph Smith, *Word* 32, 71f. By way of contrast, see Duane L. Christensen, "The Acrostic of Nahum Reconsidered," *ZAW* 87 (1975): 17-30. Christensen offers a reconstruction *metri causa*, based on syllable count.

depreciated the effect of this model on the understanding of Nah 1:2-8.[36]
2) More recently, one notes a trend to conceive the acrostic elements as
only one of several stylistic techniques employed by Nahum.[37] Adherents
claim someone as creative with poetic techniques as Nahum would be free
to depart from slavish adherence to an alphabetic hymn. Against this
argument two objections should be raised. First, for the most part, these
claims stem from preconceived notions against the redactional growth of
prophetic books. Second, this view treats the creation of acrostic poetry too
casually. The creation of such poetry in any language requires considerable
deliberation and creativity. It is highly improbable that a poet would
deliberately choose to write a poem which is *almost* acrostic. The corollary
is also enlightening. An acrostic poem, once recorded, is a subtle literary
technique. It is therefore much more conceivable that an editor working
with sources would overlook or ignore this device than that its creator
would almost utilize it. 3) The *redactional growth* model holds the most
promise for explaining those places where the acrostic breaks down. Yet
the redaction model has been applied to Nahum from two opposing
perspectives. Schulz sees the growth of the text constructively in relation
to Nah 1:2-8, while Jeremias treats it destructively in relationship to the
acrostic elements.

    Schulz argues that the hymn in Nah 1:2-8 is not from one layer, but
that the acrostic features are a redactional creation.[38] He maintains an
original hymn may be isolated (1:2a,3b-6), which consists of a core (1:3b-5)
and a frame (1:2a,6) whose structure (A/B/A) marks off a closed unit that

---

[36] Despite his devaluation of the acrostic, Haldar, *Studies in the Book of Nahum*, 15-87,
was in no small measure responsible for this shift in Nahum. For specific arguments,
see the text-critical notes to Nah 1:2-8 in Nogalski, *Literary Precursors*, 40.

[37] Oswald T. Allis, "Nahum, Niniveh, Elkoch," *Evangelical Quarterly* 27 (1955): 69. Allis
discusses the so-called alphabetic hymn of Nahum from the conservative standpoint of
preserving the text. He goes to considerable length, primarily on the basis of style, to
prove that the hymn is not a corruption of a formerly semi-acrostic poem. His main
arguments are that as follows: 1. In verses 1:2-6 only five of the ten metrical lines give
clear evidence of alphabetic sequence. 2. If Nahum would have wanted to have
alphabetically sequential lines it would have been simple for him to have done so. The
required changes are minor. 3. The difficulty of 1:2b-3a is for him a tremendous
obstacle for the proponents of an acrostic hymn, because these are by no means part
of any alphabetic structure. See also De Vries, *VT* 16 (1966): 476-481. Haldar, *Studies
in the Book of Nahum*, 15-28, may also belong to this group, although he is less explicit
about what to do with existing alphabetic elements than with combatting emendation
on the basis of these elements.

[38] Schulz, *Nahum*, 9-11.

is characterized by its concern over the jealousy, wrath, and scorn of YHWH (1:2a,6), theophanically manifested in natural disturbances (1:3b-5). According to Schulz, Nah 1:2b,3a,7f introduce new elements into the poem, namely the wrath of God against an enemy and the patience of YHWH for those who are faithful. These themes appear in this new frame in chiastic order (vengeance/patience — goodness/destruction). These observations point to a complicated structure of the hymn, which may be represented in the letters AacBAca. Schulz maintains that only with this expansion was the alphabetic principle utilized, but that it was not consistently applied. Several problems pose difficulties for the views of Schulz. Most importantly, the criteria for his division of the hymn into layers appear contrived. Schulz goes too far when he claims the mention of wrath against the enemies and God as refuge are "foreign" to the core of the hymn.[39] In addition he falls prey to the relativization of the acrostic by claiming those responsible for the near alphabetic order are the very ones responsible for the inconsistency of that same order.

Jeremias presents a much more plausible scenario.[40] He argues that an originally intact semi-acrostic poem has received redactional accretions in the process of its incorporation into the book of Nahum. He acknowledges this hymn has numerous stylistic and theological elements which distinguish it from the Nahum speeches elsewhere in the book, and he goes on to relate at least some of these accretions to other later redactional material in Nahum. Jeremias proposes that a redactor placed 1:2-2:3 at the beginning of the Nahum speeches as an introduction and re-interpretation for the late exilic, early pre-exilic community. Jeremias' basic model needs to be enlarged from two perspectives: first, while he only treats 1:2b-3a in this redactional context, the remaining interruptions to the acrostic should be investigated from this perspective as well; and second, rather than seeing this redactional work merely on the level of the isolated book, it should be viewed in its context inside the Book of the Twelve.

4.3. A Semi-Acrostic Hymn: Nah 1:2-8

The alphabetic structure of the hymn in Nah 1:2-8 may be graphically illustrated:

---

[39] Schulz, *Nahum*, 9.
[40] Jeremias, *Kultprophetie*, 16-19. See also Seybold, *Profane Prophetie*, 75f.

אל קנוא ונקם יהוה   א

נקם יהוה ובעל חמה

נקם יהוה לצריו

ונוטר הוא לאיביו

יהוה ארך אפים וגדול־כח

ונקה לא ינקה יהוה

בסופה ובשערה דרכו   ב

וענן אבק רגליו

גוער בים ויבשהו   ג

וכל־הנהרות החריב

אמלל בשן וכרמל   ד

ופרח לבנון אמלל

הרים רעשו ממנו   ה

והגבעות התמגגו

ותשא הארץ מפניו   ו

ותבל וכל־ישבי בה

לפני זעמו מי יעמוד   ז

ומי יקום בחרון אפו

חמתו נתכה כאש   ח

והצרים נתצו ממנו

טוב יהוה   ט

למעוז ביום צרה

וידע חסי בו   י

ובשטף עבר

כלה יעשה מקומה   כ

ואיביו ירדף־חשך

The acrostic pattern in Nah 1:2-8 falters in four places: two extra bi-cola have been inserted between the א and ב lines; the ד line begins with א; and the ז line begins with ל, although the second word in that line begins with ז; the י line begins with ו. A notable phenomenon within these breaks in the acrostic must be born in mind, namely *all four* interruptions can be explained as deliberate alterations to an existing poem, and at least two of the remaining interruptions (possibly all three) can be tied directly to the redactional process of linkage to Micah 7. The easiest disruption to explain is the fourth disruption, the presence of the ו in the י line. Someone incognizant of the acrostic nature could have added the ו to conform the text to more typical syntax. Two of the three remaining interruptions (Nah 1:2b-3a; 1:4b) contain words appearing in Micah 7. The remaining break (1:6a) contains no words from Micah 7, but can be plausibly, if not conclusively, explained as the result of an insertion into the preceding line. These three remaining interruptions deserve more careful consideration.

The first interruption is the insertion in 1:2b-3a, or the two bi-cola between the א and ב lines. Not only does 1:2b-3a visually break the acrostic, it contains the words "enemies" and "anger," both of which appear later in the theophany (1:6,9) and also in Micah 7 (7:8,10,18). This phenomenon raises the possibility that the insertions were motivated by the desire to attach the theophany (and the book of Nahum) to Micah 7. To evaluate the emphasis brought to the semi-acrostic by this insertion, it is first necessary to look at the purpose of the hymn *prior* to the insertion.

Excursus: The Independence of the Theophanic Hymn

How does one account for the semi-acrostic poem at the beginning of the Book of Nahum? Was the poem originally independent or was it, from the outset, written for incorporation into the book? The vast majority of scholars agree that the hymn originated independently of the book, and there seems to be no rationale to challenge this consensus.[41] The disappearance of the alphabetic sequence, the lack of integral connections to other parts of the book, and specifically the lack of Nineveh among the constellation of participants are cited as reasons for this independence. Some discussion should be given to the function of this poem from the perspective of its independence, from the perspective of its incorporation into Nahum, its relationship to other portions of the Book of the Twelve, and to Isaiah.

Methodologically, the independence of the poem requires that the interruptions of the acrostic be set aside temporarily from the discussion. The semi-acrostic frame dominates the structure, but the poem also describes a theophany. As such, it depicts YHWH's appearance for judgment, and it presents this appearance in terms typical for later stages of this genre.[42] The poem begins

---

[41] This majority includes those who see the Nahum book as a "collection" of speeches (e.g. Rudolph) as well as those who see the final form of the book as a later work (Jeremias, Schulz).

[42] Jörg Jeremias, *Theophanie: Die Geschichte einer Alttestamentlichen Gattung*, WMANT 10 (Neukirchener Verlag, 1965), 123-125. For his history of the *Gattung*, see 150-64, especially 157 for the implications and changes with the incorporation into prophetic traditions. Traditional elements common to prophetic use of the portrayal of theophanies appearing in Nah 1:2-8 are the wrath of YHWH, the fire, an emphasis on the storm, and the day of YHWH. One missing feature typical of the latest use of the theophany is the portrayal of YHWH as king. In Nah 1:2-8, he still appears to be portrayed as divine warrior. See also the discussions in Fritz Stolz, *Strukturen und Figuren im Kult von Jerusalem. Studien zur altorientalischen vor- und frühisraelitischen Religion*, BZAW 118 (Berlin: De Gruyter, 1970); and John Day, *God's Conflict with the Dragon and the Sea: Echoes of a Canaanite Myth in the Old Testament* (Cambridge: Cambridge University Press, 1985), 60f. Day is specifically interested the theophanic

with a short depiction of YHWH as jealous and avenging (1:2a), followed by a depiction of his arrival in the storm (1:3b). YHWH tames the sea and the rivers (1:4), the mountains and the hills (1:5a), and the earth (1:5b). YHWH is a refuge on the "day of trouble" (1:7). The imagery of YHWH's arrival originates from chaos-battle and day of YHWH traditions. However, the diverse imagery indicates that the theophanic language does not describe a single event, e.g. a cultic re-enactment of the chaos battle. Rather, the theophanic descriptions *take up these images in summary and abbreviated fashion.* This recognition has significance for the way one interprets the inner thought movement of the hymn. The hymn uses the theophanic images as a type of evidence to describe YHWH's power. The author's purpose does not appear until the rhetorical question in 1:6 crystallizes the poem's message by asking: "If YHWH has done all this, then who can withstand his indignation on the day of distress?" The phrasing of the question clearly implies that no one can escape, and the following bi-cola serves to confirm this implication by graphically describing the power of his wrath which is "poured out like fire." Yet this wrath is not a fatalistic judgment, since the author portrays a discerning god who distinguishes his enemies from his worshippers. It is in this sense that 1:7-8aa should be read: "YHWH is good, a refuge in the day of distress; he is the one who knows those seeking refuge in him when he is passing over in the flood." The poem concludes with a summary of the main theme: "he will make a complete destruction of it, and pursue his enemies into darkness."

The insertion in Nah **1:2b-3a** does not dramatically alter the essential message of the hymn, but it serves to highlight the recipient of judgment described later in the theophany (his enemies), while simultaneously exhibiting a perspective which is not present in the original hymn, namely the aspect of the *temporal delay* of the judgment. The insertion begins with an affirmation of YHWH's vengeance ("avenging is YHWH to his enemies"), but is then followed by three bi-cola, all three of which exhibit a certain awareness that vengeance has not yet occurred. The verb נטר appears idiomatically in Nah 1:2bb in the sense of holding a grudge or reserving wrath:[43] YHWH reserves anger for his adversaries. Nah 1:3a evidences this tension more explicitly, again making use of idiomatic expressions: "YHWH is *slow to anger,* but great in strength; though he leaves unpunished he will not leave unpunished."[44] Noting this temporal

---

images in Nah 1:4, which he sees as part of a larger development of the *Chaoskampf* motif into a reference to YHWH's work at creation. He understands function of the entire hymn as a means of providing "the cosmic background against which his (YHWH's) judgment on Nineveh must be seen."

[43] Jer 3:5,12; Lev 19:18; Ps 103:9.

[44] In the first instance the redactor has adapted the more typical idiom: YHWH is slow to anger, and great in lovingkindness (Exod 34:6; Joel 2:13; Jonah 4:2; Ps 86:15; Ps 103:8; 145:8; Neh 9:17). The change to "great of strength" is very much in keeping with

awareness by no means militates the basic message that YHWH will judge his enemies. It only serves to demonstrate that the redactor is working with a broader time frame than was the author of the semi-acrostic poem. This delay of YHWH's salvation by no means reflects a modern skepticism. Rather, it illustrates a subtle hermeneutic which both recognizes that the promised deliverance has not yet occurred, but nevertheless affirms strongly that YHWH will act on behalf of his people.[45]

The subtle sense of delay present in Nah 1:2b-3a appropriately relates to the recognition of the delay of salvation implicit in Mic 7:18-20. The perspective differs only slightly because both passages demonstrate the interests of their respective contexts. Mic 7:18-20 recognizes the delay of the salvation of YHWH's people:

> Who is a god like you, bearing iniquity and passing over transgression to the remnant of his possession? He does not strengthen his anger forever, for he delights in mercy. He will return his compassion on us. He will subdue our iniquity.

Nah 1:2b-3a exhibits the same awareness of delay and affirmation of YHWH's action, but from the perspective of vengeance upon his enemies.

The second break in the acrostic appears in the ד line (**Nah 1:4b**), which begins with א in its current form. Those emending Nah 1:4 must select from several words which do not fit the evidence of the versions, while those who recognize the problems of emendation must concede this line interrupts the acrostic pattern.[46] In trying to account for this interruption, one must note, however, that in addition to the acrostic interruption, several observations set this line apart literarily, making plausible the suggestion that this entire line has been substituted for one which did not adequately serve the redactor's purpose. First, this line is the only line in the entire poem containing no reference to YHWH. Second, the entities Carmel, Bashan, and Lebanon are not intrinsic to Old

---

the context of Nahum. In the second instance, the idiom of temporarily leaving unpunished also appears elsewhere (Exod 34:7; Num 14:18; Jer 30:11 — see also above discussion of Joel 4:21; and Obad 16). The presence of both of these phrases in the Sinai theophany of Deut 34:6f, presumably serves as backdrop for these phrases, but they have clearly been adapted for use in the context of Nahum where they treat YHWH's enemies, not his covenant people.

[45] See further elaboration of this theological perspective in Robert P. Carroll, "Eschatological Delay in the Prophetic Tradition?," *ZAW* 94 (1982): 47-58.

[46] See text notes to this verse in Nogalski, *Literary Precursors*, 40.

Testament theophanies.[47] Third, the passive use of אמלל stands out from
the active verbs elsewhere in the hymn, giving this line a *situational*
character, rather than one which depicts the reaction to YHWH's
appearance. Fourth, the reference to the withering of Bashan, Carmel, and
Lebanon take up literary traditions appearing elsewhere. Scholars typically
interpret the withering of these three areas only via traditions associating
these regions with fertility. However, this interpretation ignores two
essential elements of this metaphor, the political and literary implications.

The literary combinations of Carmel and Bashan have already been
discussed.[48] Deuteronomistic traditions, especially as expanded in Isaiah,
associate the loss of these regions with the political aggression of the
Assyrians. Numerous references leave little doubt that "Lebanon" elicits
notions of fertility and splendor, and represents the source of commercially
valuable commodities.[49] However, other well attested traditions
concerning Lebanon play a role in understanding the full impact of Nah
1:4b. Several Old Testament texts utilize Lebanon in parables and
metaphors to describe political power.[50] Additionally, several passages
depict Lebanon as part of the ideal territorial extent of Israel. While a
certain tension exists, demonstrating awareness that Lebanon was seldom
a part of the kingdom, there is nevertheless decisive emphasis given to the
conviction that the region was included in the promised land, and that,
under Solomon, it belonged to the united kingdom of Israel.[51] Carmel,

[47] Jeremias, *Theophanie*, treats no other passage containing Bashan or Carmel as
theophanic. Day, *God's Conflict*, 113-119, suggests a possible Canaanite tradition of
the mountain of Bashan (Mt. Hermon) as the dwelling place of the Gods. His only
biblical evidence, however, is his interpretation of Ps 68:23, which he himself admits is
debatable (118). Amos 1:2 does mention Carmel, but this association relates more to
the redaction of the book than a specific tradition. See the previous discussion of the
involvement of Amos 1:2 with the macrostructure of the book.

[48] See discussion of Mic 7:14 in Nogalski, *Literary Precursors*, 158ff.

[49] Cant 4:11,15; 5:15; 7:5; Ezek 27:5; Hos 14:6,7,8; Jer 18:14; 22:6; Pss 72:16; 92:13;
104:16.

[50] See Judg 9:15 (Shechem); 2 Kgs 14:9 (=2 Chr 25:18) (Judah and Israel); Ezek 17:3
(Judah); Ezek 31:3,15f (Assyria); Isa 2:13 (the nations).

[51] Descriptions of the *ideal* Israel whose boundaries include Lebanon appear in Deut 1:7;
3:25; 11:24; Josh 1:4; 11:17; 12:7; 13:5f; Judg 3:3. Whereas Josh 11:17; 12:7 assume
Joshua captures the region, Josh 13:5f and Judg 3:3 contradict this view by stating
explicitly that at the end of Joshua's life Lebanon was among those regions which
Joshua did not capture. The Deuteronomistic history places Lebanon under Solomon's
rule (1 Kgs 9:13 = 2 Chr 8:6). For a discussion of the historical problems with this
picture, see Miller-Hayes, *History of Israel and Judah*, 308f. For a discussion of other

Bashan, and Lebanon appear only one other time together, significantly in Isa 33:9.[52] In Isaiah, the political overtones are clearer, but other parallels point to the awareness of Isa 33 by the redactor of Nah 1:2-8,9-11,12f.[53]

All of these observations concerning Nah 1:4b create an interesting picture, which bears much in common with Mic 7. Both depict a situation utilizing Carmel and Bashan metaphorically to depict the political weakness of the *Northern regions*. Both passages mix images of fertility with a political concern for the re-unification of the monarchy to its Davidic-Solomonic glory. Both passages assume Assyria as the political power which causes the disruption. For Nahum, these emphases are best explained as redactional implants into the theophanic semi-acrostic poem. The assumption of Assyria as the enemy in the theophanic hymn comes from its position in the book where both the superscription and the majority of the stock material in the remainder of the book clearly point to Nineveh/Assyria as the chief opponent.

The third break in the acrostic appears in the ז line (**1:6a**). Typical suggestions for the restoration of the acrostic pattern in this line is to read לפניו (before him) rather than לפני, and/or to presume the dislocation of the preposition (ו)לפני.[54] This argument is appealing, but, as it is normally presented, it lacks a clear explanation of what precipitated the dislocation of an entire word.[55] Two possible explanations may be

---

examples of the restoration of the Northern kingdom, see David C. Greenwood, "On the Jewish Hope for a Restored Northern Kingdom," *ZAW* 88 (1976): 376-385; and Benedikt Otzen, *Studien über Deuterosacharja*, Acta Theologica Danica 6 (Copenhagen: Munksgaard, 1964), 130-134.

[52] Bosshard, *BN* 40 (1987): 34, interprets Nahum and Habakkuk in the context of parallels between the Book of the Twelve and Isaiah. Bosshard notes the considerable interplay of vocabulary and theme between Nahum and Habakkuk and chapters 32-33 in Isaiah, which, like Nahum and Habakkuk, shift the portrayal of the dominant power from Assyria to Babylon. In Isa 33:9, the valley of Sharon appears as well.

[53] In addition to the withering of Bashan, Carmel, and Lebanon, several other parallels appear. Both passages share images of YHWH's wrath which is poured out "like fire" (Nah 1:6; Isa 33:11); the imagery of thorns (Nah 1:9; Isa 33:12), stubble (Nah 1:10; 33:11), and double rhetorical questions asking who can withstand YHWH's anger (Nah 1:6; Isa 33:14).

[54] Some prefer simple transposition, e.g. Christensen, *Transformation of the War Oracle*, 168f. Others claim the original position of לפניו followed יאמוד, see text notes in BHS.

[55] See for example, Duane Christensen, *Transformations of the War Oracle in Old Testament Prophecy*, Harvard Dissertations in Religion 3 (Missoula, Montana: Scholars Press, 1975), 168f.

offered: one linguistic, the other redactional. The linguistic explanation recognizes the tension created by the original hymn's author when the choice of זעמו to fit the acrostic strained the syntax of the remainder of the sentence. Presumably, this strained syntax *could* have been alleviated by a redactor (or copyist) who was unaware of the semi-acrostic pattern.[56] An alternative explanation suggests the presence of לפני could have resulted from the insertion of the phrase "and all the inhabitants in it" (ישבי־בה וכל) in 1:5bb. The removal of this phrase could explain how לפניו became לפני, and the resulting parallelism would be more exact. The earlier form of 1:5b would thus have read: "The land (הארץ) is lifted up before him (מפניו) and the world (תבל) before him (לפניו)." The resulting sentence exhibits a more precise synonymous parallelism (abc/bc).[57]

One important observation on the earlier bi-cola of 1:6aa requires comment, namely the necessity of the preposition לפני. While the presence of this preposition is syntactically more pleasing, it is *not syntactically mandatory*. Not only does the poetry follow syntax less rigidly than prose, but other Old Testament passages use the construction עמד + Object with no preposition. This construction implies that עמד carries the nuance "to stand before" and does not necessarily require the presence of a preposition to be meaningful.[58] The earlier form of 1:6b would thus have read: זעמו מי יעמוד. The meaning of this sentence would be exactly the same as MT. זעמו would have been accented by virtue of its position, and it would have corresponded with the acrostic. A similar accentuation of the object and conformity to the acrostic appears in the very next line with the object חמתו.

Granted, the insertion of "all the inhabitants in it" could have precipitated the dislocation of לפניו and its simultaneous or subsequent change to לפני. The question remains, why would a redactor insert the phrase into a perfectly understandable poetic line? Two factors shed light upon this question. First, the redactor was consciously shaping the book of Nahum to continue the message of Mic 7:8-20. Therefore, the insertion emphasizes that the implied judgment of the theophany portrayal is directed against the "inhabitants" of the world. It almost certainly picks up

---

[56] Such a correction would represent a similar technique to the manner in which someone added a ו to the י line.

[57] Counter-arguments that the second bi-cola would be too short are not convincing since other lines in the poem also have second lines which are noticeably shorter than the first. See especially 1:8a with 1:7b, and also 1:5ab.

[58] For example, Gen 19:27; Jer 48:11; Hab 3:11; Exod 33:9; Josh 20:4. Also many of these constructions have theophanic elements present in the context.

the theme from Mic 7:13, that the coming desolation of the "world" was the result of the deeds of "its inhabitants." Second, the universal aspect of the judgment of Nah 1:5b differs from the narrower perspective described in Mic 7:13, but it corresponds to the more typical interpretation of 7:13.[59] This observation implies that the redactor who added the phrase "all the inhabitants in it" to Nah 1:5 was not the same person who composed the liturgy of Micah 7. The implications of this observation will be further elucidated later, but first it is necessary to consider the reshaping of the semi-acrostic hymn in relationship to the remainder of the first chapter and to the book.[60]

4.4. Nah 1:9f,11-14; 2:1-3

Nah 1:9f discontinues the acrostic pattern of 1:2-8, separating it from the hymn, although Nah 1:9-10 presupposes the presence of that hymn. Nah 1:9 takes up the end of the hymn (עשׂה ... כלה), and the reference to distress (cf 1:7, צרה). The verses take up 1:11 by virtue of an *inclusio* between 1:9,11 (חשׁב). Nah 1:11 currently continues directly from 1:10, and addresses Nineveh directly, but the form of this address — the 2fs suffix in ממך — presupposes the mention of Nineveh in 1:1a. Additionally, the reference in 1:11 to the one going forth functions smoothly — with 1:12a — as the rationale for judgment against the king of Assyria in 1:14. Nah 1:9f therefore provides the transition to the Nineveh material in the remainder of the book, by shifting from general remarks to the specific applications against Nineveh. The 2mp addressee in (1:9a) gives way to a third person description of the destruction (1:10), but abruptly turns to a direct address of Nineveh (1:11):

[9]Whatever you (2mp) devise against YHWH, he makes a complete end. Distress will not rise up twice. [10]Indeed unto interwoven thorns and like their liquor (are) the drunkards. They are consumed like stubble completely withered. [11]From you (2fs) has gone forth one devising evil against YHWH, one advising worthlessness.

---

[59] See the explanation of Mic 7:13 and its relationship to the Hezekiah tradition Nogalski, *Literary Precursors*, 148-50,165-68. The fact that the redactor of Nahum understood Mic 7:13 universally is not surprising, given the fact that Mic 7:8-20 already existed, and that it can be understood either universally or nationally, depending upon how closely one associates 7:13 with the preceding verses.

[60] See below, beginning page 115.

In light of the relationship between Mic 7 and Isa 10, it is not surprising that many of the puzzling images in these verses find explanations when read in conjunction with Isa 10.[61] The one devising evil against YHWH in Isa 10:6f refers to Assyria (and to its king) who has overstepped its role as the instrument of punishment. These verses constitute part of the woe oracle against Assyria with YHWH as the speaker:

> I send him (Assyria) against a godless nation and commission him against the people of my fury ... Yet he does not so intend, and his heart does not so *devise* (חשב), rather it is his purpose to cut off many nations.

Assyria becomes prideful, and opts to destroy Jerusalem (Isa 10:11), but YHWH limits the punishment to Jerusalem (10:12), after which time he will "punish the fruit of the arrogant heart of the king of Assyria." Description of this destruction culminates in 10:16-18, an important part of which reads:

> [17]And the light of Israel will become a fire and his holy one a flame, and it will burn and *devour his thorns* and his briars in a single day. [18]And he will destroy the glory of his forest and of his thicket.

The imagery in Nah 1:9-10 stems in part from this picture, although it is not slavish literary dependence. The thorns and briars in Isa 10:17 explain the interwoven thorns in Nah 1:10. Also the reference to the destruction in a single day in Isa 10:17 has a content parallel in Nah 1:9, which says distress will not be raised up twice.[62] Further, Isa 10:23 specifies that YHWH will make a complete end (כלה ... עשה) within the entire land (כל־הארץ) before turning vengeance upon Assyria. These emphases appear in the transition and in the original acrostic (Nah 1:6,8,9).

---

[61] See also the discussion of Rudolph, *KAT* 13/3, 156f, who relates Nah 1:9-11 to Senacherib's siege and to the message of the remainder of Nahum. Further, see the treatment of the intertextuality between Mic 7:8ff and Isa 9-12 in Nogalski, *Literary Precursors*, 155ff.

[62] The obvious corollary to this statement is that distress will be lifted up once (and only once). The reference to distress in Nah 1:9 serves as the counterpart to the reference to the day of distress in 1:7, which is part of the acrostic hymn. The message in 1:7 is that those who rely on YHWH in the day of distress will find refuge, the implication of 1:9 is that YHWH's destructive power will make an end of those purposing evil. The tenor of 1:9-11 is primarily one of threat making this interpretation more likely than one which sees the phrase as only an implicit promise of deliverance. Given the fact that it is addressed to Assyria, the phrase "distress will not be raised up twice" should here be read essentially as a threat as well.

Nahum 1:9-11, in its present form, thus makes the transition to the specific subject of Nineveh's destruction prevalent in the remainder of the book. It presupposes the presence of the acrostic poem and uses a hermeneutic derived from Isa 10 to make this shift. The same subtle use of motifs and images appears in Mic 7, creating a high probability that those responsible for the redactional shaping of Nahum 1:2-8,9-11 were quite aware of the canonical position of this passage next to Mic 7, and were aware of the relationship of Mic 7:8ff to Isa 10.

The probability of an intentionally created relationship between Mic 7 and Nah 1 continues to grow when one recognizes the role of Nah 1:12,13,14. The messenger formula signals a new unit, and with this unit comes new addressees. These verses approach the subject of Assyrian domination from the *perspective of Jerusalem*, and they utilize a liturgical style very similar to that of Micah 7:8ff. First, YHWH addresses Jerusalem directly (1:12b,13 [2fs]) and then the king of Assyria (1:14, [2ms]). Significantly, YHWH tells Jerusalem, "I will shatter his (the king of Assyria) staff (מטהו) from upon you." This verse, as with Mic 7:14, plays off of the Isaiah traditions describing Assyria as YHWH's rod. The imagery of the rod as the king's scepter also plays a role. Thus punishment described in Mic 7 is completed. Assyrian domination shall be removed from Jerusalem.

Nah 1:12ff uses terms to describe the liberation from Assyrian bondage which bear a striking resemblance to Deutero-Isaiah's description of Jerusalem's redemption in Isa 52.[63] There Zion is admonished to shake the bonds from her neck (52:2; cf Nah 1:13); there is an historical allusion to the oppression of Assyria (52:4; cf Nah 1:12b); and the herald's proclamation (52:7) which has its parallel in Nah 2:1, as already noted.[64] In a very real sense, the language is appropriated from Isa 52 as a theological reflection upon YHWH's action in history. The Assyrian threat against Jerusalem is removed in Nahum in precisely the same manner as the lifting of Babylonian oppression in Isa 52.

Nah 2:1-3 also impacts the extended composition of Nah 1. Nah 2:1-3 currently functions as the introduction to the victory song in 2:4-13. Nah 2:2 provides an announcement of battle that depends upon the quote in 2:1. Nah 2:3 offers YHWH's motivation for the attack on Nineveh, namely to restore the Jacob and Israel.[65] This emphasis upon the restoration of the

---

[63] Further elaboration in Jeremias, *Kultprophetie*, 14f.

[64] See above discussion of Nah 2:1 and Isa 52:7, page 97.

[65] Literally, MT reads "YHWH will return the pride of Jacob like the pride of Israel." This sentence is not comparative, rather it seeks to correlate YHWH's saving action

Northern and Southern regions corresponds to the redactional emphases
of both Nah 1 and Mic 7, particularly in the references to Jerusalem,
Carmel, and Bashan. This emphasis, together with the dependence upon
Isa 52, creates a strong impression that Nah 2:1-3 is not the original
introduction to the victory song in Nah 2:4ff. This impression may be
strengthened further by two observations: 1) The reference to "his" warriors
in 2:4 fits better with the address to the king in Nah 1:14 than it does to
2:1-3. 2) Nah 2:3 alludes to Joel 1, as will be demonstrated briefly.[66]

When one removes these later elements from consideration it is
possible to determine an earlier frame (1:11-12a,14) which introduced the
victory song of 2:4-14.[67] This frame addresses Nineveh directly to say that
one has gone forth (the king) who councils evil against YHWH (1:11), but
the numerical strength of Assyria will provide no help. They will be cut off
and he will pass away (1:12a). Nah 1:14 announces the immanent death of
the king and the preparation of his grave. Based upon further observations
in the remainder of the corpus, it is possible to place this framework within
the realm of the compilation of the early Nahum corpus, and not merely as
an introduction of the victory song in 2:4-14. The bulk of chapters two and
three present parallel descriptions of the destruction of Nineveh, but the
last several verses of the third chapter conclude the corpus with precisely
the same thematic combination as in 1:11-12a,14:[68]

A.1.		1:11-12a The numerical strength of Nineveh will not deliver it from destruction
A.2.		1:14: The preparation of the grave of the king of Assyria
	B.	2:4-14 (Eng: 2:3-13): First description of Nineveh's destruction
	B.	3:1-15: Second description of Nineveh's destruction
A.1.		3:16-17 The numerical strength of Nineveh will not deliver it from destruction
A.2.		3:18f Mocking funeral dirge at the grave of the king of Assyria

---

on *both* regions. See the interpretation of in Watts, *Joel, etc.*, 109; contra Rudolph, *KAT*
13/3, 160; and Coggins, *Israel Among the Nations*, 36, both of whom claim Nahum
exhibits no interest in the North.

[66] See discussion below, page 116.

[67] The later elements mentioned here are those which draw from Isa 52 (Nah 1:12b,13;
2:1f) and from Joel (Nah 2:3).

[68] For further details concerning the structural similarity of Nah 2-3, see page 123ff.

All of these observations, when taken together reinforce the belief that the independent semi-acrostic poem (1:2-8), with its literary transition (1:9f), was redactionally incorporated into a pre-existing Nahum corpus.

5. The Role of Nah 1 in the Book of the Twelve

The previous discussions have demonstrated that the interruptions in the acrostic pattern of Nah 1:2-8 arise as the result of a redactional process which shaped these verses slightly to fit their position in the Book of the Twelve. This process, together with Mic 7, evidences a strong awareness and utilization of Isaiah and Deutero-Isaiah traditions with regard to the destruction of the Northern and Southern kingdoms and Assyria's role in that process. This attitude differs from the view of the early Deuteronomistic corpus which utilizes Samaria as the symbol of idolatry responsible for introducing these practices to Judah. It likely represents a later stage of development when there was hope for re-unification of the regions under Judean control.

The use of theophanic material to introduce the book parallels Amos 1:2 and Mic 1:2-7. Theophanic material also appears at the end of Hab 3. The Nahum theophany differs in that it depicts a universal judgment, but this depiction results from the selection of a pre-existing hymn, where it serves a rhetorical purpose to cause the hearer to "seek refuge" in YHWH. By contrast, the theophanies of Amos and Micah more explicitly presume judgment against the North. However, one may note that the Nahum theophany also presupposes a wider literary horizon than just Mic 7:8ff. The reference to withering of "Carmel" (1:4b) plays off Amos 1:2 in which "the *summit* of Carmel dries up."[69] It also takes up motifs from Hos 14 with its reference to the "blossom of Lebanon" (1:4b).[70]

The redactional material in Nah 1:3a contains two stereotypical phrases, both of which play a role in other writings in the Book of the Twelve. Joel 2:13 and Jonah 4:2 use the phrase more typical formulated:

---

[69] This use of Carmel specifically refers to the mountain and does not presuppose the thicket/fertility tradition described for Mic 7:14 and Nah 1:4.

[70] Excluding Nah 1:4b, only two other passages contain the root פרח in association with Lebanon, Isa 35:2 and Hos 14:6,8. Both passages contain verbal forms of פרח in promises of restoration, which are specifically tied to parallel statements about the desert (Isa 35:2) and Israel (Hos 14:6,8).

"YHWH is slow to anger and abounding in lovingkindness." The reference in Jonah almost certainly comes later, and uses this stereotypical formula as a direct contradiction to Nahum.[71] Several other factors, however, raise the possibility that Nah 1 drew from Joel or perhaps that it was even part of the same redactional movement. First, Nah 1:3a contains another phrase which also appears in Joel 4:21, albeit in a different form, where YHWH promises to avenge the actions of Egypt and Edom against Judah and Jerusalem.[72] Joel 4:21, in its context, provides the same theological slant affirming YHWH's salvation in the face of an implicit recognition of the delay of the fulfillment of that promise. Second, much of Joel exhibits a liturgical awareness and style like the redactional material in Nah 1:9ff. Third, Joel exhibits the same redactional adaptation of pre-existing blocks for its own eschatological purpose. Fourth, the specific reference in Nah 2:3 to the destruction of the vine branches of Jacob and Israel comes very close to the imagery of Joel 1, especially 1:7.[73] Fifth, the reference to drunkards and their liquor in Nah 1:10 has a counterpart in Joel 1:5, except there the drink belongs to references to the destruction of Israel. Sixth, the feasts of Judah mentioned in Nah 2:1 do not belong to the parallel to Isa 52:7. However, the call to Judah to celebrate feasts makes sense when read in light of Joel 1-2. According to Joel, the feasts have been removed (see Joel 1:5ff), but the promise is given that the Northern army will be driven from the parched and desolate land (Joel 2:20) *if* the people repent (2:12-14). This imagery may help explain the call to pay the vows in Nah 2:1 as well. Finally, the use of specific motifs found in Joel appears again in the connection between Nah 3 and Hab 1.[74]

All of these observations add further weight to the argument that the redaction of Nah 1 was cognizant not only of its position adjacent to Micah 7, but that it was aware of a larger corpus including Hosea, Joel, Amos, and Micah. The awareness of Joel plays a stronger role. The major problem prohibiting the direct correlation of Nah 1 with Joel is that Joel is more

---

[71] See the literary discussion of the purpose of Jonah.

[72] See discussion of Joel 4:21 and its relationship to 4:19.

[73] The vocabulary is not such that it represents an exact quote, but it nevertheless provides evidence of awareness. Joel 1:7 says "It made my vine to destruction, and my fig-tree to splinters ... and its branches have become white." Joel uses שׂריג, having the branches of the fig-tree more in mind while Nahum's use of זמורה reflects the branches of the vine. Nevertheless the plural devastators of Israel in Nah 2:3, used in connection with the stripping of branches presents the same image, and is not inherently part of the military description of 2:4-14.

[74] See discussion of Nah 3:15-17 below, page 120.

apocalyptically oriented. However, this distinction may be explained by the function of the two books. Nah 1 explicitly denotes YHWH's action against one enemy in particular (Assyria) within the framework of historical events, while Joel, on the other hand, has a wider interest in portraying the antagonism of all the surrounding nations.

6. The Literary Units in Nah 3:1-19 (Nineveh's Imminent Destruction)

Nah 3:1-19 contains a woe oracle against Nineveh (3:1-4) with an oracular response (3:5-7), a compositional taunt song to Nineveh (3:8-17), and an ironic burial lament to the king of Assyria (3:18f). Nah **3:1-4** contains all the typical features of the woe oracle: the introductory הוֹי, the nominal subject of the woe (3:1a); a short accusation of its wretchedness (3:1ba); a description of the trouble to befall the city (3:2f); and an explanation of the cause (3:4).[75] The city is consistently mentioned in 3fs, which distinguishes the woe oracle in style from 3:5ff, however the relationship of 3:1-4 with the following verses deserves more attention. Nah 3:1-4 has been deliberately woven into the collection of Nahum sayings with a literary awareness of the context. This weaving did not effect the shape of 3:1-4, rather 2:14 appears to have been composed as a transition verse preparing the reader for the woe oracle which so graphically depicts Nineveh's military defeat. Nah 2:14 takes up catchwords from the previous unit, particularly "young lion" and "prey."[76] In addition, 2:14 takes up specific words from the woe oracle in 3:1-4: it refers to "prey" (3:1); "sword" (3:3); "chariot" (3:2). Nah 2:14 also uses the same opening formula as the oracle in 5-7, increasing the likelihood that the oracle (3:5-7) was attached to the woe (3:1-4) prior to its incorporation into the Nahum collection.[77]

---

[75] The use of the nominative rather than the participle as the addressee is unusual, but by no means unique. The participial constructions in 3:2-4 are in keeping with the *genre*, as is the singular reference, in this case 3fs. See the discussions of the structure of the woe oracle in W. Eugene March, "Prophecy" in *Old Testament Form Criticism* (San Antonio, Texas: Trinity University Press, 1974, 141-177), 164f; Claus Westermann, *Basic Forms of Prophetic Speech* (London: Lutterworth Press, 1967), 190-194.

[76] Compare the lion imagery throughout 2:12f with the use of "prey" and its verbal root טרף in 2:13.

[77] Nah 2:14 and 3:5 begin identically: הנני אליך נאם יהוה צבאות (Behold I am against you, utterance of YHWH Sebaoth).

A divine judgment oracle (**3:5-7**) follows the woe oracle. Both the 2fs address to Nineveh and the divine first person separate these verses stylistically from 3:1-4, but two observations suggest this change does not require a separate origin for the two sections. First, form-critical studies demonstrate a clear tendency for the woe proper to be followed by a divine oracle.[78] This divine response oracle affirms the woe, and often changes to direct address, whereas the typical style of the woe is the 3rd person. Second, the content of 3:5-7 very vividly takes up the harlotry imagery of 3:4. The harlotry condemned in 3:4 receives appropriate punishment: she is stripped and exposed to the nations for what she is. The stripping of Nineveh metaphorically depicts its destruction, as seen by 3:7, which in turn demonstrates awareness of 3:2-4.[79]

Nah **3:8-17** is best classified as a taunt song to Nineveh, but strong clues suggest that the "song" is composed of several independent elements, and that not all of them entered the collection at the same time. The intended speaker of this song is difficult to determine with certainty. The rhetorical question in 3:8 provides a marker that a new unit begins, but there are no concrete grammatical signals identifying the speaker. The divine first person style of the judgment oracle ceases in 3:7, and is not continued anywhere in the remainder of the book. However, there are also no references to YHWH in any of this material which specify whether the prophet or YHWH is understood as the speaker. In all probability, the prophet should be presumed as the speaker, but one should not draw too fine a distinction in this passage between the prophetic and divine words.[80]

Nah **3:8-11** compares Nineveh with Thebes, whose destruction in 663 B.C.E. offers the only concrete date in Nahum.[81] The satire of this unit is evident from the opening rhetorical question, "Are you better than No-Ammon?" (Thebes), which is so phrased as to demand a negative answer.

---

[78] See Erhard Gerstenberger, "The Woe Oracle of the Prophets," *JBL* 81 (1962): 253.

[79] The reference in 3:7 which says "Nineveh" is devastated presupposes the judgment for the harlotry as well as the reference to "this city" in Nah 3:1.

[80] This lack of distinction of the prophetic and divine speeches is by no means surprising since prophets considered themselves deliverers of divine messages, but it serves to contrast the style of this passage with others such as Joel 4:7-17 or Hab 1:1-17, where a dialogue between prophet and YHWH takes place.

[81] Jeremias argues this comparison was originally addressed to Jerusalem, but most commentators reject his claim. The similarity of vocabulary to other descriptions of Jerusalem's destruction he cites can be explained on the basis of the Jerusalem setting of Nahum (cf 2:1). See Jeremias, *Kultprophetie*, 50f. See also the critiques of Schulz, *Nahum*, 148-153; and Rudolph, *KAT* 13/3, 184.

The fact that this question is addressed to Nineveh, the power center for the very country which was responsible for Thebes' overthrow, creates the satirical mood of the passage. This device is certainly utilized for the benefit of the audience, who would presuppose that the reason Nineveh is not better than Thebes is because YHWH controls the destiny of both cities. The prophet implies that just as YHWH used Nineveh to overthrow Thebes, YHWH can and will use another instrument to overthrow Nineveh. As shall be demonstrated, this same theme receives further attention in Habakkuk.

Following the rhetorical question (3:8), the comparison of Thebes continues with a description of Thebes' might and its downfall (3:9f). The climax of the unit explicitly states that Nineveh will receive the same fate as Thebes (3:11). Often, scholars attempt to reconstruct the description of Thebes' power because 3:8 refers to the sea as the fortress of Thebes. Since it is 400 miles from the Mediterranean and over 100 miles from the Red Sea, the argue that "fortress" makes no sense.[82] Such reconstruction is neither necessary nor desirable in light of the metaphorical nature of the description, and in light of the following descriptions incorporating the surrounding regions, which effectively stretch to the Mediterranean and Red Seas.[83] Thebes thus serves as symbol for an entire region, "whose fortress was the sea."

Nah **3:12-15ab** presupposes 3:8-11, and expands the implications of the destruction of Nineveh announced in 3:11. The verses combine a botanical metaphor with the threat of a military attack to taunt Nineveh. The verses mock Nineveh's fortifications as a fig-tree with ripe fruit ready to be devoured (3:12); followed by a taunt comparing her people to women (3:13aa), implying the inability to withstand attack. This inability of both the fortress and the people to withstand a threat leads to the explicit statement that the entire land will be overrun. The sexual connotations implicit in 3:13a take up the imagery of the divine oracle in 3:5-7.[84] The

---

[82] Keller, *CAT* 11b, 130; Sellin, *Das Zwölfprophetenbuch*, 325; Marti, *Dodekapropheton*, 321; Horst, *HAT* 14, 162; Rudolph, *KAT* 13/3, 181, comes close to Maier, *Nahum*, 314-318, in associating the sea with the Nile.

[83] Thus Ethiopia, Egypt, Somalia, and Libya provide the expansion of Thebes as the center of the entire region, not merely as a large city. A general consensus now exists that the location of פוט and לובים refer approximately to the regions of Somalia and Libya. See Coggins and Re'emi, *Israel Among the Nations*, 52f; and earlier commentaries for the discussion of this identity.

[84] Embarrassing though the language may be, the parallelism of the "your people" as women with the "gates of your land" which are opened wide euphemistically serves as

fact that 3:13a alludes to 3:5-7, and interrupts more specific concerns with the city fortifications (3:12,14-15ab), suggests that a redactor of the Nahum collection deliberately strengthens the connection between the various units of the chapter. Nah 3:13b alludes to Amos' oracles against the nations, further enlarging the scope of this passage. The allusion to Amos is not an exact quote, but a theological reflection which seeks to actualize Amos' oracles as an appropriate message for Assyria.[85]

Nah 3:14-15ab mockingly commands Nineveh to make battle preparations: draw water for the siege, strengthen the fortifications, and prepare brick. The satirical tone manifests itself strongly in 3:15, where even in the midst of this preparation, the destruction arrives. These verses depict a frantic battle preparation which begins too late to fend off the attack. This same motif is evident in 3:18f, although there it is addressed to the king of Assyria.

The tenor and imagery changes substantially in Nah **3:15ac-17**. Nah 3:15ac ("It will devour you like the locust") provides a relatively clumsy transition from the threat of military attack prevalent in the preceding verses to the locust metaphors in 3:15b-17. This phrase does not correspond grammatically or pictorially to the destruction by fire and sword mentioned in 3:15ab, although it does presuppose its presence. Nah 3:15a contains three phrases, the first two of which form the conclusion of the military attack imagery from the preceding unit, while the third one stands out notably: "There the fire (fs) will devour (fs) you; the sword (fs) will cut (fs) you down; it will devour (fs) you like the locust." The lack of a subject for the last phrase presupposes the presence of the first two, but it is not tied directly to either one.[86] Neither does the transition in 3:15ac tally with the locust material in the majority of 3:15b-17. The transition stresses destruction caused by the locusts, whereas the majority of the material in 3:15b-17 stresses the multitude or the numerical strength of the locusts.

---

double entendre to the derogatory stripping of the harlot in 3:5f. Compare the similar euphemism in Gen 29:31; 30:22; and especially Cant 5:5.

85 Nah 3:13b reads: "Fire consumes her gate bars." The language of this allusion comes closest to the first oracle in Amos 1:3-5, against Damascus, where 1:4f says: "I will send *fire* upon the house of Hazael. It will *devour* the citadels of Ben-hadad. And I will shatter the *gate bar* of Damascus..."

86 The preposition "like" makes clear that the locust is not the subject. Grammatically, one would expect the antecedent of "it will devour" to be the sword, but the metaphorical association of a locust with a sword is difficult to conceive. The association of locust with fire would make more sense, but this requires ignoring the reference to sword. Cf. for example, Joel 2:3 in context.

One significant exception appears in 3:16b with the phrase, "The creeping locust (ילק) strips and flies away." This phrase, as with the transition phrase in 3:15ac, accentuates the destructive power of the creeping locust, and is equally unnecessary, syntactically and pictorially, to its context.[87]

The remainder of 3:15b-17, as already stated, concentrates upon the numerical strength of the locusts. The verses command Nineveh (3:15b) to multiply itself until it is as numerous as locusts. This command then leads to a hyperbolic description (3:16a,17), depicting Nineveh's traders, guardsmen, and marshals to be as numerous as locusts. The irony is obvious in that the writer makes clear that even though they are more numerous than the stars of heaven, their numerical strength will not save them. Destruction is near (but not from the locusts). The sun will rise and they will flee, and their place will be destroyed.[88] This change to locust imagery — particularly the tension between the numerical strength of the Nineveh-locusts and the destruction of the attacker-locusts — raises the question of the relationship of these verses to the remainder of the chapter. Often, the change in tenor and vocabulary has been taken as a sign of later interpolation, particularly on the basis of later vocabulary, however, caution must be exhorted.[89] It will be necessary to return to these questions.

---

[87] The use of the verb פשט in Nah 3:16 is particularly provoking in the context of Nah 3, since it can be used both in the sense of "stripping off" clothes (1 Sam 19:24; Lev 6:4; 16:23) as well as the raiding action of an army (Judg 9:33,44; 20:37; 1 Sam 23:27; 27:8,10; 30:1,14). Both of these images fit aptly in the metaphor of a locust-army attacking Nineveh: the locust strips the branches the same as the army that raids the city (cf similar images in Joel 1:7), but this is precisely the problem with the metaphor. The majority of the locust imagery in 3:15b-17 presumes Nineveh as the locust, not the attacking army.

[88] The phrase "and his dreadful place is not known," is best understood as a reference to the destruction, not to the hiding of the locust. See text note 3:17b&c in Nogalski, *Literary Precursors*, 44. The use of the 3ms suffix with "his place" as a reference to the locust makes the 3mp suffix of MT very difficult to explain, and presumption that the consonants should be pointed as the adjective אים (dreadful, cf Hab 1:7) make more sense and do not alter the consonontal text.

[89] The problems of dating this passage are manifold. On the one hand, the vocabulary appears elsewhere in exilic literature, or later, while on the other hand the involvement of these verses within the earlier structure of the collection of Nahum oracles (see discussion below, page 123) raises the suspicion that they predate the destruction of Jerusalem. "Marshal" appears elsewhere only in the oracle against Babylon in Jer 51:27. The context there specifically expects a coalition of the kings of the Medes (cf 51:28) to overthrow Babylon, an event which never occurred, and which must have also pre-dated not only the Persian overthrow of Babylon in 539, but also the earlier Persian conquest of the Medes. See Holladay, *Jeremiah*, vol 2, 422. The word מנזר, normally

The last two verses, Nah **3:18-19**, rather unexpectantly address the king of Assyria. The verses are best classified as an ironic burial lament. They depict a situation in which the king is addressed as though already dead or very close to death (hence the domination of the perfect and the reference to the incurable wound). Nah 3:18 depicts a situation in which the nobles and the leaders have fallen asleep with no one to lead the scattered people. This basic attitude of the imminent destruction of Assyria is very much in keeping with the message of the Nahum collection, in spite of the fact that it addresses the king of Assyria rather than the personified Nineveh. In fact, these verses offer highly significant evidence that Jeremias' view of a collection of Nahum speeches that has been reworked is a better model than Schulz' view of a single composition. These two verses, together with Nah 1:11-14, actually form a frame of the earlier blocks of this Nahum collection prior to the incorporation of the theophanic hymn (1:2-8) and its interpretive transition (1:9f).[90] Nah 3:18f shares much in common with 1:14 in particular since both address the king of Assyria directly, and since both accent the imminent death of the king. With this observation, the stage has now been set to look at the relationship of the various parts of chapter 3 to one another, to the book as a whole, and to its relationship to the Book of the Twelve.

---

translated guardsman, is a *hapax legomenon*. רכלים (traders) appears more frequently, but again in texts later than the 7th century. Above all the word appears in Ezekiel's oracles against Tyre (27:3,13,15,17,20,22,23,24). Compare also the parable in Ezek 17:4; and 1 Kgs 10:15; Cant 3:6; Neh 3:31; 13:20. However, as with "marshal," Ezekiel's oracle against Tyre can be dated with a high degree of probability between 587-571. See Zimmerli, *BK* 13/2, 638. See also the discussion of this passage in Schulz, *Nahum*, 41, 103; and Jeremias, *Kultprophetie*, 43. A possible solution to the dilemma suggests itself in the acceptance of a late 7th century dating of this early Nahum corpus. A date near the time of 612, probably shortly after Nineveh's destruction would be no more than 30-40 years removed from the Jeremiah and Ezekiel passages, putting it relatively close chronologically. In addition, it would account for several important aspects of Nahum: namely that Nineveh is portrayed as a historical entity; the destruction of Nineveh appears imminent, meaning it was a current topic; and the mocking tenor of chapters 2-3 strongly exhibits real *Schadenfreude* over the fate of Nineveh.

[90] See the discussion of this frame above (page 114) and in the discussion of the growth of Nah 3:1-19 which follows immediately.

7. The Growth of Nah 3:1-19

Strong indications of the remnant of a previous structure strengthen the suggestions of Jeremias and Seybold that an earlier corpus of Nahum has been expanded. Taking the clue from the observation that Nah 3:18-19 functions as *inclusio* to 1:14, it is also possible to demonstrate that the earlier material in 1:11ff has thematic affinity to 3:16-17, and that Nah 2:4-13 parallels Nah 3:1-14 compositionally.

1:11-14* Though the Assyrians are numerous The king will perish.	
2:4-8 Description of battle Stripping of Nineveh Her handmaids mourn	3:1-4,5-7 Woe oracle with battle description The stripping of Nineveh No one mourns
2:9-11 The sacking of Nineveh Comparison of Nineveh to pool of water Plunder of treasure without end Fear of the people	3:8-11 Comparison to the sacking of Thebes Thebes' strength was her water fortress There was no end to Thebes' allies Thebes' people were devastated
2:12-13 Nineveh collected prey (to devour) (Lion metaphor)	3:12-15a Nineveh will be devoured
2:14 Transition	
	3:16-17,18-19 Though Assyrians are numerous (Locust metaphor) The king will perish

These compositional observations provide a starting point for understanding the growth of the Nahum corpus. They indicate that it had a structured literary form prior to the post-exilic reshaping, which added the theophanic hymn and the allusions to Joel and Deutero-Isaiah.[91] They indicate the literary unity of most of Nah 2-3 in this early corpus. The early corpus had a frame predicting the death of the king in spite of the Assyrians' numerical strength (1:11-12a,14; 3:16f,18f). The material inside this frame offers two

---

[91]   See the discussion of Nahum 1:2-8,9-14; 2:1-3, beginning on page 101.

parallel depictions of the destruction of Nineveh, although the backgrounds and interests are not identical. Both passages begin with vivid depictions of battle scenes (2:4-8; 3:1-4); both continue with references to the sacking of cities (2:9-11; 3:8-11);[92] both contain metaphors of devouring, although Assyria functions differently in these portrayals (2:12f; 3:12-15a).[93]

This schema creates several significant implications for understanding the current shape of Nahum. Clearly, the majority of the growth of the corpus appears at the beginning of the book, where a redactor attached the theophanic hymn (1:2-8), a transition (1:9f), and simultaneously reworked the introductory passages in light of Deutero-Isaiah, in order to proclaim an end to *Assyrian* oppression. By contrast, the majority of Nah 2-3 were left essentially intact. Their message of Nineveh's imminent destruction suited the redactor's purpose. The hermeneutical interest had a dual purpose, establishing YHWH's control of the world (hence the theophany) within an historical framework (hence the connection to Mic 7:8ff). Nineveh, whose destruction was part of YHWH's divine plan, symbolizes the entire period of Assyrian domination.[94]

One place in chapter three, however, illustrates redactional emphases which transcend the earlier framework. The reference to the destruction caused by the creeping locust (ילק) in 3:15ac,16b introduces a distinct shift in the function of the locust metaphor from the early material. This early

---

92 Nah 2:9-11 relates directly to the sacking of Nineveh, while 3:8-11 evidences a broader perspective with its comparison to the Assyrian sacking of Thebes and the exile of its population.

93 Again, the perspective of these units are different. The first (2:12f) pictures Assyria as the lion who has devoured everything in its path, and collected prey to support its own appetite. The passage implies that this unsatiated appetite provides the reason for the judgment which will befall them. The second (3:12-15a) portrays Assyria/Nineveh as the one who will be devoured. It thus serves as thematic counterpart to the lion metaphor: the hunter becomes the hunted. Several commentators argue that the locust metaphor in 3:15b-17 functions as the counterpart to the lion imagery, since both utilize animal metaphors. Insofar as these observations go, they are correct, but the focus of the locust metaphor illustrates Assyria's numerical superiority and thus functions as the recollection of the theme of Assyrian numerical strength (1:12a). Only short gloss-like comments (3:15ac,16b) reflect the destructive power of the locusts.

94 This divine plan included the punishment of his people by means of Assyria (the destruction of Samaria and the threat of Jerusalem's destruction). The destruction of Assyria, represented by Nineveh, resulted from the arrogance it demonstrated in overstepping the task YHWH had given it (here the allusions to Isa 10 and the Hezekiah traditions play a significant role). This unfolding story of salvation history continues with Habakkuk, see the discusssion of the redactional adaptation of Habakkuk for the Book of the Twelve in the next chapter.

metaphor inherently stresses the numerical strength of the locusts, and the
futility of this numerical strength in light of impending judgment. The
creeping locust phrases, however, both allude to the destructive power of
this insect. What is more, this destructive insect attacks Nineveh, unlike the
insects in the remainder of the metaphor.[95] This observation has
significance beyond the question of Nah 3. Scholars often claim that the
locust imagery in Nah 3:15-17 has a certain affinity to Joel, where locusts
also represent invading armies.[96] However, one must acknowledge that
this *affinity* is in reality very much dependent upon the two phrases treating
the destructive force of the creeping locust, not upon the futility of
Nineveh's numerical strength. Question thus arises as to the purpose and
function of these two phrases.

Most understand the character of these ילק phrases as simple glosses,
but there are good reasons for seeing them in a wider perspective.[97] First,
they reinterpret the early metaphor so that Nineveh's metaphorical locusts
are raided by a more destructive locust. Second, they are not literally well
integrated into their context.[98] Third, they take up a motif which depends
upon another writing in the Book of the Twelve, namely Joel 1-2. The
manner in which this motif is taken up supplies evidence that the redactor
had a specific purpose in mind in adding the ילק phrases. The pertinent
material for the allusion stems from Joel 1:4: "The left-over of the gnawing
locust, the swarming locust has eaten. And the left-over of the swarming
locust, the creeping locust has eaten. And the left over of the creeping
locust, the stripping locust has eaten."[99] Leaving aside the question of the
historicity of the locust plague, discussed elsewhere, one thing is certain:
whatever the original setting of Joel 1:4, this imagery came to symbolize,

---

[95] Hence, even though the earlier metaphor also refers to the creeping locust among
others, the locusts are all symbols of Assyrian/Ninevite groups. The two phrases of
destruction, by contrast, both draw on images of the creeping locusts *attacking* Nineveh,
not as representative of Nineveh: "It will devour you like the creeping locust. ... The
creeping locust strips and flies away."

[96] Compare the observations of Schulz, *Nahum*, 27,41; Coggins and Re'emi, *Israel among
the Nations*, 56. Jeremias, *Kultprophetie*, 43, does not explicitly note relationship to
Joel, but remarks that the phrases clearly stem from a later time than the metaphor in
the remainder of 3:15-17. The relationship to Joel is seen most clearly in the selection
of ילק (Joel 1:4; 2:25), rather than the more common term אברה, and in the similarity
of the descriptions of stripping and flying to Joel 1:7.

[97] Compare *BHS* text notes.

[98] See discussion above, page 120.

[99] Compare also the related passage, Joel 2:25, where the different order relates back to
the effects of the locusts in 1:4.

not locusts as such, but the armies which invaded Judah.[100] When viewed
from a broader historical perspective, there can be little doubt that both
Assyria and Babylon were included in this litany of locust invaders.
Whereas Joel writes from the perspective of Judah, or more precisely
Jerusalem, Nahum functions as a specific message to Nineveh (Assyria)
within a historically influenced literary framework in the Book of the
Twelve. Nahum predicts that Nineveh will be destroyed, and by picking up
the allusions to Joel this redactor intimates that it will be destroyed by
another locust army, namely the Babylonians.[101]

The question arises, how do the redactional ילק comments in Nah
3:15ab,16b relate to the heavy redaction work at the beginning the book of
Nahum, particularly the theophany? Are these part of the same redactional
interest or do they stem from the interests of another layer? The question
is not an easy one to answer in light of the peripheral nature of the
creeping locust comments, but some observations at least increase the
likelihood that they come from the same layer. The primary question for
relating the creeping locust material to that of the theophany concerns the
perception of the judgment on Nineveh. Simply stated, the theophany
implies YHWH's direct intervention, while the creeping locust comments
suppose an army attacking Nineveh. However, one must guard against
distinguishing these two variations too radically. The theophany was an
independent block brought into the corpus to introduce the judgment on
Nineveh. Redactionally, its chief purpose serves to announce judgment, not
to portray the actual unfolding of the events of that judgment.[102]
Additionally, Nah 2:2, with its reference to the "one who scatters," has the
Babylonians in mind in depicting the army attacking Nineveh, while at the
same time entering the corpus with the theophany and Deutero-Isaiah
allusions.[103] Finally, YHWH's use of other nations as a manifestation of

---

[100] Above all see Joel 1:7; and the description of the army in locust terms present in Joel
2:2-10. For discussion of the problems of Joel 1:4 as a reference to a historical locust
plague, see literary discussion of Joel 1.

[101] The selection of the ילק to portray Nineveh's destruction makes sense in light of Joel
1:4 (and 2:25), where its position, neither first nor last, coincides with the ongoing cycle
of invaders.

[102] This distinction between the events portrayed in the hymn and the intention of the
redactor is most noticeable in 1:9-11, where in spite of the fact that the destruction of
the entire world has been announced in 1:8, this passage creates a transition to
judgment upon Assyria.

[103] See by implication Smith, *Word* 32, 82f.

his judgment, has numerous parallels in Old Testament literature.[104] It thus is not only possible that the coming of YHWH can be manifested in the military attack of a nation (under YHWH's commission), but references elsewhere in Nahum to an attacking army, which presuppose the presence of the hymn, point toward a single layer which incorporated both the theophany and allusions to the Babylonians to accomplish the specific purpose of judgment against Nineveh.[105]

8. Dating the Layers of Nahum

The fundamental question for dating Nahum revolves around the various elements which point in different directions. The theophany and its transition, along with the allusions to Deutero-Isaiah, represent the latest redactional reworking. The remnants of a clear structure offer solid evidence of an existing structure which pre-dated the incorporation of this material. Dating even this earlier corpus poses a difficult task. On the one hand, references to the destruction of Thebes seemingly indicate the middle of the 7th century, and a lack of Deuteronomistic language has been cited as evidence that the book pre-dated Josiah's reforms.[106] On the other hand, the language of the locust metaphor seemingly indicates the early exilic period.[107] In addition, other linguistic arguments have been garnered to argue for a later origin.[108] A determination of the date for

---

[104] Compare most significantly, YHWH's reference to Assyria as "my rod" used to punish Israel in Isa 10.

[105] The reason for two different pictures may lie in 1) the fact that the basic Nahum material clearly intended a human military invasion, and 2) the historical events underlying Nineveh's destruction did not, for the redactor, need to be denied in order to affirm YHWH's universal control.

[106] So for example, Richard Coggins, "An Alternative Prophetic Tradition?," in *Israel's Prophetic Tradition: Essays in Honour of Peter Ackroyd*, Richard Coggins, and others, eds (New York: Cambridge University Press, 1982, 77-94), 83.

[107] See literary discussion above (this chapter, note 89), and Jeremias, *Kultprophetie*, 43.

[108] So especially, Schulz, *Nahum*, 48f. Note also the descriptions of battle, especially in Nah 3:1-4, which presume calvary action. Only with the Persians did full-scale calvary actions a play major role, but already the Assyrians used calvary troops, particularly with regard to chasing fugitives. See the discussions of H. Weippert, "Pferd und Streitwagen," in *Biblisches Reallexikon* (Tübingen: Mohr, [2]1977), 250-255; and Yigael Yadin, *The Art of Warfare in Biblical Lands in the Light of Archaeological Study*, 2 vols (New York: McGraw-Hill, 1963). The Assyrian artifacts and reliefs noted by Yadin

Nahum must somehow come to terms with these various elements. Several observations can help to strike needed balance between these elements. First, the recognition of two formative layers goes a long way in determining the date. The theophanic hymn and the allusions to Deutero-Isaiah are at least late exilic elements, more likely post-exilic, particularly in light of the reflective use of the Deutero-Isaiah allusions and quote. Concerning the date of the earlier corpus, the best option still appears to assume a date somewhere around the time of Nineveh's actual destruction (612). Such a dating can account for the language found in the locust metaphor, since it would be only thirty plus years removed from parallels in Jeremiah and Ezekiel. The time around 612 could still account for the reference to Thebes, since monumentous events can live a long time in the collective consciousness of a people. The use of Thebes becomes important for another reason as well. Their selection for comparison can be understood much more readily prior to the destruction of Jerusalem, after which time the destruction of Thebes would pale quickly.[109] Of utmost significance for dating the earlier portions of Nahum around the time of Nineveh's destruction is the basic tenor of the passages which treat the city Nineveh as a political entity, not as symbol for all nations. In addition, there is a very real sense of unbridled joy at the thought of Nineveh's destruction (3:6,19) and reference to the longstanding suffering under Assyrian oppression (3:19).

More precise dating of the reshaping of Nahum must await discussion of other passages, since only by the comparison of several different texts, which share certain characteristics can one hope to shed light on the texts beyond mere speculation. Some of the elements which will play an important role for comparison for Nahum are the relationship of Nah 3 to catchwords in Habakkuk 1; the relationships of the theophany which begins Nahum to the theophany which concludes Habakkuk; and the question of the date and unity of Joel.[110]

---

which reflect calvary troops, demonstrate that calvary was a weapon employed by the Assyrians more than is evident from the article by Weippert.

[109] Contra Schulz, *Nahum*, 49.

[110] Nah 3:15ab,16b allude to Joel 1-2, and those chapters are often dated earlier than Joel 4, and the question must be asked if this distinction is valid, and if so what effect that has in relationship to Nah 3.

Habakkuk

1. The Macrostructure of Habakkuk

Habakkuk divides readily into three major sections, although their relationship to one another provokes considerable discussion.[1] After the superscription (1:1), the book commences with an extended dialogue section (1:2-2:5), followed by a series of five woe oracles with commentary (2:6-19). This second block closes with a concluding verse (2:20) to the literary corpus of 1-2, but begins immediately anew with a second superscription (3:1) introducing the "prayer of Habakkuk the prophet." In order to understand how these divergent parts fit together, the respective sections deserve more descriptive treatment.

In its present form, scholars often portray 1:2-2:5 as a unity containing two complaints (1:2-4,12-17) followed by two divine oracles (1:5-11; 2:1-5).[2] However, simply designating the material as a unity poses serious problems, and fails to do justice to the diversity within these verses. It has long been noted that the themes found in the complaints and oracles are not

---

[1] For a comprehensive summary of the history of research on Habakkuk, see Peter Jöcken, *Das Buch Habakuk. Darstellung der Geschichte seiner kritischen Erforschung mit einer eigenen Beurteilung*, Bonner Biblische Beiträge 48 (Köln: Peter Hanstein Verlag, 1977). No attempt will be made here to match the breadth of viewpoints covered in this volume. Rather, selections will be made on the basis of typical arguments and of significant literature which has appeared since Jöcken's work.

[2] A selection of authors supporting this view of integrity includes: William W. Cannon, "The Integrity of Habakkuk cc. 1.2," *ZAW* 43 (1925): 62-90; Hubert Junker, *Die zwölf kleinen Propheten*, vol 2, 32; Rudolph, *KAT* 13/3, 195. Others believe the section represents a composition from the hand of the prophet: Karl Elliger, *ATD* 25, 24f, believes the work is a liturgical unity; Georg Fohrer, *Die Propheten*, vol 2, 37, follows Weiser; Donna Dykes, *Diversity and Unity in Habakkuk*, Vanderbilt University Dissertation, (1976), 103, apparently believes that the two oracles belong inherently to the complaints which they follow, although she separates the two complaints by some years; J.H. Eaton, *Obadiah, Nahum, Habakkuk, Zephaniah*, Torch Bible Commentary (London: SCM, 1961), 81, also believes the "unity" stems from the prophet. Jeremias, *Kultprophetie*, 78ff believes 1:1-17 originally had a two-fold structure (1:2-4 parallels 1:12f; 1:5-11 parallels 1:14-17). He believes the two parts were complaint and pronouncement. Admittedly, form critical questions in 1:14-17 disturb his theory, but he attempts to solve this disruption through the supposition of minor textual corruption, which led to a "new understanding" of the latter verses as complaint.

consistent. The first complaint decries the violence and prosperity of the wicked. The oracles, on the other hand, deal with the ferocity of the Babylonians. Some scholars go even further, seeing two entirely different attitudes toward the Babylonians, with the first denoting the Babylonians as a tool of YHWH's punishment (1:5-11) followed by the second attitude depicting the Babylonians in a much more negative light (1:14-17).[3]

Equally problematic are form-critical implications stemming from the designation of 1:5-11 and 2:1-5 as the original oracular responses to the complaints in their current form. The complaint proper is the complaint of an individual treating the question of the prosperity of the wicked. By contrast, the oracular response in 1:5-11 has a communal frame. YHWH addresses the congregation (2mp) directly in 1:5, and the congregation responds corporately (1cp) in 1:12. All of these problem areas, and more, raise two questions immediately: 1) Should this "dialogue" be viewed more realistically as a redactional composition?   2) On what level is this composition related to the remainder of the book?

The second major block (2:6-20) is organized around a cycle of five woe oracles and a conclusion to the corpus containing Hab 1-2.[4] At least some of the oracles in 2:6-19 demonstrate the same expanded viewpoint evidenced in the dialogue section. The first woe (2:6-8) condemns the one who gets rich on borrowed money (2:6), since he does not realize that the creditors will rise up and demand their investment (2:7). Hab 2:8, however, reinterprets this pseudo-wealthy individual as a personified nation, or king.[5] The identity of this nation deserves further treatment, but prudence demands holding the question open until the remainder of the woe oracles have been noted.   The language of this verse finds close parallels in

---

[3]   Already Wellhausen, *Die kleinen Propheten*, 161f, evidences this view when he ties the wicked in 1:2-4 with the Babylonians in 1:13, and sees 1:5-11 as an earlier oracle. See also Dykes, *Diversity and Unity*, 103, who also claims this anti-Babylonian oracle "antedates" the oracle predicting their arrival "by a number of years in order for the Israelites to have experienced the violence which is lamented." This reasoning is not at all clear, resting on the assumption that 1:2-4 presumes Babylonian violence. Eckart Otto, "Die Theologie des Buches Habakuk," *VT* 35 (1985): 279, isolates an anti-Babylonian layer which post-dates the material in 1:5-11.

[4]   On the independence of Hab 3:1ff, see below 133, as well as a more thorough discussion later in the chapter.

[5]   The 2ms addressee of 2:8 follows the person and number of 2:7. The masculine suffix would indicate a country or king by virtue of the content of 2:8, where the crime is reinterpreted such that it no longer designates the pseudo-wealthy individual of 2:7, but one who has "looted many *nations*," and who is responsible for "human bloodshed." See further discussion in Otto, *VT* 35 (1985), 281.

prophetic literature, but these parallels do not by themselves shed any light upon the identity of the nation.[6]

The second woe (2:9-11) also has an underlying critique against a wealthy individual, with wisdom vocabulary parallels, although the woe is thoroughly prophetic.[7] This critique also receives reinterpretation (2:10b) along the lines of the first oracle, which broadens the primary thrust of the critique from the social to the political sphere.[8] The precise identity of this individual, even in the earlier form of the woe, needs clarification. The context of the next oracle raises the possibility that this "house" could intend the Judean dynasty, in other words the king and his household.[9] Such anti-royal attitudes would certainly be more typical for prophetic than wisdom literature. At any rate, this house metaphor receives reinterpretation which clearly understands "house" as a political metaphor (2:10b).[10]

---

[6] For example, the verse shares linguistic similarities with Mic 3:10, where the rulers of Judah are intended, and Mic 7:2, where the wicked is the leading class of Jerusalem. Likewise, the expression "city of bloodshed" in Nah 3:1 could imply Assyria. See also Ezek 22:2; 24:6,9 where the "city of bloodshed" refers to Zion. Also Isa 26:21 announces YHWH's arrival to reveal the bloodshed of the earth.

[7] Jeremias, *Kultprophetie*, 68, notes the vocabulary stems from the wisdom tradition (cf Prov 1:19; 15:27). Rudolph, among others, *KAT* 13/3, 225, forces 2:9-11 into a simple condemnation of Babylon. Such attempts fail to convince. The reference to the cry of the stone, the wall, the rafter, etc. (2:11) play too intricately upon the house metaphor. The metaphor of the stone crying out and the rafter's response implies these elements belong to the house (which received the evil gain), but that they reject the evil gain brought into the house. It is difficult to understand this rejection by the elements of the house if Babylon were the original subject. This understanding implies Babylon rejected its king (the one bringing evil gain), but even metaphorically, it is unlikely that the prophet would have established a dichotomy between the political action of the Babylonian king and the subsequent rejection of that action by the kingdom.

[8] The phrase "by cutting off many peoples" implies aggressive military action. The rationale for obtaining the "evil gain" in 2:9, however, further isolates 2:10b. According to 2:9, the rationale for obtaining the "evil gain" is defensive: "to be delivered from the hand of evil;" whereas in 2:10b the crime is offensive: cutting off many peoples.

[9] See discussion of 2:12-14 in the following paragraph. Rudolph, *KAT* 13/3, 225, may be correct in understanding "house" as dynasty, but not the Babylonian dynasty. Contrast Jeremias, *Kultprophetie*, 68, who ties a wisdom background for "house" to the extended family of every individual. An answer to the question of identity hinges largely upon whether one views these oracles as part of a literary composition, or the collection of isolated prophetic sayings.

[10] This expansion cannot refer to Judean royalty, since the dates in question, late 7th century to post-exilic times, do not readily lend themselves to a political offensive of this magnitude which would have been condemned by prophetic tradents. This reference could only be to an military invasion from a foreign power. The fact that this

The third woe (2:12-14) also manifests prophetic intentions, even though some of its language has a certain affinity to wisdom traditions. This woe has also received expansions, with 2:13 presenting an almost exact doublet to Jer 51:58, and Hab 2:14 bringing a strong hint of post-exilic traditions.[11] This short woe experiences radical transformation as a result of these expansions. In its earliest form, the clearest parallel to Hab 2:12 appears in Mic 3:10, where the context clearly refers to the heads of Judah "who build Zion with bloodshed (בדמים) and Jerusalem with violence (בעולה)." Since this is the second time the primary layer of the woe oracles takes up Mic 3:10, the verse receives considerable importance and offers evidence that the original woes did indeed reflect an animosity toward Jerusalem's leaders.[12] The addition in 2:13, takes up Jer 51:58, thereby reinterpreting 2:12, by changing the critique against Judean leaders to a critique against Babylon.[13] Hab 2:14 provides the purpose of YHWH's action, the universal recognition of YHWH. It presupposes the preceding verses syntactically and thematically, and provides an optimistic motivation in the midst of the woe cycle.[14]

The fourth woe (2:15-17) also begins with the illicit behavior of the wicked who get their neighbors drunk to look upon their nakedness (2:15), a practice which leads to disgrace rather than honor (2:16a). This woe against despicable ethical behavior receives two expanded sentences which

---

power devastated "many peoples" presumes a world power, and eliminates all but the Babylonians and Assyrians as possible subjects.

[11] See Jeremias, *Kultprophetie*, 63, who cites: Isa 60:1-3; 66:18; 11:9f; 35:2; 40:5.

[12] For the first reference to Mic 3:10, see note 6 above.

[13] It is not wise to follow Rudolph, *KAT* 13/3, 226f, by dividing Hab 2:13, precisely because both halves of the verse are involved with the citation of Jer 51:58. In context, Jer 51:58 ends a collection of condemnations against Babylon, and brings unimpeachable evidence of the strength of the connection of this verse to an anti-Babylonian tradition. The implication of the verse in 2:13 asks rhetorically, whether YHWH has the power to control the destinies of nations. The question's phraseology (הלוא) indictes that the expected answer is yes. YHWH decides who will be punished. This theme appears also in Hab 1:11, where the critique clearly implies that Babylon is "he whose strength is his god." Both 1:11 and 2:13f carry implicit, yet evident, threats that part of the reason Babylon receives punishment is its refusal to recognize YHWH's control of universal destiny.

[14] The כי clause ties 2:14 with 2:13, and the universal aspect of 2:14 relates more closely to 2:13 than 2:12. However, the verse could be the thematic counterpart to 2:12 as well. If such were the case, the thought would have been condemnation against those filling the town with violence when YHWH desires the entire earth to be filled with knowledge of his glory. This verse quotes Isa 11:9.

bring in themes from elsewhere in the Book of the Twelve. Hab 2:15b brings in the theme of the punishment of the cup of YHWH's right hand, which played an important role in Obad 15ff (via dependence upon Jer 25 and 49), and 2:17 introduces the "violence done to Lebanon," a theme which elsewhere appears most notably in the interruption of the acrostic in Nah 1:4, and relates to the legacy of the *Assyrian* hegemony.[15]

The fifth woe (2:18f) presents a considerably different structure than the others. It does not begin with the typical introductory element (הוֹי), but with an introduction (2:18). This introduction prepares the reader for a shift to an anti-idolatry motif. Likely, these verses reflect later tradition, particularly Deutero-Isaiah.[16]

Hab 2:20 functions doxologically, on the one hand as the counterpart to the anti-idolatry oracle in 2:18f, and on the other to the entire corpus to that point. The verse contrasts those speaking to idols, which do not speak back, with a command to keep silent before YHWH, who is in his holy temple. Simultaneously, the verse resolves the essential dilemma begun in chapter one. The fact that YHWH is in his holy temple implies that everything is in its proper order, and implies that YHWH has everything under control. The verse belongs best with the early material treating the question of the prosperity of the wicked, and essentially affirms the traditional view that YHWH will punish the wicked.

A general description of Hab 3:1-19 will suffice here as an overview, since Hab 3:1-19 will be treated in more detail later.[17] The chapter begins with a new superscription (3:1), has its own subscription (3:19b), and exhibits three סלע markers (3:3,9,13). All three of these elements have demonstrable relationships to psalmic literature, and point toward a separate history for this portion of the book.[18] The content of the chapter brings a theophanic portrayal of YHWH's arrival for battle which draws heavily upon mythological allusions to portray this event. The depiction of this theophany is framed with prophetic "I" sayings that provide clues as to how the chapter is to be understood in the context of the Habakkuk corpus. In essence, one must recognize a dialectic between two events, *both of which lie in the future*, namely the attack of the enemy and YHWH's

---

[15] See above discussion of the interruptions of the acrostic.

[16] See Jeremias, *Kultprophetie*, 64f.

[17] See below, beginning page 154.

[18] Considerable debate exists whether this separate history resulted from the cultic adaptation of Hab 3 or whether this separate history *predated* the inclusion of the psalm into the Habakkuk corpus. A fuller discussion is provided below (154ff), here the separate origin of Hab 3:1-19 is presumed as a result of that investigation.

salvation of his people. The content and purpose of the hymn make it clear that this portion of Habakkuk is not interested in the wisdom-related question of the prosperity of the wicked, meaning that it did not enter the corpus at least until the time of the Babylonian expansion.

Even this cursory overview of Habakkuk demonstrates a remarkably well-crafted work which intertwines two separate motifs: the prosperity of the wicked in various facets of society, and the attack and oppression of the Babylonians. This investigation must ask, how are these themes intertwined from a technical perspective? What forces motivate their combination? Before turning in detail to the first section, a brief summary of the traditional positions for dating the Habakkuk corpus will serve as an orientation from which to evaluate the growth of the book.

2. Dating Habakkuk: Traditional Arguments and Problems

Traditional arguments place Habakkuk roughly contemporary with Jeremiah, largely on the basis of the reference to the Chaldeans in 1:6.[19] Since the Chaldeans could not have posed a serious military threat to the Assyrian control of Palestine prior to the late 7th century, this date serves as an irrefutable *terminus ab quo*. Opponents of a late 7th century dating of Habakkuk have not been particularly numerous, but they raise some significant objections which are not often given the credence they deserve, in part because their proponents combine these objections with substantial emendations to conform the text more readily to theories of late date.[20] While suggested emendations of the Chaldeans have been dismissed on the

---

[19] Several examples suffice to typify the line of reasoning, when the question of date is not separated from the question of the compositional elements or when the authors maintain the diversity stems from a single author: Lawrence Boadt, *Jeremiah 26-52, Habakkuk, Zephaniah, Nahum*. Old Testament Message 10 (Wilmington, Delaware: Michael Glazier, 1982), 162; Elliger, *ATD* 25, 22f; Paul Humbert, *Problèmes du livre d'Habakkuk* (Neuchâtel: Secréteriat de l'Université, 1944), 247f; Eduard Nielsen, "The Righteous and the Wicked in Habaqquq," *Studia Theologica* 6 (1952): 60-64; Keller, *CAT* 11b, 140; Rudolph, *KAT* 13/3, 194.

[20] Duhm, *Das Buch Habakuk: Text, Übersetzung, und Erklärung* (Tübingen: J.C.B. Mohr, 1906), 19, remains the classic example. He changes the reference to the Chaldeans to the Kittim, and proceeds to interpret the Hab 1:6 as a reference to the Greeks. 1QpHab also *interprets* the Chaldeans as the Kittim, but attests to the Chaldeans in the text proper (as opposed to the commentary).

basis the other versions, the objections themselves, which arose from a careful reading of the text, do not receive adequate treatment in current literature.[21] Some of these objections should be noted, not so much to make a determination of their validity prior to looking carefully at the text, but in order to keep them in mind in the following literary analysis. Those objections relating most prominently to the dialogue in 1:1-2:5 can be summarized in three statements: 1) The Babylonian depiction does not correspond in detail to the historical circumstances of the invasion. 2) The presence of "Torah" in 1:4 argues for a date later than the 7th century. 3) The name "Habakkuk" is itself of Babylonian origin, pointing to a time after Babylon became the dominant power of the region.

One recent work argues the diversity of Habakkuk comes not from the growth of an early corpus, but from the prophet's incorporation of ancient pre-existing material. Hiebert claims that chapter three is an independent composition, which *predates* the remainder of the work, but which was attached and incorporated into the corpus by the prophet.[22] This model has little effect upon the question of 1:1-2:5, but will be treated more fully in the discussion of Hab 3:1ff and its connection to Zephaniah.

Despite this strong agreement on the date of Habakkuk, the deduction of the *terminus ad quem* for the formation of the book is not so readily solved. Jeremias posits that Habakkuk, like Nahum, has a late 7th century core, which receives expansions in the late exilic period. Jeremias goes so far as to suggest that the same circle edited both Nahum and Habakkuk.[23] Jeremias postulates an oral transmission of Habakkuk which did not record the speeches of Habakkuk until the end of the exilic period in order to account for thoroughness of this reinterpretation.[24] The use

---

[21] Duhm's theory, originally followed by Sellin and others, that Habakkuk prophesied in the time of Alexander was convincingly discounted even prior to the discoveries at Qumran. See already, M.J. Gruenthaler, "Chaldeans or Macedonians? A Recent Theory on the Prophecy of Habakkuk." *Biblica* 8 (1927): 129-160; 251-289; and W. Staerk, "Zu Habakuk 1:5-11. Geschichte oder Mythos?" *ZAW* 51 (1933): 1-28. However, Duhm did not begin by changing the reference to the Chaldeans to correspond to a *preconceived* idea that the book stemmed from a later period. Rather, he sought to change that reference in response to the literary problems in the remainder of the chapter. Recent commentaries typically shelve Duhm's conclusions with a brief dismissal of his emendation, but do not treat the tensions in the text adequately. See for example, Allen, *Joel, etc.*, 148.

[22] Theodore Hiebert, *God of My Victory: The Ancient Hymn in Habakkuk 3* (Atlanta: Scholars Press, 1986).

[23] Jeremias, *Kultprophetie*, 108-110.

[24] Jeremias, *Kultprophetie*, 87f.

of other prophetic material (particularly Jer 51:38 in Hab 2:13) make many of Jeremias' arguments plausible, but the preponderance of catchwords in the Babylonian sections, which share images and vocabulary with Nahum raise the question if Jeremias is correct in limiting the expansions to the woe oracles in chapter 2, and relatedly if the *terminus ad quem* can be so firmly placed in the late exilic period rather than the post-exilic period.[25]

3. Literary Observations on Hab 1:1-2:5

As already noted, the dialogue section of Habakkuk contains readily demonstrable units, but the original relationship of these units poses problems. A closer analysis reveals the units stem from separate contexts, and are first combined on a redactional level. The first unit is the superscription in **Hab 1:1**. Unlike many of the other superscriptions in Book of the Twelve, Hab 1:1 shows no signs of growth. Its syntax is simple and straightforward: "The oracle which Habakkuk the prophet (הנביא) saw." The verse functions as a title, with no syntactical connection to the verses which follow. The extent of the corpus for which this superscription functions causes debate. This debate arises from the model used for Hab 3:1-19, where 3:1 attests a second superscription. Those who treat Habakkuk as an original literary composition generally assume or argue that 1:1 intends the entire book.[26] Most of these scholars argue that the superscription in 3:1, along with the psalmic elements in that chapter, were added when 3:2ff — ostensibly because of its presumed popularity — was utilized during worship services apart from the context of the other two chapters. They argue that chapter three relates integrally to the vision depicted in 2:1-5. However, this rationale fails to account for the lack of these cultic notations in the remainder of the book, or in prophetic literature in general. This forceful evidence of a separate transmission history outweighs the arguments that Hab 3:1-19 was used in worship services apart from Hab 1-2, while still remaining anchored to the corpus.

---

[25] Jeremias is not entirely clear with regard to why he places Habakkuk solidly in the late exilic period, while maintaining that Nahum is either late exilic or early post-exilic. The confusion is heightened dramatically when Jeremias says that the same group was responsible for the expansions of the two works.

[26] See Rudolph, *KAT* 13/3, 199, 239-242, who relates the use of חזה in Hab 1:1 with the visionary elements in 2:1 and 3:16.

When one recognizes the different transmission history of Hab 1-2 and 3, then the question must be asked how to explain the fact that Hab 1:1 and 3:1 both refer to "Habakkuk the prophet." Several possibilities exist. Both could stem from the same cultic personage;[27] 3:1 could derive from 1:1; or 1:1 could derive from 3:1. Given the separate transmission history, style, content, and traditions in the two sections of Habakkuk, it appears unlikely that they originate from the same author.[28] On the other hand, the use of the unparalleled phrase "Habakkuk the prophet" rules out any accidental occurrence of entirely independent origin of 3:1 and 1:1. It is not possible to answer the question of which verse depends upon the other for the identity of its author with absolute certainty, since neither 1-2 or 3:1-19 delve the personality of the prophet. Elsewhere, it has been shown that the information in the superscriptive elements was often derived from the writing itself, meaning that a redactor who intended to incorporate chapter three could easily have begun the writing with a superscription which took up the identity of the prophet from 3:1.[29] On the other hand, a redactor affixing chapter three to Hab 1-2 could presumably have had 1:1 from which to draw, and could have simply inserted the name, perhaps replacing Habakkuk for another name. When viewed in terms of probabilities, however, the scales tip toward the second option. The content of 1:1 is more general than 3:1, but it can be explained in relation to Hab 1-2.[30] Additionally, the combination of חזה with משא in Hab 1:1 appears also in Nah 1:1, which when combined with other similarities in the two works, argues that the superscription in Hab 1:1 came at the level of a common tradent.[31] It is highly significant, however, that these similarities imply the

---

[27] For a discussion of the cultic background of Habakkuk see Jöcken, *Das Buch Habakkuk*, 377-400.

[28] For fuller discussion of how these elements differ from chapters 1-2 see the literary discussion of Hab 3:1-19, below page 159ff.

[29] See the discussion of Amos 1:1 Nogalski, *Literary Precursors*, 76-78.

[30] Many interpret חזה in Hab 1:1 as a reference to 2:1-5 *and* to 3:7. For example, Rudolph, *KAT* 13/3, 199. See also Wilson's description of the function of משא in Robert R. Wilson, *Prophecy and Society in Ancient Israel* (Philadelphia: Fortress, 1980), 257-259. However, given the weight of the arguments of separate transmission histories, there is no reason to assume 3:7 had to be a part of the corpus to refer to the "vision" of Habakkuk.

[31] See also Isa 13:1, which introduces "The oracle against Babylon (as in Hab 1:1) which Isaiah the son of Amos saw." This similarity provides another link between the Isaiah tradition and the Book of the Twelve. This similarity provides more evidence of common transmission circles for Isaiah and the Book of the Twelve, but again not in the macrostructural sense described by Bosshard.

combination of both parts of Nah 1:1. Since the second portion of Nah 1:1 has already been determined as an expansion, it makes more sense that Nah 1:1 imitated Hab 1:1 than the other way around. By contrast, Hab 3:1 is very genre specific (the prayer of Habakkuk) in a way which can only relate to the frame (3:2,18f) surrounding the theophanic portrayal (3:3-17). It is quite possible that the name Habakkuk the prophet was inserted into this context. Thus, in all likelihood, Hab 3:1 draws upon the identity of the prophet mentioned in 1:1 for its formulation.

Hab 1:2-4 comprises the second unit, and may be classified as an individual complaint. The complaint begins with a direct question to YHWH in which the prophetic "I" speaks consistently. This unit extends until 1:5 begins a divine retort in oracular form. In 1:2-4, the prophet demands pointedly that YHWH respond to an unjust situation. The language combines legal, wisdom, and prophetic motifs to confront YHWH with the prosperity of the wicked. The prophet expresses great impatience with the delay of punishment on those doing "violence," causing the prophet to look upon iniquity and wickedness. Strife and contention exist so that תורה is ignored, justice is not upheld, and the wicked surrounds the righteous. This complaint has a clear aim: it seeks to goad YHWH to respond in order to change an unjust situation.

The identity of the wicked in these verses has elicited considerable discussion in scholarly circles.[32] The verses themselves do not state specifically what group they consider as the wicked, or which group they consider the righteous. The "crimes" depicted, however, do point toward an inner-Judean perpetrator of wickedness. The term "violence" has a juridical background. The mention of "law" and "justice" point in similar directions. However, the theological terms "iniquity" and "righteous," combined with the address to YHWH, indicate that the complaint's purpose is theological from the beginning. For this reason, most commentators correctly see a group of Judeans as the original cause of the complaint. The righteous are likewise to be understood as another, smaller, group of Judeans. Hence, Hab 1:2-4 depicts an unjust situation in which one Judean group oppresses another. The prophet stands in the middle and implores YHWH, as intermediary for the righteous, while at the same time belonging to that group.

---

[32] In addition to inner-Judean suggestions, theories on the identity of the wicked have included Scythites, Egyptians, Babylonians, Assyrians, and Greeks. These theories rest not on 1:2-4, but primarily upon interpretations of the material in the remainder of the book. See Jöcken, *Das Buch Habakuk*, 116-284.

The prophet confronts YHWH with his accusation that the wicked, and not the righteous, continue to prosper. Not only does this situation offend the prophet, in part because of the duration of the prosperity, but the prophet blames YHWH for the prosperity of the wicked.[33] These themes presupposes the traditional wisdom contention that the righteous will prosper and the wicked will be punished, but the verses seek to reconcile this contention with the the the current situation, where justice is perverted. In spite of the blame laid at the feet of YHWH, the prophet also operates with an implicit assumption that only YHWH can change the situation. Therefore the confrontation takes on a very personal character in the form of direct address to YHWH.

The incorporation of the numbing of "Torah" in 1:4 raises interesting tradition-historical questions. The major question of importance centers on the understanding of Torah in this context. Does Torah imply the written Pentateuch? If so, how much of the "law" does it imply? Johnson suggests that Hab 1:4 refers not to a law of commandments but to the promise contained in the Deuteronomic law.[34] This idea, while intriguing, overlooks the depiction of the crimes in 1:2-4, particularly strife and contention. These crimes do not take up the Deuteronomic "promise." Traditional understandings of תורה as "law," need not be modified. The particular manifestation of for the writer of Habakkuk in its early form should be treated in general terms. Unlike many passages in Deuteronomy, there is no indication that the author speaks of a written תורה.[35] Rather, the parallel word "justice" places the two on a narrower level, much more in keeping with texts such as Hag 2:11, which specifies priestly rulings upon specific questions. Literarily, Hab 1:4 appears to be related to Zeph 3:4, although 3:4 presupposes Hab 1:4 when it refers to Zion's prophets and

---

[33] Hence in 1:1 where the prophet demands to know: "How long will I call for help, and you will not hear?" touches on the offense and duration of the prosperity, while 1:2, "Why do *you* make me look on iniquity, and cause me to look on wickedness?", places the blame on YHWH.

[34] Marshall D. Johnson, "The Paralysis of Torah in Habakkuk 1:4," *VT* 35 (1985): 257-266. This promise for Johnson (262) includes the 1) retention of the promised land; 2) security from foreign oppressors; 2) security of the king; and 4) the continuance of the covenant and of divine חסד.

[35] Contrast the parallels Torah and justice in Hab 1:4 with the clear literary manifestations in places in Deuteronomy designating torah as the code or the book as a whole (1:5; 4:8,44; 17:18; 27:3,26; 28:58; 29:21,29; 30:10; 31:9,11-12; 32:46). See also Johnson's discussion of תורה and משפט, *VT* 35 (1985): 265.

priests: "Her prophets are reckless, treacherous men; her priests have profaned the sanctuary. They have done *violence to torah*."[36]

The divine speech in **1:5-11** incorporates a socio-political dimension with the punishment. YHWH's speech begins in 1:5, although the speaker in the MT can only be deduced from the context.[37] Hab 1:6 indicates unreservedly that YHWH delivers the address in that verse. Since 1:5f demonstrates no compelling syntactical reasons to suppose a literary break — whereas the use of the plural imperative separates 1:5 from 1:2-4 — one may confidently state that YHWH also speaks in 1:5.[38]

---

[36] Interestingly, all three of these passages omit the definite article ("the law") which typically appears in the Deuteronomy passages. Only one place in Deuteronomy omits the article, Deut 33:4.

[37] Contra Brian Peckham, "The Vision of Habakkuk," *CBQ* 48 (1986): 617-636, who argues 1:5 is still part of the prophetic complaint. Problems for determining the speaker in 1:5 arise from the lack of a formal literary marker and from the confusion of the versions. While the addressee in 1:5 leaves no doubt, the only place which could help clarify the speaker is open to various interpretations. The phrase כִּי־פֹעַל פֹעֵל can mean either "for a work works ..." or it can mean "for he is working a work ..." The latter initially appears the most likely on the basis of other Old Testament texts. Ps 44:2 is the only other place where both noun and verbal forms of פָּאל occur together in the same syntactical expression, but it also suggests that the expression in 1:5 should be understood as a stock formula. Additionally, Ps 44:2, together with other passages, indicates that the nominal form "work" would likely be understood as the object not the subject. However, Ps 90:16 provides evidence that "work" can also function as the subject, although the verb is different: "let your work appear (יראה) to your servants." The versions complicate the issue even further since both G and S have "*I* am working a work ...," meaning either 1) the 1cs pronoun has fallen out of the MT; 2) the verbal form was originally imperfect (אֶפְעַל); or 3) that both G and S have interpreted YHWH as the speaker. 1QpHab is often cited as being in agreement with MT, but the evidence there is not as clear cut as one might desire. The verse in question is missing in the Qumran text. Brownlee's reconstruction (*The Midrash Pesher of Habakkuk*, 53) of the text line follows MT, with the exception that he twice reconstructs the *plene* spelling of the conjunction כי with כיא. Brownlee does not explain why he uses this particular spelling in 1:5, whether by convention or for reasons of space, but the plene spelling need not have been present, especially in light of the fact that the very next line contains כי, not כיא. If the two additional occurrences of א were not present in the 1QpHab text, then there would have been room on that line for the 1cs pronoun אני, or most assuredly for the imperfect form. Nothing in the פשר itself allows a further decision, meaning that the evidence from 1QpHab *must be labelled inconclusive*. In summary, given the uncertainty of 1:5, with its multiplicity of possibilities, and given the clear signal in 1:6 that YHWH speaks, the most cautious approach would be to grant priority to 1:6 and interpret YHWH as the speaker.

[38] See also text notes to Hab 1:5 in Nogalski, *Literary Precursors*, 45.

A significant shift of perspective, compared with 1:2-4, arises from the change of characters in 1:5. Whereas 1:2-4 instigates a complaint in which the prophetic "I" addresses YHWH directly, 1:5 begins with a series of commands addressed *to the people*, which completely bypass the prophet's question and person. This sudden shift often gives rise to theories that the prophet functions as intermediary, and that this response to the people merely reflects an implicit recognition of this function.[39] Others assume the verse is transitional and that the prophet speaks the words, not carefully distinguishing between the role of the prophet delivering the oracle and YHWH as the intended speaker.[40] Yet such harmonizations neglect several literary markers which imply clearly that 1:5-11,12b has been inserted into the context.

The plural in 1:5 appears again in 1:12ab,b, except the people respond to YHWH: "*We* will not die. You, YHWH, have set him to judge. You have decreed him a rock to correct." The congregational *frame* of this YHWH speech thus contains references to the people at both ends, but does not address the prophet.[41] Moreover, it does not directly address the prophet's question, in spite of the fact that its position and form indicate that those who added the verses intended that they *function* as an oracular response. Whereas 1:2-4 questioned YHWH over the prosperity of the wicked, this oracular response pronounces judgment upon all of Judah.

Not only does the plural addressee alter the perspective of these verses, but the incorporation of the Babylonians in response to 1:2-4 comes as a tremendous shock. Apart from the communal frame, 1:5-11 is a speech depicting Babylonian ferocity. YHWH continues as the speaker, consistently speaking about the Chaldeans in 3ms. The depiction uses vivid imagery to demonstrate the unparalleled strength, speed, and cruelty of the Babylonian military machine. The real shock comes when YHWH decides to punish the wicked in 1:2-4 in a way which implies that all of Judah will suffer. The coming of the Babylonians is not an act of the deliverance of the oppressed or punishment of the guilty, but represents, from start to finish, an act of national punishment.

Serious questions regarding the integrity of 1:5-11 arise only in 1:11, which suddenly introduces the question of Babylonian guilt.[42] This twist

---

[39] So Rudolph, *KAT* 13/3, 205.

[40] So apparently Watts, *Joel, etc.*, 126; Elliger, *ATD* 25, 29.

[41] Below, page 142, it will be demonstrated why 1:12a belongs with the earlier layer of Habakkuk.

[42] Otto, *VT* 35 (1985): 281, does not assign Hab 1:11 to his anti-Babylonian layer with

in the action does indeed stand out, given the fact that the Babylonians come at YHWH's instigation (1:6), however, this twist *does not* represent a later addition to the unit. Rather, the change appears to be a deliberate shift on the part of the redactor who incorporated 1:5-11. The redactional insertion of 1:5-11 delineates a two-stage development. Babylon will punish Judah, but Babylon will be held guilty. This second stage is introduced in 1:11 by the adverb אז (then). The purpose of the shift, while surprising, is explainable in the literary context. Hab 1:12b represents the response of the people to 1:5-11 in general, but specifically, it presupposes 1:11.[43] The double aspect of a punishment against Judah by the Babylonians and Babylon's subsequent punishment is entirely understandable when read against the backdrop of similar motifs in Mic 7:8ff and Nah 1-3, where the same dynamic was portrayed for Assyria. These works have structured historical epochs redactionally: Judah is punished by Assyria; Assyria oversteps its role, bringing its own destruction.[44] Now Hab 1:5-11 brings these same motifs in condensed form. Judah sins (1:2-4) and YHWH uses Babylon to punish (1:5-10), while at the same time predicting Babylon will also fall because it too will overstep its role as YHWH's instrument (1:11,12b).[45] This structuring of history represents much more than an impromptu prophetic vision. It very much presumes a reflective literary technique used in conjunction with this portion of the Book of the Twelve. The literary nature of this perspective should become evident in the following sections which look at the remaining units of the dialogue and the relationship of the catchwords in 1:5ff to Nah 3:1ff.

The key to solving many of the compositional questions of Habakkuk appears in the composite complaint in 1:12-17 and the second oracular response in 2:1-5. The second complaint, Hab **1:12-17**, is composite, evidencing two distinct literary layers, the wisdom-oriented material which continues the initial encounter with YHWH from 1:2-4 and the commentary

---

1:15-17, despite the fact that it represents the same negative attitude toward the Babylonians. Jeremias, *Theophanie*, 78f, correctly notes the parallel functions of the motif of Babylonian power in these verses.

[43] Hence 1:12 may affirm "we will not die" on the basis of the punishment of the Babylonians pronounced in 1:11.

[44] See above discussion of Mic 7:8ff and its relationship to Isa 10 and the Hezekiah tradition.

[45] For a fuller discussion of this relationship see below, page 146, on the relationship of the *Stichwörter* to Nah 3:1-19. In addition, note the double expectation in Hab 3, which concentrates upon YHWH's future overthrow of the enemy, while at the same time displaying full cognizance of a future judgment against Judah (see especially Hab 3:16).

material which again focusses upon the ferocity of the Babylonians. The wisdom-oriented layer may be readily delineated by its use of the prophetic first person and its theme of the prosperity of the wicked. This layer continues the thoughts, style, and form of 1:2-4. This wisdom-oriented layer contains 1:12a*,13-14, and when seen beside the remainder of the complaint, the compositional character is readily observable:

Wisdom-oriented Layer	Babylonian Commentary
1:12a*: Truly you are from everlasting YHWH, my god, my holy one.	
→	1:12a*,b: We will not die. You, YHWH, have set him to judge. You have decreed him a rock to correct.
1:13-14: Too pure of eyes to see evil, and you are not able to look on trouble, Why do you look on the ones dealing treacherously, (or) become silent when the wicked swallows one more righteous than he? And have you made man like the fish of the sea? Like creeping things with no ruler over him?	←
→	1:15-17: All of them he brings up with a hook, and he drags him away in his net, and then he gathers him with his fishing net. Therefore he will rejoice and be glad. Therefore he will sacrifice to his net, and he will burn incense to his fishing net, because in these his portion grows robust, and his food becomes fat. Will he therefore empty his net, indeed continually slay nations without sparing?

When these elements are placed side by side, the differences become considerably clearer. Not only are the different themes recognizable, but also much of the confusion over the identity of the "he" clarifies itself. The wisdom-oriented layer continues the prophet's penetrating questioning of YHWH over the continued prosperity of the wicked. The same stylistic aspects are present in 1:12a,13-14 as in 1:2-4. The prophet speaks directly to YHWH (1:12a*): "my god, my holy one." The durative aspect of continued prosperity is thus present in 1:2-4,12a*,13f.[46] The prophet appeals to YHWH's holiness in order to provoke YHWH into response: "your eyes are too pure to look upon evil." (1:13) This appeal functions similarly to the affirmation of confidence so prevalent in complaints, and yet its continuation in the remainder of 1:13f consists of a series of pointed rhetorical questions which color the expression of confidence with more than a hint of sarcasm, providing a provocative tenor to the passage.[47] These rhetorical questions are themselves not the end of an original literary unit, rather their literary presence is assumed by 2:1-5, as will be noted briefly, and it is these questions for which the prophet receives a response, in the form of the wisdom-oriented foundational layer of woe oracles in 2:6ff discussed above.[48]

By contrast, the Babylonian commentary in 1:15-17 evidences none of the stylistic or thematic traits of the wisdom-oriented layer.[49] This commentary takes up the fish imagery in the last rhetorical question in the wisdom-oriented layer as the basis for a continuation of the depiction of Babylonian ferocity. As in 1:5-11,12b, Babylon is mentioned in 3ms. One must carefully distinguish the two referents in 1:15, both of which are mentioned in 3ms, the Babylonians and אדם (from 1:14).[50] In 1:16f the 3ms references all intend the Babylonians. The fact that 1:15 assumes the

---

46 Hence in 1:2 the prophet asks "How long YHWH?", and in 1:13 the prophet's question "Why are you silent when the wicked swallows one more righteous than he?"

47 The realization of the function of 1:13a as a quasi-affirmation of confidence negates the arguments of critics who deny two or more hands to this passage on form-critical grounds by saying the wisdom-oriented material contains no affirmation of confidence. Most of these scholars overlook 1:13, presumably because they consider it related to the Babylonian commentary in 1:15-17. See for example, Dykes, *Diversity and Unity in Habakkuk*, 82; Elliger, *ATD* 25, 26,34f. Elliger's contention that the expanded references to YHWH in 1:12a argue against an original continuation of 1:2-4 is not convincing enough to overcome the remaining similarities of style and theme.

48 See discussion of this material above beginning on page 130.

49 Peckham, *CBQ* 48 (1986): 618, correctly understands and labels this expanding layer as commentary, including 1:14-17. However, his assignation of much of 1:5-11 as a prophetic vision is far less convincing in light of the clear indications of its role and form as a divine speech. The same must also be noted with regard to why he assigns 1:14 to the commentary, when it is tied thematically and stylistically to the wisdom motifs.

50 Thus 1:15 intends the Babylonians as subject and אדם as object in when it says "he drags him away..." and "he gathers him..."

presence of 1:14 naturally implies that 1:15-17 was never an independent unit. Rather, 1:15-17 presents its own message as a continuation of the questions of the earlier layer, in much the same manner as the woe oracles receive reinterpretations in light of the attack of a foreign nation, as noted in the discussion of Habakkuk's macrostructure.

Hab 1:15-17 metaphorically portrays Babylon with fishing imagery. Babylon captures אדם with hook and net and rejoices. This rejoicing introduces another theme important to this depiction of the Babylonians, namely the false attribution of success to its own prowess. Hence the sentence, "He burns incense to his fishing net," metaphorically depicts what was already said in 1:11: "... he whose strength is his god." This idolatrous action reinforces the depiction of Babylon as having overstepped its role as YHWH's correcting instrument. The imagery culminates in 1:17, another rhetorical question directed to YHWH, which asks concerning Babylon: "Will he therefore empty his net, and continually slay nations without sparing?" On the basis of the common theme and style of 1:5-11 and 1:15-17 they should not be generically divided as indicative of two separate strata, positive and negative, toward the Babylonians. Rather, the tension of YHWH's selection of the Babylonians to punish YHWH while at the same time condemning them for not recognizing the source of this commission derives from the intention of both 1:5-11 and 1:15-17.[51]

The final unit of the dialogue section is the second oracular response in **Hab 2:1-5**. Not surprisingly, this response contains evidence of both the wisdom-oriented concerns and an expanded commentary style. The commentary material in this section may be assigned to the periphery since the primary aim of 2:1-5 relates very distinctly to the earlier wisdom-oriented material in 1:2-4,12a,13f. The appearance of the prophetic "I" in 2:1 places the opening of the unit in the stylistic realm of the wisdom-oriented layer. From there, the common interests continue. Whereas 1:14 brought the complaint about the prosperity of the wicked to a climax with a rhetorical question directed to YHWH, the prophet in 2:1 now prepares to receive an answer from YHWH. More telling still, the answer which the prophet receives very pointedly takes up the problem of the wisdom-oriented material by treating the "proud one" and "the righteous" (2:4). Indeed, unlike 1:5-11, the action in 2:1-5a involves only the prophet and YHWH. The people appear only in 3rd person references, and are not

---

[51] Contra Wellhausen, Dykes, Otto, etc. See introduction of Habakkuk's macrostructure, note 3.

directly involved.[52] For these reasons, 2:1ff may best be described as the *original* literary response in oracular form to the complaint of the wisdom-oriented layer.

Hab 2:1-5 not only presupposes the questions of the wisdom-oriented layer from Hab 1:2-4,12a,*13f, it also introduces the early layer of the woe oracles in 2:6ff. One readily recognizes that the addition of 2:5b,6a stems from the hand of the Babylonian commentator. Its political interest relates back to the Babylonian commentary, when it reinterprets the "haughty one" as the one who "gathers to himself all nations and collects to himself all peoples."[53] Hab 2:6a presupposes 2:5 with its claim that "these" will take up a taunt song against him. "These" must refer to the nations and "him" to the Babylonians. However, the first woe oracle proper (beginning in 1:6b) condemns the one who grows rich from loans, which ties in quite well with the haughty man who enlarges his appetite like Sheol in 2:5a.

In summary, literary observations on the dialogue section of Habakkuk demonstrate strong evidence that a redactional hand has taken a theological treatise questioning the prosperity of the wicked, and expanded it through the incorporation of oracular and commentary material which announces both YHWH'S use of Babylon for punishment, *and* the subsequent destruction of Babylon because it overstepped its role as YHWH's tool. A further step should now be taken which analyzes the common words between Nah 3:1-19 and Hab 1:1-17.

4. Hab 1:1-17 and the Relationship to *Stichwörter* in Nah 3:1-19

Having analyzed two literary layers in the dialogue section of Hab 1:2-2:5, it is possible to turn to the question of the relationship of Hab 1:1ff to Nah 3:1ff. In an attempt to evaluate the nature of the relationship, three questions arise: 1) Do the common words appear accidentally? 2) Has a *collector* merely placed two similar passages beside one another, influenced by their *pre-existing* similarities? Or 3) Has a *redactor* deliberately created

---

[52] Note 2:1f where the prophet's autobiographical style dominates and also in 2:2 where the response to write the vision appears in singular, not plural as in 1:5.

[53] This depiction is almost universally recognized as a reference to Babylon since even those who consider the book an original unity would be hard pressed to find a Judean expansion in the late 7th century. See Jeremias, *Kultprophetie* 65f. See also Rudolph, *KAT* 13/3, 216f, who relates this half-verse to the Babylonians despite the fact that he considers chapters 1 and 2 as separate literary pieces.

this similarity, and if so, for what reason? The consistent pattern of common words in the seams of the Book of the Twelve makes the first possibility unlikely. Already enough evidence has been brought in other connections to make one suspicious of an accidental relationship. A glance at the *Stichwörter* in light of the preceding literary observations dramatically decreases the possibility that the catchwords appear merely as the result of a collecting principle since the common words between the two passages occur *almost exclusively in the Babylonian layer.* Thus, an initial evaluation indicates the third possibility is the most likely. Further discussion will both strengthen this supposition and provide insights for determining the rationale motivating this connection.

If one looks at the catchwords noted in the translation of this passage, only three words appear in both Nah 3:1-19 and the wisdom-oriented layer in Hab 1: the verb "see" (Nah 3:7; Hab 1:3,13), "evil" (Nah 3:19; Hab 1:13a); and "sea" (Nah 3:8; Hab 1:14). All these words are too common, and too well embedded in their context, to carry much weight as deliberate connecting words between Nahum and Habakkuk. Of these three only, "sea" in Hab 1:14 can possibly have a more dynamic relationship to Nah 3, but that is only true if one compares "sea" in conjunction with the extended fishing metaphor in the Babylonian commentary which follows.[54]

Much more significant are the number and frequency of the catchwords appearing in the Babylonian oracle and commentary. Not only does this layer contain substantially more words, the words themselves and the images they provoke are much less likely to be attributed to an accidental occurrence. These words include: "nation(s)" (Hab 1:5,6,17), "horses," "horsemen," "gallop," "fly," "devour," (1:8), "horde," "captives" (1:9), "kings," "rulers," "fortress" (1:10), "strength" (1:11), "continually," "slay" (1:17).[55] Simply noting the presence of these words in the Babylonian material does not suffice, however, in understanding their relationship to Nah 3:1ff. One cannot refute the existence of these words and synonyms, but that is not the only similarity. Formulation of these words, in their context, relies upon interplay with Nah 3:1-19. The relationship between these two passages must be explained by their intention. Specifically, when compared with Nah 3:1-19, the Babylonian layer in Hab 1:5-11,12b,15-17

---

54   More below on the use of sea metaphors in both Nah 3:8f and Hab 1:15f.

55   These words appear in Nah 3:1-19 as well: "nation(s)" (3:4,5), "horse" (3:2), "horsemen" (3:2), "gallop" (see פרש in 3:18), "fly" (3:16), "devour" (3:8), "horde" (3:9), "captives" (3:9), "king" (3:18), "rulers" parallels "shepherds" in (3:18), "fortress" (3:8,12), "strength" (see "strengthen" in 3:14), "continually" (3:19), and "slay" (synonym in 3:3).

appears to be formulated in such a manner that it presents a *heightened parallel* to the announcement of the destruction of Nineveh.

The heightened parallel between Nineveh's destruction and Babylon's attack deliberately builds upon the images of Nineveh's fear and destruction in Nah 3:1ff, but in such a way that it heightens Babylon's portrayal as an enemy. Hence Nah 3:8f mocks Nineveh's *fortress* as a fig-tree ready to be picked, and its people as women afraid to fight. By contrast, Hab 1:10 depicts Babylon as one who mocks the leaders of other nations, and who laughs at every *fortress*. The fact that historically, Babylon was the one who destroyed Nineveh makes this parallel quite poignant. Another example of the way in which Habakkuk takes up and escalates the imagery of Nah 3:1ff appears in the use of the locust imagery. Nineveh's "locusts" hyperbolize its apparent numerical strength in order to dramatize its military weakness (Nah 3:15-17). By contrast, the "horde" of Babylonians moves forward in an unstoppable mass, collecting captives at will (Hab 1:9). Nineveh's preparations for the defense of its fortress are futile gestures (Nah 3:14), whereas Babylon pauses only to *laugh* at *every* fortress on its constant march of destruction (Hab 1:10). Nineveh is compared to Thebes, whose strength lay in its political alliances and secure location (Nah 3:8f), but Babylon's own strength is its god (Hab 1:11). Nineveh's people are scattered (פוש, niphal) in fear (Nah 3:18), while Babylon's military force creates fear by galloping (פוש, in qal) in to attack. The Ninevites grovel in the mud inside their fortress as it falls down around them (Nah 3:14), while the Babylonians laugh at every fortress, like so much dirt piled up for their amusement (Hab 1:11). Nah 3:18f evokes images of the mortal wound of Assyria's king, and it does so with more than a hint of mockery. Hab 1:10 depicts Babylon as the one who laughs at kings and rulers as a matter of course.

Some of the motifs in Nah 3:1ff are down-played or modified in the Habakkuk context. Nah 3:4-7 exposes Nineveh as a harlot who first seduces, then sells nations. This harlotry motif in the Old Testament carries strong connotations of idolatry, a motif which appears also in Hab 1:15f. The idolatry in that passage, again metaphorically portrayed, adapts itself to the Habakkuk context by re-emphasizing Babylon's belief in its own divinity (cf also 1:11). The motif in Habakkuk 1:15f owes its particular formulation to the fact that it comments upon 1:14: "(Why) have you made man like the *fish of the sea*?" This image serves as the backdrop to 1:15f where Babylon catches "fish" with hook and net, and then offers sacrifice to its own net, as though the net were a God.

The comparison of Nineveh to Thebes (Nah 3:8-11) plays no direct role, but this omission is understandable in light of the intention of the entire Babylonian material, which portrays Babylon as an incomparably destructive force. Whereas Thebes and, by extension of the metaphor, Nineveh relied on a network of alliances and a commanding fortress, Babylon relies on its own military muscle.

Another element which plays a significant role in the heightening of the parallelism between Nineveh and Babylon is the temporal aspect. Nah 3:18f leaves the indisputable impression that Assyria's destruction is imminent. The images in these verses presuppose that Assyria no longer poses a threat.[56] Its power and threat lay in the *past*, and its final condemnation, in the form of a rhetorical question, makes it clear that Assyria is condemned for the universal wickedness it *continually* perpetuated (3:19). By contrast, the Babylonian layer in Hab 1:5-11,15-17 not only portrays Babylon as a greater power, but the threat of its arrival lies in the immediate *future* (1:5). This future threat is accentuated by the same rhetorical device. Hab 1:17 presents a rhetorical question which underscores both the threat and the parallel to Nah 3:19 when it asks if Babylon will "*continually* slay nations without sparing?"

The threat Babylon poses, like the depiction of its power, plays off Nahum. Nineveh's crime was the way it treated the nations (Nah 3:4,5,19), but denunciation of this crime is filtered through a Judean lens (Nah 2:1). Habakkuk (in its combined form) implies this same dialectic. Babylon's wickedness is directed universally (Hab 1:6,10,17), although inner-Judean circumstances provoke the oracle (1:2-4) and the pungency of the threat lies in the fact that it *includes* YHWH's people (1:5,12ab, see also 3:16b). This inclusion of judgment recognizes implicitly *both* the historical destruction of Jerusalem *and* the theological interpretation of that destruction as a result of the people's sin. It also implies a destruction which would leave only a remnant. Thus, the communal response in 1:12b ("*We* will not die."), curious though it might be, evidences a conviction which has parallels elsewhere in the Book of the Twelve: a punishment is coming which will purify Jerusalem and Judah, but which will ultimately lead to salvation. This same curious expectation of deliverance in the face of destruction has its nearest parallels in Mic 7:11-13 and particularly in Hab 3:16b: "I will wait quietly for the day of distress, for the people to arise who will invade

---

[56] In a certain sense the entire chapter, and even the entire book, may be seen in this light, but the images are particularly strong in 3:18f. Compare also Nah 2:1.

us." This expectation is one of the underlying motifs helping to fashion a literary "story-line" through the Book of the Twelve.[57]

The expanded structure of Habakkuk, which includes both the wisdom-oriented material and the Babylonian commentary, fits well into the section of the Twelve which runs from Micah to Habakkuk. This section intertwines lament or complaint with theophanic material, as already noted in the discussion of the Nahum acrostic. After a discussion of Hab 3:1-19, this pattern will be evaluated in more detail. Here, it need only be noted that the portrayal of Babylon as YHWH's instrument of punishment against his recalcitrant people corresponds with the prediction of Assyria as YHWH's rod of punishment in Mic 7:14, and it brings to fruition the prediction in Mic 7:12f that there will be a day when they will come from the Euphrates (among other places) to make the land a desolation.

5. Redactional Summary and Re-evaluation of the Date of Hab 1:1-17

Recognition of two literary layers in Hab 1:1-17 greatly alleviates many of the tensions in the dialogue section of Habakkuk. The two layers separate readily from one another in terms of theme, style, vocabulary, and interests. The wisdom-oriented layer (1:2-4,12a,13-14) existed in literary form, and led directly to the response oracle described in 2:1ff, which in turn introduced the early form of the series of woe oracles (2:6ff).[58] The

---

[57] Other passages indicate remnant theology as well, although perhaps not on the same literary level. However, at least some of these would have already been present in the corpus, and would have helped further this aspect. See especially Amos 9:10. This literary element climaxes in Zephaniah, but does not disappear entirely. Rather, there appears to be a certain redactional interest in drawing attention to the fact that just as YHWH punished you once he can do it again if you do not obey. See Zech 1:6; 8:14-17, Mal 1:5ff.

[58] Compare not only the literary observations and the macrostructure described above, but also recent works, whose own observations come relatively close to recognition of the same layered division of Habakkuk. See especially, A.H.J. Gunneweg, "Habakuk und das Problem des leidenden צדיק." ZAW 98 (1986): 400-415; Eckart Otto, "Die Theologie des Buches Habakuk." VT 35 (1985): 274-295. Both of these articles differ from the present construction in certain details, most notably Otto's isolation of more than two layers. Such dissection into numerous layers, however, appears unlikely on the basis of the preceding analysis. Gunneweg's article offers a very perceptive interaction with both Otto and Jeremias (Kultprophetie), properly correcting Jeremias assertion that the initial Überarbeitung was directed against the Babylonians

unexpanded oracles dealt specifically with the question of the suffering of the righteous.[59]

The Babylonian layer (1:5-11,12b,15-17) presupposes both the wisdom-oriented material and Nah 3:1-19. It provides a heightened parallel to the picture of Nineveh in Nah 3:1ff, while contrasting the past threat of Nineveh with the ferocity of the imminent Babylonians threat. Most of the comparative material appears in 1:5-11. The Babylonian commentary to the second complaint primarily plays off Hab 1:14, although the final rhetorical question is formulated on the basis of Nah 3:19, with תמיד serving as *inclusio*.

While Hab 1:1-17 does not paint a positive picture of Babylon, neither does it polemicize against them. The announced judgment is directed at Judah. Only 1:11 pronounces judgment against Babylon, but this verse makes clear that Babylon's judgment will come only after they invade Judah. The remainder of the layer portrays Babylon as a power against which no human ruler can stand. Two other places insinuate the *eventual* downfall of Babylon: the communal assertion of confidence (1:12b) intimates the survival of at least some of the people while simultaneously recognizing the punishment to come; and the plea, in the form of the rhetorical question in 1:17 hints of a future beyond the punishment. This rhetorical question in particular serves a major role in understanding the negative pronouncements against Babylon in the expanded woe oracles. The rhetorical question serves to introduce the divine response in 2:1ff. In this sense, it reinterprets that reply, from one in which the prophet waits for YHWH's response to the question regarding the prosperity of the wicked (1:13f), into a response to the question whether Babylon will destroy nations forever. Hab 1:17 phrases the question such that a negative answer is expected: Babylon will not continually slay nations forever. The expanded woe oracles presuppose this hermeneutic, providing prophetic condemnation of Babylon. Hab 3:1ff, as will be shown, brings another dimension to this same portrayal — YHWH will deliver his people, but they will be punished first.

By recognizing the Babylonian layer, and particularly its function regarding Nah 3:1-19, one shifts the perspective considerably with regard

---

(Gunneweg, 405f). He also accents Otto's contention that 1:5-11 belongs to the reworking of the basic material. Also significant is Gunnewg's discussion, throughout his article, which seeks to explain the mixture of wisdom and prophetic traditions.

[59] See the careful development of the *Grundbestand* of Hab 1-2 in Gunneweg, *ZAW* 98 (1986): 400-415, particularly §5-7 (407-414).

to the date of Habakkuk. On the one hand, the objections to a traditional 7th century date, mentioned at the beginning of the discussion of Habakkuk, can now be more readily explained. On the other hand, the assignation of a precise date for Habakkuk becomes considerably more complicated. This complication stems in part from the function of the Babylonian layer as a heightened parallel to Nah 3:1-19. This layer deliberately seeks to shape history according to an epochal schema corresponding essentially to the portrayal of the Deuteronomistic school, which placed the blame for Babylon's destruction of Jerusalem upon Judah's rulers.[60] This epochal depiction of history, using prophetic forms, represents a considerably later perspective than one from the 7th century. Indeed, when one recognizes the use of the Chaldeans to portray this history, combined with the fact that it reinterprets a pre-existing *literary* work, one can no longer regard the Habakkuk book as the work of a contemporary of Jeremiah. Hence, the use of a Babylonian name for a prophet, the presence of Torah, and the imprecise portrayal of the Babylonians could be explained as stemming from the post-exilic period.

The implications of the secondary and interpretive nature of the Babylonian layer complicates the dating of Habakkuk still further by the fact that the elimination of the reference to Babylon as part of the *early Habakkuk corpus* also eliminates essentially the only *concrete* dating criteria from the book. After the Babylonian layer is suspended from consideration, the remaining material in Hab 1-2 presents a very general picture of the prosperity of the wicked while the righteous suffer. One must then rely on an evaluation of internal criteria to delimit the date of Habakkuk further. Several observations point toward the post-exilic period as a likely date for the early corpus. One of the most significant is the reference to תורה in Hab 1:4, used with legal implications, which coincides well with Hag 2:11, whose early post-exilic date is beyond repute.[61] This significant sentence — "Ask now the priests for a ruling" (תורה) — implies a priestly decision, not the book (see Hag 2:12). This same connotation fits Hab 1:4, where the complaint that the priestly decisions, along with משפט, are not taken seriously.

A second observation pointing toward a post-exilic time-frame regards the use of the Babylonian name "Habakkuk." Simply stated, the name

---

[60] See 2 Kgs 25:1ff, and the negative portrayal of the kings throughout the Deuteronomistic history, with the only real exceptions being Hezekiah and Josiah. Relatedly, see Jer 50:17f.

[61] See discussion below of the date of Haggai.

implies cultural interaction with Babylon, yet the further away one gets from the period of Babylonian domination, the less understandable the name becomes. The name does not appear to presume a symbolic interpretation, meaning that its use is best explained by Babylonian interaction with Judean culture in some way.[62] One would be safe to presume that the naming of a child with a Babylonian name took place after the immediate emotions against Babylon as conqueror had passed. Caution must be exercised, however, since one does not know precisely how this interaction took place.[63]

A third observation regarding the dating of the early corpus appears in 2:1 with reference to the guardpost (משמרת) and bulwark (מצור). Hab 2:1 clearly belongs to the early corpus, and assumes a situation in which some type of defence structure exists around the city. This sentence, particularly with the unaccented manner in which these structures are mentioned, all but eliminates the exilic period from consideration, since these terms must presuppose the presence of the city wall, the temple, or both at the time of the original composition. The use of משמרת increases the likelihood of post-exilic origin, given the preponderance of examples in P, and its relationship to Levitic responsibility for the temple.[64] The use of מצור in this sense likely relates to prophetic functions, and although a

---

[62] Habakkuk distinguishes itself somewhat in this regard from other writings such as Obadiah, Malachi, and Nahum, all three of which have been interpreted by some as having symbolic associations with their book. These suggested associations are difficult to prove in light of the sparsity of knowledge regarding the naming of prophets and cult officials. See discussions of the superscriptions.

[63] Babylonian influence could have come in many different forms, and one cannot even assume the birth took place in Babylon. Several scenarios would place Habakkuk's ministry well into the Persian period. One example will suffice, if "Habakkuk" was named in Babylon as the son of Jewish parents, who shortly thereafter returned to their homeland, then the ministry of "Habakkuk" could easily be placed in the first quarter of the 5th century. Even with this scenario, it is not impossible to imagine an older man writing closer to the middle of the 5th century. The fact that many Jewish exiles remained in Babylon when others returned could push an explanation of "Habakkuk" even further into the Persian period.

[64] See J. Milgrom and L. Harper, "משמרת," ThWAT, vol 5, 78-85. Their article draws attention to the fact that the term appears mostly in later Biblical materials. They also demonstrate a close connection of the term with the Levites. They assign Hab 2:1 to pre-exilic material (84), but their contention that only pre-exilic texts exhibit the nuance "Wachposten," appears problematic in light of the other example they cite as pre-exilic. They cite Isa 21:8 as pre-exilic, but its prediction of the fall of Babylon must stem from the late exilic or early post-exilic period.

date is less determinative for this word, the Biblical evidence appears strongly slanted toward post-destruction literature.[65]

One final observation deserves mention briefly, namely, that the deep questioning of YHWH concerning the prosperity of the wicked which dominates this dialogue has its closest thematic parallels with post-exilic wisdom literature, particularly with Job. This relationship does not manifest itself in literary form, but one basic question dominates both — "Why does YHWH allow the wicked to prosper?"   While the vast majority of commentators argue for a post-exilic composition of Job, the lack of agreement on a specific date, combined with the non-literary relationship do not allow specific deductions regarding the date of Habakkuk.[66]

In summary, a precise date for Habakkuk poses real difficulties, although there is a strong likelihood that the *both* the wisdom-oriented layer and its Babylonian expansion are post-exilic. This evidence rests upon the manner in which the Babylonian layer portrays itself upon the basis of Nah 3:1ff, and upon the vocabulary and thematic parallels of the wisdom-oriented layer.   Further evidence for such a dating comes when one considers the function which Hab 3:1-19 serves in the Habakkuk corpus and in its position in the Book of the Twelve.

6. Cultic Transmission of Hab 3:1-19

Habakkuk 3:1-19 combines many diverse images.   In order to understand how these images fit together compositionally, one must first

---

[65] Jeremias, *Kultprophetie*, 105f, demonstrates the background of the word, but his reliance strictly upon parallels outside Biblical literature eschews the fact that the word appears most frequently in exilic or post-exilic Biblical passages: e.g. 2 Chr 8:5; 11:5; Ezek 4:2; Mic 4:14; Zech 9:3. At the very least, this would indicate the word was in use for a period of time so extended that it cannot be used as evidence of pre-exilic origin. The two passages normally attributed to an exilic setting (Ezek 4:2; Mic 4:14) refer back to the destruction of Jerusalem, a feature which distinguishes them from Hab 2:1, where the prophet simply says he will go to the מצור.

[66] See discussion of the problems for dating Job in Norman C. Habel, *The Book of Job*, OTL (London: SCM, 1985), 40-42. The problems stem from the lack of historical events or the use of other Israelite traditions, which has led to more cautious statements regarding the precise date of Job. See the particularly strong polemic of J.J.M. Roberts, "Job and the Israelite Religious Tradition," *ZAW* 89 (1977): 107-114. See also the cautious statements of Otto Kaiser, *Einleitung in das Alte Testament. Eine Einführung in ihre Ergebnisse und Probleme* (Gütersloh: Gütersloher, 1969), 305f.

separate them from one another. Given the divergent backgrounds of the various images in this chapter, prudence demands beginning with elements which are the easiest to isolate before moving into more debated areas. In Hab 3:1-19, the elements most readily delimited are the cultic notations.

The evidence of cultic transmission in Hab 3:1-19 appears in the trifold use of סלה (Hab 3:3,9,13), in the superscription (3:1), and in the postscription (3:19b). The word סלה demonstrates a cultic connection, since elsewhere the word appears only in the Psalter. Several suggestions with regard to its meaning have been offered, and while no single solution has created a consensus, the most common suggestions demonstrate the word should be associated with the cultic performance of psalms.[67] The word occurs almost exclusively in Pss 3-89, or the first three books of the Psalter.[68] The ruling theory suggests that one sweeping redaction of the Psalter was responsible for the vast majority of these notations.[69] Scholars universally agree, however, that סלה was added to the pss in which it appears, and do not believe it was a part of the original composition.

The presence of סלה in Hab 3:3,9,13 carries considerable implications for both the transmission history and dating of Hab 3:1ff. Its presence provides a clear link to those responsible for the transmission of cultic songs. This link is undeniable since סלה appears elsewhere only in the Psalms. However, caution must be exercised since it is not yet clear what function סלה serves in Hab 3:3,9,13, and how this function relates to the question of the literary unity of the chapter. Until these questions are answered one cannot specify on what level and how intricately this cultic transmission affected the shape of Hab 3:1ff, or how this cultic transmission relates to the question of the *Stichwörter* between Hab 3:1ff and Zeph 1:1ff. The presence of סלה implies redactional work on the passage during a relatively limited time period. Evidence from the psalter demonstrates the

---

[67] Two suggestions appear most frequently, although these two ideas are not necessarily treated as mutually exclusive: (1) those who understand סלה as the mark of a refrain, and (2) those who see סלה as a notation for accompanists. Further discussion may be found in R. Gyllenberg, "Die Bedeutung des Wortes Sela," *ZAW* 58 (1940/41): 153-156; Norman H. Snaith, "Selah," *VT* 2 (1952): 43-56; Sigmund Mowinckel, *The Psalms in Israel's Worship*, vol 2 (Oxford: Basil Blackwell, 1962), 221; Walter Beyerlin, *Der 52. Psalm. Studien zu seiner Einordnung*, BWANT 111 (Stuttgart: Kohlhammer, 1980), 124f.

[68] The only two exceptions are Pss 140 and 143.

[69] See Beyerlin, *Der 52. Psalm*, 124f. Even if the "single redaction" proposal is perhaps too simplified, one may say confidently that the use of סלה was limited to a specific time period. Beyerlin's arguments that the Levitical temple singers were the group responsible for this marking appears quite plausible.

word is essentially limited to the first three books of the psalms, and is not spread equally over the entire psalter.[70] This isolation of סלה implies the word was "in vogue" for a relatively short time span. The ruling consensus is that this סלה redaction occurred in the Persian period.[71] This opinion provides a relatively fixed element for dating one portion of Hab 3:1ff which must be born in mind after it can be determined how intricately this cultic handling of Hab 3:1ff effects the text and the connection to Zephaniah.[72] It is easily demonstrated that סלה, as in the Psalter, is not intrinsic to Hab 3:1-19. What is perhaps more significant still is the fact that these cultic notations are all limited to the theophanic hymn (3:3-15), and not to the literary frame (3:1f,16-19). This isolation raises the question whether the presence of סלה is more properly understood as a part of the history of the theophanic hymn than of its current literary position within a prophetic writing.[73] One must acknowledge, in any case, that the inclusion of סלה in Hab 3:3,9,13 was cultically influenced. In addition to סלה there are two other examples of the cultic handling of this text (the superscription and the postscription) which strongly suggest that cultic transmission was more than peripheral.

The superscription (3:1) also demonstrates a connection to the cult with its reference to "prayer," the prophet (הנביא), and the expression "according to Shigionoth." The use of prayer (תפלה) highlights a certain perspective of the chapter. The designation leads one to suspect direct communication between the prophet and YHWH, but one must assess this supposition with caution. Often the superscriptive titles of the psalms are not closely related to the contents within.[74] Simple designations of source on the basis of address to or about YHWH are not therefore easily achieved. Elsewhere, the description "prayer" in the psalter can also demonstrate this same admixture of perspective.[75]

---

[70] The word סלה appears around seventy times in the first three books of the psalter, but afterwards only in Pss 140:4,6; 143:6.

[71] See Beyerlin, *Der 52. Psalm*, 124.

[72] This time frame is strengthened further by evidence from the subscription which places that cultic element within the same general sphere. See below, note 81.

[73] For discussion of this literary frame and the relationship to the hymn, see below 159ff and 173ff.

[74] See Klaus Seybold, *Die Psalmen. Eine Einführung*, Urban Taschenbücher 382 (Stuttgart: Kohlhammer, 1986), 93.

[75] As superscription, the word תפלה appears in Pss 86:1; 90:1; 102:1; 142:1, but it does not allow a definite conclusion. The characteristics of those pss are as follows: Ps 86 is in prayer style throughout, and is formulated in individual style. Ps 90 is communal,

In the case of Hab 3:1-19, direct address of the prophet to god does appear in 3:2,8-15, but not in 3:3-6,16-19. The designation "prayer" could have been a simplifying characterzization of a complex mixture of material. If so, this simplification attempts either to isolate certain parts of the chapter or, more neutrally, merely attempts to classify complex material with some general term. A second possibility is that the designation could indicate an earlier form which was perhaps more consistent in its presentation of material as a "prayer" between YHWH and the prophet. Of these two alternatives, the first option appears by far the more likely, because the cultic material appears in both the 2ms and 3ms material. One of the סלה (3:3) and also the postscript (3:19b) occur in material which does not exhibit direct address to YHWH, while the two remaining סלה (3:9,13) and the superscription (3:1) appear in 2ms oriented contexts.

The word "prophet" (נביא) is normally associated with cult prophecy. There is strong Deuteronomistic attestation of the office, but the word is not frequently used of the writing prophets.[76] This infrequency has sometimes been used to impose a dichotomy between cult prophets and "genuine" prophets of God.[77] However, work in recent years has liberated the term from such polemics.[78] The use of the term applied to Habakkuk does not by itself argue for a specific date, although its presence in the book is somewhat troublesome for dating the book as pre-exilic.[79]

---

but likewise consistent with its designation — with the psalmist speaking explicitly for the congregation, but always directly to God. Careful distinction must be drawn between the style, which addresses YHWH directly, and the content, which seeks to interpret the present situation to the congregation (see 90:7). Ps 102:16-24 interrupts the direct address to YHWH present in the remainder of the psalm (1-15,25-29) with an extended section (16-24) which talks about YHWH. Ps 142 begins with statements about YHWH (2-3), but continues with direct address (4-8).

[76] For statistics and analysis of the occurrences see Robert R. Wilson, *Prophecy and Society in Ancient Israel* (Philadelphia: Fortress, 1980), 136. See however Jer 1:5; and the superscriptions in Hag 1:1; Zech 1:1).

[77] Also playing a factor in this negative evaluation of cult prophecy was certain inner Biblical polemicizing against "prophets." See, for example, Amos 7:14.

[78] See Gene M. Tucker, "Prophecy and Prophetic Literature," in *The Hebrew Bible and Its Modern Interpreters* (Chico, California: Scholars Press, 1985), 348-350; Wilson, *Prophecy and Society in Ancient Israel*.

[79] Jeremias, *Kultprophetie*, 104, points out that it is noteworthy that Habakkuk is the only pre-exilic prophet whose superscription names the author as a נביא. Wilson, *Prophecy and Society*, 136-138, attributes the term to the influence of the Ephraimite tradition, although he admits it usage was not limited to that tradition.

A third sign of cultic transmission in 3:1 is the word "Shigionoth." The noun appears elsewhere only in Ps 7:1, and there it occurs in the singular. Its meaning is not easy to determine. In Ps 7:1 it appears to be a type of poem, but the preposition עַל and the plural form in Hab 3:1 would appear to indicate musical instruments. Complicating the issue still further is the fact that several textual traditions understood the term as a reflection of the mental state of the author.[80] Still, combined with the use of סלה, it adds to the assumption of the cultic transmission of Hab 3:1ff.

In addition to the superscription and the presence of סלה, the postscript (3:19b) also contains evidence of cultic transmission. The postscript refers to the choir director and to stringed instruments, both of which have strong connections to the psalter.[81] Both words correspond to the aspect of cultic performance present with the use of סלה. Interestingly, the presence of a postscriptive element in Hab 3:19b has no correlation to the first three books of the Psalter. Only a few psalms have postscripts, and even fewer have both superscription and postscript.[82]

Thus the third chapter of Habakkuk has an undeniable relationship to the cult. The cultic evidence appears at the beginning, in the middle, and at the end of the chapter, but nowhere else in the Habakkuk corpus or in the book of the Twelve. These special markings in a prophetic text argue very strongly that Hab 3:1ff had a transmission history separate from the rest of the book. The tendency of scholars to assume this chapter exhibits a literary unity with the remainder of the book is extremely difficult to reconcile with the peculiar transmission history it has received. It strains

---

[80] See the discussions in Rudolph and Robertson. Rudolph, *KAT* 13/3, 232f, demonstrates the complexity of the problem from a text-critical perspective. O. Palmer Robertson, *Nahum, Habakkuk, Zephaniah*, NICOT (Grand Rapids: Eerdmans, 1990), 215, tries to balance the cultic with the ecstatic, and cautiously postulates an emotional poetic form.

[81] "To the choir director" (למנצח) is the most common superscriptive element of address in the Psalter, appearing 55 times. As with סלה, the use of the term is limited almost exclusively to the first three books of the psalter. Only three times does it appear in the last two books of the psalter (109; 139; 140). Outside the Psalter, the choir director appears only in Hab 3:19 and 2 Chr 34:13, part of the Chronicler's account of Josiah's reforms. Although not as frequent, the reference to stringed instruments is also typical of superscriptions in the psalter, see: Ps 4:1; 6:1; 54:1; 55:1; 67:1; 76:1.

[82] See Gerald Henry Wilson, *The Editing of the Hebrew Psalter*, SBL Dissertation Series 76 (Chico, California: Scholars Press, 1985), 242f. Wilson, 236f, also compares Hab 3:1+19 with the typical order of the superscriptive elements in the Psalter, but does not take up the question why the elements are separated. None of those psalms bearing subscripts contain the elements found in Hab 3:19b. These elements appear only as superscriptive elements in the psalter.

the imagination to believe that the chapter received this cultic treatment after it was already incorporated into the Habakkuk corpus, since this manner of reworking does not exist elsewhere in the book.   This conceptualization would require a very strange redactional process. Much more plausible is the assumption that the cultic handling of this text occurred *prior* to its incorporation into the corpus. This explanation, however, complicates the question of the literary relationship of 3:1-19 to the remainder of the book. If the chapter as a block had a separate pre-history from chapters 1-2, then one must ask on what level the literary relationship exists. This question can only be addressed after some consideration of the literary units inside the material has been evaluated.

7. The Literary Units in Hab 3:3-15

An overview of the macrostructure of Hab 3:1-19 reveals that the prophetic "I" speeches in 3:2,7,16,18f provide the dominant framing device. In Hab 3:2 the prophetic "I" addresses God directly. The prophetic "I" in Hab 3:7 reports a vision, in which Cushan and Midian under distress.[83] Hab 3:7 includes the prophet in the action of the theophany more directly than the remainder of the prophetic "I" material (3:2,16,18f).   The prophetic "I" in Hab 3:16 offers a response of fear, but the response does not appear entirely appropriate to the immediate context of the theophanic psalm (3:8-15). Hab 3:18-19a also brings a reaction which, in its present position, follows the mention of the infertility of the land in 3:17, but 3:17 is so isolated thematically that a great many scholars label it as an addition.

The remainder of the chapter separated by the prophetic "I" speeches combines diverse theophanic traditions. Hab 3:3-6 describes YHWH's judgment theophany and the effect of that arrival. Hab 3:8-15, a poetic theophany in which direct address to YHWH dictates the style, contains images from a different tradition-historical background than 3:3-7. Despite these differences, most do not assign 3:3-7 and 3:8-15 to separate sources. They speak more of a blending of traditions.[84] Unanimity does not exist

---

[83] The problem of identifying these enemies is discussed below.

[84] Jeremias, *Theophanie*, 44f, typifies this perspective. He argues: "Es sind in Hab. 3 Vorstellungen ganz verschiedener Art miteinander verflochten worden. Der Verfasser konnte gar nicht genug Material sammeln, um die Herrlichkeit und Furchtbarkeit des Kommens Jahwes zu beschreiben und den grenzenlosen Schrecken alles Seienden

on this question, however, and there are those who do separate the passages on the basis of their differences in style and tradition.[85] Hab 3:3-7 takes up the Sinai theophanic traditions such as Judg 5:4f and Deut 33:2. By contrast, Hab 3:8-15 utilizes imagery from the victory over chaos, and has a more universal interest.[86]

In sum, while the prophetic "I" sayings function as a unifying element of the chapter, these sayings themselves exhibit several areas of tension which require some attempt at explanation, both from the context of the individual units and from their position in the chapter. Pragmatically, it will be necessary to look first at the two theophanic sections (3:3-7,8-15) in more detail before turning to the literary frame (3:2,16-19).

Hab **3:3-7** presents the first theophanic description, which begins suddenly with no preparation. The internal flow of the description as well as certain inclusionary elements indicate the unit extends to 3:7.[87] The lack of transition from 3:2, the change of style, and radically different content all argue against an integral connection to the preceding verse. The question as to whether 3:3 could ever have existed apart from 3:2, however, is complex. The announcement of a theophany can and does begin elsewhere with a statement of the arrival of the divinity which begins as abruptly as 3:3, but such is the exception not the rule.[88] Significantly, the presence of סלה does not argue definitively against the independent origin of Hab 3:3ff, since its usage in the Psalter can also appear at or near the opening sentence of a work.[89] However, such functions for סלה are

---

auszumalen." See also 94-97.

[85] See for example, William F. Albright, The Psalm of Habakkuk," *Studies in Old Testament Prophecy, Presented to Professor Theodore H. Robinson, by the Society for the Old Testament Study on his 65. Birthday August 9th, 1946.* H.H. Rowley, ed. (Edinburgh: T&T Clark, 1950), 8f.

[86] These images appear frequently in Old Testament texts, in large part due to the age of the traditions which have been repeated and adapted throughout the ancient near east. See above all, Fritz Stolz, *Strukturen und Figuren im Kult von Jerusalem. Studien zur altorientalischen vor- und frühisraelitischen Religion.* BZAW 118 (Berlin: De Gruyter, 1970). For a more narrowly directed discussion, concentrating on the Old Testament material, see also John Day, *God's Conflict with the Dragon and the Sea: Echoes of a Canaanite Myth in the Old Testament* (Cambridge: Cambridge University Press, 1985).

[87] See discussion of 3:7 below.

[88] Compare for example, Amos 1:2.

[89] See Ps 67:2, where the position of סלה comes after the opening bi-cola of the hymn. Other occurrences near the beginning of a work add to the impression that the position of the word in the hymn was not an essential factor in its usage: see Pss 3:3; 82:2.

not typical. In the end, form critical observations argue that 3:2 should likely be seen as an introductory verse and not separated from 3:3 as a later addition.[90] Hab 3:3 thus belongs with Hab 3:2.

Hab 3:3 announces a theophany of God's arrival from Teman/Edom.[91] The use of בוא with the preposition "from" implies origin of movement, that is, God comes from Teman. Other theophanies from the Edom area indicate a relationship with the Sinai tradition.[92] Hab 3:3b implies a positive image (the heavens and earth are full of his praise), which is somewhat surprising, in light of the fact that elsewhere in the Twelve, Edom does not play a positive role.[93] Even more surprising, the area in question also plays no significant role in Hab 1-2. Hiebert, and others, are thus correct in questioning the assumption of an integral connection of all of Hab 3:1-19 with the same author as the first two chapters.[94]

Hab 3:4 continues the positive image, although the tenor begins to change. Following the pronouncement of his splendor and praise, the description of his awe-inspiring appearance is natural. However, the

---

[90] See discussion of Hab 3:2 below, page 173.

[91] The use of the word אלוה is unusual in the prophetic writings. It appears frequently in Job, but also appears in the context of other songs: Ps 18:32; 50:22; 114:7; 139:19. Of some significance perhaps is the fact that the Song of Moses also uses the word (Deut 32:15,17). Its selection for Hab 3:3 may perhaps be attributable to the phonetic considerations of the poet: see Hiebert, *God of My Victory: The Ancient Hymn in Habakkuk 3*, Harvard Semitic Monographs 38 (Atlanta: Scholars Press, 1986), 84, who notes the strong phonetic interplay of 3:3 with 3:7.

[92] Cf Deut 33:2; Judg 5:4f. See the discussion of the problems with the identification of the precise locations of Teman and Paran in Theodore Hiebert, *God of My Victory*, 84-88. See also Jeremias, *Theophanie*, 9f.

[93] Teman is specifically mentioned in Obad 9; Amos 1:12. Elsewhere Edom receives condemnation in the Book of the Twelve: Amos 9:12; Joel 4:19; Obadiah; Mal 1:2-4. It not impossible, given the work of Bosshard, *BN* 40 (1987), 34, that this reference was *intended to be read* as implying Edom's downfall in much the same manner as Isa 34:5ff, but more definite statements cannot be made at present. The presence of other theophanic traditions connected with the region rule out the possibility that the original intention of this passage intended one to presume the destruction of Edom, but its position near the Isaiah parallels (Isa 32-33) noted by Bosshard could certainly point in this direction. Further support appears only insofar as one can clearly say that the only other passage concerning Edom in the Book of the Twelve still to come, Mal 1:2-5, presumes judgment on that nation has already occurred.

[94] Hiebert, *God of My Victory*, 1f; see also Lawrence Boadt, *Jeremiah 26-52, Habakkuk, Zephaniah, Nahum*. Old Testament Message 10 (Wilmington, Delaware: Michael Glazier, 1982), 162.

inclusion of military imagery introduces a different dimension than 3:3. The reference to the hiding place of his strength definitely implies a threat.

Hab 3:5 makes the threat explicit. With pestilence and plague as the accompaniment, the arrival of God arrayed for battle has an entirely different character from the positive beginning of the announcement. Comparison with other ancient near eastern theophanies demonstrates Deber and Resheph once functioned as more than metaphors for plague and pestilence. They were at one point lesser gods accompanying the arrival of the divinity.[95] Until now, the poem has not mentioned the recipient of God's wrath.

Hab 3:6f provides the reaction of the cosmos and of humanity to YHWH's appearance. The cosmic reaction appears in the collapse of the mountains and hills, while 3:7 describes the fear of the nomadic peoples of the desert. That the poem intends Midian and Cushan as references to nomads may be deduced from the fact that the poem describes both entities with reference to nomadic dwellings (the tents of Cushan; the tent curtains of the land of Midian). The exact identification of these two regions in the mind of the writer is not possible, since Cushan does not occur elsewhere in the Old Testament and Midian is used to cover a wide area.[96] One may say, however, that Midian at least has strong connections

---

[95]   See John Day, "New Light on the Mythological Background of the Allusion to Resheph in Habakkuk 3:5," *VT* 29 (1979): 353-355; Hiebert, *God of My Victory*, 92-94. It should be noted that Resheph and Deber, as they appear in Hab 3:5, however, have long since lost this function, and here serve only as personifications of pestilence and plague respectively.

[96]   See fuller discussion of the both difficulties and the suggestions offered for the locations in Hiebert, *God of My Victory*, 83-92. Hiebert argues plausibly for the location of 3:3-7 in the Southern Transjordan, based upon his interpretations of 3:3-7. His geographical observations and compilation of Biblical data are illuminating, if not always as incontrovertible, with regard to date, as he would imply. Note particularly the statements (91) regarding Deut 33:2, which he considers one of the "archaic" passages (together with Judg 5:4 and Ps 68:9). This verse is not universally regarded as archaic. Almost all commentators assign Deut 33:1ff as a later addition to the book, and although many see the sayings in the chapter (6-25) as ancient, most are much more cautious about the hymnic frame (33:2-5,26-29) which surround the sayings. See Eissfeldt, *Introduction*, 228; Smend, *Entstehung*, 71; Fohrer, *Einleitung*, 71f. Hiebert is concerned with finding the archaic form and meaning of the poem in Hab 3:3-15, and therefore he concentrates upon the likely geographical locations of Teman, Paran, Midian, and Cushan in earlier Biblical and geographical data, even to the point of ascribing later Deuteronomistic and Priestly usages as unreliable and artificial (86f) where they conflict with earlier traditions. Hiebert does not address the question, however, as to what these place names would have meant to those who incorporated

with Moses and conquest traditions.[97] In order to understand Cushan's significance, one must consider extra-biblical evidence which points in different directions. What little geographical evidence can be brought to bear on the question indicates a location in the Southern Transjordan is possible for the poem on its *independent* level.[98] At the other end of the spectrum, the LXX and Vulgate both understand the region as Cush (Ethiopia). All told a firm determination of the original intent cannot be reached since neither suggestion indisputably explains the peculiar form of the word, and even the Biblical evidence is capable of different interpretations.[99] One is on firmer ground, however, in asking about the understanding of the redactor who selected the poem for placement with Hab 1-2. In all likelihood, given the fact that Cush in later writings clearly refers to Ethiopia, one suspects that, whatever the intention of the original

---

the theophany into the Habakkuk corpus. Since this incorporation would have occurred much closer to the time of Deuteronomistic and Priestly activity, the question carries considerable significance whether one accepts the late 7th century date typically ascribed to Habakkuk or the later reworking of an existing corpus during the Persian period. Logic leads one to accept that the incorporation of the poem would also have been unaware of the exact location of the place names.

[97] Outside of genealogical passages (Gen 25:4; 36:35; 1 Chr 1:32,46), the story of Gideon's defeat of the Midianites figures prominently in the references to Midian (Judg 7-8; Ps 83:10). Midian is also the place to which Moses fled after killing the Egyptian (Exod 2:15, which offers the only other use of the phrase "land of Midian" as in Hab 3:3). Num 25:15; 31:1-11 also attest to hostilities between Israelites and Midianites. On the other hand, Isa 60:6 uses the term "Camels of Midian" as a description of the "wealth of the nations" (60:5) which will be brought to Zion when the Diaspora ends.

[98] See Hiebert, *God of My Victory*, 89f; L.M. Muntingh, "Teman and Paran in the Prayer of Habakkuk," *Oud-Testamentiese Werkgemeenskap van Suid-Afrika* (1969): 64-70; William F. Albright, "The Land of Damascus between 1850 and 1750 B.C.," *BASOR* 83 (1941): 34. Both Hiebert and Albright make reference to an Egyptian list of enemies from the reign of Ammenemes III (1842-1797 B.C.) that cites a tribe of *kwšw* in the region of Moab. Hiebert argues certain literary discrepancies between Cush and Midian in the Moses traditions (Exod 2:15-22 and Num 12:1 cite the origin of Moses' wife as both Midianite and Cushite), may be explained if Cush was also the name of a group located in the Southern Transjordan, which was essentially the same region as Midian. This suggestion, while possible, must still explain the form Cushan as opposed to Cush or Cushu. Additionally, most of the texts connecting Midian and Cush are equally as explainable through the supposition of a trade link between the Arabs and the Ethiopians, who were separated only by the Red Sea.

[99] The most important observation is that different Biblical traditions associate the Midianite region with the Ethiopians. Not only the Moses tradition, as explained by Hiebert, but also later tradition places Midian (or at least Arabs in the same general area) in association with Ethiopia (e.g. 2 Chr 21:16).

author, that the compiler understood the reference to African Cush and not a region of the Transjordan. In addition, the writings on either side of Habakkuk both manifest an awareness of Ethiopia (Nah 3:9; Zeph 2:12; 3:10), whereas there is no further mention of Midian in the Twelve.

Hab 3:3-7 reaches a climax with the reaction of Midian and Cushan. The geographical designations, aural similarities, and poetic style unite the verses.[100]   Sinai and conquest traditions portray God's arrival for judgment. The climax is misleading, however, in that while the nations (3:6) and Cushan and Midian respond in fear, the verses do not explicitly state that the judgment of the theophany is directed against them. The responses they display parallel the response of the hills and the mountains in 3:6. To this point, the poem has proclaimed God's arrival, but no actual battle has occurred. The battle is described in 3:8-15, but the background and style change dramatically.

Hab **3:8-15** comprises the second, and concluding, stanza of the theophanic poem. Several aspects separate it from 3:3-7 and from the literary frame which follows (3:16-19a). First, the style of the passage shifts noticeably. While 3:3-7 speaks about "God" in the third person, Hab 3:8-15 directs the speech to YHWH.[101]   Second, the two sections use different designations for the divinity: Hab 3:3 refers to אלוה, while 3:8 addresses YHWH. Third, the imagery of the two sections changes dramatically. Hab 3:3-7 utilizes traditions most closely associated with the Sinai theophanic material, Moses traditions, and conquest motifs. Hab 3:8-15, by contrast, draws upon images and motifs which have roots in Canaanite and Ancient Near Eastern mythology.[102]   Theophanic depictions unite the two sections

---

[100] Hiebert, *God of My Victory*, 69-71, 84 overstates the symmetrical structure of the verses, yet his observations on the *inclusio* between 3:3,7 does add validity to his arguments.

[101] The only vacillation from this pattern occurs in the stylistically awkward transition at the beginning of 3:8 where the verb חרה literally asks, "Was YHWH angry against the rivers?" Still, the second bi-cola has the parallel expression "or *your* anger against the rivers?" This variation inside the parallelism militates against a division of either portion as secondary. The change should likely be attributed to the function of the verse as a transition between the 3ms and 2ms sections of the poem.

[102] Considerable time and energy has been devoted to the question of whether Hab 3:(3-7),8-15 drew from Babylonian or Canaanite mythological motifs. Several argue on both sides of the question. For example, William A. Irwin, "The Psalm of Habakkuk," *JNES* 1 (1942): 10-40, argues Babylonian origin on the basis of the story line. Irwin reacts vigorously against the work of Umberto Cassuto, "Chapter 3 of Habakkuk and the Ras Shamra Texts," *Biblical and Oriental Studies*, vol 2 (Jerusalem: Magnes Press, 1975), 3-15, who argues that the chapter draws from the Baal/Mot cycle on the basis of the characters involved (Nahar, Yam, etc.). While most scholars have tended to support

of the poem, albeit loosely. Most commentators recognize the difficulties inherent in ascribing the poem's diverse traditions to separate sources, yet they simultaneously acknowledge the incongruity of the images. Hab 3:8 does not appear to begin an independent poem, and Hab 3:7 does not provide an appropriate ending.[103]

The second stanza reaches to 3:15, where the *inclusio* back to 3:8 has often been noted.[104] This device functions similarly to the relationship between 3:3 and 3:7. Hiebert argues the use of inclusion shapes the entire structure of 3:8-15.[105] However, this inclusion does not take shape in typical chiastic or parallel fashion, rather the four parts (3:8-9a; 3:9b-11; 3:12-13a; 3:13b-15) have a more intricate system of *inclusio*, in which the two outer sections relate to one another, while the two inner sections relate to the outer portions.[106] This structured inclusion, as Hiebert sees it may be diagrammed as follows:

There are problems with Hiebert's interpretation of this structural schema, but his analysis is insightful with regard to the inner relationship of the constituent parts, and it does reflect a coherency within these verses of the poem. It will, however, be necessary to return to the question of the relationship of these parts following a discussion of the individual verses.

Hab 3:8 asks a series of rhetorical questions that take up the theophanic imagery of YHWH as warrior. Was YHWH's anger directed against the rivers? Or was it against the sea? The questions are phrased

---

the views of Cassuto, recent studies approach the text from the perspective of the peculiarly Israelite form which the myth developed. Instrumental in this shift was the work by Stolz, *Strukturen und Figure im Kult von Jerusalem*. He compares relevant texts from ancient cultures with Old Testament passages relating to this mythological motif. See also the recent work by John Day, *God's Conflict with the Dragon and the Sea*, which likewise catalogues similar Old Testament passages, although this work does not bring the comparison with other cultures to the extent of the work by Stolz.

[103] The attack of the warrior in 3:7 is yet to occur, while the "anger" in 3:8 presupposes YHWH's coming in anger, which must require Hab 3:3-7.

[104] The reference to YHWH riding on the sea with his horses appears in both verses.

[105] See Hiebert, *God of My Victory*, 71-76.

[106] Hiebert divides the units somewhat differently. He sees them as 3:8-9a; 3:9b-11a; 3:11b-13a; 3:13b-15, but his separation of 3:11a from 3:11b is particularly confusing given the close grammatical connection which exists.

rhetorically such that they lead the hearer to expect a negative answer.[107] In this context, the author apparently wishes to say that YHWH did not go forth to battle the sea or the rivers. The background of these terms in Canaanite mythology, however, provides an interesting point of departure for further consideration. Yam (sea) was the Canaanite God of Chaos who was also called Judge Nahar (River). In the Canaanite version, Baal clearly does battle the sea and the river.[108] If the theophany battle in Hab 3:8ff is not directed against the sea or the river, then against whom is it directed? Perhaps it is best to see here an anti-Canaanite polemic standing behind the verses. At the very least, the phraseology provides a clear linguistic marker, that the following section should not be read simply as an account of the *Chaoskampf* of the warrior YHWH battling the forces of chaos.[109]

Hab 3:9 creates considerable difficulty for translation, although the sense of the verse may be deduced readily from the context and from a comparison with the accounts of the *Chaoskampf*. It belongs to the warrior YHWH motif, and pictures YHWH preparing to do battle by drawing his bow. Most scholars understand the strangely formulated phrase ("The curses of the 'rods' are said") to be related to the previous line about the bow, and despite the strange syntax, it does indeed fit that context.[110] The image of the warrior YHWH with bow and "rods" corresponds to a battle scene. More significant, this same picture recurs in 3:11 with the more explicit mention of YHWH's arrows and spear.[111] The context

---

[107] *GK* §150d.

[108] See Pritchard, *ANET*, 130. For a pictorial example of how this battle was envisioned (and an analysis of the picture), see Othmar Keel, *The Symbolism of the Biblical World: Ancient Near Eastern Iconography and the Book of Psalms* (New York: Crossroad, 1985), 47f.

[109] Contra those who try to explain away the expected negative answer: Hiebert, *God of My Victory*, 102f. See explanations more in keeping with the grammatical expectations, and relating to an historical enemy, in Rudolph, *KAT* 13/3, 244f; and Robertson, *Nahum, Habakkuk, Zephaniah*, 231.

[110] Note the cosmic background of the portrayal in light of the fact that the spear is lightning. See the Baal myth. In the Canaanite version of the Chaos battle YHWH has two shafts with names Yagrush and Ayamur. Pritchard, *ANET*, 131.

[111] It is interesting that the plural of rod appears in this context. It is normally understood as either a reference to the arrows or spears. The plural conjures images of the commissioning of the YHWH's instruments of punishment in Nahum (see also Mic 7:14) and Habakkuk, but the phrase, at least in its entirety, does not appear to be redactionally inserted. It is too embedded in the context. It also presents a different image, in that it portrays YHWH himself as the one preparing to attack, not the rods. The images are also embedded in the context of the Canaanite myth. These

clearly demonstrates that YHWH is here presented as entering into a cosmic battle. Next, YHWH acts by cleaving the earth with rivers. This imagery remains in the realm of the cosmic battle, although its precise background against the myth is not easy to ascertain.[112]

Hab 3:10 describes the reaction of the cosmos to the sight of YHWH's arrival for battle. In Hab 3:10a the mountains quake as the flood passes over. The quaking of the mountains is typical of theophanic material.[113] The image of the flood of waters in 3:10a shares much in common with Nah 1:8. Both refer to the flood passing over (עבר), and although they use different words for flood, the contexts of the two passages make it clear that the background of both refers to the primal waters, although in their context these waters represent specific enemies.[114] In 3:10b the deep utters its voice in fear. The expression "utter its voice" is the same one as in Joel 4:16 and Amos 1:2, but with two essential differences. First, Tehom, the great deep, and not YHWH is the subject. Second, the phrase is used in the context of giving up in fear, not to denote the coming in power as in Joel and Amos. Tehom also lifts its hands in

---

observations point away from any redactional insertion of the line, but it does not eliminate the possibility that the redactor was aware of the similarity of images.

[112] Vuilleumier, *CAT* 11b, 172, notes the problem that it is difficult to understand "rivers" as both the enemy (as in the Baal cycle) and as the weapon. He therefore suggests that the root נהר (2) be read, and that the word be translated with "lightning." While the root certainly exists, it is by no means common. In the Old Testament, the only equivalent noun from this root appears only once (Job 3:4). His argument is aided by the fact that the word is the feminine נהרה, which would correspond to the feminine here (as compared with the masculine in 3:8). Nevertheless, the noun נהרה in Hebrew and Aramaic means "light," not lightning. See also the examples cited by Paul Humbert, *Problèmes du Livre d'Habakkuk*, 222, who notes נהר can appear in the same context with both masculine and feminine endings. Rudolph, *KAT* 13/3, 245, and Robertson, *Nahum, Habakkuk, Zephaniah*, 234, both explain the imagery as references to an overabundant cosmic rainfall which causes the groundwater to overflow and the clouds to lose their water. This picture of a cosmic flood relates well with the passage, but this difference along with others, means that one must be careful not to try to force the events described in Habakkuk into the narrative development of the Baal cycle.

[113] Some examples include Mic 1:4; Pss 18:8; 46:4.

[114] See also the discussion of 3:13-15, beginning page 168. The relationship of Nah 1:2-8 and Hab 3:3-15 is significant. There are many similarities, but one should not see these similarities as signs of a single author. More likely, the similarities are due to the same redactional movement using a similar technique: the incorporation of pre-existing independent theophanic hymns into a context to expand the viewpoint already established by the connection between Micah and Zephaniah in the Deuteronomistic corpus.

resignation and fear. In 3:11 the sun and the moon retreat at the sight of YHWH arrayed for battle. All of these images portray cosmic responses to YHWH's appearance.

The next section, Hab 3:12-14, describes the actual battle, and finally, the rhetorical question in 3:8 becomes clear. Hab 3:12 demonstrates unequivocally that the anger of YHWH was directed against the nations, when it states: "In indignation you march the earth. In anger you tread the nations." Unlike 3:8-11 with their cosmic imagery, the picture here enters into the "real" world with reference to the nations, yet the metaphorical imagery makes it difficult to determine with absolute precision the identity of these nations. The use of the nations, in contradistinction to the cosmic imagery, has several possible explanations. (1) The inclusion of the nations could be part of a later literary reworking of the cosmic material; or (2) The nations could represent a separate theophany. Against both of these explanations one must note the fragmentary character of the passage if the poem is separated into sources based upon the enemy. (3) The inclusion of nations can refer to the accompanying forces from the Chaos battle motif. In the chaos battle of the Jerusalem tradition, the nations appear as an integral part of the battle motif from a relatively early stage of the development.[115] Apart from the thematic shift, no real literary tension appears strong enough to argue that the nations were not part of this literary piece from the beginning. Indeed the fact that 3:6f also incorporated nations motif, argues that the nations play a pivotal role for the understanding of the poem in 3:3-15.

Hab 3:13 continues to blend references to the enemy as the chaos power and the nations. The salvation of his people motivates YHWH's attack, and leads one to think the enemy is at least quasi-historically intended. However, "the head of the house of evil" points to a single enemy, not the plural nations. As such it is perhaps more in keeping with the cosmos motif, but the head of the house of evil would be a strange designation for Yam.[116] The description of the death of the enemy has strong affinities with both the Babylonian and Canaanite versions of the cosmic battle, as has frequently been noted.[117] However, several authors

---

[115] Stolz, *Strukturen und Figuren*, 92.

[116] Hence, those who argue for an early date and closer association with the actual myth are forced to radical emendation or excision of the entire phrase. See for example, Hiebert, *God of My Victory*, 36-38.

[117] This verse particularly has sparked discussions on the similarity between Hab 3:8-15 and the Mesopotamian and Canaanite versions of the myth, where the divinity destroys the chaos enemy. While the similarity is striking, it has often detracted from a

correctly point out this verse is most understandable as a reference to Babylon's destruction.[118]

The reference to "your anointed" in 3:13 does not necessitate the assumption of a pre-exilic date.[119] The argument that the phrase refers to the king must be balanced from two sides. First, the bi-cola parallels YHWH's anointed with his people, making it possible that the "anointed" in this case does not explicitly assume the king. Second, and probably more likely, the hope for the restoration of a kingdom with a Davidic king is a theme which outlasted the presence of a Davidic king in Judah.[120]

Hab 3:14 poses even more translation difficulties, with the result that its precise interpretation is uncertain. Several approaches typify the uncertainty. 3:14b is so fraught with images that defy understanding in this context that Hiebert simply omits translation.[121] Rudolph emends the text beyond recognition.[122] Robertson translates the text faithfully, but virtually ignores the problems it poses for comprehension.[123] Jeremias believes the verse relates to the guilt of the wicked inside Israel.[124] The

---

discussion of the use of this motif in the context of Hab 3:3ff. See especially, William A. Irwin, "The Psalm of Habakkuk." *JNES* 1 (1942): 10-40; and Umberto Cassuto, "Chapter 3 of Habakkuk and the Ras Shamra Texts" *Biblical and Oriental Studies*, vol. 2, 3-15.

[118] Day, *God's Conflict with the Dragon and the Sea*, 105; Jeremias, *Kultprophetie*, 85f. The arguments rely heavily upon the presumed date of the material and the relationship of the chapter to the remainder of the book.

[119] Contra Hiebert, *God of My Victory*, 134f.

[120] Note the treatment of Zerubbabel in Haggai and Zechariah as the representative of Davidic lineage, the reference to the pardon of Jehoiachin in 2 Kgs 25:27-30; and specific mention of the king in Zech 9:9f, to name but a few locations.

[121] Hiebert, *God of My Victory*, 9,43-46. His rationale for the omission are the text-critical difficulties themselves. He certainly demonstrates the wide variety of textual readings of the phrase (43-46), but these difficulties themselves merely point to a difficult text, not one which can be omitted from consideration of the literary context.

[122] Rudolph, *KAT* 13/3, 237.

[123] Robertson, *Nahum, Habakkuk, Zephaniah*, 241. He relates the entire passage to the enemies mentioned in 3:7 and the "me" in 3:14b to the prophet himself.

[124] Jeremias, *Kultprophetie*, 86, distinguishes between the destruction of the wicked in Israel and the true Israel who will escape destruction. The wicked, for Jeremias, are intended as the wicked house. They are accused of pride. Jeremias may have a point in applying the judgment to the wicked inside Israel. The pride of Judah's wicked fits with portions of Zephaniah (2:3, salvation for the humble; also 3:11-12). This understanding would help account for the prophet's response in 3:16 — which presumes an attack on the nation — but it creates too many other problems, particularly since there are no convincing criteria to separate the destiny of YHWH's people in 3:3-15.

verse in MT consists of three parts: 1) YHWH pierces the head of the enemy throng with the enemy's own rod; 2) a parenthetical description of the attack of the army ("They stormed in to scatter me."); 3) The secret gloating of the enemy over the oppressed.

The first element causes the fewest problems since it fits the imagery of the context.[125]   YHWH has killed the leader of the "house of evil" (3:13), and in 3:14 the battle action continues uninterrupted. YHWH picks up the fallen enemy's own "rod" and uses it against the remainder of the attacking army.[126]

The second and third element actually transport the battle-action one step backward. In spite of the fact that YHWH has already struck and defeated the enemy and the army, the author has deemed it necessary to add further (albeit enigmatic) imagery to the account. "They stormed along to scatter me" obviously understands the enemy and his army collectively, hence the plural form of the verb. The confusion stems from the 1cs reference to "me," which despite many suggested emendations cannot be explained away.[127]   Those who opt for MT as it stands have difficulty explaining the identity of "me." They normally understand it as a reference to the prophet.[128]   However, "me" in this context cannot refer to the prophet as in 3:2,16ff because the imagery does not allow a singular person as the recipient of the verb "to scatter." The very meaning of the verb *demands* a corporate identity for the speaker. Logic dictates scattering requires more than one entity or more than one piece of a single entity. The well-attested use of the verb "scatter" in connection with Babylon and the overthrow of Jerusalem further buttress the supposition that the images

---

[125] See also text-critical notes in Nogalski, *Literary Precursors*, 49.

[126] In spite of the fact that the battle imagery fits the context, it is significant that the word "rod" appears in this connection. The "rod" of YHWH motif introduced in Mic 7:14 can well have played a role in the formulation of this verse or at least in its selection, particularly in light of the fact that the word does not normally connote an instrument of battle. One possibility which can only be suggested at this point is that the imagery in Hab 3:14 plays off the "rod of YHWH" motif as appointed by YHWH (Assyria in Isa 10), and the anti-Babylonian polemic in Habakkuk which depicts Babylon as relying upon its own strength. The fact that YHWH then takes the "rod" of Babylon would then see the scepter as symbol of power (He whose strength is his God — Hab 1:11), which YHWH then turns against the leader's own army.

[127] See discussions in Hiebert, *God of My Victory*, 44f; Rudolph, *KAT* 13/3, 238.

[128] So Robertson, *Nahum, Habakkuk, Zephaniah*, 241. The same arguments would have to be applied to those who see the song as a victory song for the king (so Hiebert, even though he does not indicate that he considers the king as the speaker in this context).

of this verse must be read in connection with the Babylonian invasion.[129] The identity of a corporate personified speaker include either a personified Judah or a personified Jerusalem, with the latter being the more plausible, because of its frequency in exilic and post-exilic prophetic texts. Such an interpretation would coincide with the poem as a whole, and especially with 3:8-15, given the recurrent acknowledgement that these verses utilize cosmic imagery as a reference to Babylon.[130] This interpretation furthers the observations of those who see 3:3-15 as an independent poem, because the corporate "I" of this song is not entirely consistent with the individual "I" of 3:2,16-19 in its original form. It seems much more plausible to recognize the "I" here as stemming from a cultic setting in much the same manner as other psalms where the "I" takes on corporate characteristics.[131]

The third element in Hab 3:14 concerns the secret gloating of the enemy over the oppressed. Like the previous element, this line must prefigure the battle-action in 3:13 where YHWH annihilates the enemy and his army. Of the three elements, this one is the most difficult to comprehend. The crux of the problem lies in the secrecy in which "they" seek to devour the oppressed. When one recognizes the common usage of "oppressed" in other contexts as a metaphor for the suffering following the Babylonian occupation, the images may be clarified somewhat.[132] The devouring of the oppressed in 3:14 should not be taken literally, but metaphorically in keeping with the remainder of the chapter. Jeremias, as already noted, believes the enemy here refers to an inner Israelite oppression.[133] He does so by reading this chapter in light of chapter one. However, it appears much more likely that the line may be better understood in its near context in relation to the battle imagery. One has to distinguish between the two-fold threat which YHWH defeats, namely the head of the house of evil and the leaders of the army. In light of the earlier references to the nations in the hymn (3:6,12) it seems wisest to understand the nations as those who stormed in to scatter Zion's oppressed. The role of the nations in the events of the Babylonian occupation played a significant role in increasing nationalistic feelings against surrounding

---

[129] See discussion of פוץ in relationship to Babylon in the discussion of Zeph 3:9ff.

[130] Day, *God's Conflict with the Dragon and the Sea*, 104-109; Jeremias, *Kultprophetie*, 86.

[131] See other examples in prophetic literature of similar devices, such as Mic 7:1ff and Isa 33. See also explanations of the use of "I" in the Psalter.

[132] See for example Zeph 3:12 which refers to the righteous remnant, and Isa 51:21; 54:11, where the term is used of the personified Zion herself.

[133] See above, footnote 124.

nations.[134]   This interpretation of the metaphorical reference to the
surrounding nations coincides with the strange formulation of the verse in
the MT. Given the official Babylonian rule of the area, these raids and
advances were presumably viewed as deceitful on more than one level. Not
only did they infringe upon Judah's territory, but they would also have had
to be carried out in such a manner that the Babylonians did not feel
threatened. As the Babylonian power waned in the region, the frequency
and intensity of this "storming" could well have increased. Hence, Hab 3:14
cannot only be read as it stands so that it is consistent with the remainder
of the context of Babylonian rule, as 3:12-14 is normally interpreted, it also
fits well with late exilic Judean experience.

Hab 3:15 returns abruptly to the cosmic imagery of the chaos battle,
and initially stands somewhat at odds with its context. Nevertheless, it
should be read as the conclusion to the theophanic poem and not the
beginning of a new unit.[135]   The summary character of the verse along
with the function it plays in recalling 3:8, make it a fitting conclusion to the
verse and to the original poem. The role of 3:15 is interesting in that it
appears to stand at odds with the rhetorical question in 3:8 which expects
a negative answer to the question whether YHWH's anger was wrought
against the sea or the rivers. Yet this tension all but disappears when one
reads 3:15 as the concluding statement of the poem which has from start
to finish taken the images of the *Chaoskampf* and interpreted them in light
of Babylonian domination. Stated succinctly, 3:8 implies YHWH did not
battle the sea, 3:9-14 amplifies these thoughts by interpreting the Chaos
imagery to say: YHWH will destroy Babylon. Finally, Hab 3:15, almost in
midrashic style, ends the poem with one last verification that YHWH did
tread his horses on the sea, but only in its reinterpreted form.

---

[134] This role included the involvement of other nations by the Babylonians prior to the
destruction (see Miller/Hayes, *A history of Ancient Israel and Judah*, 407), and their
apparent use of other nations in some fashion during and immediately after the
destruction of Jerusalem and the temple. See especially Lam 1:9 (cf also Obad 10-14;
and many of the oracles against the nations in Jeremiah and Ezekiel). It also included
the hostile actions of those countries which saw an opportunity to gain land and slaves
by preying upon Judean territory and people. Here Edom and Tyre apparently played
an active role. Naturally, nationalistic rivalries were not limited to the period after the
destruction, but they were greatly accentuated.

[135] Here commentators are virtually unanimous, although a few exceptions such as Watts,
Joel, etc., 150f, who argues the verse begins the final argument. However, his
translation, or at least that of the New English Bible upon which he comments, is not
consistent with the Hebrew text. The translation "When thou dost tread ..." adds a
conjunction which is neither present in nor necessary to the text.

In summary, 3:3-15 is a poem with two stanzas (3:3-7,8-15), whose origin is independent of the Habakkuk corpus. There are occasional indications that the formulation *may have been* influenced by either the incorporation of the poem into the Habakkuk corpus or by an awareness of the broader literary horizon of the Book of the Twelve, however, these possible reformulations are too few and too open to multiple interpretations to claim that they are more than possibilities. It is much more likely that a pre-existing poem has been incorporated *en bloc*. The literary frame (Hab 3:2,16-19) manifests demonstrable links to both the Habakkuk corpus and to other parts of the Book of the Twelve. Likely, this frame was composed with an awareness of both position and function for the explicit purpose of relating to a larger context. However, this composition adapted a pre-existing form of the frame through insertions.

8. The Literary Frame (Hab 3:2,16-19a)

Hab 3:2 contains the strongest connections to Hab 1-2 in Hab 3:1ff, but these connections are almost always *assumed* to be the result of an awareness of those chapters. Hiebert has correctly called this assumption into question, although his own conclusions need to be modified.[136] He argues the entire chapter was an ancient victory hymn that was interpreted by post-exilic editors and subsequently subsumed into the Habakkuk corpus. The majority of his arguments for dating the hymn as "ancient" rest too heavily upon an all too neatly defined distinction between archaic and newer Hebrew poetic forms, but his observations that the tensions between Hab 3:2 and the remainder of the corpus are greater than the similarities are insightful and to the point. He notes that most of these assumptions presuppose that chapter 3 must be understood as a prophetic vision (3:3-15) inside a prayer of supplication. Hiebert argues that the chapter can be understood better as a recitation of God's acts than as a prophetic vision, although he probably overstates the distinction for Hab 3:1ff.[137] Regardless, he correctly asserts that the current context of the psalm in Habakkuk has influenced its interpretation, and that this context (and

---

[136] Hiebert, *God of My Victory*, 144-149.

[137] In 3:1ff, Hiebert distinguishes too sharply between these two *Gattungen*, especially since he agrees (138) with Jeremias' observation that it is difficult at times to distinguish between the two. See Jörg Jeremias, "Theophany in the OT," *IDB Supp*, 896-898.

relatedly the interpretation) is secondary to the original setting of the poem. As evidence, Hiebert cites not only the cultic transmission of 3:1ff, but he observes that the vision in 2:1, to which almost all commentators relate 3:2, occurs on the city fortifications, not in the temple, where the prayer would have been offered. He also points out that the vision anticipated in 2:1 was already received and recorded in 2:2-5. He also describes how the process of interpreting the poem as a "vision" based on the remainder of the book became more pronounced in the LXX and later works.

Additionally, two observations should be added to those of Hiebert, namely, the vocabulary of 3:2 is not unusual for theophanic material. This is true not only for the verbs, "hear" and "see," but also for the noun "work" (פעל) in the context of the Divine Warrior motif.[138] This adds weight to his argument that the song is more readily understandable as an independent composition. While many are willing to grant the independent origin of 3:3-15, it is difficult to believe that 3:3 begins the "prayer," or that 3:2 was redactionally inserted. Elsewhere in the Psalter, all of the other examples of תפלה have lament characteristics, and offer some type of introductory element which states the situation of the person offering the prayer (individual or communal) which makes use of the first person.[139] Thus, there are good reasons for seeing Hab 3:2 as the original introduction to the "prayer," and not a redactional addition.[140]

The composition in 3:16-19a contains material from very divergent backgrounds, yet several observations provide evidence that the author of these verses is aware of the context of both the Habakkuk corpus and of the Book of the Twelve. Hab 3:16 affords relatively solid criteria to establish its relationship to other parts of the book. As noted above, it describes the prophetic reaction. However, the verse stands in tension to its immediate context since the direct address to YHWH in much of 3:8-15 does not call for a prophetic response. The prophet does not respond to a message from YHWH. In the 2ms material, the prophet addresses

---

[138] For example, compare Pss 44:2f; 74:12.

[139] See Pss 86:1; 90:1; 102:1; 142:1.

[140] With Hiebert, one has to accent the fact that the "prayer" has a certain affinity which lends itself to a vision interpretation, but the poem itself can better be comprehended as an independent piece than one *written* for its place in the Habakkuk corpus. See also the work of Umberto Cassuto, "Chapter 3 of Habakkuk and the Ras Shamra Texts," 5, who argues that there there are two polarities in Jewish traditions regarding the use of this Canaanite material. 1) These battles appear as ancient remote events before creation (e.g. Ps 74:12-15). 2) They are projected into the future where God's victory will be renewed and last forever (Isaiah 27:1).

YHWH, but YHWH never speaks in chapter 3. Logically the prophet must be responding to the theophany. The loud noise to which the prophet responds could correspond with the chaos motif (cf 3:10), or it could respond to the battle noise involving the nations.

The prophet in 3:16 does not respond, however, to the contents of the theophanic poem in more than general terms. Hab 3:16, at least in its present form, reinterprets the theophany to one of judgment, in spite of the reference to salvation mentioned in 3:13. Both the chaos battle motif and the battle against the nations are positive traditions in their background. The chaos battle motif celebrates YHWH's victory over the primordial sea and the forces of chaos.[141] While not all prophetic literature uses the motif positively, 3:8-15 demonstrates no negative intention.[142] The tenor of the hymn is one of awe and fear before the mighty acts YHWH performs. In typical presentations of YHWH's battle against the nations, YHWH fights on the side of his people, not against them. The positive aspect of these traditions makes the prophetic intention of judgment stand out all the more dramatically in 3:16b. There are, however, strong indications that 3:16b does not belong to the original layer of this poem's frame. The presence of אשר grammatically disturbs the context. This half-verse contains the only plural reference to the congregation in the entire chapter.[143] The sentence as a whole varies thematically both from the theophany and from the positive reactions in 3:18f. A single nation will attack, unlike the "nations" in the theophanic poem. Also, this attack does not pick up on the mythological material, rather it presupposes a real historical attack while at the same time interpreting the hymn as a representation of this attack. The profession of the fear of the coming attack of "a people," following a depiction of YHWH's victory over the nations and chaos, surprises the reader familiar with these traditions and with the contents of 3:8-15. Hab 3:8-15 contains no real indication that an attack by a single nation is directed at the prophet's people.[144]

The perspective of 3:16b, while not at home with most of the chapter, coincides with the redactional activity in the first two chapters of the corpus. The pre-existing wisdom material was expanded to interpret the Babylonian invasion. The single "people" of 3:16b therefore presupposes

---

[141] See Stolz, *Strukturen und Figuren im Kult von Jerusalem*, 86-101.

[142] Above all Jeremiah negates the chaos motif's positive depiction, and turns these battle imagess against Judah. See Stolz, *Strukturen und Figuren im Kult von Jerusalem*, 90-92.

[143] Hab 3:16b: "... when I wait for the day of trouble, for the people rising up to attack us."

[144] The poem concerned Babylon *and* the surrounding nations (3:7,12,14).

these images, not the images of the poem. Also, the battle account uses the expression, "the day of trouble." Significantly, this phrase appears in the eschatological framework of Zeph 1:15, which also combines Jerusalem's destruction with the motif of universal judgment. This expanded literary horizon separates 3:16b further from its immediate context and allows the tentative assignation of a redactional insertion to this sentence.

Hab 3:17 introduces another new perspective into chapter 3, but unlike 3:16b, one which is not at home in the book of Habakkuk. Hab 3:17 introduces agricultural fertility. The withering of fertile regions is a motif which appears in other theophanic contexts, but in Hab 3:1-19 only 3:17 contains this motif. Scholars have puzzled over the inexplicable incursion of this thematic intrusion, and have proposed various suggestions.[145] If one considers the larger literary horizon of the Book of the Twelve, the verse takes on new significance. Similarly to redactional insertions in Nahum, Hab 3:17 takes up vocabulary and motifs which appear in Joel 1-2. The vocabulary is not so uncommon that one can declare literary dependence without hesitation. Nevertheless the probability rises dramatically when one recognizes that the agricultural images in Hab 3:17 and in Joel's laments, both relate agricultural distress to the attack of an enemy people (cf Joel 1:6f) with a decidedly eschatological perspective.

---

[145] Earlier authors overwhelmingly rejected this verse as essential to the context. Elliger, *ATD* 25, 51, he considers the verse a "harmless" and "weak" addition to the portrayal of the final judgment. Recent attempts have focussed on trying to maintain the verse, although with considerable hesitation. Hiebert, *God of My Victory*, 113f, has substantial difficulty with the verse. He believes it is original, based upon its archaic character, but he concedes the strength of the arguments it was added. Jeremias, *Kultprophetie*, 98, also acknowledges the arguments for insertion, but still believes the verse is genuine. He argues: 1) The motif that danger to the world order effects the harvest, appears too generally in ancient near eastern complaints to separate the verse on purely thematic grounds. 2) The prophet would have been functioning not as an individual, but in an official function, most likely at a "*Volksklagefeier*" on a day of fasting, similarly to chapter one. Rudolph, *KAT* 13/3, 240f, an author not prone to excision, considers this verse as a secondary addition. He believes it has no organic relationship to the preceding or to that which follows. He answers Jeremias' suggestion that it fits the general ancient near eastern theme with a significant argument that the motif of desolation makes little sense after the promise and description of help in 3:8-15. Robertson, *Nahum, Habakkuk, and Zephaniah*, 245, apparently sees no tension since his interpretation assumes a relationship to 3:16, and he nowhere hints that the verse might indeed be secondary. Despite the attempts by some recent scholars, the older predominant arguments are more convincing that Hab 3:17 is a later insertion.

Additionally, the themes appear periodically in other significant portions of the Book of the Twelve.

The vocabulary relationships to Joel are substantial. Hab 3:17 reads:

> Though the fig tree will not bloom,
> And no produce will be on the vines,
> (Though) the yield of the olive has failed,
> And the fields do not produce food,
> (Though) the flock is divided from the field,
> And there is no cattle in the stalls, ...[146]

Almost every phrase in Hab 3:17 has a corresponding element in Joel 1-2. The fig tree which does not blossom corresponds to similar images in Joel 1:7,12; 2:22, but also appears in gloss-type redactional insertions elsewhere in the Book of the Twelve.[147] "No produce on the vines" also shares this wider perspective. Produce is an unusual word in prophetic literature, with only four occurrences. While the word does not occur in Joel, three of the four occurrences appear in the Book of the Twelve (Hag 1:10; Zech 8:12; and Hab 3:17).[148] Concern for the vines, particularly in a metaphorical description of the aftermath of military invasion does, however, occur in Joel 1:7,12; 2:22.[149] The "yield of the olive fails" uses vocabulary which is also understandable in the context of the Book of the Twelve.[150] The image is closely related to Joel 1:10, in spite of the fact that the vocabulary varies slightly.[151] The expression, "the fields produce no food" describes the situation as depicted in Joel 1:16.[152] The same phenomenon repeats

---

[146] The current continuation of 3:17 in 3:18 is discussed below, beginning page 178.

[147] Compare the verb from Hos 14:6, and especially 14:8; Nah 1:4, in one of the broken acrostic lines; Hag 2:19, in a phrase which is very unusually stated; Hos 2:14, although the anti-Baal polemic of that chapter likely predates this redactional layer. Compare further Hos 9:10; Amos 4:9 which contain similar vocabulary, but not in redactional passages.

[148] The other prophetic use of produce (Ezek 34:27) appears in connection with the idiom produce of the land.

[149] Compare also the examples of variations of this metaphor elsewhere in the Book of the Twelve: Mal 3:11; Hos 2:14; 10:1; Hag 2:19; Zech 3:10; 8:12.

[150] Compare the pictures of olive in Hos 14:7; Amos 4:9; Mic 6:15; Hag 2:19; and of the verb grows lean: Hos 9:2.

[151] The significant phrase in Joel 1:10 translates "the fresh oil is languished," but the phrase is synonymous with the picture in Hab 3:17 since the fresh oil (יצהר) is certainly part of the "yield of the olive." See 2 Kgs 18:32.

[152] Further expansion of this metaphorical image could conceivably have included Mic 1:6 and 3:12 which depict the destroyed "fields" of Samaria and Jerusalem. While this

with the phrase "the flock cut off from the fold." The verb גזר does not appear in Joel,[153] but the word for flock (צאן) and the picture of the cattle cut off in the "drought" appears in Joel 1:18.[154] The phrase "no cattle in the stalls" further fills out the images in Joel 1:18.[155] Also, the images of the destruction of the cattle form part of the connection to Zeph 1:3, where the universal aspect of the judgment (as in Hab 3:16) comes into play as well. The fact that all of the phrases manifest a relationship to Joel, in roughly the same order as in Joel, combined with the fact that Hab 3:17 disturbs its context, argues strongly that Hab 3:17 serves a redactional unifying function and is more than an isolated gloss.[156]

Hab 3:18 offers an affirmation of confidence. In its present position, it offers the conclusion to 3:17, but given the uniqueness of 3:17, one must ask if 3:18 fits better with that verse or with the earlier material in 3:16.[157] The question of original unity is complicated, since 3:18 has a grammatical connection to 3:17 stronger than to 3:16 in its present form.

---

supposition cannot be proven, the presence of the unusual plural form in Hab 3:17 could be thus explained more plausibly than other attempts to relate the word to geographic cites for the practice of idolatry, so Manfred R. Lehmann, "A New Interpretaiton of the Term שדרמות." *VT* 3 (1953): 361-371. See the similar, but not literarily related, motif in Mal 1:12.

[153] The use of this verb appears significantly in the final servant song in Isa 53:8, which in its context also uses an extended sheep metaphor for the cutting off of the servant from the land of the living (53:8). The servant/sheep was taken away from the fold silently (53:7) for the transgression of the people.

[154] Although perhaps not so literarily dependent, the promise in Mic 2:12f must nevertheless also be brought into view at this point. These two verses provide metaphorical background and hermeneutical keys for understanding the intention of Hab 3:17 as promise to the remnant following Jerusalem's approaching destruction: "...I will surely gather the remnant of Israel. I will put them together like sheep in the fold." See also Mic 7:14, where the flock also appears as metaphor for people. The flock, in spite of future salvation, must first experience the shepherd's "rod."

[155] "Cattle" appear elsewhere in the Book of the Twelve, and may also have played some role in the image in Hab 3:17, but direct influence is hard to establish. The closest image comes in Amos 6:4, where punishment will come to those who have eaten cattle from the stall. Amos 6:4 stems from early layers of Amos and could have influenced the image in Hab 3:17, but the words for "stall" are different.

[156] It is interesting that a recent article relates much of the botanical imagery in the Book of the Twelve to similar motifs, but does not relate it to the redactional transmission of the corpus. See Izak Cornelius, "Paradise Motifs in the 'Eschatology' of the Minor Prophets and the Iconography of the Ancient Near East. The Concepts of Fertility, Water, Trees, and 'Tierfrieden' and Gen 2-3," *JNSL* 14 (1988): 41-83.

[157] Hab 3:17 creates a grammatical relationship of the 3:18 in the form of an interrelated series of clause ruled by a single construction: "Though ... then ..." See *GK* 159bb.

Nevertheless, there are good reasons for believing the original connection existed between 3:16a and 3:18. First, 3:16b,17, as already demonstrated, stand in considerable tension to the context of the poem. Second, Hab 3:18 read in its adversative function is not grammatically inconsistent with 3:16a.[158] Third, when 3:16a,18 are read together they form a consistent ending to the theophanic poem of 3:3-15:

> [16a]I heard and my inward parts trembled. At the sound my lips quivered. Decay entered into my bones, and beneath me I trembled, ... [18]but I will exult in YHWH. I will rejoice in the God of my salvation.

The "God of my salvation" in 3:18 takes up the images of the battle against the nations in the theophanic hymn, and particularly 3:13-14, which depicts YHWH as battling for the salvation of his people. The tension of the expectation of an attack by a single nation thus disappears, and the poem thus contained an appropriate response to the theophany proper.

Hab 3:19a concludes the poem, prior to the cultic subscriptive elements in 3:19b. This verse represents no mere appendage. It follows grammatically on 3:18, and continues the affirmation of confidence. The similarity of the language of this affirmation with the promise of conquest in Deut 33:29 and the deliverance from an enemy military attack in Ps 18:34, provides a further touchstone with the theophanic poem, coinciding with the Moses and Sinai traditions of Hab 3:3-7, and the attack of the nations in Hab 3:6,12-14.[159]

---

[158] By contrast, the verse is logically and grammatically inconsistent with a direct attachment to 3:16b, providing indications that 3:16b,17 stem from the same redactional hand. The change of theme between these two verses is due to the expansion of the literary horizon.

[159] Deut 33:29 appears at the end of Moses' blessing of the individual tribes just prior to the account of his death (Deut 34:1-12). As Moses prepares the people to enter Canaan, he states: "Blessed are you Israel: Who is like you, a people saved by YHWH, who is the shield of your help, and the sword of your majesty! So your enemies will cringe before you, and you shall *tread upon their high places.*" This phrase in Deuteronomy is closely connected to Hab 3:17 on the basis of the common verb they share (דרך), while Ps 18:34 provides the metaphor of the feet of the hind.

9. Summary of Redactional and Temporal Observations

Despite the diversity of style and the strangeness of many of the images within Hab 3:1-19, careful examination reveals that the "prayer" of Habakkuk need not be subjected to massive textual emendations, nor has it undergone an extraordinarily complex redaction history. Suggestions from Hiebert and others that the chapter underwent a separate transmission history from the Habakkuk corpus go a long way toward explaining the very diverse combination of motifs from the Sinai theophany and *Chaoskampf*. This separate transmission is most clearly evidenced by the cultic trappings the poem has received (3:1,3,9,13,19b), all of which are consistent with their usage in the Psalter. Emerging evidence on the compilation and redaction history of the Psalter, argue that the early Persian period provides the most likely period when these terms (particularly סלה) would have been added to the work, while it was still independent of the Habakkuk corpus.

Internal indications from the poem (especially in the metaphors of 3:8-15) indicate the strong possibility that the poem's original composition was probably the late exilic period or early post-exilic period, with the former being perhaps the more likely, because the poem readily implies the lessening of Babylonian power while at the same time condemning the surrounding nations. There is also no emphasis upon the return of the exiles, nor strong evidence of the influence of Deutero-Isaiah.

While there are one or two isolated places whose formulation *could have been* influenced by the incorporation of the poem into the Habakkuk corpus, the evidence is for the most part inconclusive. Only Hab 3:16b-17 stands out significantly enough from the basic tenor and content of the poem to assert with conviction that it does not belong to the original form of the poem, but has been inserted into the existing context. The fact that 3:16b-17 demonstrates an awareness of the literary context of Habakkuk 1-2 and of its position in the Book of the Twelve implies that these additions were deliberately added to connect the hymn to its current context in the canon. These verses reinterpret the hymn in light of the "coming" attack of the Babylonians (3:16b),[160] and in light of a paradigmatic reading of Joel 1-2 (Hab 3:17) that functions as a literary enactment of Joel's continuous locust attacks (metaphors for nations) which ruin the land.[161]

---

[160] Note the future attack in both Hab 1-2 and 3:16b is a literary construction about the Babylonian invasion and destruction to come. Also the "day of distress" relates to the eschatological destruction of Jerusalem as depicted in Zeph 1:15.

[161] See the interpretation of Joel as literary anchor in the conclusion of this work.

One more note regarding this adaptation of the poem warrants consideration. In the previous chapter a very similar technique was noted to the technique used here. Namely Nah 1:2-8 was a pre-existing hymn which was incorporated into a prophetic corpus. The similarities of these two works extend considerably beyond this formal observation. Both hymns in their original forms exhibit signs of cultic transmission. Both provide very similar perspectives of universal judgment in the form of a theophanic portrayal of the attack of the Divine Warrior. Both experience modification of the universal aspect of universal judgment by incorporation into contexts where the judgment is more narrowly focussed on the ruling world power of the period which each represents (Assyria and Babylon respectively). Finally, the redactional modifications in both Nah 1:2-8 and in Hab 3:16b-17 demonstrate a literary awareness which deliberately cites Joel. This last observation (when seen in relationship to the other similarities) strongly implies that Nahum and Habakkuk entered the corpus of the Book of the Twelve simultaneously. It also significantly increases the likelihood that both entered simultaneously with Joel. The date of Joel is debated, but there are good reasons for believing it stems from a time well into the Persian period. This date then provides a date before which these works could not have entered a common corpus.[162]

---

[162] See the discussion of the problems of dating Joel above in the discussion of Joel 4:1-21.

Malachi

1. The Macrostructure of Malachi

Scholarly opinions concerning the macro-structure of Malachi agree extensively regarding the number and extent of its units, although consensus cannot be claimed regarding the character of these units or of the writing as a whole.[1] Following the superscription, six units provide the skeletal frame for Malachi, to which is added a two-layered appendix. The units (1:2-5; 1:6-2:9; 2:10-16; 2:17-3:5; 3:6-12; 3:13-21) rely heavily upon a question/response format most often classified as disputation speeches.[2] The disputations normally begin with a statement followed by a rhetorical question and a further explication of the statement.[3] Paraphrasing this question/response structure provides an overview of the thematic interests, and it demonstrates the extent to which this stylistic device shapes Malachi.

---

[1] A recent article challenges this consensus. Erich Bosshard, and Reinhard Gregor Kratz, "Maleachi im Zwölfprophetenbuch." *BN* 52 (1990): 27-46, argue that Malachi exhibits three redactional layers, each with their own particular literary horizon. The *Grundschicht* (Mal I) contains the majority of the writing, but it receives an expansion in a second layer (Mal II), which contains two further units (2:17-3:5; 3:13-21). A final layer (Mal III) includes several smaller insertions (Mal 1:1,14a; 2:10-12; 3:22-24). They argue that all three layers presuppose Malachi's role as conclusion to the Book of the Twelve, but from different perspectives. They argue that Mal I was never a separate book on its own, but was originally the redactional continuation of Zech 7-8. Only with the inclusion of the superscription with the final layer did the material take the form of a separate writing. The majority of the redactional expansions they describe fall outside Mal 1:1-14, the immediate interest of this study. Nevertheless, an attempt has been made to dialogue with Kratz and Bosshard in appropriate places below.

[2] Egon Pfeiffer, "Die Disputationsworte im Buche Maleachi. Ein Beitrag zur formgeschlichtlichen Struktur," *Evangelische Theologie* 19 (1959): 546-568, documents this form in detail and classifies Malachi as a well-developed example of disputation speeches. Hans Jochen Boecker, "Bemerkungen zur formgeschichtlichen Terminologie des Buches Maleachi," *ZAW* 78 (1966): 78-80, attempts to soften the terminology by classifying them as discussion speeches, but the strident rhetoric in many of the speeches argues against Boecker's treatment. See Beth Glazier-McDonald, *Malachi: The Divine Messenger.* SBL Dissertation Series 98 (Atlanta: Scholars Press, 1987), 20f.

[3] Mal 2:10-16 stands as a slight exception in that 2:10 begins immediately with a question.

Verses	Statement	Question	Response
1:1	Superscription		
1:2-5	I have loved you (Israel).	But you say, "how have you loved us?"	I have loved Jacob and hated Esau.
1:6-2:9	A son honors his father and a servant his master.	Where is my honor? You say, "How have we despised your name?"	You present defiled food.
2:10-16	Judah has committed an abomination. (2:11)	Why do we profane the covenant of our fathers? (2:10)	May YHWH cut off those bringing false offerings.
	YHWH will not accept an offering from your hand. (2:13)	You say, "Why?" (2:14)	Because you have mistreated the wife of your youth. I hate divorce, so take heed.
2:17-3:5	You have wearied YHWH with your words.	You say, "How have we wearied him?"	When you say, "Everyone who does evil is good."
	I will send my messenger to clear the way before me.	But who can endure the day of his coming?	He will purify the sons of Levi so that they may present offerings to YHWH in righteousness.
3:6-12	I do not change. Return to me.	You say, "How do we return?	With (proper) tithes and offerings.
3:13-21	Your words have been arrogant against me.	You say, "What have we spoken against you?"	You said, "It is vain to serve YHWH."
3:22-24 [4:4-6]	Conclusion		

Even this brief outline demonstrates the dominance of the question/answer schema in shaping Malachi, but it also shows that the style is not fixed as an absolute pattern with no deviation. The structural frame of Malachi varies in several ways. It sometimes diverges in the compounding of questions (e.g. 2:10), sometimes in the repetition of the question/answer schema as a whole within the individual sections (e.g. 2:17-3:5).

The relationship of the individual parts to the whole creates a certain controversy. Some explain the relationship as a mosaic of independent speeches whose placement creates a "reading logic."[4] Others consider the disputation speeches as an original literary device.[5] Whatever the original

---

[4] Cf Rudolph, *KAT* 13/4, 250; Pieter A. Verhoef, *Haggai and Malachi*, 162f, 166.

[5] So already Wellhausen, *Die Kleinen Propheten*, 195. See also discussion Gerhard Wallis, "Wesen und Struktur der Botschaft Maleachis," *Das Ferne und Nahe Wort. Festschrift Leonhard Rost* (Berlin: Töpelmann, 1967), 232.

relationship between oral pronouncements by Malachi and the recording of those pronouncements, the consistency of the question/answer schema argues strongly against treating these units as *simply* the recording of oracles delivered over an extended period. Unless one presumes this prophet spoke only in disputation style — an highly dubious assumption — one must acknowledge that these oracles in their present form evidence literary interests. Even if one holds to the opinion that they accurately reflect the oral message of Malachi, they have been shaped to such an extent that they are now related by a consistent literary frame which identifies the "writing" stylistically.[6]

The themes of the individual oracles vary. Mal 1:2-5 discusses Israel's election in terms of Edom's destruction. Mal 1:6-2:9 exhibits several themes, but the condemnation of the priestly abuses dominate the unit.[7] Mal 2:10-16 centers on the theme of divorce, although there is considerable debate whether these images are to be taken literally or figuratively.[8] Mal 2:17-3:5 announces the coming of a messianic figure to purify the sons of Levi (3:3) and the people of Judah and Jerusalem (3:4f). Mal 3:6-12 calls for the repentance of the people, specifically with regard to the tithes and offerings they should bring to the temple. Significantly, this passage shares much common vocabulary and imagery with Haggai and Joel, so much so, that one must ask to what extent this passage reflects the literary awareness of a larger corpus.[9] Mal 3:13-21 deviates significantly from the disputation style in a manner which is often overlooked. This unit begins similarly to the others with the question/answer style prevalent in Malachi (3:13-15), but the continuation deviates in a manner more readily categorized as *narrative-like* because it describes the response of the faithful to the message of the prophet (3:16ff).[10] The actions of this response depict a situation in which

---

[6] For further discussion of the problem of drawing too stringent a distinction between oral and written prophecy, see Helmut Utzschneider, *Künder oder Schreiber? Eine These zum Problem der »Schriftprophetie« auf Grund von Maleachi 1:6-2:9*. Beiträge zur Erforschung des Alten Testaments und des Antiken Judentums 19 (Frankfurt: Peter Lang, 1989), 20f.

[7] See discussion below, page 194.

[8] See the summary of opinions in Glazier-McDonald, *Malachi*, 113-120. Most take these references as literal reference to the problems of intermarriage attested in Ezra and Nehemiah, but a substantial minority note the sense of the images is much sharper when it is related to the question of religious fidelity.

[9] See discussion below, page 204.

[10] Failure to recognize the change in function has caused confusion on several fronts. The LXX of 3:16 is sometimes cited as evidence for a different text, because it begins with ταῦτα, normally translated as "these things," while MT has זֶא ("then"). Compare e.g.

a righteous group of the whole (those fearing YHWH) respond properly to the disputations (they spoke among themselves and a book of remembrance was written). This proper response corresponds with the cessation of the disputation style. It will be necessary to return to this response in more detail following discussion of several other elements.[11] The remainder of the unit reflects a division among Israel, between the wicked and the righteous, with explicit descriptions of YHWH's future arrival to judge the wicked.

The conclusion to the book (3:22,23f) has won general recognition among scholars as two separate appendixes, the one (3:22) legal in its orientation and the other (3:23f) prophetic.[12] The former receives general recognition as an intentionally created conclusion to an extended portion of the prophetic canon.[13] This consensus rests in large part on stylistic differences to the writing of Malachi and on the similarity of 3:22 with Josh 1:2,7, the beginning of the former prophets.[14] Most interpret the reference to the coming of Elijah in 3:23f as a later addition still because its association of Elijah with the end times comes so close to Elijah's role in the New Testament.[15]

The appendix to the book (3:22-24) is the only passage which commands wide acceptance as a later addition, but some other passages have been suggested as interpolations, most frequently Mal 1:11-14. The

---

Elliger, *ATD* 25, 201. However, the fact that ταῦτα is a neuter plural which elsewhere can mean "for this reason" makes it unwise to accept these suggestions (cf Liddell and Scott, *Greek-English Lexicon*, under οὗτος). Rudolph, *KAT* 13/4, 286f, relates the verse to the actions of the past, understanding אז in the sense of "damals, als ...," but the context does not suit this interpretation.

[11] See the discussion of Mal 3:16ff below, page 206.

[12] This distinction refers to the content of the verses, not the literary function, in which Mal 3:22 seemingly attempts to combine the beginning of the prophetic corpus with the law.

[13] Examples include Elliger, *ATD* 25, 205; Mason, *Haggai, Zechariah, and Malachi*, 159f; Rudolph, *KAT* 13/4, 250; Horst, *HAT* 14, 253, 267. Some do disagree, e.g. Glazier-McDonald, *Malachi*, 262-270; Verhoef, *Haggai and Malachi*, 337f.

[14] Rudolph, *KAT* 13/4, 291, suggests 3:22f forms the conclusion of the prophetic corpus. For rationale for treating the verses as secondary, see also Elliger, *ATD* 25, 205f; Mason, *Haggai, Zechariah, and Malachi*, 159f. See also the summaries and discussions of Glazier-McDonald, *Malachi*, 243-270; Verhoef, *Haggai and Malachi*, 337f.

[15] Cf. Matt 11:14; 16:14; 17:3ff; 27:47,49; Luke 1:17; John 1:21,25. Malachi was likely not consciously selected by Christians as the conclusion to the Old Testament. Manuscript evidence is much too complicated to allow such a simple conclusion. See Graham Ogden and Richard R. Deutsch, *A Promise of Hope — A Call to Obedience: Joel and Malachi*, International Theological Commentary (Grand Rapids: Eerdmans, 1987), 117f.

reasons for this suggestion will be discussed below.   Other passages
suggested as secondary include parts of 2:11-13, and 3:1bb.[16]

2. The Date of Malachi

The consensus on the units also extends to the date of Malachi, at
least in relative terms. Almost universally, scholarship dates Malachi to the
fifth century, but there is considerable disagreement, or hesitation, about
dating it more narrowly than 480-430. Internal evidence strongly suggests
a fifth century date for several reasons: the ruling power is the Persian
governor (פחה); the temple is rebuilt, placing the date after 515; yet there
is no fervor over its existence. Rather, considerable cultic abuse has set in,
and economic conditions bear a general similarity to those in Nehemiah.
Hesitation over more specificity arises from several factors: the uncertainty
of the dates of Ezra and Nehemiah; the relationship of Malachi to Ezra's
reforms; and the long-term effects of those reforms.[17]   Attempts to date
Malachi on the basis of the destruction of Edom (1:2-5) are as problematic

---

[16] See discussions in Rudolph, *KAT* 13/4, 250f and Verhoef, *Haggai and Malachi*, 163f.

[17] While scholars are typically cautious in dating the book too precisely, most state a
preference for a specific time. Most attempt to discuss Malachi in relation to the
primary personages of the fifth century, Ezra and Nehemiah, but they disagree whether
Malachi preceded these two, followed them, or worked contemporary with them. A
sampling of suggested dates include the following: Glazier-McDonald, *Malachi*, 17
cautiously suggests Malachi appears between 460-450. W.J. Dumbrell, "Malachi and
the Ezra-Nehemiah Reforms," *Reformed Theological Review* 35/2 (1976): 42-52, is more
forceful in his conviction that Malachi served as instigation for the Ezra-Nehemiah
reforms, and he dates the book around 460. Verhoef, *Haggai and Malachi*, 156-160,
prefers 433, a date which he considers falls between the two visits of Nehemiah.
Rudolph, *KAT* 13/4, 248f, only narrows the parameters between 450 and 420. Horst,
HAT 14, 255, assumes Malachi came several decades after the work of Haggai and
Zechariah, but preceded Ezra (458/7) and Nehemiah (445), since Malachi contains no
references to them or their work. Elliger, *ATD* 25, 177f, similarly, believes Malachi
worked in the first half of the fifth century. Mason, *Haggai, Zechariah, and Malachi*,
137-139, is more cautious than most. He concludes that one may, with certainty, only
say that Malachi falls somewhere between Haggai and Zechariah 1-8 and Zechariah 9-
14. Mason notes that concrete reference to Malachi comes only with the second
century, and that the description of the problems does not tally completely with those
in Ezra or those in Nehemiah, despite some general similarities. Smith, *Word* 32, 298f
opts for the middle of the fifth century, but his qualifications for this date are more
involved than his arguments for it, placing him almost in the position of Mason.

as dating the work of Ezra and Nehemiah.[18]   When all the evidence is balanced, it would seem best to accept the general consensus for dating Malachi somewhere in the middle decades of the fifth century, at least for the majority of the writing.[19] Those who consider the writing to have been reworked or to have received additions (such as 3:22-24) would then date those additions subsequent to 430.[20]

3. Literary Observations on Mal 1:1-14

Mal 1:1-14 contains numerous words which link it with Zech 8:9ff.[21] It is thus necessary to look at the literary units in which Mal 1:1-14 appears. Mal 1:1-14 stretches across three distinct units of Malachi: 1:1, 1:2-5, 1:6-2:9. The superscription in **Mal 1:1** has been subjected to a great deal of scrutiny because of its similarity to Zech 9:1; 12:1.[22]   Additionally, the question of the identity of the prophet has created debate.[23] To be sure, the similarity of the superscriptions in Mal 1:1; Zech 9:1; 12:1 delimit three consecutive blocks of material, and creates the strong impression that these superscriptions play a role in shaping of the Book of the Twelve, but the exact nature of that relationship needs evaluation. The superscriptions share the same style, otherwise unattested, since they all begin with same

---

[18] See discussions in Smith, *Word* 32, 258; J.R. Bartlett, "The Brotherhood of Edom," *JSOT* 4 (Oct. 1977): 2-27; and John Lindsay, "The Babylonian Kings and Edom, 605-550 B.C.," *Palestine Exploration Quarterly* 108 (1976): 23-39.

[19] Despite the call for caution from those such as Mason and Smith, the arguments for this general date still appear convincing.

[20] Most who recognize Mal 3:22-24 as an addition date it in the Greek period.

[21] Zech 8:9ff and Mal 1:1-14 both contain at least twelve words and phrases which, with their recurrences, appear more than thirty times between the two passages: your hands (Zech 8:9,13; Mal 1:9,10,13); people (Zech 8:11,12,20,22; Mal 1:4); fruit (Zech 8:12; Mal 1:12); curse (Zech 8:13; Mal 1:14); nations (Zech 8:13,22,23; Mal 1:11); evil (Zech 8:14; Mal 1:8); father (Zech 8:14; Mal 1:6); return (Zech 8:15; Mal 1:4); gates (Zech 8:16; Mal 1:10); love (Zech 8:17,19; Mal 1:3); I hate (Zech 8:17; Mal 1:3); entreat the face (Zech 8:21,22; Mal 1:9).

[22] See, e.g., Fohrer, *Einleitung*, 511; Kaiser, *Introduction*, 284; Eissfeldt, *Introduction*, 440.

[23] This debate rests in no small measure on the LXX translation of מלאכי as "his messenger" rather than a proper name. Additionally, from an early time people have posited various suggestions as to the identity, with the most frequently suggested person being Ezra. For a collection of the evidence, consult Eberhard Nestle, "Miscellen." *ZAW* 27 (1907): 115.

three word: מַשָּׂא דְבַר־יהוה (oracle of the word of YHWH). They also introduce blocks of material roughly the same size. In spite of this similarity there are some differences in the three superscriptions.

Zech 9:1	Zech 12:1	Mal 1:1
The burden of the word of YHWH is against the land of Hadrach, with Damascus as its resting place (for the eyes of men, especially all the tribes of Israel, are toward YHWH).	The burden of the word of YHWH concerning Israel, declares YHWH, who stretches out the heavens, lays the foundation of the earth and forms the spirit of man within him.	The burden of the word of YHWH to Israel through Malachi.

The words form part of a nominative sentence in Zech 9:1, whereas in both Zech 12:1 and Mal 1:1 the phrase serves a titular function. Yet even the two titular usages distinguish themselves from one another. Zech 12:1 exhibits an expanded style which gives the impression that it has been inserted into an existing context, whereas Mal 1:1 presents a simple title affixed to the head of the writing.[24] Both Zech 12:1 and Mal 1:1 mention Israel in the title specifically, but Zech 12:1 implies Israel as the subject (עַל) while Mal 1:1 implies it as the recipient (אֶל). Zech 9:1 also mentions the "tribes of Israel," but in a parenthetical expression, not in the title proper. In its earlier form, Zech 9:1 likely introduced only 9:1-7.[25] Finally, the expression "through Malachi" in Mal 1:1 recalls similar phrases in Hag 1:1; 2:1, but has no counterpart in Zech 9:1; 12:1.

As already noted, the similarities of the three superscriptions cause a large number of commentators to postulate a relationship, but distinctions have caused others to question whether a relationship really exists between the three elements.[26] An important clue to explain both the similarities and the differences appears in the double title in 12:1 and the strained syntax in Zech 9:1. Rudolph argues correctly that the phraseology of these

---

[24] The second title in Zech 12:1a stands before (but not syntactically integrated with) the doxological hymnic piece in 12:1b. This doxological material comes very close to the style found in Amos 4:13; 5:8f; 9:5f, although those hymns stand at the close of units, not the beginning. Rudolph, *KAT* 13/4, 219, correctly notes that 12:1a has been inserted into a context in which the doxological material in 12:1b served as the conclusion to the shepherd allegory (11:4-17; 13:7-9). The transposition of 13:7-9 from its original position at the conclusion of the shepherd allegory has long been recognized (see discussion in the chapter on Zech 9-14).

[25] See discussion of Zech 9:1ff in the following chapter on Zech 9-14.

[26] Such as Verhoef, *Haggai and Malachi*, 154.

two passages reflects a interest to shape Zech 9:1; 12:1 after Mal 1:1.[27]
This redactional shaping accounts for the similarities and the differences if
one assumes that 9:1 was modified and 12:1 was added when they entered
the Book of the Twelve.[28] It is here suggested that Zech 9-14 entered an
existing corpus in which Proto-Zechariah and Malachi already existed side
by side.[29] The reasons for this inclusion, while currently somewhat
hypothetical, nevertheless provide better explanations for several factors,
such as the existence of catchwords between Zech 8:9-23 and Mal 1:1-14,
and the fact that Zech 9-14 post-dates Malachi considerably.[30]

---

[27] Rudolph, *KAT* 13/4, 218f, 253. Mason, *Haggai, Zechariah, and Malachi*, presumes Mal
1:1 imitated Zech 9:1; 12:1, but this appears unlikely in light of the syntactical problems
of those two verses. Fohrer, *Einleitung*, 511, ascribes all three to a redactor of the
Book of the Twelve, but assumes that the proper name Malachi was added to make a
Twelfth book. This opinion, often cited, accounts for the similarities but does not
account for the differences or for the catchword connections between Proto-Zechariah
and Malachi. Bosshard and Kratz, *BN* 52 (1990): 45, place Mal 1:1 in their final layer
because it functions similarly to 3:22-24 which concludes the prophetic corpus (see
above, page 185). In addition to its syntactical clarity, the formulation of Mal 1:1
evidences a resemblance to Haggai (ביד) which argues more strongly that it was
present before the inclusion of Zech 9-14, since Zech 9:1 and 12:1 do not exhibit these
similarities. A summary of the formation of the Book of the Twelve in the final
chapter will suggest that the writings of Joel, Obadiah, Nahum, Habakkuk, and Malachi
entered the Book of the Twelve together with a specific purpose. The combination of
the superscriptions of these writings might also shed some light on the peculiar form
of Mal 1:1. The use of דבר יהוה could tie in with Joel 1:1, while the use of משא
could derive from Nah 1:1 and Hab 1:1.

[28] One may assume the redactor added משא in Zech 9:1, because its elimination leaves
a clearer syntax. Zech 9:1 involves the title in a nominative sentence, whose reference
to the "land of Hadrach" leads directly into the oracles in Zech 9:1-7 (See discussion
in the chapter on Zech 9-14). In Zech 12:1, the question is more complicated since the
doxological material in 12:1b once concluded the shepherd allegory. It is unlikely that
12:1b began an entire complex, since נאם־יהוה does not function as an introduction
elsewhere, and since its doxological style functions more appropriately as a conclusion.

[29] This theory runs contrary to the presumption that Proto-Zechariah and Zech 9-14 were
a single corpus prior to their inclusion into the Book of the Twelve, and contrary to
those who assume that Malachi and Zech 9-14 all entered the corpus simultaneously,
with Malachi gaining special status to create the twelfth book. See, e.g., Fohrer,
Einleitung, 511; Kaiser, *Introduction*, 284; Eissfeldt, *Introduction*, 440.

[30] Later, this chapter will discuss the rationale and implications for this understanding of
Zech 9-14 as they relate to why Malachi retained its position at the end of the corpus
(see below, page 204). The following chapter will discuss some of the hermeneutical
forces at work in the compilation of Zech 9-14.

The next unit, **Mal 1:2-5**, begins typically with disputation statement, and continues until the next statement (1:6) marks a decided change in theme. The unit is unified thematically, but has no formula marking either the beginning or the end of the unit. YHWH speaks in first person style throughout these verses, although at times he quotes the objections of his opponents.[31] The unit may be subdivided structurally into two parts (1:2-4,5), but these parts are not independent from one another, since the entire unit is syntactically and thematically cohesive. Mal 1:2-4 represents a tightly-knit speech dominated by an antithetical chiastic structure.[32]

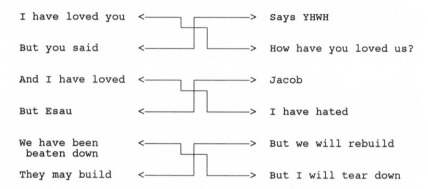

```
I have loved you   <----------   ---------->  Says YHWH

But you said       <----------   ---------->  How have you loved us?

And I have loved   <----------   ---------->  Jacob

But Esau           <----------   ---------->  I have hated

We have been       <----------   ---------->  But we will rebuild
  beaten down

They may build     <----------   ---------->  But I will tear down
```

The chiastic statements are part of the overall dialogical frame in which YHWH confronts Israel's accusation that YHWH has not treated them properly. Mal 1:5 climaxes the unit, providing a suitable closure in the process by the *inclusio* it creates (again antithetically) with 1:2. Whereas in Mal 1:2, YHWH quotes Israel's accusation, 1:5 uses the same style and a similar formula ("but/and you say") to quote Israel's proper response — that of praise.[33] The structure of Mal 1:2-5 thus progresses step-by-step from the people's improper attitude to a proper attitude toward YHWH.

While the structural frame of Mal 1:2-5 demonstrates its intention to bring Israel to a proper recognition of YHWH, the content of these verses exhibits a decidedly negative attitude toward Edom as an example of YHWH's action on behalf of his people. Several comments about the

---

[31] Hence in Mal 1:2, YHWH quotes the people ("but you say ...") and in Mal 1:4 he quotes Edom.

[32] For further elaboration on minor chiastic element which appear in these verses as well, see S.D. Snyman, "Antitheses in Malachi 1:2-5," *ZAW* 98 (1986): 436-438.

[33] Mal 1:2 contains the accusation, "... but you say, 'how have you loved us?'" Contrast this with Mal 1:5, where YHWH quotes a changed Israel, "... and you will say, 'YHWH be magnified beyond the borders of Israel.'"

background of this animosity are in order. Historically, post-exilic Judah treated Edom with contempt because of the collective memory of Edom's role in the destruction of Jerusalem.[34] Tradition-critically, these verses presuppose knowledge of the Jacob-Esau tradition in Genesis.[35] Literarily, and for this study most significant, Mal 1:2-5 explicitly takes up the book of Obadiah. Specifically Mal 1:4, which quotes Edom's resolve to "rebuild," plays off Obad 3-4:

> Your insolent heart has deceived you, the one dwelling in the hiding places of the cliffs, the height of his dwelling, saying in his heart: "Who can bring me down to earth?" Though you *build* as high as the eagle, and though your nest is placed among the stars, from there I will bring you down — utterance of YHWH.

The destruction of Edom in Obad 3f clearly lies in the future, whereas in the dialogue in Mal 1:4, the destruction of Edom has already occurred (or is a least in a very advanced stage), but the language of Mal 1:3-5, especially 1:4 alludes quite clearly to Obad 4. The reference to Edom as Esau derives ultimately from the Genesis traditions, but it is not at all a common designation in the prophetic literature, since it only occurs within

---

[34] For a discussion of the historical circumstances surrounding Edom's participation in Jerusalem's destruction, see the treatment of Obadiah above (chapter three).

[35] The Jacob-Esau narratives play a role in the selection of epithets Jacob and Esau. It does not appear, however, that the content of the narratives serves as a literary backdrop for Mal 1:2-5. For an analysis of the growth of the Jacob/Esau traditions, see J.R. Bartlett, "The Brotherhood of Edom," *JSOT* 4 (Oct. 1977): 2-27. See also the article on this passage by G. Johannes Botterweck, "Jakob habe ich lieb," *Bibel und Leben* 1 (1960): 28-38. Bosshard and Kratz, *BN* 52 (1990): 31,35f, consider Mal 1:2-5 as part of Mal I because it functions as a type of exposition on the framework in 1:6-2:3 and 3:6-12. Further, they note the presupposition of the Jacob/Esau tradition in Mal 1:2-5, but they do so on the basis of the argument that it draws from Hos 11:1ff and the reference in Hos 12:4 to Jacob's wrestling with God at Bethel (which is part of the Jacob/Esau cycle). However, their presentation overlooks the fact that Mal 1:2-5 (also) draws from Obadiah in a manner which is much more direct literarily in light of the particular formulations in that writing. (See below, note 36). The reason for this oversight might be linked to the fact that they believe (36) Obadiah (as well as Joel, and Zephaniah) entered the larger corpus later than Malachi. This conclusion differs from the evidence presented in this study. See also the discussion of the dependence of Mal 3:10f on Joel motifs (below, page 205). Since Bosshard and Kratz recognize Mal 1:2-5 and 3:10f as part of the *Grundschicht*, and since these passages depend upon Obadiah and Joel respectively, it seems more plausible that Joel and Obadiah already formed part of the corpus when Malachi entered. Bosshard and Kratz provide striking evidence, however, that Malachi is very much a literary text created for its position as the conclusion to the Book of the Twelve.

the prophetic writings in Mal 1:2-5 and in the two related passages of Obadiah and Jer 49:8,10. The reference to the mountains of Esau in Mal 1:3 and Obad 8,18 occurs only in these two places.[36] Obadiah and Malachi share other terminology as well.[37] The conditional statement in Mal 1:4 corresponds with the same conditional style in Obad 4f. Finally, the motif of Edom's self-deception plays a dominant role in both Obadiah and Malachi.[38]

One question remains uncertain, namely, how does one explain Malachi's use of Obadiah? Should it be viewed tradition-critically or redactionally, i.e. does Malachi simply draw on Obadiah's prophecy to accentuate the historical situation of the time, or does Mal 1:2-5 reflect a theological conviction implanted into a literary context? Is Malachi better understood as the record of a prophet's speech, or as a type of "written" prophetic literature drawing upon other texts in its attempt to portray a message?[39] If the latter, was Malachi's adaptation of Obadiah already part of a larger corpus, or only to be understood in the context of Malachi alone? Several factors complicate a decision. Arguing for a more narrow

---

[36] There are good reasons for supposing that Mal 1:3 alludes to Obadiah, and not to the parallel text in Jer 49:16. First, the transmission history of the Book of the Twelve makes this assumption the more natural one. Second, while the two passages (Jer 49:14-16,9; Obad 1ff) naturally share much common vocabulary, complicating a decision on the question of dependency, the reference to "his mountains" in Mal 1:3 with the antecedent Esau is more readily explainable in light of the references to the "mountain of Esau" in Obad 8,18. Elsewhere these terms do not appear together, arguing that the primary focal point was Obadiah.

[37] Obad 10 states that Edom will be cut off forever (לעולם) which parallels the statement in Mal 1:4 naming them a people against whom YHWH is indignant forever (עד עולם). Obad 7 predicts Edom will be driven from the territory (literally to the border [עד הגבול]), whereas Mal 1:4f contrasts the wicked territory (גבול) of Edom with the power of YHWH over the territory (גבול) of Israel.

[38] Obad 3 portrays Edom as self-deceptive in its delusion over the security of its lofty dwelling place. Mal 1:4 takes this deception one step further by portraying Edom as still suffering under the misapprehension of its strength. In spite of the fact that YHWH has beaten them down (רשש), they try to claim they will rebuild their ruins (note the antithetical relationship involving the height of Edom's dwelling in Obad 3 contrasted with their lowly stature in Mal 1:4. However, YHWH refuses to allow their bravado to go unchallenged.

[39] At least one other passage in Malachi points in the direction of the latter. Utzschneider has documented how Malachi's use of various scriptural passages in Mal 1:6-2:9 informs the interpretation of those verses. See Utzschneider, *Künder oder Schreiber*? More significantly, Bosshard and Kratz, *BN* 52 (1990): 27-46, demonstrate how the entire writing is cognizant of its position in the Book of the Twelve.

view in which Mal 1:2-5 is read only in light of the composition of Malachi, one must admit the similarity of style in Mal 1:2-5 points in the direction of a relatively homogenous compositional frame. The question-response style plays as important a role in Mal 1:2-5 as in the remainder of the writing. Also, the unit makes sense as it stands, i.e., it is self-contained. On the other hand, several observations argue in the other direction, namely that Mal 1:2-5 functions better as literary prophecy within the Book of the Twelve than in an isolated reading in Malachi alone. The Edom pericope stands out considerably from the remainder of Malachi, which has a strong cultic orientation. Mal 1:2-5 exhibits no such orientation. As for the dominance of the question-response style, one can observe that it is *so dominant* a redactor would certainly not have been oblivious to its presence, and could easily have adopted the same style for an insertion. Finally, the argument that Mal 1:2-5 is self-contained can be turned around, since it also reveals Mal 1:2-5 has no intimate relationship to the immediate context, although some argue that its *position* prior to the statement in Mal 1:6 is logical, even if not presupposed.[40]

It is thus difficult to determine criteria as to how to "read" Mal 1:2-5. One observation does shed further light on the pericope in relationship to Malachi, but this observation also leads to further complications. It is true that Mal 1:2-5 has no direct relationship to its immediate context, but a passage later in the writing indicates an awareness of Mal 1:2-5. Mal 3:15 mentions the "doers of wickedness" (עשׁי רשׁעה) who are built up (נבנו) when they test god and escape. This verse appears to contain a deliberate play on words with Mal 1:2-5 in which Esau (עשׂו) is called a territory of wickedness (רשׁעה) who threatens to rebuild (בנה) after YHWH destroys their dwelling place. Since Mal 3:17 refers back to 1:6 with a similar play on words it seems plausible that these passages form a deliberate *inclusio* from the beginning to the end of Malachi.[41] It is thus not wise to say that Mal 1:2-5 is so isolated that it comes from a different compositional layer from the remainder of the writing. The complication created by this

---

[40] So for example, Verhoef, *Haggai and Malachi*, 210. Rudolph, *KAT* 13/4, 250, presents a typical position when he states that the speeches are on the whole loosely ordered one after another, but the *position* of 1:2-5 exhibits a certain logic because it functions as a disputation of the skepticism regarding YHWH's love for his people, which serves as the basis for a call to observe pure cultic rites in thankfulness (1:6-2:9; 3:6-12) and other religious obligations (2:10-16). The certainty of YHWH's love should also serve to prevent any doubt regarding YHWH's justice (2:17-3:5; 3:13-21).

[41] See discussion of similar phenomena in the macro-structure of Amos and the early version of Nahum.

observation results from the context of 3:13-21. This unit raises as many questions about its *function* as Mal 1:2-5. On the one hand, the passage presupposes its context in Malachi, but on the other hand one should ask if this pattern of Malachi has a broader literary interest. Such would seem to be the case, in large part because of numerous references near the end of Malachi which transcend the book.[42] These observations, together with many of those made by Bosshard and Kratz, argue that Mal 1:2-5 (indeed, the entire book) should be read in context as the conclusion to the Book of the Twelve.

The next unit, **Mal 1:6-2:9**, may be subdivided into five parts (1:6,7,8-10,11-14; 2:1-9), but these subsections should not necessarily be presumed to be independent in origin.[43] Mal 1:6 serves as the introduction since the main words in this verse are taken up in the subsequent subsections.[44] Mal 1:7 presents two images, the first in 1:7a refers to the defiled material brought for sacrifices, and the second in 1:7b refers to the priests who say that the table of YHWH should be despised. Mal 1:8-10 takes up the theme of 1:7a, the bringing of impure sacrifices. These verses also contrast the gifts brought to the governor with those which come before YHWH. Several commentators describe Mal 1:11-14 not only as thematically unusual, but also as formally independent, stating or implying it was added later.[45] Thematically, the verses take up the question of the name of

---

[42] See the discussion below, beginning on page 204, on the literary indications that Malachi indicates an awareness of its position as the conclusion of the Twelve.

[43] With the probable exception of Mal 1:11-14, see discussion below. Other commentators sometimes divide the sub-units of this section somewhat differently. I follow Utzschneider in these subdivisions in light of his careful analysis of the text markers and the thematic cohesion. Utzschneider, *Künder oder Schreiber?*, 35-37, Utzschneider divides the text into four main themes: 1) The priests make the name of YHWH despised rather than honored or feared. 2) YHWH's name is great among the nations. 3) The command for the priests is therefore, that since they do not take the honor of the name of YHWH to heart, the curse will come upon them. 4) YHWH will make the priests despised to the degree that they do not follow in his ways.

[44] Compare "glory" (כבוד) in 1:6 and 2:2; "fear" (מורא) in 1:6 and 2:5; "name" (שם) in 1:6 and 1:11,14; 2:2,5; "despise" (בזה) in 1:6 and 1:7,12; 2:9.

[45] Such as Utzschneider, *Künder oder Schreiber?*, 31f, 41f, 84-87. Utzschneider considers Mal 1:11-14 (84-87) as a probable addition (based on typical arguments), and dates this passage somewhere between 300-162 because this period evidences other temples (Elephantine [in Persian Period]; Gerazim in Lachish, Leontopolis in Egypt; "Qasr el -ᶜAbd" in East Jordan.) See Volkmar Fritz, *Tempel und Zelt. Studien zum Tempelbau in Israel und zum Zeltheiligtum der Priesterschrift* (Neukirchen: Neukirchner Verlag, 1977), 76-93. Others who see these verses (or parts of them) as later additions include: Horst, *HAT* 14, 259; Elliger, *ATD* 25, 187f. By contrast, others argue that it does not

YHWH among the nations, but they do so with many of the words from Mal 1:6-10. This anaphoric relationship is coupled with a cataphoric relationship to 2:1-9, and implies an awareness of the context, even though the theme changes.[46] Mal 2:1-9 should be seen primarily from the perspective of its function as the verdict over the situation described in 1:6-14.[47] From this perspective the catchwords with Mal 1:6 play an important function in this section.

Utzschneider probes 1:6-2:9 to demonstrate its literary cohesion *and* its dependence upon other texts. A brief summary of his conclusions will facilitate the discussion of the entire unit before turning to Mal 1:6-14 in particular. Utzschneider begins by recognizing that *"Schriftprophetie"* as a concept challenges traditional understandings of prophetic literature, but one which cannot be ignored, since one must not only come to terms with the speeches of particular prophets, but also with a process of transmission and editing, which in most cases, extended well beyond the life of the prophet. Utzschneider pointedly asks whether one can or should isolate as "prophetic" only that which can be found in the extraction of the orally delivered message, or whether the written "interpretation" has prophetic qualities as well.[48] Utzschneider presents his thesis that in the Old Testament there were also "writers" whose function was "prophetic."[49] As example, Utzschneider investigates Mal 1:6-2:9 first from the perspective of its inner cohesion and then from the perspective of its intertextuality.[50] Examples of this intertextuality Utzschneider finds include:[51]

---

disturb the context, and should therefore not be regarded as secondary: Mason, *Haggai, Zechariah, and Malachi*, 144f; Rudolph, *KAT* 13/4, 262. Glazier-McDonald, *Malachi*, 55-64; and J.G. Baldwin, "Malachi 1:11 and the Worship of the Nations in the Old Testament," *Tyndale Bulletin* 23 (1972): 117-124, try to avoid the problems by treating the verse as an eschatological expectation.

[46] Utzschneider, *Künder oder Schreiber?*, 31f, discusses the various words in their context. Anaphoric refers to the repetition of words which appear above the current text, while kataphoric refers to those which refer below.

[47] See also Glazier-McDonald, *Malachi*, 47.

[48] Utzschneider, *Künder oder Schreiber?*, 12.

[49] Utzschneider, *Künder oder Schreiber?*, 17.

[50] Utzschneider, *Künder oder Schreiber?*, 18f, offers three rationale for selecting Malachi in general: 1) Several scholars have questioned whether Malachi is a purely scribal creation. 2) The long-recognized difficulty over the identity of the author stems largely from understanding Malachi as a name rather than a title. 3) Malachi depends upon other parts of the Old Testament.

[51] Utzschneider, *Künder oder Schreiber?*, 42-71. See also his graphic presentations of the texts involved, pages 97-102.

Receiving Text	Source Text
Mal 1:6b-7	Ezek 44:6f,15f
Mal 1:6bb-8a	Deut 15:20f
Mal 1:8b-10	Gen 32f (esp 32:14,21f,31; 33:10)
Mal 1:11f	Ezek 36:20-23; Ps 113f
Mal 1:13	Exod 18:8; Num 20:14; Neh 9:32
Mal 2:2-4	Deut 33:8-11; Num 25:10-13; 2 Sam 2:31

Utzschneider summarizes his conclusions from three perspectives.[52] First, the texts which he finds related to Mal 1:6-2:9 are not isolated to one part of the canonical literature. Second, the transmitted form of the intertextuality varies. It can relate to common sayings, to formulas from worship services, and to catchword associations with texts which correspond to the written form of those texts which are utilized meaningfully. Third, he considers the type and function of the intertextuality. He notes that the relationship is always anonymous. Functionally, the catchwords from the source texts are woven meaningfully into the context of Mal 1:6-2:9, and thus one cannot unqualifiably label these associations as "interpretation" of the source text. Rather, they *presuppose* an interpretation of the source text in order to clarify the position of the receiving text. Nevertheless, the relationship between the two texts is often contradictory (especially with Ezekiel), sometimes explanatory, and sometimes simply utilizes a word play.

Utzschneider demonstrates the extent to which Israel's scriptural traditions had begun to effect the form of prophetic literature by the time of Malachi. The author of Malachi was well-versed in these traditions and freely drew from them in creating his work. Having noted how both 1:2-5 and 1:6-2:9 fit together as a unit, and how they rely upon other texts to sharpen their point, it is now possible to turn more explicitly to Mal 1:1-14 in light of the end of Proto-Zechariah, in order to seek determine the relationship of the two passages.[53]

---

[52] Utzschneider, *Künder oder Schreiber?*, 72-74.

[53] The comparison is limited to Mal 1:1-14 in part because of space, in part because of the number of words, and in part because of the logical breaking point 1:6-14 affords with its function as the accusation section of the larger unit.

4. Contrasting Motifs in Mal 1:1-14 and Zech 8:9-23

On the surface, these two passages provide an impressive array of common words, but literary analyses alone do not immediately reveal criteria for deciding how to evaluate the question of intentionality.[54] Are the common words merely attributable to accident, or do they represent deliberate attempts to coordinate the two passages in some manner? A comparison of several of the motifs in the two passages adds to the impression that they are related in some way, since these motifs paint a picture in which the two passages present *contrasting images*. Both passages incorporate the priests and the people as addressees.[55] The Zechariah passage demonstrates no animosity toward either the people or the priests, while anger and confrontation against the priests dominate Mal 1:6ff. Zech 8:9ff addresses the people with encouragement, and the tone is hopeful. By contrast, Mal 1:2-5 exhorts the people to recognize YHWH's sovereignty in a decidedly more negative tone in which they are confronted with their own skepticism. Zech 8:21f and Mal 1:9 both contain the phrase "to entreat the favor" (חלה + פני) in relation to the divinity, but the contrast between the two passages is quite marked. In Zech 8:21f, the nations will come to Jerusalem to entreat YHWH's favor, in part because of the positive example of YHWH's people. This image is positive, and assumes that YHWH will accept their entreaty. The phrase in Mal 1:9 is part of a series of combative rhetorical questions which reject the entreaty of the priests because of the negative manner in which they bring the offering.[56]

---

[54] For a list of catchwords, see above, note 21. See also the discussion of Zech 8:9ff in Nogalski, *Literary Precursors*, 257ff, which is presumed in the following discussions.

[55] Mal 1:2-5 addresses all Israel while Mal 1:6ff is directed primarily against the priests, for their acceptance and encouragement of abuses. The extended context of Zech 7:1-8:23 demonstrates that the priests and inhabitants are the recipients of this extended speech as well. Compare Zech 7:3,5 and the *inclusio* to the end of chapter eight incorporating the two chapters as a single "event."

[56] When one compares the specific form of the phrase in the two passages, one cannot help but note the irony of the fact that the nations entreat the favor of YHWH, and will be accepted, while the priests entreat the favor of god (אל), but will be rejected. The fact that post-exilic texts use אל primarily as a designation for foreign gods makes this irony even more pronounced. (See Frank M. Cross, "אֵל," *ThWAT*, 278). Utzschneider, *Künder oder Schreiber?*, 50-53, sees the Malachi passage as a deliberate play on Peniel in Gen 32:31. Since this word is part of several words and phrases related to Gen 32f, one cannot dismiss this possibility lightly. While it is possible that Mal 1:8-10 could play off both Gen 32f and Zech 8:21f, it is *more likely* that the Zechariah passage is the later of the two (see literary analysis) and would thus

Both Zech 8:18f and Mal 1:6ff treat the question of the observance of cultic rites and ceremonies, and again Zechariah treats the theme in positive images (the fasts will become feasts of joy), while Malachi portrays the entire relationship to the cult in negative terms in which the priests and people conspire to bring defective offerings which do not please YHWH.[57] Both Zech 8:20-23 and Mal 1:14 introduce highly positive, and highly unusual, attitudes toward the nations. Yet, even these verses offer a contrast with regard to the different attitudes toward YHWH's people they present. Zech 8:20-23 portrays the nations making a pilgrimage *to Jerusalem* to entreat YHWH's favor because of the fame of the deeds YHWH has performed for the city (20-22), and because they can follow YHWH's people. By contrast, Mal 1:11-14 provides for the possibility of offerings in a way which explicitly avoids Jerusalem, and treats the nations as better examples of proper attitudes than YHWH's own people.[58]

The economic situation of Zech 8:9ff and Mal 1:1ff also demonstrates a progression which moves from the positive to the negative. In Zech 8:9-13, the economic prospects have begun to change for the better, particularly when compared with the situation of the past. The agricultural outlook has changed for the present generation (Zech 8:11), and by implication from the reference to the past time when their was no wage too be had (Zech 8:10), the economic situation was also improved. Malachi offers both a progression and a contrast to the situation in Zechariah. The progression is visible in that while Zechariah marks a transition from bad to normal economic conditions, Malachi presupposes relatively stable economic

---

presuppose this portion of Malachi. The fact that Mal 2:2 explicitly uses אל when referring to the "daughter of a foreign god" makes it possible that Mal 1:8 deliberately selected the word to create this irony, and that Zech 8:21f accentuated the irony by associating the entreaty of the nations with YHWH.

[57] The contrast between the positive and negative relationship to the cult could very well help account for the extended *inclusio* in Zech 7-8. The redactional placement of the response to the question of Zech 7:3 in 8:18f not only creates an effective envelope for the two chapters, the placement of the cultic material nearer the end of chapter eight also serves to highlight the contrast with Malachi's negative images.

[58] The question as to how this contrast was created is complicated, since both passages manifest tension thematically with their respective contexts. Possibly, Zech 8:20-23 demonstrates awareness of Mal 1:11-14, since it already evidences a broader literary perspective with its bracketing function to 7:1-3. Additionally, 8:20-23 affords a positive view toward the nations, but it also differs in one aspect from Mal 1:11-14. It depicts the positive relationship of the nations more typically for Zion theology, with a pilgrimage of the nations to Jerusalem. Another model presupposes Malachi as a redactional *Fortschreibung* of Zech 8:9ff. See footnote 61.

conditions have existed for some time.[59]   The contrast between the two passages derives from the actions of the priests and the people. Stated tersely, Zech 8:9-13 marks the transition away from the time when the people had nothing to offer YHWH, while Malachi presumes they have the means to offer YHWH his due, but that they only bring what is defective (Mal 1:8f). The ability to bring acceptable sacrifices is not at issue in Malachi, but the dishonesty of the priests and the people who give only what they find undesirable contrasts markedly with Zech 8:9-13 where the transition was a sign of hope for the future. In Malachi, there is no sense of gratitude to YHWH for changed circumstances, no sense of the gift that YHWH had returned to them. The picture is one in which any obligation to YHWH is perfunctory at best.

In addition to these contrasting constellations and motifs, several of the catchwords further the contrasts between the two passages.[60]   Zech 8:17 warns that YHWH hates evil, while in Mal 1:8 the priests perform evil. The gates of the city in Zech 8:16 are a place of peace, while the gates of the temple in Mal 1:10 should be closed because of treachery and abuse. Zech 8:9 exhorts the priests and people to strengthen their hands, while in Mal 1:9,13 YHWH refuses to accept the offering from the hand of the priest.

Given that these two passages consistently use the same vocabulary to contrast radically different situations, and that one can sometimes detect one or the other passage appears to be shaping the contrast, the question arises: *why* do the two passages contrast situations as they do?[61]   In

---

[59]   One may legitimately deduce the relative stability of the economic situation from the fact that offerings and sacrifices are being brought in Mal 1:6ff. These items require not only a functioning cult, but the availability of the items themselves.

[60]   Not all the words can be accounted for in this manner. "Father" refers to YHWH in Malachi, but Zechariah uses the plural to refer to the previous generation. The contrast of hate/love in the two passages likewise does not relate directly. Zech 8:17 creates this contrast in relationship to ethical commands while Mal 1:2f uses the contrast in comparison between Jacob and Esau. The use of שׁוּב to mean "again" in Zech 8:15 and Mal 1:4 is somewhat antithetical, but not so direct that one can maintain a deliberate relationship. Zech 8:15 offers a promise that YHWH will "again" return to Jerusalem, while Mal 1:4 asserts that Edom will not "again" build up its ruins.

[61]   In most instances, the text in Malachi creates these opposing perspectives. See Kratz and Bosshard, *BN* 52 (1990): 32ff. Kratz and Bosshard properly correct my previous suggestions that Zech 8:9ff created the contrast. See James D. Nogalski, *The Use of Stichwörter as a Redactional Unification Technique in the Book of the Twelve*, ThM Thesis (Rüschlikon, Switzerland: Baptist Theological Seminary, 1987), 124. They correctly observe this suggestion approached Malachi from too narrow a perspective,

response to this question one should consider the respective position of these passages in the context of the Book of the Twelve. The Haggai-Zechariah (1-8) corpus depicts a very hopeful and positive view of the times surrounding the building of the temple. To be sure, Haggai must rally a sluggish people to build the temple, but the end of the work presupposes their compliance to a certain extent. Zechariah likewise contains elements of warning to the current generation, but generally assumes obedience. Zech 7-8 presume that a change has already started to occur, although greater blessings lie in the future. Malachi, with its portrayal of the abuses of both people and priest, presents a shocking contrast to the hope in Zechariah. This contrast works hermeneutically in much the same fashion as the typical pattern of the alternation of judgment/salvation in the Deuteronomistic corpus, which formed the basis of what later became the Book of the Twelve.[62] When seen in this larger perspective, particularly following the hope of Zechariah and the rebuilding of the temple, Malachi's confrontation of the current generation presents an even more dramatic contrast. The situation has gone full circle, as if Jerusalem's destruction and YHWH's subsequent deliverance had been for nought. The circular pattern of judgment, punishment, and deliverance begins again in precisely the place where one would expect a different, more hopeful, beginning. In this light, the calls of Zechariah to learn from the mistakes of the fathers (especially 1:2-6; 7:9-14; 8:9-13,14f) appear even more poignant, precisely because they went unheeded, despite the optimism with which they were delivered. Further, it is significant that Malachi does not end with salvation for all Israel. Beginning in Mal 3:1, the book increasingly distinguishes between the righteous and the wicked within Israel. This observation goes beyond the context of Mal 1:1-14, and cannot be treated in detail, but it is necessary to note several indicators which reflect awareness of Malachi's function as the conclusion to the Book of the Twelve.

---

while the primary formation of Zech 7-8 is best attributed to the Haggai-Zechariah corpus. These chapters, according to earlier investigation, did receive some adaptation on the basis of the Joel motifs in the Book of the Twelve (cf especially Zech 8:12). See Nogalski, *Literary Precursors*.

[62] The vacillation of judgment and salvation plays a highly significant role in the Deuteronomistic corpus. It plays a dominant role in Hosea (Israel) and Micah (Judah), as well as in the editorial expansions of Amos and Zephaniah. Further, Joel, Obadiah, Nahum, and Habakkuk all assume this motif in some form, but add to it the punishment of the nations as well.

5. A Haggai-Zechariah-Malachi Corpus?

Pierce has written two provocative articles in which he maintains that the three writings, Haggai, Zechariah, and Malachi form a single corpus.[63] Pierce investigates Haggai, Zechariah and Malachi to demonstrate their literary and thematic interrelationships. He finds five literary connectors common to Haggai, Zechariah, and Malachi. These five include: 1) The precise *dating techniques* utilized in Hag 1:1,15; 2:1,10,20; Zech 1:1,7; 7:1. 2) The literary and *thematic unity* of Zech 1-14.[64] 3) The *oracle titles* of Zech 9-11; 12-14; Mal 1-3. 4) The *interrogative elements* in Haggai, Zechariah, and Malachi.[65] 5) The *"narrative genre"* of Haggai, Zechariah, and Malachi.[66] Pierce argues that a type of story line begins in Haggai with the initial prophetic charge which elicits a reluctant response from the

---

[63] Ronald Pierce, "Literary Connectors and a Haggai-Zechariah-Malachi Corpus," *JETS* 27 (1984): 277-89; and "A Thematic Development of the Haggai-Zechariah-Malachi Corpus," *JETS* 27 (1984): 401-11. Pierce's selection of the term "corpus" is somewhat unclear, since he *deliberately* avoids "questions concerning authorship, original intent, and canonical compilation," and prefers instead "to understand how the books function in their extant form and canonical arrangement." (278) Despite this disclaimer, Pierce treats the works as a single corpus in an effort to demonstrate that "this post-exilic element within the minor prophets" ... should be treated "in a unified fashion with respect to its literary and thematic characteristics."

[64] Again Pierce purposefully avoids the question of the authorship of 9-14, but he investigates 9-14 according to *linking elements* connecting it to Zech 1-8, and the remainder of the Haggai, Zechariah, and Malachi corpus. The unifying elements Pierce finds include: 1) Literary dependence upon preexilic prophets in Zech 1-8 and 9-14: 1:4, 1:12 (cf Jer 25:11; 29:10); 11:13 (cf Jer 18:1-3; 19:1; 32:6-15). 2) The unity of the message in Zechariah lies in the proclamation of salvation. 3) The sobering charge to covenant fidelity is joined with the salvation message: 1:2-6; 3:7; 5:3-4; 6:15; 7-8 (esp 7:5-7); and 11 (which Pierce considers the pivotal chapter).

[65] Hag 1:3-11 with its two-fold response (5-6, 7-11); 2:1-9 also with a two-fold response (4-5, 6-9); 2:10-19 again with a two-fold response (15-17; 18-19). Pierce notes the "element of prophetic dispute is present in veiled fashion" in 2:20-23 (283); Zech 1:5f. Pierce lists eight places in the visions; in addition to 7:1-14; and 8:1-23. He admits there are *none present in Zech 9-14*. The six sermons in Malachi also utilize this feature (cf the sections beginning in 1:2,6; 2:10,17; 3:6,13.

[66] Pierce chooses a poor term to describe the message-carrying portion of Haggai, Zechariah, and Malachi. He describes a *"profile* painted in a literary fashion via the collection of the encounters of the prophets of the return with the post-exilic community. The kind of literature, therefore, may rightly be termed *narrative."* (p. 287) Pierce believes the books demonstrate a "third-party objectivity." Pierce fails to note that such is missing from Zechariah 9-14. The frequent use of the prophetic first person in the visions of Zechariah makes this assertion highly questionable.

people. This response is followed by the warning of Zech 1:2-6 not to behave like their parents. Next comes the "generous offers for an age of salvation" in the night visions of Zechariah, but the response is still moderate (cf interrogative style of Zech 7-8). Zech 9-14 climaxes the story line with its more traditional oracles "in which the remnant is portrayed as a miserable flock of sheep doomed to slaughter (Zech 11). Malachi is "anticlimactic, depicting in much the same fashion in which the corpus began, a community in disharmony with the word of YHWH that came by the hand of his messenger."[67]

In the second article, Pierce continues his earlier work and treats the theme of Haggai, Zechariah, and Malachi in more detail by investigating what he considers to be the major unifying factor, namely the question/ answer schema, together with the periodic interludes (which he calls narratives).[68] He believes Zech 9-14 holds the "key to the central thrust of the work as a whole."[69] He divides his treatment into sections on the 1) sermons of Haggai, 2) the visions and sermons of Zech 1-8, 3) the oracles of Zech 9-14, and 4) the oracle of Malachi. Pierce summarizes the function of Haggai, arguing that it depicts the people (the generation of the returnees) as capable of changing from disobedience to reverence, and then back to fear and uncleanness, all within three months.[70] He sees in this portrayal a dilemma which only finds its outcome in a continued reading of the adjoining literature. Pierce argues Zech 1:1-6 places the message within the context of salvation-history, and that it "forms an introduction to the visions, linking them with the Haggai corpus."[71] In the remainder of Proto-Zechariah, Pierce concentrates upon the interrogative material as the key to understanding the intention of the complex.[72] As for Zech 9-14,

---

[67] Pierce, *JETS* 27 (1984): 289.

[68] Pierce defines these interludes as Hag 1:12-15; 2:20-23; Zech 6:9-15; Mal 4:4-5; and Zech 9-14.

[69] Pierce, *JETS* 27 (1984): 401.

[70] Pierce, *JETS* 27 (1984): 404.

[71] Pierce, *JETS* 27 (1984): 405.

[72] In the night visions, sometimes the prophet asks the angel (1:9,19,21; 2:2,4,11,12; 5:6,10; 6:4); and sometimes the angel questions the prophet (3:2; 4:2,5,7,13; 5:2). The climax comes in the fifth vision because it and the response contain so much interrogative material. Pierce treats Zech 7-8 separately because of the dating element in 7:1. Pierce denies that the passage falls into easily defined units based on the introductory formulas "Then the word of the Lord of Hosts came, saying" (7:4,8; 8:1,18) and "Thus says YHWH Sebaoth" (7:9; 8:2,3,4,6,7,14,19,20,23). He claims that the repetition of these formulas make it "difficult to distinguish where mere repetition for emphasis differs from a valid introductory usage." He notes this style is similar to Haggai. See

Pierce treats it on a par with Zech 1-8. He maintains that the contention that Zech 9-14 presupposes a different set of historical circumstances from Zech 1-8 is too strong literarily, since "the reader has been prepared from the outset for a failure on the part of the people."[73] This preparation appears in the "tragically accurate" comparison to the former prophets, who also spoke to a generation which would not listen.[74] Pierce believes there is a disappointing conclusion to Malachi, similar to the conclusion of Samuel-Kings. At the end of that corpus there is a confession that the people failed prior to the captivity. In Haggai-Zechariah-Malachi, a similar confession must be made for the post-exilic remnant community.

Several problems should be raised with regard to Pierce's treatment, but it should also be acknowledged that he illuminates a consistent hermeneutic running through the majority of these works.[75] Perhaps the most troublesome problem is his insistence on treating Zech 9-14 on the same level as the remaining material. From the perspective of his own formal criteria, these chapters differ decidedly from the remainder of the corpus. They lack the interrogative style which is so important for Pierce in the remaining sections. The connecting literary elements he notes are rather broad or questionable.[76] If the books exhibit a "third-party objectivity," as he claims, then several portions of Zech 9-14 depart from this pattern.[77] Finally, the "narrative," or story line, he describes is more appropriate for Haggai, Proto-Zechariah, and Malachi, given the thematic contrast of Zech 8:9-23 and Mal 1:1-14 described above.

---

also Mason, "The purpose of the Editorial Framework of the Book of Haggai," *VT* 27 (1977): 413-421. Rather than the formula, Pierce argues that, in light of the importance of the interrogative elsewhere in Haggai, Zechariah, and Malachi, that it is likely that the two questions in 7:5 and 8:6 should be viewed as the "literary indicators marking the main sections of the sermons." (406)

[73] Pierce, *JETS* 27 (1984): 409.

[74] Pierce, *JETS* 27 (1984): 411.

[75] Pierce's work remains much truer to the text, for example, than the arguments of House, *Book of the Twelve*, 109, 124, 160, who argues Haggai, Zechariah, and Malachi center on restoration, and who sees Malachi as an "optimistic" conclusion to the Book of the Twelve.

[76] 1) Literary dependence upon preexilic prophets; 2) Salvation as the unifying message in Zechariah; 3) The sobering charge to covenant fidelity. The first two are rather general and the third is questionable since Zech 11, a passage which Pierce considers central, announces the breaking of the covenant.

[77] Again, the most obvious exception appears in the prophetic "I" of Zech 11, which Pierce cites as a transitional passage.

Pierce also stops short of an adequate definition of what he means by "corpus." Ackroyd, Beuken, and Mason have demonstrated a relatively high probability of a Haggai-Zechariah corpus, but much of their work centers on the evidence for a common transmission that deliberately shaped these works. Although Pierce deliberately avoids these questions, one is hard pressed to explain why these three works together constitute a corpus without addressing the questions of authorship and redaction.[78]

If Pierce's observations are generally sound, but need clarification, and if, as is maintained in this study, the story line is clearer without Zech 9-14, then how does one explain the addition of these chapters into the writing of Zechariah, and not at the end of Malachi? This question will be addressed from the perspective of Zech 9-14 in the next chapter, but it is helpful at this point to explore some observations which might explain the incorporation of 9-14 between Proto-Zechariah and Malachi. First, Pierce claims Malachi is "quite anti-climactic," but this is an overstatement. It has already been demonstrated that Malachi reverses the situation of Zech 8:9-23 dramatically and poignantly.[79] Second, there are places in Malachi, beyond 1:1-14, which lead one to consider whether the "corpus" responsible for creating the hermeneutic Pierce describes is the Book of the Twelve rather than the three writings alone. Briefly, some discussion of these observations will illuminate this possibility further.

6. Further Indications of a Wider Literary Awareness in Malachi

The final chapter of Malachi cannot be treated in detail, but it contains several hints that it included a literary horizon which extends well beyond the book itself. As already noted, **Mal 3:22-24** plays off the opening verses of Joshua, the beginning of the former prophets. This allusion implies a sense of canon at the time when these verses entered the corpus, although Malachi's quotation of Joel 3:4 indicates that the incorporation of the legal and the prophetic canon is not its only concern.[80] More closely

---

[78] At one point, Pierce, *JETS* 27 (1984): 278, *intimates* that the three writings should be seen in light of the Book of the Twelve, but he neither clarifies nor develops these thoughts, so that one is not entirely clear if he considers this corpus as part of the Book of the Twelve or a corpus which had its own transmission history.

[79] See also Pierce, *JETS* 27 (1984): 289.

[80] The question of the extent to which this relationship effects the question of original unity cannot be treated here in detail. It is possible that the "foreignness" of this verse

related to the topic at hand is **Mal 3:10f**, which very explicitly take up
motifs from Malachi *in combination with Haggai and Joel*. Mal 3:10f reads:

> [10]Bring the whole tithe into the *storehouse*, so that there may be food in *my house*,
> and test me now in this, says YHWH Sebaoth, (to see) if I will not open for you the
> windows of heaven, and I will pour out for you a blessing until it overflows. [11]And
> then I will rebuke *the devourer* so that it may not *destroy the fruits of the ground*, and
> so that the *vine* will not abort for you in the field, says YHWH Sebaoth.

These verses rely on the immediate context in that they take up the
question of the full payment of the tithe in much the same manner that
Hag 2:18f uses the founding of the temple as the starting condition of
YHWH's blessing. More significant are the relationships to Joel. Mal 3:10
demands the tithe be brought into the storehouse (בית האוצר) in order
that there is food in the temple. Contrast this statement with the situation
in Joel 1:16f, where the food has been cut off, causing lamentation for the
"house of our God," and causing the storehouses (אצרות) to become
desolate. According to Mal 3:10, if the tithes are brought, abundant
showers will result. The promise in Mal 3:10 corresponds to the promise
of Joel 2:23-25, where YHWH promises to send an abundance of showers
to make up for the years that the locusts devastated the land. More explicit
still, YHWH promises in Mal 3:11 to "rebuke the devourer," which, given
the other references to Joel, clearly refers to a metaphorical understanding
of the locusts/armies devouring the land that are mentioned in Joel 1:4,7;
2:25.[81] These verses depict a series of locust plagues invading the land in

---

stems more from its incorporation of this wider literary horizon than from the necessity
of a later hand. This idea gains more credibility when it is realized that Mal 3:23 not
only predicts the coming of Elijah, but it does so with a quote from Joel 3:4 when it
places Elijah's coming before the "great and terrible day of YHWH."

[81] For an appreciation of how these locusts in Joel have been (re-)interpreted as armies
of foreign powers, see Joel 1:6f and the discussion of Joel elsewhere in this study. The
particular formulation of Mal 3:11 in its context is also instructive. Reference to the
removal of the "devourer" depends upon the reaction of the people to bring the entire
tithe into the storehouse (3:10). This dependence makes 3:11 difficult to interpret if
one looks only at the immediate context. There is no indication in 3:8f that the means
to offer the tithe are not present to the people. Rather, 3:8 appears to imply just the
opposite, namely that the people withhold what "by rights" belongs to YHWH. Mal 3:9
promises a blessing of abundant showers (3:10), which is followed by another promise
to rebuke the one devouring (3:11) so that it does not destroy the "fruit of the land."
By this means Israel will become blessed (3:12). Most commentators interpret "the
devourer" as a locust, but do not draw any literary implications from the association.
They interpret the situation literally. Yet, if one attempts to interpret this passage

which each invasion "devours" what little the other had left. The fact that
the Assyrian and Babylonian occupations were already designated/revealed
in the Book of the Twelve through redactional allusions to the locust
imagery in Joel makes this allusion appropriate for its position in Malachi
at the end of the Book of the Twelve, as a reiteration of the promises of
Joel to restore wealth and bounty to Israel if the country (led by the
priests), would but return to YHWH.[82]

One further section deserves brief treatment in light of possible
implications for the Book of the Twelve as a whole. As already noted in
the description of the macro-structure of Malachi, the question/response
schema which dominates the writing actually concludes with 3:15.[83] Mal
3:16-21,22-24 do not evidence this stylistic technique. Rather, beginning
with **Mal 3:16-18**, the book concentrates on the response to the debates as
a whole. The verses shift to a soteriology which implicitly recognizes the
failure of all Israel to change, with the result that there will be a division
within Israel between the righteous and the wicked at the final judgment.

> [16]Then those fearing YHWH spoke, each one with his neighbor. And YHWH gave
> attention and heard. And then a book of remembrance was written before him for
> those fearing YHWH, and for those esteeming his name. [17]And they will be mine,
> says YHWH Sebaoth, for the day when I make a possession, and I will have
> compassion upon them, just as a man has compassion upon his son who serves him.
> [18]So you will again distinguish between the righteous and the wicked, between the
> one serving God and the one who does not serve him.

The key to understanding these verses in the Book of the Twelve centers
around Mal 3:16, and understanding the book of remembrance written for
those fearing YHWH. Normally, scholars interpret this verse is as though
this "book of remembrance" contains the names and/or deeds of those

---

literally as a locust-plague (e.g. Glazier-McDonald, *Malachi*, 198-202; Rudolph, *KAT*
13/4, 284f), one is left with a series of events which do not coincide with one another.
Rain would be an appropriate response to drought, but would do little to stop a locust
onslaught. However, this vacillation between drought and locust-plague provides yet
another touchstone with Joel 1:4ff, which intertwines the two images of drought and
locust attack.

82   This observation, together with the discussion of Mal 3:16-18 below, gives serious cause
to question the consensus of dating on Malachi, particularly since criteria in Joel
appear best suited for a date after 400, not closer to the middle of the fifth century.
See discussion concerning the date of Joel elsewhere in this work.

83   See above, page 184.

fearing YHWH who will be delivered at the final judgment.[84]   While this interpretation is undeniably one of the possibilities, it is not the only way to view this passage, nor is it the best contextually.   Consideration of another perspective involves the re-evaluation of several aspects.

First, the term "book of remembrance" (ספר זכרון) has no *exact* parallel, but the nearly identical "book of remembrances" (ספר הזסרנות) appears in Esth 6:1, where the context indicates that this book refers to a writing which records events of the king's reign: "During that night the king could not sleep, so he gave an order to bring the book of remembrances, and they were read before the king."[85]   Thus, a phrase nearly identical to Mal 3:16 implies a record of events, not a listing of names.

Second, the Hebrew of Mal 3:16 is rather strained if one attempts to interpret the scene and the phrase as a listing of the names of "those fearing YHWH." The book is written before YHWH *"for* those fearing YHWH..." not *"concerning* those fearing YHWH." The difference reflects how one perceives the contents of the "book of remembrance." A simple listing of the names of those fearing YHWH appears to be excluded by the parallel expression in Esth 6:1, but the question remains how one should view the "remembrance" itself. Most assume the remembrance would list the deeds of those fearing YHWH, to the aim that YHWH will remember them at the final judgment. This supposition stands in tension, however, with the two-fold use of the preposition ל, whose root meaning "to," "for," or "on account of" does not entirely coincide with the typical interpretation of this phrase. A more plausible interpretation linguistically would be that the book is written "for" those fearing YHWH, and not for YHWH himself. This picture is syntactically more probable.[86]   If one takes this observation seriously, then the contents of the book would hardly contain the deeds of

---

[84]   So for example, Glazier-McDonald, *Malachi*, 220f; Rudolph, *KAT* 13/4, 288; Horst, *HAT* 14, 266.

[85]   The context indicates that the reading of these records provoked the king's memory of an incident for which he had not rewarded Mordecai.

[86]   Glazier-McDonald, *Malachi*, 206, typifies those opting to interpret the contents of the book in Mal 3:16 as relating to the righteous. She translates the preposition as, "regarding those ..." Both "regarding" and "for" are linguistically possible for the preposition (cf Prov 10:7 and Ps 111:4), but the particular expression to "write a book" used with ל elsewhere means to write a book *with the intention that they receive said writing*. Compare the formulation in Deut 24:1,3 where the context illustrates this point: "When a man takes a wife and marries her, and it happens that she finds no favor in his eyes because he has found some indecency in her, then *he writes for her a book of divorce* (וכתב לה ספר כריתת), and puts it in her hand and sends her out from his house."

the individuals, rather the "remembrance" would be a remembrance of YHWH, not of those fearing YHWH.

Third, this book of remembrance for those fearing YHWH coincides readily with other passages depicting writings given to the faithful as a guide for the future.[87] These passages most often appear in apocalyptic literature.[88] However, even in apocalyptic literature, writings about the past are understood as relating events which effect the present and the future.[89] Perhaps the closest parallel understanding appears when Moses was commanded to write the law as a testimony for future generations.[90] This same idea appears with YHWH depicted as the "writer" in Jub 30:21, in which YHWH says to Moses, "All this account I've written for you and commanded you to say to the children of Israel." The same verse offers a rationale for the writing which includes a soteriological perspective, and thereby provides a further parallel to the context in Malachi, when it says, in order "that they should not commit sin, nor transgress the ordinances, nor break the covenant which has been ordained for them, but that they should fulfill it and be recorded as friends." Thus, it is even possible to combine the two forms of writing, the one a type of revelation to explain YHWH's intention for his people, and the other a heavenly record of who has followed the instruction.

Fourth, the context of Mal 3:16-18 more closely fits an interpretation that the book of remembrance should serve as an aid to YHWH's loyal servants. Mal 3:17 presents a soteriological perspective that YHWH desires to deliver them on the day of his final judgment.[91] One should not, however, jump to the conclusion that the reference to the final judgment implies only YHWH's recollection of his servants. Mal 3:18 demonstrates the book's purpose in a manner often overlooked. The purpose of the

---

[87] The following arguments do not deny the existence of the idea of a heavenly book containing the names and/or deeds of the faithful. Clearly, this tradition exists as well. Cf Pss 69:29; 139:16; Neh 13:14. Dan 7:10; Isa 4:3.

[88] For example, in 1 Enoch 82:1f, Enoch commands Methuselah to write his vision in the book, in order to preserve it, and to pass it on to the "generations of the world." In 1 Enoch 93:2, Enoch begins to recount from the books that which what was revealed to him about the future.

[89] Compare, for example, the citation of earlier authorities in TAsh 2:10: "For this is what God has said on the tables of the commandments." In TLevi 5:4, Levi says, at that time I put an end to the sons of Hamor as is written in the tablets of the fathers."

[90] For example, see Exod 24:4-7; Jub 23:32.

[91] Mal 3:17 is often interpreted, in light of 3:16, as an implication that the names were recorded in YHWH's book. For example, Glazier-McDonald, 220f; Rudolph, *KAT*, 288f; Ogden and Deutsch, *Malachi*, 109.

book is to be an aid to the faithful, so that "you can again distinguish between the righteous and the wicked, and between one who serves God and who does not serve him." From this verse, it is clear that the writing was to serve an instructional purpose.

Mal 3:16-18 thus depicts a scene in which a book is written with the intention that it serve as instruction to help distinguish between the righteous and the wicked. What book is intended here? The easiest answer is, of course, the writing of Malachi. However, one should not be too quick to accept this idea glibly. Several observations indicate that the Book of the Twelve is also a possibility when one asks about the identity of this "book." First, given the parallel in Esth 6:1, one would not be wrong in expecting some type of royal annal for the "book of remembrance." This observation adds further weight to the linguistic and contextual arguments above that it is YHWH who is remembered since, in the constellation of Mal 3:16-18, only YHWH has any claim to royalty. Second, one is hard pressed to interpret Malachi as a royal annal by itself, in light of the disputation style utilized in the majority of the work. Third, the Book of the Twelve as a whole, because of the historical frame it utilizes, could very well be classified as a *type* of annal of YHWH's reign. Fourth, YHWH's decision to spare those fearing him in Mal 3:17 coincides with a significant verse in Joel. Joel 2:18 marks the transition from judgment to promise in that writing.[92] The promises of Joel begin with the assurance that after destruction, and after repentance, then "YHWH will be zealous for his land, and will have compassion (חמל) on his people." Joel's promise finds an echo in Mal 3:17, where YHWH promises: "I will have compassion (חמל) upon them as a man has compassion (חמל) upon his own son who serves him."[93] Fifth, even if one cannot build an absolutely airtight case that the book originally intended was the Book of the Twelve and not Malachi, one can say that these verses are certainly appropriate as a conclusion to the Book of the Twelve. These verses, perhaps together with 3:22-24, offer a strong rationale as to why Zech 9-14 was inserted in front of Malachi. Additionally, these verses could help to account for the conviction at the time of Sirach that the Book of the Twelve, despite its many passages of judgment, was *en toto* a book of hope.[94] When all of the observations on

---

[92] See discussion of the macro-structure of Joel in the chapter on the Hosea-Joel connection.

[93] The combination of allusions here relates back to Joel 2:18 and to the rhetorical question in Mal 1:6.

[94] Sir 49:10 says that the Book of the Twelve "comforted the people of Jacob and

the concluding passages of Malachi are taken into account, there do seem
to be good reasons for believing that Malachi is quite cognizant of its place
at the conclusion of the Book of the Twelve.

7. Summary and Reflections on Proto-Zechariah and Malachi

This chapter has sought to demonstrate that the incorporation of
Malachi into the Book of the Twelve affected its shape and literary thrust
substantially. The beginning and end of Malachi demonstrate awareness of
the Book of the Twelve. The results of this chapter are mixed. Positively,
a number of observations have been developed which show a hermeneutical
logic contrasting the situation of hope at the end of Proto-Zechariah with
the situation of a return to the abuses of the past in Malachi. This
contrasting of elements occurs so frequently, often involving the catchwords
between the two writings, that one gets the distinct impression that the two
passages deliberately create this hermeneutic. Negatively, the task of
separating literary layers in these two passages has proven considerably
more difficult than in many of the other connections. Three possible
explanations could explain this difficulty. *First*, the hermeneutic could have
resulted from the placing of two completed works next to one another,
works which had been selected specifically for their antithetical comments.
While this option has some appeal because it eliminates the need to explain
the passages in detail, other observations argue more strongly against its
acceptance. The sheer number of words involved, the consistency of the
contrasted themes and motifs, the existence of places where there are
reasons to suspect more than one editorial hand, and the use of passages
from elsewhere in the Book of the Twelve all argue against this option.
One cannot help but suspect that editorial perspectives and activity have
helped shape these passages, because they function too well in their
respective positions. A *second* possibility argues that one or both passages
were written from the beginning for the Book of the Twelve. Like the first,
this option eliminates the need to explain different perspectives in the text,
by simply noting one is later than the other. The fact that both passages
relate to specific situations whose function is not exclusively literary raises
some doubts about the likelihood of this option. The delegation sent from
Bethel forms the backdrop for Zech 7-8, and the vehemence with which

---

delivered them with confident hope."

Malachi addresses the priests in 1:6-2:9 seem to have very explicit situations in mind, which admittedly reflect more of an orientation toward current historical circumstances than the literary context of the Book of the Twelve. The *third* option argues that the redactional shaping has been accomplished by adaptation of pre-existing material which skillfully integrated the perspective of a larger corpus with the book of which it was a part. This option would of course imply the deliberate adoption of the style and vocabulary of the respective writing, but this assumption does not appear as far-fetched as some might argue in light of the fact that both Zech 7-8 and Malachi have a style which is so dominant that not to adopt it would make any addition stand out notably. This option has the advantage that it more readily accounts for the places noted in the text which do reflect the interests of the expanded corpus, while still accounting for the formulations conforming to the immediate context. However, the allusions to other parts of the Book of the Twelve are fully embedded in the macrostructure of Malachi.[95] Each of these possibilities brings its own set of problems, but the most likely solution appears to be the second option, that Malachi was composed for its position as the conclusion to the Book of the Twelve.[96]

As with the literary character of the passages, the question of the identity of the redactors and the date of their work is not without problem. There is a strong consensus that both passages reflect Persian period conditions, at least in their core forms. There is also convincing evidence

---

[95] Such as Mal 1:2-4; 3:16-24.

[96] Herein lies both the similarities and the differences to the conclusions in this chapter to those of Bosshard and Kratz. See also Odil Hannes Steck, *Der Abschluß der Prophetie im Alten Testament. Ein Versuch zur Frage der Vorgeschichte des Kanons*. All of these studies, mine included, see Malachi as the redactional continuation of Zech 8:9ff. I differ with their conclusions in that I sense this redactional work already takes place in the Book of the Twelve, and not with the Haggai-Zechariah corpus alone. Mal 1:2-5 and 3:10f meaningfully utilize Obadiah and Joel respectively. Both of these passages appear in their description of the *Grundschicht* of Malachi, incidating the intricacy of involvement in the literary form of Malachi. In addition, I have argued that the three superscriptions in Zech 9:1; 12:1; and Mal 1:1 do not come from the same layer, but that Zech 9:1; 12:1 immitate Mal 1:1. By contrast, Mal 1:1 demonstrates awareness of Haggai, Nahum, and Habakkuk. Thus, I see the composition of Malachi as a deliberately created conclusion to the larger corpus. I suspect that some of the tensions Bosshard and Kratz cite which lead them to separate Mal II from Mal I can be resolved with the wider literary horizon of this larger corpus. These minor differences notwithstanding, the similarities shared by the respective studies, together with Utzschneider, independently conclude that Malachi is a literary construction which manifests canonical awareness in its compositional process.

that Zech 7-8 owes portions of its formulation to the time well after the prophet when the temple was completed and functioning. Some have argued that one could even place this shaping almost as late as the Chronicler.[97] However, there is a strong consensus that Malachi reached its written form between 480-420. Complicating the problem, both the end of Proto-Zechariah and Malachi draw upon Joel, a writing which probably stems from the first thirty years of the fourth century (400-370).[98] For this reason, it is not possible to accept the consensus of a middle fifth century dating for the *final form* of Malachi, despite the arguments that the majority of Malachi seemingly reflects the situation and concerns of that period. However, since a large number of scholars have long claimed Mal 3:22-24 as a later addition to the book, and given the affinity of Mal 3:16ff to later writings, it is by no means inconceivable to argue that the book was reworked (or even composed) later than is normally conceded. A later Persian period date still seems more probable than a date in the Hellenistic period, since the addition of Zech 9-14, normally considered a product of early Greek period, interrupts the Proto-Zechariah/Malachi connection.[99]

Several characteristics of the groups responsible for creating the connection between Proto-Zechariah and Malachi may be gathered here for evaluation at some later point. The redactors had access to works which have a strong concern for the cult (i.e., the Haggai-Zechariah corpus and Malachi), and they were centered in Jerusalem. They had a high regard for the historical awareness of the mistakes of past generations. This group also manifests a sense of the apocalyptic division between the righteous and the wicked. Malachi exhibits a strong anti-priest polemic, which is certainly not modified by later work (compare also Joel 1:1ff), while simultaneously upholding the true covenant of Levi (Mal 2:8). These observations paint a picture relatively consistent with other work in the Joel-related layer of the Book of the Twelve.

---

[97] On the problems of dating the work of the Chronicler, see the discussion of Joel 4:9ff.

[98] The date of Joel is of course debated, with suggestions ranging from the eighth century to the second. For my rationale for accepting these dates, see the chapter on Joel.

[99] See the following chapter.

Zech 9-14

1. Zech 9-14 Distinct from Zech 1-8: A Brief Summary of Research

Zech 9-14 exhibits considerably different interests than Zech 1-8, a fact which led to special treatment for these chapters early in the critical period.[1] Early theories regarding separate authorship of Zech 9-14 came from England. Mede was the first to argue relatively scientifically that Zech 9-11 did not come from the author of 1-8.[2] Based in part on the attribution of Zech 11:12f to Jeremiah in Matt 27:9f, Mede argued these chapters corresponded more closely to the time of Jeremiah. Kidder and Whiston followed Mede's position, and argued the same was true for Zech 12-14.[3] Newcombe moved the date for 9-11 to the eighth century, and claimed 12-14 came from shortly before the destruction of Jerusalem.[4]

Flügge was the first on the continent to take up these theories of separate authorship. He argued there were actually nine prophecies which came from different times, but were preserved by Zechariah or his followers.[5] Bertholdt explicated this theory more precisely, arguing that Zechariah ben-Jeberechiah (a contemporary of Isaiah [8:2]) was the author.[6] He argued that these chapters were attached to Zech 1-8, which were attributed to the prophet named Zechariah ben-Iddo. At that point the second name, ben-Berechiah, was added to Zech 1:1. Subsequently,

---

[1] The following sketch has been adapted in part from the thorough summary by Hanns-Martin Lutz, *Jahwe, Jerusalem und die Völker. Zur Vorgeschichte von Sach 12:1-8 und 14:1-5*, Wissenschaftliche Monographien zum Alten und Neuen Testament 27 (Neukirchen: Neukirchener Verlag, 1968), 1-7). Some of these works from the 17th, 18th, and early 19th centuries were unavailable for verification.

[2] Joseph Mede, *Dissertationum Ecclesiasticarum Triga: ... Quibus accedunt Fragmenta Sacra* (London: 1653).

[3] Richard Kidder, *The Demonstration of the Messiah*, vol. 2 (1700), 199; William Whiston, *An Essay towards Restoring the True Text of the Old Testament* (1722), 94f.

[4] William Newcombe, *An Attempt towards an Improved Version, a Metrical arrangement and an Explanation of the Twelve Minor Prophets* (1785), 194f.

[5] Benedikt Gilbert Flügge, *Die Weissagungen, welche den Schriften des Propheten Zacharias beygebogen sind, übersetzt und critisch erläutert, nebst einigen Abhandlungen* (1784).

[6] Leonard Bertholdt, *Historischkritische Einleitung in sämmtliche kanonische und apokryphische Schriften des Alten und Neuen Testaments*, vol. 4, (1814), 1697-1728.

Ewald, Bleek, von Ortenberg, Davidson, Steiner-Hitzig, and von Orelli propagated the idea that Zech 9-14 involved a collection of works from several pre-exilic authors.[7]

Late in the 18th century, Corrodi became the first to argue for the post-exilic authorship of Zech 9-14.[8] He argued 9-13 came from the time of Alexander, while 14:1-21 was composed during the reign of Antiochus Epiphanes (175-163 B.C). Eichhorn, Vatke, Geiger and Böttcher also supported post-exilic authorship of 9-14.[9] Massive articles by Stade in 1881 provided detailed arguments that the chapters arose during second half of the Diadochoi wars between 306 and 278.[10] Stade's contributions were significant because he maintained the unity of authorship for all six chapters, and named them Deutero-Zechariah. Stade's work sparked a flurry of subsequent writings reflecting various opinions, particularly on the questions of post-exilic date and unity of authorship.[11]

20th century scholars have severely questioned the unity of these chapters, but their arguments for doing so vary considerably. Some, like Eissfeldt and Sellin-Rost, argue for two authors in 9-11 and 12-14.[12]

---

[7] George August Ewald, *Die Propheten des Alten Bundes*, vol. 1 (1840), 308-324, 389-398; Friedrich Bleek, "Über das Zeitalter von Sacharja Kap 9-14," *TThStKr* 25 (1852): 247-332; Friedrich Bleek, *Einleitung in das Alte Testament*, ([4]1878), 439-449; E.F.J. von Ortenberg, *Die Bestandteile des Buches Sacharja*, (1859), 68ff; Samuel Davidson, *An Introduction to the Literature of the Old Testament*, vol. 3 (1863), 329ff; Heinrich Steiner and Ferdinand Hitzig, *Die zwölf Kleinen Propheten*, ([4]1881), 367-374; Conrad von Orelli, *Die zwölf Kleinen Prepheten*, ([3]1908), 178f.

[8] H. Corrodi, *Versuch einer Beleuchtung der Geschichte des jüdischen und christlichen Bibelkanons*, vol. 1 (1792), 107.

[9] Johann Gottfried Eichhorn, *Einleitung ins Alte Testament*, vol. 4 ([4]1824), 427ff, 444ff; Wilhelm Vatke *Die biblische Theologie, wissenschaftlich dargestellt. Die Religion des alten Testaments nach den kanonischen Büchern entwickelt*, vol. 1 (1834), 553; Abraham Geiger, *Urschrift und Übersetzungen der Bibel in ihrer Abhängigkeit von der innern Entwicklung des Judentums*, (1857; [2]1928), 55f, 73f; Friedrich Böttcher, *Neue exegetisch-kritische Aehrenlese zum Alten Testamente*, part 2, 1864, 215f.

[10] Bernhard Stade, "Deuterozacharja. Eine kritische Studie," *ZAW* 1 (1881): 1-96; *ZAW* 2 (1882): 151-72, 275-309.

[11] Several whose arguments were similar to Stade were Gerrit Wildeboer, *De letterkunde des Ouden Verbonds*, (1893; [2]1896), 417; Kuiper, *Zacharia 9-14* (1894), 163; Carl Heinrich Cornill, *Einleitung in das Alte Testament* ([7]1913); Karl Marti, *Das Dodekapropheton* (1904), 396ff. Some who disagreed with Stade included Julius Wellhausen, *Die kleinen Propheten, übersetzt und erklärt* (1892; [3]1898), 188-203; Rubinkam, *The Second Part of the Book of Zechariah*, (1892), 83f.

[12] Otto Eissfeldt, *Einleitung in das Alte Testament* ([3]1964), 594f; Ernst Sellin-Leonhard Rost, *Einleitung in das Alte Testament* ([9]1959), 138.

Others argued for two authors, but divide the parts differently.[13] Still others argue for four or more different authors.[14] Some scholars, such as Nötscher and Bič, are not so easy to categorize with regard to either authorship or unity.[15] Otzen also considers Zech 9-14 as the product of several authors, ranging from late pre-exilic to post-exilic periods.[16] He argues that 9-10 come from a Judean circle in the time of Josiah. Zech 11, according to Otzen, stems from the time right before the fall of Judah. Zech 12-13 come from the early exilic period.[17] Zech 14 demonstrates an affinity to Trito-Isaiah and comes from a later post-exilic period.[18]

Lamarche strains heavily to argue for a literary unity which forms a consistent pattern.[19] He finds twelve units which center on four themes: the nations; idols and false prophets; war and victory for Israel; and king and shepherd. Lamarche visualizes one structural principle for all twelve sub-units, which organizes these four themes around an axis running between 11:4-17 and 12:1-9. This structural pattern utilizes elements of symmetry, parallelism, and chiasm as techniques to accomplish its aims. Lamarche dates Zech 9-14 between 500-480.

Ellul maintains Zech 9-14 represents a compilation centered around the theme of holy war.[20] He argues a series of five different battle scenes transform the portrayal of YHWH from a mythical God to a historical God, from a national God to a universal God, from a territorial and political God

---

[13] The following separate chapter 14 from 9-13: Wilhelm Nowack, *Die kleinen Propheten* ([3]1922), 364-367; Otto Procksch, *Die kleinen Prophetischen Schriften nach dem Exil*, ([2]1929), 98f; and (in his commentary) Ernst Sellin, *Das Zwölfprophetenbuch*, vol. 2: *Nahum-Maleachi* ([3]1930), 538f.

[14] Hinckley G. Mitchell, *A Critical and Exegetical Commentary on Haggai and Zechariah*, ICC (1912), 218-220, 232-259, esp 258f; Elliger, ATD 25,2 (1967), 143f; Theodore H. Robinson-Friedrich Horst, Die HAT I/14 ([3]1964), 212f. Also Th. Chary, *Les prophètes et le Culte à partir de l'exil* (Paris: Desclée, 1955), 218-220, argues for two primary parts (9-11, 13:7-9; and 12-14), considers the possibility of several authors.

[15] Friedrich Nötscher, *Zwölfprophetenbuch oder Kleine Propheten*, 144, holds a single author responsible for 9-14, but does not mention the time; Bič, *Das Buch Sacharja*, 11f, 115, supposes post-exilic dating, but is silent about authorship.

[16] Bernard Otzen, *Studien über Deuterosacharja*, Acta Theologica Danica 6 (Copenhagen: Munksgaard, 1964).

[17] Otzen, *Studien über Deuterosacharja*, 226f, subdivides these chapters into independent complexes, 12:1-13:1; 13:2-6; 13:7-9.

[18] Otzen, *Studien über Deuterosacharja*, 212.

[19] Paul Lamarche, *Zacharie 9-14. Structure Littéraire et Messianisme*, Études Biblique (Paris: Gabalda, 1961).

[20] Danielle Ellul, "Variations sur le thème de la guerre sainte dans le Deutéro-Zacharie," *Etudes Théologiques et Religieuses* 56 (1981): 55-71.

to a cosmic and cultic God. These five battles (9:1-10; 9:11-17; 10:3b-11:3; 12:1-13:9; 14:1-21) include the majority of material within these chapters. Only 10:1-3a and 11:4-17, according to Ellul, do not specifically take up these motifs.

Hanson treats Zech 9-14 as the collection of several independent pieces, dating from the mid-sixth century to around 425.[21] He sees Zech 9-14 as the evidence of a development of apocalyptic consciousness. He believes the culmination in Zech 14:1-21 to be the work of visionaries "disenfranchised from the official Jerusalem cult."[22] According to Hanson, only the assumption of inner-Israelite conflicts accounts for the anticipated destruction of Jerusalem in chapters 12 and 14. He believes chapters 9-11 and 12-14 have independent histories, each representing a collection of oracles based on theme and catchwords.

The wide variety of opinions on the date and authorship allows no claim to a consensus, but one may say that the work of Elliger provides the groundwork for the dominant opinion of the last forty years, at least for the question of the date. Elliger argues that considerable portions of Zech 9-14 come from the beginning of the Hellenistic period.[23] The reference to the Greeks as a world power (Zech 9:13) makes this date the most acceptable starting point for the date of the complex.[24] The question of authorship

---

[21]   Paul D. Hanson, *The Dawn of Apocalyptic* (Philadelphia: Fortress, 1975), 280-401. He dates Zech 9:1-17 to the middle of the sixth century (324) because it predicts the salvation of the entire nation, prior to "the bitter conflict between visionary and hierocratic elements in the post-exilic community." On the other hand, he thinks 14:1-21 reflects of the inner-Israelite conflicts which resulted from the exclusiveness of the Zadokite priesthood. Hanson (400) dates 14:1-21 between 475-425 (with a preference for the end of that period). He bases this dating on the abatement of struggles between the visionaries and the hierocrats, which Hanson places at the end of the fifth century.

[22]   Hanson, *Dawn of Apocalyptic*, 392.

[23]   Karl Elliger, "Ein Zeugnis aus der jüdischen Gemeinde im Alexanderjahr 332 v. Chr.," *ZAW* 62 (1949/50): 63-115. See also his commentary, *ATD* 25, 133-135. The dating suggested by Elliger is followed by Ina Willi-Plein, *Prophetie am Ende. Untersuchungen zu Sacharja 9-14*, Bonner biblische Beiträge 42 (Köln: Hanstein, 1974), 120f; Rudolph, *KAT* 13/4, 163-64, modifies this date further into the Diadochoi period, but (as with Elliger) refuses to push it into the Maccabean period.

[24]   While Elliger goes perhaps too far in trying to harmonize 9:1-8 with the Alexandrian campaign, those such as Hanson and Otzen, who argue for an earlier date create real problems by trying to explain away the reference to the Greeks as the chief adversary of chapter nine. While there were long-standing relationships between Greece and Palestine, Zech 9:13 clearly pits Judah, Ephraim, and Jerusalem against Greece using military imagery implying Greece as the chief threat, i.e. political power of the time. This is difficult to harmonize with any known historical events prior to the time of

and the intentions behind the collection and/or compilation of the various units in these chapters requires a discussion of those units.

2. Preliminary Observations Concerning Zech 9-14

Before describing the macrostructure of Zech 9-14, several preliminary observations should be made. First, the similarity of the superscriptions in Zech 9:1; 12:1 and Mal 1:1 point toward a deliberate shaping on the part of a redactor who adapted both superscriptions in Zech 9:1 and 12:1 rather mechanically to conform to Mal 1:1.[25] This observation generates certain implications for the shape of Zech 9-14. One the one hand, someone deliberately divided Zech 9-14 into two parts relatively equal in length. On the other hand, the literary problems of Zech 12:1 in particular lead to the assumption that this superscription has been implanted into a context in which 11:17 and 12:1b already stood side by side.[26] The implication derived from this last observation predisposes one to consider that Zech 9-14 already existed in a form which contained more than chapters 9-11 at the time of the incorporation of the superscription into the Book of the Twelve. The likelihood of this presumption will need to be tested against the text, and the question must be raised whether this block existed independently of the Book of the Twelve.

Second, in addition to the superscriptions, Zech 9-11 and 12-14 concentrate upon different entities. Zech 9-11 emphasizes Judah and Ephraim, while demonstrating considerable interest in the ideal boundaries of the Davidic Kingdom. By contrast, Zech 12-14 deals exclusively with Jerusalem, Judah, and "the nations." Within this constellation of entities, Jerusalem receives special honor in the vast majority of material. This observation leads to the assumption that one must reckon, at the very least,

---

Alexander. By contrast, those who argue for an earlier date are forced into rather fanciful hypotheses and emendations. For example, Otzen, *Deuterosacharja*, 45-58, argues that the reference to the Greeks in Zech 9:13 refers to the Greek troops used by the Egyptians in the 7th century. Hanson, *The Dawn of Apocalyptic*, 298, deletes reference to the Greeks as a dittographical error. Hanson bases his deletion on what he perceives as disturbed meter, a suggestion which is dubious.

[25] See discussion of Mal 1:1 in the previous chapter.

[26] Previous discussion (see Mal 1:1) demonstrated 12:1b is logically and stylistically appropriate following 11:17 or 13:7-9, but linguistically inappropriate following 12:1a as the introduction to a new unit. For discussion 13:7-9, see below, page 234.

with collection principles which have guided the accumulation and ordering of the units in Zech 9-14. At this point, one cannot rule out the possibility that the thematic consistency of these two larger blocks represents compositional intentions rather than compilational interests. In other words, the thematic shape of 9-11 and 12-14 requires a fundamental decision as to whether Zech 9-14 results primarily from the redactional placement of pre-existing independent units, or whether it stems primarily from the hand of a single author.

A third preliminary observation concerns the inversion of typical prophetic ordering principles in Zech 9-11. Zimmerli demonstrates that prophetic corpora generally follow one of two organizational patterns.[27] Either they reflect the pattern judgment/oracles against the nations/salvation or they reflect the pattern judgment/salvation/oracles against the nations. Both of these patterns may be characterized, from the perspective of YHWH's people, as a movement from the negative to the positive. By contrast, Zech 9-11 does not follow either pattern. Rather, its ordering pattern would best be characterized as oracles against the nations/salvation/ judgment.[28] Thus, the macrostructural pattern of these chapters moves from the positive to the negative. One question which should be kept in mind regarding this observation is whether this inversion reveals a deliberate shaping of Zech 9-11 alone, indicating a very negative and disillusioned message, or whether this pattern serves as precursor to a larger salvation section more thoroughly depicted in chapters 12-14.

A fourth observation relates to the extended units of Zech 9-14. One is immediately struck by the *impression* that the thought units, particularly of 9-11, appear as an amalgamation of short sayings and oracles in which subjects shift suddenly and often. Unlike 12-14, Zech 9-11 displays no dominant formulaic device as an organizational guide.[29] In Zech 9-11, one must pay careful attention to the changes in subject, addressee, and style

---

[27] Walter Zimmerli, "Vom Prophetenwort zum Prophetenbuch," *ThLZ* 104 (1979): 481-496.

[28] Zech 9:1-7 announces YHWH's judgment against the nations (with an eye toward the restoration of the Davidic kingdom). Zech 9:8-10:12 announces salvation for YHWH's people. Zech 11:1-17 concludes the section with negative images of judgment against the nations and YHWH's people.

[29] Contrast this lack of consistent formulaic devices with the dominance of the formula ביום־ההוא in Zech 12-14. This formula appears in 12:3,4,6,8,9,11; 13:1,2,4; 14:(1),4,6, 8,9,13,20,21. By contrast, this formula appears only once within chapters 9-11 (9:16). However, the phrase in 9:16 does not appear as an introductory element, as it does in most of the occurrences in Zech 12-14.

in order to determine the extent of these thought units, and just as importantly, to explain their relationship to one another.[30]   With these observations, it is now possible to turn to the units within these chapters.

3. The Units within Zech 9:1-17 and Their Literary Relationships

The first recognizable extended unit encompasses **Zech 9:1-7**, which scholars regularly classify as a series of short oracles against the nations. However, these oracles do not represent typical examples of this genre, but have their own particular character, which may be characterized by several observations.[31]   First, the brevity of the condemnation of the individual locations appears mild in comparison to other oracles.[32]   Second, the order of the entities exhibits a definite movement from regions northeast of Judah to the southwest along the Mediterranean coast.[33]   Third, the geo-political interest in the selection of these verses lies in the fact that they formed part of the ideal Davidic/Solomonic kingdom, not in the delivery of a precise account of a military campaign.[34]   Fourth, these verses cluster

---

[30]   Note for example, the careful delineation and application of criteria by Willi-Plein, *Prophetie am Ende*, 38-43, based in part on the foundations of Richter.

[31]   The accentuation of various aspects in these verses leads to different ideas about their form and function.   Contrast the discussions in Saebø, *Sacharja 9-14*, 161-175, who accents the *Gestalt* of the material in order to discuss its growth, with Otzen, *Studien über Deuterosacharja*, 62-123, who centers on the geo-political toponyms in order to place the oracles in the time of Josiah.

[32]   Condemnation of Tyre (9:3) together with its punishment (9:4) is the most severe, but still relatively mild.   Tyre is criticized for building up wealth, but compare, for example, the more acrimonious threats against the same city in Ezek 26:1-28:19.   Zech 9:5 implies that the "crime" of the Philistine entities of Ashkelon, Gaza and Ekron resulted in their reliance upon Tyre.   The major complaint against Hadrach, Damascus, and Hamath is not stated explicitly, but apparently emanates from the author's belief that they belong to the "tribes of Israel," with the implication that they do not acknowledge this relationship.

[33]   For depiction of the location of the regions Hadrach and Hamath northeast of Judah, see Otzen, *Deuterosacharja*, 70.

[34]   So Otzen, *Deuterosacharja*, 69, correctly observes, although his attempt to force the date of the passage into pre-exilic times creates more problems than it solves.   Elliger, *ZAW* 62 (1949/50): 63-115, overstates the military similarity to the campaign of Alexander as the purpose behind these verses.   See the critique of Otzen, *Deuterosacharja*, 66-68.   However, the centrality of Tyre's destruction (9:3), which serves to frighten Ashkelon, Gaza, and Ekron (9:5), makes it difficult (given the other

toponyms to the point that one must either postulate that these oracles
have been expanded by the occasional insertion of place names into the
existing literary context, or that the author uses this clustering effect as a
deliberate device to describe entire regions. In the case of Zech 9:1-7, the
latter appears the more likely.[35]

The train of thought within Zech 9:1-7 defies a simple explanation.
On the one hand, it announces YHWH's judgmental intentions against the
various regions.[36] On the other hand, both the beginning and ending of

---

evidence for the late character of Zech 9-14) to ignore an allusion to Alexander's
conquest. Compare Zech 9:13.

[35] Both options create difficulties that are not easily resolved. For example, scholars often
suggest that either the reference to Tyre or Sidon in Zech 9:2b has been added because
the singular suffix relates back to the toponym. Otzen, *Deuterosacharja*, 237, and
Rudolph, *KAT* 13/4, 169, however, correctly treat the singular suffix in 9:2b as a
reference to the entire region. This possibility accounts for the tension better than the
suggestion of a mechanical insertion, because it is equally difficult to postulate that
either entity results from scribal incorporation of a gloss. Syntactically, Sidon would
appear to have priority because the presence of the ‎ן before it would more naturally
mark a new bicola, but the tradition of wisdom in 9:2b is more often associated in
Biblical passages with Tyre, arguing just as strongly for Tyre as the original reference
if one accepts the interpolation model for this passage. Both of the other "regions"
addressed in Zech 9:1-7 refer to larger regions with singular suffixes, which increases
the likelihood that the same phenomenon occurs in 9:2b. In Zech 9:1-2a, the author
refers to Hadrach with Damascus as *its* (3ms) capital, while simultaneously maintaining
the confusing belief that Hamath borders on *it* (3fs), meaning the region of Hadrach,
including Damascus. Since Hamath actually lay between Hadrach and Damascus (see
Otzen, *Deuterosacharja*, 70), one must either assume mistaken geography or that the
reference in its current form results from a later interpolation (so Saebφ, *Sacharja 9-
14*, 1969, 46f). In Zech 9:1-2a, the assumption of a geographical mistake on the part
of an author could readily be accounted for with the acceptance of the dominant
opinion that the passage stems from some time after the beginning of the campaigns
of Alexander. In this case, the archaic language — the titles of the regions in 9:1-2a
correspond to the titles in the last half of the seventh century — creates the impression
that the author utilized toponyms with which he was not entirely familiar. Zech 9:7
also uses singular suffixes (3ms) and pronouns to refer to the Philistine region.
Syntactically, these singular references assume the masculine construct "exaltation of
the Philistines" at the end of 9:6 as the antecedent. Thus, whether referring to the
Syrian interior, the Phoenician coastal region, or the Philistine coastal area, the author
of 9:1-7 uses singular pronouns and suffixes to reflect the broader districts.

[36] YHWH's word is *against* the land of Hadrach (9:1). Tyre will be dispossessed and her
wealth thrown into the sea (9:4). The Philistine cities also have judgments pronounced
against them (9:5): they will be afraid and writhe in pain; lose their king and their
inhabitants; and lose their ethnic purity.

the unit reflect another, more positive, presupposition, namely, that the actions of YHWH intend the punishment to bring the rebellious regions under control, not to annihilate them.[37]   Zech 9:7 even utilizes the theologically potent root שאר (to be a remnant) with the Philistine regions, a term normally reserved for Israel.[38]   Thus, Zech 9:1-7 employs the *Gattung* of prophetic oracles against the nations, but places these short oracles within a frame which manifests YHWH's control over the ideal limits of the Davidic/Solomonic monarchy.

Zech 9:8 changes the subject dramatically with the introduction of the motif of YHWH's defense of his house against an oppressor, but significant relationships within this verse suggest that it serves a bridging function between the oracles against the nations and the pronouncement of weal to Jerusalem, Judah, and Ephraim which follows in 9:9f. In other words, in spite of the fact that Zech 9:1-7 introduces punishment against the nations, the literary context precludes the assumption of 9:1-7 as an independent unit. The question remains, how far this relationship extends.

Superficially, Zech 9:8 attaches directly to 9:7 by means of a *waw* adversative, setting up a contrast between the preceding judgment and the announcement of salvation which follows. Zech 9:8 presumes the existence of the threat of punishment in 9:1-7, forming the logical culmination of the geographical movement depicted within those verses.[39] The text prepares the reader for this logical movement. Zech 9:8 follows a certain logic by turning to YHWH's kingdom after mentioning the Philistines in relationship to Judah and the Jebusites (= Jerusalem) in 9:7. In so doing, Zech 9:8 not

---

[37] Zech 9:1 states that the "eyes of man and all the tribes of Israel belong to YHWH." In Zech 9:7, the positive goal appears even more explicitly, namely, the Philistine region will become like a clan in Judah.

[38] The author of these verses uses this term theologically as opposed to purely military terminology. The image does not portray the destruction of the region, rather 9:7 claims that "it will be a remnant for our God," implying punishment of the region and yet its treatment like YHWH's people. Note the comparison of Ekron to the Jebusites (9:7), a reference to the tradition of the Davidic conquest of Jerusalem (2 Sam 5:6f/ 1 Chr 11:4-6). The Jebusites continued dwelling in the city (Josh 15:63; Judg 1:21).

[39] This movement, as in Amos 1-2, deliberately takes the reader from the nations to the fate of YHWH's people, but unlike Amos, salvation, not judgment, represents the climactic intention of the author. Not surprisingly, several scholars note the similarity to the oracles against the nations in Amos. So for example, Willi-Plein, *Prophetie am Ende*, 68f; Saebø, *Sacharja 9-14*, 166f. In addition, the final line of Zech 9:8 — for now my eyes have seen — serves as an affirmation linked to the statement in Zech 9:1 — the eyes of man and all the tribes of Israel belong to YHWH.

only attaches to 9:1-7, it also anticipates the change of subject to the
defense of YHWH's kingdom centered in Jerusalem in 9:9-13,14-17.[40]

Zech 9:9f, often cited for its messianic character, marks another
significant shift in the style of the passage. YHWH addresses personified
Zion directly, promising the impending arrival of her king. Reading these
verses presents a certain tension, but they should be understood as
YHWH's words to Zion about the king.[41] The dialectic created by the
divine speeches deserves note. The royal imagery draws upon expectations
of the return of a ruler, almost certainly of Davidic lineage, but the
presentation deliberately portrays the arrival of the king as one of peace.[42]

---

[40]   Hence YHWH proclaims his positive intention in Zech 9:8: "I will encamp (for
defense) around my house." Rudolph, *KAT* 13/4, 175, correctly notes that the phrase
"my house" should not be understood as limited only to the Jerusalem temple, but to
the broader region of the land as a whole (cf Hos 8:1; 9:15). Nevertheless, Rudolph's
comments should be expanded to acknowledge that this expression presupposes a
Jerusalemite setting. Even in this motif presenting an expanded image of YHWH's
house, most passages presume YHWH's abode centers in Jerusalem. Compare the
similar use of majestic proportions in metaphorical language presupposing the image
of YHWH's footstool in relationship to Jerusalem (e.g. Ps 99:5; Lam 2:1; Isa 66:1),
where the context demonstrates the extent of area covered by YHWH's footstool varies
while still indicating the centrality of Jerusalem. Ps 99:5 visualizes the temple as the
footstool, while Lam 2:1 presupposes Jerusalem itself. Isa 66:1 explicitly states the
entire earth is YHWH's footstool, but as with Zech 9:8, assumes the centrality of
Jerusalem as part of the context and the metaphor (cf Isa 65:25; 66:6). This association
of "my house" with both the kingdom and Jerusalem (as capital or as the place of the
temple) helps to account for the current position of the Zion material in 9:9-13, which
interrupts the context of 9:8,14-17. See further discussion below, pages 226 and 229.

[41]   The confusion stems largely from a determination of the intended speaker. The verses
utilize both first, second, and third person verbal forms, causing problems for
determining the speaker with absolute certainty. Several observations argue one should
assume these verses continue the divine speech in Zech 9:8. First, the speaker must
either be the prophet or YHWH. Second, the MT indicates YHWH as the speaker in
9:10 ("I will cut off the horse from Ephraim ..."), but many commentators (e.g. Elliger,
Mason) mistakenly follow the LXX by omitting the final consonant from והכרתי. The
assumption that the LXX preserves the original reading is questionable, however, since
it presumes the MT *added* a consonant for no apparent reason. By contrast, the LXX
reading can well be understood as a harmonization of the verb form with the remainder
of the verse which utilizes third person forms. Third, the context argues that YHWH
is the speaker since clear indications of the divine "I" appear in the preceding (9:8) and
in the verses which follow (9:11,13).

[42]   Contra Rudolph, *KAT* 13/4, 181, who believes the extended lack of a Davidic ruler
argues against assuming a Davidide in this passage. The consistency of evidence from
the time of Haggai to the time of Jesus belies his rationale since the dominant image

By contrast, YHWH, not the king, performs the military actions leading to peace and to the extension of the boundary of the ideal kingdom.[43] In this regard, Zech 9:10 takes up the twice-encountered motif of YHWH's extension of the ideal boundaries of Israel (9:1,7).

The presence of the personified Zion as addressee continues to play a role in **Zech 9:11-13**, but the subject changes from the arrival of the king to the condition of Zion's inhabitants. Zech 9:11 begins with a puzzling phrase, "the blood of your (2fs) covenant," which creates problems for interpretation. Scholars typically associate the phrase with Exod 24:8, the only other appearance of דם ברית in the Old Testament.[44] However, the Zion imagery in these verses complicates a simple correlation of these two passages, since Exod 24:8 relates to the covenant obligation under which Moses placed the people of Israel.[45] Since the verse addresses Zion

---

of a human king in Jerusalem presupposes relationship to David. Additionally, the presence of the house of David in Zech 12:7-13:1 argues Davidic kingship in 9:9 is presumed. Zech 9:9-13 also relates to Mic 5:2ff, where the Davidic imagery is stronger.

[43]   Compare the extended boundaries in Zech 9:10 (from sea to sea, and from the river to the ends of the earth) to the expectations for royal rule in Ps 72:8, a psalm whose Solomonic superscription attests to the association of these traditions with the ideal boundaries of Israel's king. More significantly, several images in Zech 9:9f appear also in Mic 5:1-15, to the point that one may postulate literary awareness on the part of the writer of Zech 9:9f. Both passages reflect the return of a Davidic ruler to Zion (5:1f), which precipitates the return of those exiled (5:3) and institutes a reign of peace (5:3). Both passages likewise refer to the cutting off of (war) horses and chariots from Israel (5:10). Both passages envision YHWH's kingdom extending "to the ends of the earth." (5:4, cf also the reference to "the river" in Mic 7:12). Significantly, Mic 5:4 also introduces the rule of this king with the imagery of a shepherd and flock, imagery which plays a significant role in Zech 9-11, beginning in 9:16 and 10:2. Both passages assume the future fulfillment of the promises, but Zech 9:9f presents the fulfillment in terms of an imminent event, whereas Mic 5:4 gives the impression of the expectation of a longer period before the fulfillment (note for example "at that time" in Mic 5:4). When the two passages are compared, it appears as though the writer of Zech 9:9f wants to say, "we are fast approaching the time of fulfillment described in Mic 5:1ff."

[44]   E.g. Elliger, *ATD* 25, 143; Rudolph, *KAT* 13/4, 186.

[45]   Ernst Kutsch, "Das Sog. »Bundesblut« in Ex 24:8 und Sach 9:11," *VT* 23 (1973): 25-30, realizes the problems inherent in a direct correlation, although his explanation for Zech 9:11 does not solve the problem. Kutsch notes that the phrase דם ברית appears only twice in the Old Testament, in Zech 9:11 and Exod 24:8. He assumes that the two are related and that the key to understanding both rests in the presumption that ברית means obligation, not covenant. Kutsch (28) demonstrates from the realm of the history of religion that the rite described in **Exod 24:8** relates closely to Arabic practice of sealing a contract, in which both parties wash their hands in the blood of a sacrificed

directly, one should ask if there is any evidence for a "covenant of blood," more closely tied to Zion traditions. Such could very well be the case, although determining the precise content of this tradition proves to be as difficult as the phrase itself. The Zion imagery in Ezek 16:1-63 relates various facets of what amounts to a Zion allegory, in which both blood and covenant play a central role, and it would appear wiser to assume that traditions related to this passage go further toward explaining the imagery in Zech 9:11 than an exclusive relationship to Exod 24:8.[46]

---

animal. Kutsch (27f) notes a similar Greek practice in which military commanders obligated their company. Both of these practices aid the conceptualization of Exod 24:8, where the blood of a sacrificial animal is sprinkled onto the people by the leader in an act of obligation. In Exod 24:8, Moses places *the people* under obligation by this act. The utilization of the blood in these practices presupposes a curse on those under obligation if they fail to comply with their oath. Just as the blood of the sacrificial animal was spilled so their own blood will be spilled should they fail to comply. **Zech 9:11** uses the same expression, Kutsch disagrees that 9:11 relates explicitly to the covenant in Exod 24:8, in the sense of YHWH's covenant with the people, because then it would have to say "my covenant with you," not "your covenant." "Your covenant" points toward something other than the blood of a sacrificial animal. Since later Jewish writers relate the phrase "blood of the covenant" to the circumcision blood in Gen 17:9-14, Kutsch believes Zech 9:11 already presupposes this meaning. He translates "the blood of your obligation," meaning "the blood of circumcision." Kutsch presents convincing arguments for the understanding of Exod 24:8, but his interpretation of Zech 9:11 creates serious conceptual problems. The overriding problem against his theory lies in the fact that Zech 9:11 addresses Zion personified in *feminine* form. It is difficult to harmonize the feminine imagery of lady Zion with the practice of circumcision, particularly since Gen 17:9-14 clearly limits the act of circumcision to males, and the practice of female circumcision is not documented in ancient Judaism.

[46] Ezek 16 relates the story of YHWH's salvation of Zion after she was left for dead at birth, and her subsequent ingratitude. Three of the chief catchwords in this story which tie the various elements together are "blood" (16:6,9,22,36,38), "covenant" (16:8,59-61), and the phrase "days of your youth" (16:22,43,60). The relationship of "blood" to Zion presupposes at least three and perhaps four different conceptualizations of blood in relationship to the story of Zion: 1) The blood of her birth in which she suffered, prior to YHWH's deliverance (16:6,22); 2) The blood YHWH cleansed from her following his marriage covenant (16:9), which *perhaps* presumes the blood of her birth although the long delay and her developing beauty (16:7f) could also presume some type of blood ritual in the act of covenant along the lines described by Kutsch, *VT* 23 (1973): 28; 3) The blood spilled by Zion when she delivered her children as sacrifice to idols (16:36,38); 4) The blood of wrath and jealousy which YHWH will shed on her as punishment (16:43). Ezek 16 presupposes YHWH's "covenant" with Zion as a marriage covenant (16:8ff), which is later presumed via the phrase "days of your youth" (16:22,43,60). In Ezek 16:58-63, YHWH announces his removal of the punishment because YHWH remembers his covenant with her in the days of her youth and will now

Zech 9:11b,12 affirm that the salvation YHWH announces affects the inhabitants of Jerusalem. The content takes up promises from elsewhere in the prophetic corpus. The liberation of the prisoners mentioned in these verses has its roots in the language of Isa 42:6f; and particularly Isa 61:1ff.[47] The Isaiah passages announce the proclamation of liberty to the captives (42:7; 61:1) and the return of the double portion in the land (61:7).

Zech 9:13 climaxes the thoughts of the entire chapter to this point by explaining that the double portion promised in 9:12 means the restoration of the entire kingdom.[48] This verse takes on particular historical

---

establish an everlasting covenant with her. The result of this covenant will cause Zion to feel shame at her conduct (16:61) and to cease complaining (16:63) because forgiveness has been granted. An interesting note appears at the end of Ezek 16:61 which indicates two different covenants, by distinguishing between the covenant of YHWH and the covenant of Zion. In Ezek 16:60 YHWH establishes an everlasting covenant, and then decides to restore Zion's powers over her sisters (Samaria to the north and Sodom to the south, Ezek 16:46-52). At this point (16:61b), the text makes a deliberate point to deny that this re-elevation of Zion results from *her* covenant. YHWH explicitly states that the reward comes purely at his instigation, "and not because of your covenant" (ולא מבריתך). This distinction between the positive covenant of YHWH and the covenant of Zion, viewed negatively in Ezek 16:61, naturally raises the question of the content of Zion's covenant. Unfortunately, nothing in Ezek 16:61 indicates what this covenant entailed. It is clear, however, that while Ezek 16:61 views Zion's covenant as having no part in YHWH's decision for restoration, Zech 9:11 presumes a Zion covenant which leads to restoration (the freeing of the prisoners). It is not hard to envision that behind these two references to a Zion covenant lies a single tradition, about which only certain speculations can be made. Is it not conceivable, and perhaps even probable, given the increase of Zion imagery from the late exilic period onward, that a tradition of Zion's covenant developed which involved some type of oath of allegiance (or repentance)? Is it not also possible, in light of Kutsch's insights concerning Exod 24:8, that this tradition of Zion's covenant somehow involved the sealing of the covenant with a type of blood ritual, either similar to that of Moses in Exod 24:8 or with traditions of washing in the blood of a sacrificed animal which Kutsch describes? If so, some circles (Ezek 16:61) might view this act as ineffectual — which could also explain the reference to Zion's continual complaining in Ezek 16:63 — while other circles (Zech 9:11) might assume the act demonstrated a repentance which led to YHWH's change of heart. These observations admittedly involve speculation, but the evidence does indicate the existence of a Zion covenant tradition, whose content needs further investigation.

[47] See further discussion in Willi-Plein, *Prophetie am Ende*, 82f.

[48] The attachment of Zech 9:13 to the end of 9:12 by means of the כי clause explicitly relates the "return" of the double portion to the announcement of battle in which YHWH will use Judah, Ephraim, and Jerusalemites against Greece.

significance since it presumes Greece controls the region over which the battle is fought, which, unless one emends the text or does not take the literary context seriously, must reflect a time after the conquests of Alexander in the region (332).[49] If one does take the literary context seriously, then one must assume that the war announced against the Greeks in 9:13, which simultaneously relates to the double restoration, must be read as yet another example of the motif of the restoration of the kingdom to its ideal limits (with 9:1,7,10), even though it probably does not stem from the same literary level.

With the substitution of prophetic speech about YHWH for divine speech, **Zech 9:14-17** changes style from the preceding, but its contents appropriately follow the announcements of battle in 9:8,13. Zech 9:14-17 describes the battle and its aftermath, utilizing the portrayal of a theophany, and promises of weal for YHWH's people who participate in the battle. Stylistically, the change from the divine "I" speech in Zech 9:9-13 separates 9:14-17 significantly, but 9:14 does not represent the beginning of a new autonomous unit since its second word, עליהם ("over them"), contains a pronoun which presumes an antecedent. The nearest antecedent to which this plural pronoun could refer would be the constellation of YHWH's army in 9:13: Judah, Ephraim, and the sons of Zion. The theophanic depiction of battle in 9:14, however, differs considerably from the pronouncement in 9:13, creating a metaphorical picture which is difficult to visualize. Metaphorically, YHWH draws Jerusalem, Judah, and Ephraim as weapons (the bow and sword), this picture does not equate itself well with the announcement that YHWH will then appear *over them*.[50] Thus, Zech 9:14 introduces a juncture in the text which creates two paradoxical observations. On the one hand, Zech 9:14 cannot introduce an

---

[49] Contra Hanson, *The Dawn of Apocalyptic*, 298, who suggests emending the phrase based on meter. Compare how this perspective differs from the relatively innocuous mention of the Greeks in Joel 4:6, where the antagonism is directed against the peoples who captured and sold the slaves (Tyre, Sidon, and Philistia), not against the recipients of the slaves (Greeks, Sabeans).

[50] The picture of a warrior God appearing over a battling army (Zech 9:14) as a sign of accompaniment and protection is not uncommon in the Ancient Near East, particularly in Assyrian reliefs. See Keel, *Symbolism of the Biblical World*, plate XX. However, the metaphor of 9:13 depicts YHWH using Judah and Ephraim as a bow and the Sons of Zion as a sword, or in other words, instruments of attack that YHWH holds in his hand. It is not only difficult to visualize YHWH holding these weapons (9:13) and subsequently appearing over them (9:14), but 9:14 presumes YHWH carries different weapons than 9:13. Zech 9:14 presents YHWH using more typical theophanic images of the divine warrior with his arrows of flashing light (cf Hab 3:4).

independent unit because its pronoun requires an antecedent, and presumes an announcement of a battle.   On the other hand, despite a possible antecedent in the preceding verse, the imagery between the two verses does not readily correspond.

One can resolve this tension considerably with the assumption that the two metaphors do not stem from the same hand, but one can go further by postulating that the original antecedent of "over them" in 9:14 relates not to 9:13, but to Zech 9:8, where the same form (עליהם) relates to YHWH's protective encampment around the heart of his kingdom before battle.[51] In order to make the assumption that Zech 9:14 originally followed 9:8, then one must account for the fact, that in the current form of Zech 9:1-17, the pronoun of 9:14 is separated from its antecedent by five verses. Accounting for this five verse gap is not difficult, however, when one recognizes that Zech 9:9-13 utilizes Zion imagery which appears nowhere else in Zech 9-11.   Zech 9:9-13 addresses Zion directly in her singular personified form, whereas Zech 9:8,14-17 describes the people of YHWH as third person plural entities.   Logically, one would assume someone inserted the Zion text (9:9-13) into a pre-existing literary context.[52]

The remainder of Zech 9:14-17 treats the battle and its aftermath. The verses describe the battle in theophanic terms which presuppose traditions similar to the images found in Hab 3:3ff.[53]   Zech 9:15 formulates the battle such that YHWH's defense leads to a victory for the people.   After YHWH appears, the end comes quickly for the enemies. The latter portion of Zech 9:15 depicts the victory in celebrative, albeit gruesome images.[54]   Zech 9:16f describes the aftermath of the battle,

---

[51] The repetition of the same form in 9:15 demonstrates its importance for the thought progression in the verses.

[52] The motivation behind this insertion requires further elaboration, and it will be necessary to return to this topic following a further discussion of the larger context. See the discussion below, page 229.

[53] Above all, note that YHWH comes in the storm wind from Teman (cf Hab 3:3) with lightning (Hab 3:4) as his weapon.

[54] The dominant metaphors of Zech 9:15 describe the battle in terms of a feast and sacrifice. "They will devour ... They will drink, be boisterous, as though (drunk with) wine, and they will become full like the basin, like the corners of the altar." The images depict the victorious army, drenched in the blood of their enemies, loudly marching through the enemy ranks, meeting virtually no resistance. See Rudolph, *KAT* 13/4, 188, for a vivid description of the bloodiness of the battle, however, Rudolph and others interpret the theophanic imagery too exclusively. The plural verbs require one to envision that not only YHWH, but YHWH's people participate in the battle, or at

however, more peacefully. YHWH delivers them and they become like the "flock of his people" dotting the countryside like precious stones (9:16b). Zech 9:17 completes the description of the results of the battle with an affirmation of the goodness and beauty of his flock. The peaceful images in Zech 9:16 depicting YHWH's people as a flock dotting the land contrast sharply with the negative images of the "flock doomed to slaughter" (11:4) which appear later in Zech 10-11. Likewise, the peaceful images are neither inherent to the theophanic imagery of the battle, nor are they needed syntactically to complete the image of the victory of YHWH, since 9:16a offers a suitable climax without reference to "the flock."[55] It is not difficult, therefore, to understand the last part of 9:16 and 9:17 as an addition which serves as a literary transition to the remaining chapters. This transition introduces the metaphor of the flock into the salvific motifs of 9:1-17, deliberately helping to prepare the dramatic reversal of the following chapters.

In summary, Zech 9:1-17 provides a *relatively* consistent picture in which YHWH's punishment against the surrounding regions leads to the deliverance of his people via YHWH's own intervention as warrior.[56] This

---

least in its aftermath. See also Saebø, *Sacharja 9-14*, 195-200, for a discussion of the textual difficulties in the verse.

[55] Zech 9:16 begins with a sentence which climaxes the theophanic portrayal: "And YHWH Elohim will deliver them on that day." The continuation of the sentence with the introduction of the metaphorical imagery of the flock is syntactically awkward: "... like the flock of his people that are stones of a crown clustering upon his land." (See Koehler-Baumgartner [³1983], 664).

[56] This picture of consistency demands a particular supposition concerning the function of the enemy in order to explain the relationship between 9:1-7,8ff. This supposition requires that the judgment instituted by YHWH against the nations as punishment comes from the outside. YHWH himself does not take part in this punishment in the same manner as he participates in the theophanic battle in 9:14-17. This supposition creates a certain tension with Zech 9:3 which states YHWH will dispossess Tyre. Nevertheless, it should probably not be understood as the work of different authors. Since 9:7 does not appear to be the culmination of the oracle, which moves logically from 9:7 to 9:8,14-17, one can more readily overcome the tension in the presupposition of the author. Since elsewhere (notably, Isa 10 and Habakkuk) YHWH's instruments of punishment exceed the task for which they were commissioned, it is preferable in this case to understand Zech 9:1-8,14-17 against this background. In other words, YHWH commissions the punishment of the surrounding regions, but draws the line at the border of Judah to ensure that his instrument of punishment does not overstep its role by moving against his house. In this light, the defensive posture of YHWH in Zech 9:8 takes on considerable significance. The battle depicted in Zech 9:14-17 thus presupposes that the enemy tries to exceed the task allotted to it.

consistency points to the independent existence, in literary form, of Zech 9:1-8,14-17. Two additions to this literary unit point toward incorporation of the piece into a wider literary context. The first, Zech 9:16b-17 introduces the flock motif into the literary context of chapter nine. This addition serves as a transition to the more negative message of Zech 10-11, deliberately establishing a contrast between the peaceful flock delivered by YHWH (9:16) and the negative picture of the flock in Zech 10-11 which wanders aimlessly with no shepherd (10:2), and which is doomed to destruction (11:4). This transition may be assigned most plausibly to the hand of the collector who shaped Zech 9-11 in its inverted form which moves from positive to negative images.

The second insertion, Zech 9:9-13 addresses the personified Zion directly, introducing a motif which does not appear elsewhere in Zech 9-11. Since Jerusalem functions centrally in Zech 12-14, it seems plausible to assume tentatively that inclusion of Zech 9:9-13 into the contexts results from the combination of these two blocks. Prior to moving to a closer inspection of Zech 12-14, it seems wise to look more closely at the motivation behind the inclusion of Zion into the context of chapter nine.

4. The Position and Function of Zion in Zech 9:9-13

The Zion material in Zech 9:9-13 has been inserted into the existing literary context in a manner which exhibits considerable thought with regard to its placement within the chapter and within a larger literary context. As noted earlier, with the exception of Zech 9:9-13, Jerusalem does not play an accented role in Zech 9-11 that would suitably account for the presence of 9:9-13. By contrast, Zech 12-14 centers its messages so strongly upon Jerusalem that, at times, one almost gets the impression that these chapters do not offer salvation apart from that city.[57] Treating the combination of Zech 9-11 and the Jerusalem perspective in Zech 12-14 requires caution, however, since there are good reasons to suppose that Zech 12-14 results

---

[57] Modern readers are not alone in sensing that 12-14 stresses Jerusalem at the expense of other parts of YHWH's kingdom. Portions of 12-14 exhibit tension between Judah and Jerusalem via several corrective glosses, particularly, in chapter 12. See various explanations in Mason, *Haggai, Zechariah, and Malachi*, 113; Rudolph, *KAT* 13/4, 217; Elliger, *ATD* 25, 158f. For a different opinion, see Willi-Plein, *Prophetie am Ende*, 56.

from the combination of at least two different transmission blocks, 12-13
and 14:1-21.[58] One must not only look at the role of Zech 9:9-13 within
chapter nine, but also attempt to determine with which block of Jerusalem
material in Zech 12-14 these verses entered.

Within chapter nine, the Zion material appears at a very appropriate
point. Zech 9:1-7 brings judgment to the surrounding regions, which leads
in contrasting fashion to the announcement of protection for YHWH's
"house" in 9:8.[59] In turn, the announcement of future salvation for Zion
logically precedes YHWH's intervention in Zech 9:14-17. The specific
location of the Zion material may also have been influenced by the
reference to "my house" in Zech 9:8, given the dual traditions of kingdom
and temple which lay behind the phrase. Thus, the position of 9:9-13 fits
thoughtfully within the overall movement of the chapter.

Regarding the content of Zech 9:9-13, several additional observations
can be made which help to characterize the verses. First, more than the
remainder of the chapter, these verses brandish considerable literary
dependence upon and allusions to other portions of prophetic literature,
both inside and outside the Book of the Twelve.[60] Second, the threat
from outside comes specifically from the Greeks as world power, and
represents the most concrete historical reference within all of Zech 9-14.
The indications that this reference to the Greeks forms part of a secondary
insertion into the context complicates the question of date for Zech 9-14
still further, although it does not alter the conviction that the fundamental
literary piece (9:1-8,14-17) upon which the chapter is based stems from a
very late period, as far as Old Testament passages are concerned.[61]
Third, like the earlier portion of the chapter to which Zech 9:9-13 is added,

---

[58] See Rudolph, *KAT* 13/4, 161f; and Mason, *Haggai, Zechariah, and Malachi*, 133f.

[59] See discussion of Zech 9:8 above, beginning on page 221.

[60] In addition to the discussion above, see Willi-Plein, *Prophetie am Ende*, 93. The
remainder of Zech 9 also draws on earlier traditions, e.g. the similarity between Amos'
oracles and Zech 9:1-8. However, reliance upon particular formulations appears more
prevalent in 9:9-13. Elsewhere, only the possible literary allusion to Hab 3:3f in Zech
9:14 compares with the use of other material in 9:9-13.

[61] Several rationale still argue for the lateness of this passage, even without the Zion
material. Zech 9:1-8 plays off the oracles of Amos, and Zech 9:14 knows Hab 3:3ff.
Tyre's dominant role in Zech 9:2-4, combined with the relatively late date of Hab 3:3ff,
points toward post-exilic origin for Zech 9:1-8,14-17. Zech 9:15 takes the presence of
a sacrificial altar for granted, eliminating the possibility of exilic origin. Zech 9:1-8,14-
17 serves as the introduction to Zech 9-11 which further buttress the impression of a
post-exilic date, since 11:4-17 take up the parable of the shepherd from Ezekiel. See
also O.H. Steck, *Der Abschluß der Prophetie im Alten Testament*, 21ff, 30ff.

the Zion material presupposes that peace for YHWH's people lies in a future time, following a decisive battle in which YHWH plays an active role as warrior on the side of his people.

Looking beyond the immediate confines of chapter nine to the question of the likely origin of these verses in relationship to Zech 12-13,14, the most significant similarities appear to be those of Zech 9:9-13 with 12:1-10.[62] Chapter twelve begins with the announcement of weal to Jerusalem, despite the approaching threat of war. The depiction of events in Zech 12:1-10 bears considerable similarity to the events of chapter nine. Both passages assume a divinely inspired offensive campaign.[63] The surrounding regions play a role as antagonist in both passages, but they do not constitute the entire field of view.[64] Explicit imagery drawing upon Davidic traditions in both passages, suggests that the Zion verses were already present to the writer of 12:1ff.[65] Very significantly, one cannot help but note the parallel expressions in the two passages that YHWH "will defend" his people in 9:15 and 12:8. Zech 12:8 draws from 9:15, but mentions only the inhabitants of Jerusalem.

By way of contrast, Zech 14:1-21 utilizes different images. David does not play a dominant role in 14:1-21, unlike chapters nine and twelve. Unlike chapters nine and twelve, Jerusalem in chapter fourteen is not only threatened, it is pillaged and half of the city exiled (14:2). Only after the near destruction of Jerusalem in 14:2 (which YHWH not only allows but instigates), does YHWH intervene on behalf of the inhabitants of the city. But even in the act of intervention, the text demonstrates a significant shift from the images of chapters nine and twelve. Zech 9:9-13 and 12:6 depict YHWH's use of Jerusalem and Judah, as instruments in the battle, whereas

---

[62] On the separation of Zech 14:1-21 from chapters 12-13, see above note 58.

[63] Zech 12:6 assumes an offensive campaign in which Judah will devour "the surrounding peoples on the right and on the left." Chapter nine clearly assumes an offensive campaign against the sons of Greece in 9:13, whereas the earlier portions of the chapter point toward a defensive campaign, with 9:8 intimating defensive images (camp around my house) and 9:15 also implying a battle of defense. Compare "YHWH Sebaoth will defend (יָגֵן) them," in 9:15 with images in the Hezekiah story (2 Kgs 19:34 = Isa 37:35; and 2 Kgs 20:6 = Isa 38:6).

[64] Compare Zech 9:1-7 with Zech 12:6, both of which reflect the surrounding nations. Compare also the reference to the Greeks in 9:13 which expands the enemy explicitly, with the accentuation of "all the nations of the earth" in 12:3.

[65] Note particularly the entry of the Davidic king in Zech 9:9f and the Davidic/Solomonic boundaries in 9:1-7, also perhaps the stones of the sling in 9:15. Compare these Davidic allusions with the predictions that even the feeble of YHWH's people will be like David in Zech 12:8.

in 14:1ff, YHWH utilizes a vast array of cosmic weaponry, including his heavenly host (14:4-6). The battle in chapter fourteen results in the reconstitution of the topography so that it elevates a purified Jerusalem (whereas Zech 13:1ff describes the positive results more modestly).

5. Zech 9-13 as Corpus

With these observations, one arrives at the conclusion that the Zion material in Zech 9:9-13 entered the larger context with the addition of chapters 12-13, not with 14:1-21. It is possible to go somewhat further, and to postulate a significant intention on the part of the redactional addition of Zech 9:9-13 and the formative material of chapters 12-13, namely that Zech 9:9-13 represents a precursor to the Jerusalem emphasis in chapters 12-13, which deliberately strengthens the parallels between the two introductory passages, because they are intended to be read together.[66] In other words the writer/compiler of 12-13 simply carries the message of 9-11 further, but adds a notable shift to the climax of the message. While space does not permit a detailed evaluation, the macrostructure of Zech 9-13 does allow some significant, albeit tentative, conclusions regarding the purpose of this parallel action. These conclusions combine several of the preliminary observations regarding Zech 9-14, specifically the facts that: 1) Zech 9-11 concentrates upon the entities of Judah and Ephraim, while 12-14 centers on Jerusalem, Judah and the nations; 2) Zech 9-11 presents an inverted structure which moves from the positive to the negative. Beginning with the latter observation, there is little doubt that the culmination of Zech 9-11 reverses Ezekiel's shepherd allegory in a manner which is decidedly negative, and offers little in the way of a hopeful message.[67] These chapters culminate in the dissolution of YHWH's covenant with the nations and the annihilation of the union between Judah and Israel. As an interpretation of history from the late Persian period or early Greek period, these chapters may well have been painfully realistic,

---

[66] Contra Lamarche, *Zacharie*, 106, who implies that the similarities are stronger between Zech 12:1-9 and 14:1-15.

[67] For discussion of the relationship of Zech 11:4-17 to Ezek 37:15-28, see the commentaries and Rex Mason, "Some Examples of Inner Biblical Exegesis in Zech 9-14," in *Studia Evangelica* 7, Texte und Untersuchungen zur Geschichte der altchristlichen Literatur 126 (Berlin: Akademie-Verlag, 1982), 347-350.

but as the continuing message to YHWH's people, these chapters surely evoked strong reactions.[68] These reactions took a particular literary form in chapters 12-13, a form in which concentrates on Jerusalem and Judah.

The parallel introductory passages of 9:1-17 and 12:1-10 indicate these passages should be read in tandem, but it simultaneously points to a significant change regarding the reaction to the events described. Following 9:17, Zech 10:1-3a portrays YHWH's people as a flock which the prophet implores to turn to YHWH. These verses assume, however (even in the midst of the larger salvation sayings of chapters 9-10), that the flock will not comprehend the true source of the salvific events because of their leaders. By means of a deliberate contrast, Zech 12:10ff portrays the proper response on the part of the leaders of Jerusalem with the result that YHWH will pour out supplication and grace "on the house of David and on the inhabitants of Jerusalem" (Zech 12:10), and they will mourn (12:11-13) for what they have done to YHWH and/or his servant (12:10).[69] The repentant act of mourning involves the entire leadership of Jerusalem (12:12-14), unlike 10:2, which depicts the people without true leadership wandering aimlessly from one false religious leader to another. Contrast these images with those of 12:12-14 in which the leaders respond properly (12:12f), and then all the families that remain (12:14) behave in kind. Zech 10:1f depicts a situation in which the lack of water, which should require that the people petition YHWH, leads instead to the consultation of various idolatrous means of mediation to alleviate the problem. By contrast, the proper response of the Jerusalemites in 12:10-14 leads to the establishment of a cleansing fountain (13:1), which leads in turn to the elimination of the idolatrous elements of mediation, rather than their consultation (13:2,[3-6]). Particularly noteworthy is the accentuation of the prophets among those mediators who will be removed from the land. This condemnation points toward an interesting phenomenon in which those who are transmitting and reshaping corpora do not consider themselves to be prophets.[70]

---

[68] For a discussion of 9-11 as an inner-historical prophetic corpus, see Willi-Plein, *Prophetie am Ende*, 102-104. She determines that the historical interpretation in 9-11 differs from the eschatological material in chapters 12-14. Her observations cannot be easily dismissed, particularly since 12-14 use ביום ההוא as the dominant structuring device, whereas its sole occurrence in 9-11 (9:16) serves no such function.

[69] For discussion of the textual and literary difficulty of interpreting Zech 12:10, see Rudolph, *KAT* 13/4, 217f; Saebø, *Sacharja 9-14*, 97-103.

[70] Zech 13:3-5 calls for an end to prophecy, at least as practiced by another group which "puts on a hairy mantle in order to deceive." (Zech 13:4) Since Zech 13:3-5 functions as an expanded commentary upon Zech 13:2, one can probably assume that the literary

Given that Zech 9:9-13 and 12:1-13:6 elevate Jerusalem's response to
YHWH's salvific acts, how does one account for the re-introduction of the
more negative motifs of Zech 13:7-9, which presupposes the deliverance of
only one third of the flock? Possibly, the remnant is Jerusalem, in
contradistinction to Judah and Ephraim. This interpretation could account
for the use of three groups, but a more likely possibility suggests itself.[71]
The dominant scholarly opinion regarding Zech 13:7-9 argues it originally
formed the conclusion to the shepherd allegory of Zech 11:4-17, but was
later transposed to a new location.[72] This opinion is assumed to be
correct here for several reasons in addition to the typical arguments.

First, Zech 13:7-9 is formally more appropriate as the conclusion to
a corpus (Zech 9-11) than is Zech 11:17. It has the ring of a concluding
saying because of its application to a broader group (my people), whereas
the condemnation of the shepherd in Zech 11:17 seems too particularistic
for an appropriate conclusion to a larger block. Second, Zech 13:7-9 is
theologically more appropriate as a conclusion to Zech 9-11. The
announcement of deliverance for a remnant does provide at least some ray
of hope more in keeping with other prophetic corpora. Third, one can
explain the transposition of 13:7-9 redactionally. Zech 14:1ff, presumes the
purification of a remnant in Jerusalem, and since Zech 14:1-21 was
incorporated after Zech 12-13, it is by no means illogical to assume that

---

addition to chapters 9-11 which sought to elevate Jerusalem ended with Zech 13:2. It
later received the commentary additions against the prophets in particular. For
discussion of how these verses function as an "actualization" of Hos 2:18f, see Will-
Plein, *Prophetie am Ende*, 76f. She maintains the entire unit, Zech 13:2-6, orients itself
toward Hos 2:18f, but the literary connections appear only in 13:2. See also the
discussion below (page 235) of *13:7-9 as the earlier conclusion to Zech 9-11*. Zech 13:9
(as the conclusion of Zech 9-11) cites Hos 2:25, which helps to explain the Hoseanic
reference in 13:2. Zech 12:1-13:2(6) comments upon Zech 9-11. Not surprisingly, 13:9,
with its allusion to Hos 2:25, evokes Zech 13:2, which also cites Hos 2:18f.

[71] The destruction of two thirds of the flock could perhaps interpret Ephraim and Judah
as the two parts which would be cut off, based on Zech 9-11, but this interpretation
would fail to account for the positive incorporation of Judah into portions of 12:1ff.
The presupposition of a remnant is difficult to place in terms of chapter twelve, since
it explicitly depicts the salvation of all Jerusalem (Zech 12:12-14).

[72] So Mason, *Haggai, Zechariah, and Malachi*, 110ff; Rudolph, *KAT* 13/4, 212ff. Some
disagree: Elliger, *ATD* 25, 165; Willi-Plein, *Prophetie am Ende*, 59, but their arguments
assumpe the author of 13:7-9 is not the same as 11:4-17. Even if separate authorship
were true (which is not certain, given the specific function of 13:7-9 as conclusion), this
would not prove whether 13:7-9 originally formed the conclusion of the corpus, since
Zech 9-11 combines several pre-existing blocks. For example, Zech 9:1ff and 11:4-17
do not stem from the same hand, but they both form integral parts of the larger corpus.

.Zech 13:7-9 was transposed as an introduction to chapter fourteen, because of its remnant motif at the beginning. Fourth, the assumption that Zech 13:7-9 formed the conclusion of Zech 9-11 is literarily more appropriate from the larger perspective of the Book of the Twelve, since the particular formulation of Zech 13:9 draws upon specific literary formulations in Hosea and Malachi. Specifically, Zech 13:9b explicitly takes up Hos 1:9; 2:25:

Hos 1:9	Zech 13:9b
And YHWH said: Name him Lo-Ammi, for you are "Not my people," and I am not your God.	They will call on my name, and I will answer them; I will say, "They are my people, and they will say YHWH is my God."
Hos 2:25	
And I will say to those who were not my people, you are my people, and they will say, "You are my God."	

Additionally, the images from the initial part of the verse comes from the final chapter of Malachi:

Mal 3:2f	Zech 13:9a
But who can endure the day of his coming? And who can stand when he appears? For he is like the fire of a refiner (מצרף) ... And he will sit as a refiner (מצרף) and purifier of silver, and he will purify the sons of Levi and refine them like gold and silver, so that they may present to YHWH offerings in righteousness.	And I will bring the third part through the fire, refine (צרף) them as silver is refined and test them as gold is tested.

The dependency of Zech 13:9 upon the first and last writings in the Book of the Twelve indicates a bridging function which helps to explain the rationale behind the compilation of Zech 9-11. As noted before, the connection between Zech 8:9ff and Mal 1:1ff contrasts deliverance and promise with the return to the abominable practices of earlier generations. The transition between these two writings, however, is very sudden and abrupt, the hope of salvation immediately precedes the description of cultic abuse. By contrast, the inverted order of Zech 9-11 smoothes this transition considerably. These chapters begin with the pronouncement of salvation, taking up the dominant motif of Zech 8:9ff. Yet by the end of chapter eleven, false cultic practices (cf 10:2) based largely upon the failure of the leadership, have led to a message of judgment in which only a remnant will survive, effectively preparing the reader for the message of Malachi, which begins with an expanded description of cultic abuse (Mal 1:6ff), and leads

to the pronouncements of chapter three that only a remnant will remain.
Thus, many of the preliminary observations made earlier can be accounted
for with the postulation that Zech 9-11 was compiled for the Book of the
Twelve as a transition from Zech 8:9ff to Malachi. This transition later
received its own addition (Zech 9:9-13; 12:1-13:6) which reinterpreted
Jerusalem's role. It now remains to attempt an explanation of 14:1-21.

6. Zech 14:1-21: Positive and Negative Aspects of the Final Judgment

Zech 14:1-21 depicts a final judgment in which YHWH, Jerusalem,
and the nations play the central roles.[73] The outward structure of the text
receives a certain unifying characteristic from the multiplicity of יום
formulas within the chapter, but the variation of the function of these
formulas does not allow one to describe them as the only structural
device.[74] In addition, the most decisive thematic shift in the chapter (at

---

[73] Judah comes into play at certain points, but only peripherally. Zech 14:14,21 mention
Judah explicitly, while Zech 14:10 includes the region without mentioning it by name.
Northern regions do not receive specific treatment. Zech 14:10 encompasses territory
to the north (Geba, 10km north of Jerusalem) and south (Rimmon, 18 km north of
Beerscheba), but the limits of this territorial description do not correspond to other
traditions of the boundaries of the land. 2 Kgs 23:8 implies Geba was the northernmost
point during the reign of Josiah, but the same passage implies the limits of the territory
to the south extended all the way to Beersheba. See discussions in Rudolph, *KAT* 237;
Otzen, *Studien über Deuterosacharja*, 208, Elliger, *ATD* 25, 172. The latter two authors
treat the references as deliberate attempts to describe the territorial limits of ancient
Judah before the reforms of Josiah, while Rudolph is justifiably more skeptical. Given
the lateness of Zech 14:1-21, it is not impossible that the reference reflects the
boundary of Idumea at that time, since by the time of Judas Maccabeus (164),
Idumeans controlled Judean territory as far north as Hebron (1 Macc 4:29; 5:65).
However, lacking further data, one cannot be certain of this prospect. One can say
with confidence that the limited nature of the boundaries of Judah while accenting
Jerusalem presupposes an entirely different view of "Israel" from that pictured in Zech
9-10 and also 12:1-13:6. The images in 9-13 portray Israel more aggressively.

[74] Several different יום formulas appear in the chapter with the dominant expression
being ביום־ההוא (Zech 14:4,6,8,9,13,20,21), but these formulas do not all introduce
new thematic units. For example, 14:4 uses the phrase in the middle of a sentence, and
in 14:21 it concludes the entire section. Additionally, other יום phrases appear with
different syntactical functions: as introductory formulas for paragraphs (14:1) and
sentences (14:6,7), or as simple references within a sentence (14:3).

14:12) utilizes no יום formula at all.[75] In fact, the dominant structuring element in Zech 14:1-21 is best described in terms of theme. The final judgment overshadows all other motifs in the chapter, but within the framework of this theme, the smaller units revolve around the negative and positive aspects of the final judgment for Jerusalem and for the nations. The principal thematic units begin with the negative portrayal of the day of judgment for Jerusalem depicting the survival of only a remnant (Zech 14:1-5). The nature of the judgmental descriptions then changes to treat the positive effects of a purified Jerusalem (Zech 14:8-11). The same dynamic recurs with regard to the destiny of the nations, beginning with the negative effects of the judgment on the nations (Zech 14:12-15), followed by a short saying about the positive aspects for the remnant of the nations (Zech 14:16), who will be afforded the privilege of making a pilgrimage to Jerusalem to worship YHWH. This dialectic repeats a third time with the warning to the nations of the consequences of not going to Jerusalem (Zech 14:17-19), followed by the promise of a holy Jerusalem (Zech 14:20-21).

Having noted this thematic vacillation between the positive and the negative aspects of the final judgment, three further observations should be made regarding the relationship of the various units within this scheme. First, one section stands out conspicuously for its seeming lack of conformity to the patterns of alternations of judgmental and salvific perspectives, namely Zech 14:6f. These verses describe the peculiar character of the day with regard to whether it resembles the day or the night. Second, Zech 14:14a also stands somewhat at odds thematically with its immediate context. This line introduces the specific statement that Judah will fight against Jerusalem, and does not directly relate to the negative effects of the judgment against the nations.[76] Third, Zech 14:18f diverges from the rhetoric against all the nations in order to make a point

---

[75] Zech 14:11 concludes a positive section centering on the effects of the day on Jerusalem, while 14:12 changes the subject to the plague which effects the nations. See the discussion which follows.

[76] Zech 14:14a disturbs the thematic context no matter which position one takes regarding the translation of the preposition ב with תלחם, either "Judah will fight *in* Jerusalem" (so LXX) or "Judah will fight *against* Jerusalem" (so the remainder of the versions). Modern scholars still line up on both sides of the question. Compare Smith, *Word* 32, 290, who follows LXX; and Rudolph, *KAT* 13/4, 233, who presents a more plausible explanation that the verse is a gloss. The fact that the use of לחם with ב in the niphal elsewhere so frequently means "against" (e.g. 1Chr 18:10; Isa 30:32; 63:10, and even in the same chapter, Zech 14:3), makes the LXX reading more understandable as an attempt to dilute objectionable material.

specifically about Egypt. The character of this Egypt reference reveals further reflection upon the inappropriateness of the previously announced judgment against Egypt.[77] These tensions within an otherwise thematically consistent structure of the chapter require an explanation. Three possibilities present themselves which might explain the discrepancies: (1) A compiler incorporated material which already contained the verses as part of another context, thereby ignoring any tension when placed within this new context. (2) The tensions in the structure of the chapter reflect the growth of the text which was not explicitly interested in maintaining the vacillating perspectives, but in commenting upon specific aspects of the pre-existing components. (3) Further investigation reveals the *presupposition* of traditions which help account for the thematic tension.

Zech 14:18f allows the easiest classification of the three passages, since its reflective character upon the preceding verse, within the context of the chapter, implies someone has perceived the threat in Zech 14:17 as inappropriate with regard to Egypt.[78] The verse also exhibits a considerable literary peculiarity in relationship to the context.[79] The literary distinctiveness argues strongly against the assumption that the same author who wrote the threat in Zech 14:17 also composed the elaboration.

Zech 14:14a also demonstrates the character of a reflective gloss. The gloss accentuates Judah's participation in the battle, an interpretation which derives not from the immediate context, but from the battle descriptions of Zech 12:2b. The gloss cannot have been added prior to the combination of these two chapters. The question of Judah's inclusion as an enemy of Jerusalem probably arises from confusion within chapter twelve.[80]

---

[77] See discussions in Rudolph, *KAT* 13/4, 238f; Otzen, *Studien über Deuterosacharja*, 271; and Saebø, *Sacharja 9-14*, 124-126. The feast of booths (Zech 14:16) occurs shortly before the rainy season in Palestine, making the threat of drought particularly significant to those nations not participating in the pilgrimage to Jerusalem. The fact that Egypt depended more on the Nile flooding than on seasonal rainfall for its agricultural fate, prompts an exception for Egypt (Zech 14:18) regarding their punishment. Their potential punishment is described even more threateningly. Rather than rain, they would be punished with a plague like the nations who attack Jerusalem (cf Zech 14:12). The Targum already presupposes this interpretation: "Thus the Nile will not rise for them, rather the plague will come over them."

[78] See further elaboration in Saebø, *Sacharja 9-14*, 125f.

[79] Saebø, *Sacharja 9-14*, 125f.

[80] See the explanations of Saebø, *Sacharja 9-14*, 123,256; and Rudolph, *KAT* 13/4, 233, who understand the verse as arising from a glossator's misinterpretation of Zech 12:2b on the basis of the description of battle against the neighbor in Zech 14:13.

The categorization of Zech 14:6f represents the most difficult passage of chapter fourteen to describe. The verses begin with an introductory formula, and are separated from what follows by the same formula to begin the announcement of positive effects for Jerusalem. Coupled with the fact that these two verses play no immediately recognizable role in the thematic structure or the action of the chapter, the presence of these formulas make it difficult to avoid the conclusion that these two verses form their own thought unit. Likewise, the relationship of this unit to the immediate context offers little help in explaining its presence or location. Zech 14:6f discusses the question of the day of YHWH from the perspective of light and night. In comparison to the dynamic description of events in Zech 14:1-5, 14:6f manifests a static character, which could *almost* be read as an "academic" discussion of the luminal quality of the day of YHWH. While the "academic" or intellectual background of the verses plays a major role in interpreting the function of Zech 14:6f, one must stop short of equating the lack of "narrative" action with a lack of movement within the verses. The acadmic discussion forms a portrait against which the verses should be read, which simultaneously allows one to describe their function as transitionary to the positive account of Jerusalem's destiny.

Zech 14:6f frequently receives notice for its similarity to YHWH's promise to Noah in Gen 8:22.[81] Saebø, however, cautions against this association in light of the textual changes which it must assume.[82] Saebø more plausibly maintains that the verses should be read in light of theophanic traditions which associate the day of YHWH with the loss of light.[83] Saebø's observations open the door to a pertinent understanding of the function of 14:6f within the chapter. He notes that when one interprets the imagery from this tradition, it leaves an unmistakable tension regarding the negative portrayal of judgment of Zech 14:6 and the positive

---

[81] So Willi-Plein, *Prophetie am Ende*, 29f; Mason, *Haggai, Zechariah, and Malachi*, 127f; Otzen, *Studien über Deuterosacharja*, 268f.

[82] Saebø, *Sacharja 9-14*, 298-300, argues convincingly that the motif of darkness accompanying the theophany of Zech 14:1-5 makes it difficult to ignore the negative implications to "not ... light, and "not day" in these two verses.

[83] Note Exod 19:16,18; 20:18; 24:15,16; Deut 4:11; 5:23; Ps 18:1-12; 97:2; Josh 24:7; Isa 5:30; 13:10; Amos 5:18f; 8:8f; Jer 4:23; Zeph 1:15; Joel 2:2; 3:3f; 4:15. Particularly, this last reference in Joel 4:15 helps illuminate the reference to "precious things" understood as celestial luminaries, when it specifically mentions the sun, moon, and stars as those elements which will grow dark.

statements of 14:7b.[84] Yet Saebø insightfully argues against too hastily
treating either of these elements as an expansion. Rather, he argues that
Zech 14:7b deliberately augments the negative imagery of 14:6 with the
reversal of the theme of darkness, via a promise of light representing
YHWH's victory. When one notes that these verses appear in precisely the
point in the chapter where the subject changes from the negative to the
positive aspects of the day of YHWH for Jerusalem, one can assume that
these verses function as the deliberate transition between two thematic
subjects. Zech 14:6f serves as a poetic summary of the images in Zech
14:1-5, depicting the nations attack on Jerusalem (14:1f) and YHWH's
decisive appearance for battle (14:3-5). This appearance dramatically
changes the topography so that all must flee for their lives.[85] This unique
day of judgment (14:7a), changes to one of hope with the announcement
that "in the evening there will be light" (14:7b). This transition opens the
way for the salvific promises to Jerusalem in Zech 14:8-11.

Thus, unlike the two previous passages, investigation of 14:6f reveals
that the perceived tension reflects dependence upon traditions which
actually reinforce the observations of a thematic structure to the chapter.
Zech 14:6f forms the transition from negative to positive pronouncements

---

[84] Saebø, *Sacharja 9-14*, 299f. Saebø (303f) treats Zech 14:7a as part of a later
redactional layer (together with 14:9,10ab,b) which accentuates Jerusalem on the basis
of Isaianic and the cultic-hymnic tradition. Given the amalgamated character of the
sayings in the chapter, Saebø's assignation of these verses to a later hand does not seem
warranted.

[85] Zech 14:5 portrays the theophany such that its effects create problems, not only for the
nations, but also for YHWH's people, who must "flee just as you fled before the
earthquake in the days of Uzziah." This verse presupposes Amos 1:1, which associates
the time of Uzziah with a great earthquake, but it also presupposes a tradition about
the earthquake which exceeds the reference in Amos. See discussions in Rudolph, *KAT*
13/4, 232; and Mason, *Haggai, Zechariah, and Malachi*, 126. The problematic phrase
at the end of Zech 14:5 causes various suggested interpretations. In the MT, the phrase
"all the holy ones with you" (2fs) makes no sense because the feminine singular
reference relates neither to YHWH or the people who are addressed in the plural in
Zech 14:5. Many scholars translate "with him," and cite the versions for support.
However, this reading probably reflects a harmonization by the translators. More
likely, עמך should be read as masculine, making "with you" (2ms) a direct address to
YHWH. This reading requires no change to the consonantal text, but creates tension
with the third person references to YHWH in the passage. One can explain the
tension. Either one treats the phrase as an interpretive gloss or as another example of
the tendency of later texts to alternate styles of address, even within the same passage.
The former is more likely. At any rate, the verse reflects YHWH's arrival with his
heavenly army for battle (cf Joel 4:9ff).

to Jerusalem. Despite the diverse motifs and images, one may characterize Zech 14:1-21 as a thematic unity which portrays the positive and negative characteristics of the day of YHWH upon both Jerusalem and the nations. This cursory investigation reveals that caution must be employed, however, when referring to the *unity* of this chapter, since there are clear indications that these verses receive expansions reflecting further contemplation upon the texts after the compilation of the chapter.[86] The question of how to evaluate the role of Zech 14:1-21 within the larger literary context of the Book of the Twelve now deserves consideration.

7. Zech 14:1-21 and Its Function in the Book of the Twelve

The quotes and allusions in Zech 14:1-21 indicate that this chapter draws substantially from writings within the Book of the Twelve. The Book of the Twelve thus constitutes an authoritative source from which to draw, but those responsible for the chapter demonstrate no major interest in *shaping* the larger corpus in the same way that earlier additions to the corpus imposed particular paradigms upon the corpus.[87] Rather, as noted above, chapter fourteen's major interest is the thematic presentation of the final judgment with both its positive and negative aspects for Jerusalem and the nations. This presentation draws from a wide variety of material in order to formulate its opinions, which suggests a growing recognition of an authoritative body of prophetic literature. Despite these observations, Zech 14:1-21 belongs to the Book of the Twelve. Observations on the function of this chapter within this context are therefore in order.

Surveying recent literature on Zech 14:1-21 produces the awareness of a developing recognition that the author of Zech 14:1-21 draws heavily, though not exclusively, upon other prophetic literature for images and language. This dependence, however, does not always take the form of direct quotations, but often assumes the themes and motifs from other

---

[86] Space does not permit systematic evaluation of every piece of evidence relating to the literary tensions within the individual verses. These tensions, together with discussions of possible interpretations, are discussed elsewhere. Note particularly, Saebø, *Sacharja 9-14*, 108-127; 285-309; and Willi-Plein, *Prophetie am Ende*, 59-63; 88-91.

[87] Here one thinks in particular of the Deuteronomistic corpus with its concentration upon the respective fates of the Northern and Southern kingdoms, and the Joel-related incorporation of a paradigm for the interpretation of history.

passages.[88]   Specific examples from which Zech 14:1-21 draws include
more passages than can be treated here.[89] Nevertheless, two of the more
important passages should be noted, because of their implications for the
Book of the Twelve.   Zech 14:16ff exhibits clear similarities with Isa
66:16ff.[90] In addition, several scholars have brought Isa 2:2 and/or Mic
4:1ff into discussions of the literary background of Zech 14:1-21.[91] An

---

[88]   For example, Saebø, *Sacharja 9-14*, 285, treats the chapter as a scholarly portrayal of
conditions based on older tradition material.   He further (287f) characterizes the
"quotes" as allusions which take up themes from other passages using *Stichwörter*.

[89]   For example, Willi-Plein, *Prophetie am Ende*, 93, lists the following usages of material
by Zech 14:1-21: Gen 8:22; Deut 6:4; Isa 2:1-4; 24:23; 40:4ff; 60:19; 66:18-24; Jer 2:13;
31:38-40; 25:9; 43:28; Ezek 11:23; 43:1-3; 47:1ff; Amos 5:20; Mic 4:1-4; Zech 8:20-23;
Joel 4:17,18.

[90]   Note the variety of means by which scholars relate these two passages: Otzen, *Studien
über Deuterosacharja*, 210-212; Willi-Plein, *Prophetie am Ende*, 90f; Bosshard, *BN* 40
(1987): Bosshard and Kratz, *BN* 52 (1990): 35f,43ff; Saebø, *Sacharja 9-14*, 306f. Otzen
treats Isa 66:18ff as one of several similarities to Trito-Isaiah, which points toward a
later development of the motifs which approaches apocalypticism.   Willi-Plein argues
that Zech 14:20f and Isa 66:20 are not directly related literarily, but can only be
compared, together with Joel 4:17, in the sense of a common intellectual milieu.   She
notes, however, that the entire eschatological perspective of Zech 14:16ff comes very
close to Isa 66:18-24.   Saebø does not mention Isa 66:16ff explicitly, but characterizes
the entire chapter as a compilation of themes, almost a scribal scholastic exercise,
which — following Horst, *HAT* 14, 250 — provides the chapter with the impression of
successive additions.   Bosshard, *BN* 40 (1987): 31,36, places high value on similarities
between the two passages as part of a deliberate shaping of the Book of the Twelve
according to the structural form of Isaiah.   Bosshard observes that Zech 1ff parallels
Isa 60-62 and Isa 14:16ff demonstrates interests identical with the concerns of the
conclusion of the Isaiah corpus.   These observations coincide with a continued pattern
of similarity, which might imply (due to the lack of parallels in Malachi) that Zech
14:1-21 formed an earlier conclusion to the Book of the Twelve.   Bosshard, together
with Kratz, *BN* 52 (1990): 35f,43ff later investigate the relationship between Zech 14:1-
21 and Malachi.   They maintain that a literary relationship between the *Grundschicht*
of Malachi and Zech 8 argues a version of the Twelve ended with Malachi prior to the
inclusion of Zech 9-13,14.   Still, they maintain Isa 66:16ff forms an important element
in the formulative process responsible for the inclusion of Zech 14 and the second layer
of Malachi.   In their view (44), Zech 14:1-21 expands the nations motif in Isa 66, while
Zech 13:8f, and Mal II, expand the ideas of Isa 66 concerning YHWH's people.

[91]   Numerous authors relate the elevation of Jerusalem in Zech 14:10 to Isa 2:2ff: Mason,
Haggai, Zechariah, and Malachi, 129; Saebø, *Sacharja 9-14*, 303; Willi-Plein, *Prophetie
am Ende*, 89f; Rudolph, *KAT* 13/4, 236f.   Some also draw comparisons to the theme of
the nations' pilgrimage in Isa 2:2ff and Zech 14:16ff.   For example, Mason, *Haggai,
Zechariah, and Malachi*, 132, compares the development of Isa 2:2-4 (=Mic 4:1-3),
where the nations come to receive instruction; Zech 8:22f, where they come to entreat

interesting question arises regarding dependence on these two parallel passages. Is it possible to decide whether the author draws from Isa 2:2ff or Mic 4:1ff? It is not possible to determine with absolute certainty, but there are sound reasons which point significantly in the direction of dependence upon the Isaiah context over against the Micah context. First, the dependence upon Isa 66:16ff by Zech 14:16ff indicates that the author of Zech 14 drew freely from the conclusion of Isaiah. Second, Zech 14:20f also exhibits an awareness of Isa 2. The horses in Zech 14:20f make sense when read against the threat in Isa 2:7, which states that the land will be filled with "horses" (implying war horses). By contrast, the horses in Zech 14:20 have been sanctified, and serve as signs of peace, whereas "horse" plays no explicit role in Mic 4:1ff.[92]

These observations demonstrate Zech 14:1-21 owes its formulation to motifs appearing at the beginning and end of Isaiah. This dependence upon Isa 2:1ff and 66:1ff deserves further reflection, since the skillful combination of these two passages provides Zech 14:1-21 with the same motifs which frame Isaiah: a purified, elevated Zion will serve as the center of salvation for all the world.[93] This awareness of Isaiah creates an interesting phenomenon relating to the concluding sections of the Book of the Twelve. The relationship of the editorial circles of the Book of the Twelve to those responsible for the transmission of Isaiah has already been noted, yet the specific similarity between Zech 14:1-21 and the book of

---

his favor; and Zech 14:16ff, where they come as "fellow worshippers alongside the Jews." Rudolph, *KAT* 13/4, 238f, contrasts the attitude of the nations in Zech 14:16ff to that in Isa 2:2f, with the latter being more idealistic. Importantly for Rudolph, Isa 2:2f portrays the nations as coming to Jerusalem under their own free will, while in Zech 14:16ff, they must be threatened with punishment.

[92] See Mason, *Haggai, Zechariah, and Malachi*, 132f. Mason does not relate this observation to the context of Isa 2:7, but it does make sense when read with that passage. Note that horses, along with other animals, also play a role in returning the diaspora Jews in Isa 66:20, while Zech 14:15 portrays them as part of the attack of the nations. The formulation of Zech 14:15 takes its cue from Isa 2:7 in treating these animals as part of the camps of attacking nations, and not as the means by which the diaspora Jews are returned as in Isa 66:20.

[93] See particularly the discussion of Bosshard and Kratz, *BN* 52 (1990): 44f. Though their discussion centers on Isa 66, many of their observations apply to Isa 1-2 as well, where the centrality of Jerusalem for a new world order is already implied (see especially 1:7-9,24ff; 2:1ff). For a detailed study of the canonical implications of the relationship between Isaiah and the Book of the Twelve, see Odil Hannes Steck, *Abschluß der Prophetie im Alten Testament. Ein Versuch zur Frage der Vorgeschichte des Kanons.* Biblisch theologische Studien 17 (Neukirchen-Vluyn: Neukirchener Verlag, 1991).

Isaiah (at a very late stage of its development) evidences significant implications beyond the assumption of a common tradent.[94] A parallel phenomenon at the end of Malachi related the end of that writing to the beginning of the former prophets (Mal 3:22 and Josh 1:2,7). The fact that Isaiah begins the collection of Hebrew scriptures known as the latter prophets suggests the concluding sections of the Book of the Twelve already demonstrate a rather more developed sense of canon than is traditionally assumed.[95] Malachi concludes with allusions to the beginning of the former prophets and Zech 12-14 concludes with deliberate associations to the first writing of the latter prophets. Thus, two of the three concluding sections of the Book of the Twelve, marked by common superscriptions, allude to the beginning of major divisions in the prophetic canon. Is it possible that the third section (Zech 9-11) plays any role in this awareness of the prophetic canon?

One cannot state without qualification that Zech 9-11 conforms to the pattern of Zech 12-14 and Malachi, but certain observations strongly imply that the end of Zech 9-11 operated with an eye toward the beginning of the Book of the Twelve. Zech 9-11 concludes with the shepherd allegory which dissolves the "covenant of brotherhood between Judah and Israel" (11:14). At one point, this corpus ended with specific reference to Hos 1-2.[96] These allusions indicate that the shepherd allegory was once interpreted in light of Hosea. The question which cannot be easily answered is how long this association persisted after the movement of Zech 13:7-9 to its present location. The most logical point at which 13:7-9 was relocated occurred with the incorporation of Zech 14:1-21. It does not seem unreasonable to presume that the association of the shepherd allegory with the message of

---

[94] See Bosshard, *BN* 40 (1987): 56ff. Steck, *Abschluß*, 25-111, examines the inter-relationships between the latest material in the Book of the Twelve (Zech 9-14 and Malachi) and Isaiah in particular. He isolates eight stages of redactional activity, four in the *Mehrprophetenbuch*, three in Isaiah, and one for the prophetic corpus). These texts weave the first and last books of the prophetic corpus together in a manner which decisively demonstrates the higher unity of the prophetic canon.

[95] The basis for the following observations stems from brief comments made by Dr. John Joseph Owens in a letter dated February 24, 1986. He noted that the concluding sections of the Book of the Twelve begin with identical superscriptions (Zech 9:1; 12:1; Mal 1:1) which apparently served some organizing function. He suggests the possibility that these superscriptions might respectively introduce the concluding sections of Zechariah, the Book of the Twelve, and the prophetic corpus as a whole. His brief comments were intended to be more suggestive than definitive. The relationship of Zech 14:1-21 with Isaiah prompted certain alterations to his suggestions.

[96] Compare discussion of Zech 13:7-9 above, beginning on page 234.

Hos 1-2 still exerted influence on those responsible for the inclusion of Zech 14:1-21. Even without the specific allusion in Zech 13:7-9, the reference to the broken "covenant of brotherhood" in Zech 11:14 forms a dramatic counterpoint to the birth of Hosea's children in Hos 1:1ff. That context introduces three children, one daughter (לא־רחמה in 1:6) and two sons (יזרעאל in 1:4 and לא עמי in 1:9). One level of interpretation treats the sons as representations of Israel and Judah respectively.[97] Reference to the one leader who will again unite the land (Hos 2:2) strengthens the hermeneutical relationship between the two passages further. When this leader is seen against the background of the shepherd allegory in Zech 11:4-17, it is easy to see how the interpretation in 13:8f, relating the shepherd material to the promise of Hosea, arose from reading 11:4ff. Considering the interest in Zech 9-11 on the reunified kingdom, one can say that these chapters function as inclusio, reflecting the themes of the beginning of the Book of the Twelve.

Thus, the final three "blocks" of the Book of the Twelve all form a significant reflection to the beginning of larger sections of the prophetic corpus, working outward from the smallest to the largest. Zech 9-11 discusses the reconstitution of the monarchy, and concludes with references related to the beginning of Hosea. Zech 12-14 concludes with a chapter that unites the themes of the first book of the latter prophets, by combining the perspectives of Isa 2 and 66. Mal 3:22 deliberately takes up the beginning of the former prophets by playing off Josh 1:2,7.

If one postulates about the process which led to these reflections, a probable scenario arises which serves as summary for the observations on Zech 9-14.[98] One redactional layer incorporated Zech 9-11 into the Book

---

[97] Hos 1:4 interprets Jezreel as symbolic of "the kingdom of the house of Israel," which YHWH will bring to an end, while Hos 2:2 understands the second son as Judah because it treats the promise of 2:1 (which relates to the name לא עמי) in terms of the reconstitution of a united kingdom. It takes the promise to mean that both "the sons of Judah and the sons of Israel will be gathered together, and they will appoint for themselves *one leader*..." It thus relates to both Jezreel and to Lo Ammi.

[98] These observations are admittedly simplified since space does not permit an exhaustive evaluation of the glosses and comments which appear in these chapters. See more detailed contemplations in Bosshard and Kratz, *BN* 52 (1990): 27-46, and Steck, *Abschluß*. Despite considerable harmony in the conclusions of these works with the observations produced in this study, a few points stand out which require further reflection. First, Nogalski, Bosshard, Kratz, and Steck all conclude Zech 9-14 interrupts an existing literary connection between Zech 8 and Malachi. Nogalski argues Malachi adapts pre-existing material in 1:6ff as part of a compilational process which was aware of Malachi's function as the conclusion to the Book of the Twelve

of the Twelve in an effort to smooth the transition to Malachi. It also sharpened the division between the salvation of Zech 8 and the deplorable circumstances of Mal 1:1ff. These chapters strengthened the juxtaposition between Zech 8 and Mal 1 by interpreting the concluding allegory (Zech 11:4-17) in light of Hosea's message of election and in light of Malachi's message of a purified remnant (Zech 13:9). A second stage corrected 9-11 with a more positive attitude toward Jerusalem by adding Zech 12:1-13:2,(3-6). A third stage added Zech 14:1-21, relocating 13:7-9 to function as a transition to the remnant motif in Zech 14:2. This redactional layer took a cue from the hermeneutical relationship between the shepherd allegory and Hos 1-2, and incorporated the motifs of Isa 2 and 66. In all likelihood, this layer also incorporated the allusion to the beginning of the former prophets in Mal 3:22. Finally, one should assign the superscriptions in Zech 9:1 and 12:1 to this layer.[99]

Dates for these layers cannot be fixed with certainty, although they clearly belong to the later redactional activity on prophetic literature.[100]

---

from the outset. Bosshard, Kratz, and Steck argue that Malachi was originally a redactional *Forstschreibung* of Zech 7-8 which only received independent status as a book late in the redactional process. Relatedly, Nogalski sees Mal 1:1 consistent with other superscriptions of the Joel-related layer which immitate those of neighboring writings (see conclusion). Additionally, Nogalski argues that two passages in Malachi which form part of the *Grundschicht* of Bosshard and Kratz, already have the Book of the Twelve as part of their literary horizon (Mal 1:2-5 and 3:10f), and that at least some of the tensions which lead them to postulate different redactional layers (esp 3:16-18) may be plausibly explained with the wider literary horizon as well. In Zech 9-14, Nogalski resolves the tension inherent in the text by postulating adaptation of pre-existing material in 9-11, followed by two successive additions in 12-13 and 14:1-21. Steck, in more detailed analysis, concludes four successive redactional continuations correct and expand one another in these chapters. He divides the redactional layers as follows: 9:1-10:2; 10:3-11:3; 11:4-13:9; 14:1-21.

[99] Kratz and Bosshard, *BN* 52 (1990): 45f (see also Steck, *Abschluß*, 128f), believe Mal 1:1 belongs to the latest layer of redaction. They argue that the first layer Malachi was originally a redactional continuation of Zech 8, and was not then conceived as an independent book. It does not seem wise, however, to assign Mal 1:1 to the latest level of redaction since evidence discussed earlier indicates that Zech 9:1 and 12:1 both owe their current form to imitations of Mal 1:1. Zech 9:1 exhibits signs of literary expansion, since the original portion only mentions Damascus and the syntax does not incorporate מַשָּׂא. Zech 12:1 interrupts an existing literary context. In addition, Mal reflects awareness of the Haggai-Zechariah corpus, which is more understandable prior to the inclusion of 9-11,12-13,14, even if one concedes multiple layers for Malachi.

[100] See, however, the recent study of Steck, *Abschluß*, 73-111, who uses the relative relationships of the layers to postulate the historical conditions which prompted the

The fact that the chapters contain reflections upon the latest stages of Isaiah attest strikingly to the lateness of Zech 14:1-21. The probability that Zech 9-11 already presupposes the Greek period pushes the entire series of redactional stages into a period at the end of the fourth and beginning of the third century, although precise dating beyond this point becomes very complicated.   Clearly, Sir 49:10 fixes the date no later than 180.[101] Recent studies on the date of Isa 66 tend toward a date as late as the Ptolemaic period, although many scholars still hold to late Persian dating for Trito-Isaiah.[102]

---

various layers. Steck notes some of the layers have more explicit ties than others to historical events. By drawing upon the relative order of the passages, Steck places these redactional layers after Alexander and before the Hebrew version of Sirach, or more narrowly between 332-220.

[101] For recent discussion for the dates of Sirach, see P.W. Skehan and A.A. Di Lella, *The Wisdom of Ben Sirach*, Anchor Bible (New York: Doubleday, 1987), 8ff.

[102] Steck, *Bereitete Heimkehr*, 77f.

Jonah

The book of Jonah is unique in prophetic literature. Not surprisingly, it demands special treatment in this study. Jonah's uniqueness extends to both form and content, since no other prophetic book so extensively consists of prophetic narrative, and since no other prophetic writing so consistently portrays foreigners positively at the expense of the prophet around whom the story revolves.[1] Following a look at the macro-structure, it will be necessary to look more closely at Jonah's uniqueness because decisions about the *Gattung* of Jonah greatly effect the manner in which one treats the work. It is necessary to look carefully at the Jonah story as a whole in order to determine how best to understand the appearance of common words between Obad 10-14 and Jonah 1:4-16 in one direction, and Jonah 2:3-10 and Mic 1:1-7 in the other direction.[2]

1. The Macrostructure of Jonah

Jonah consists of a very carefully constructed narrative about a reluctant prophet, together with a hymn of thanksgiving (2:3-10) placed in the mouth of Jonah. The general outline of the narrative may be reduced

---

[1] The observations of Bosshard, *BN* 40 (1987): 36, also support this uniqueness, since Jonah does not coincide with the general parallel structure between the Book of the Twelve and Isaiah. However, Bosshard goes perhaps too far when he argues against seeing a relationship between Jonah and the narrative of Isa 36-39. To be sure, Jonah does not appear in the proper place structurally, but this deviation can be accredited to other considerations, not the least of which is Jonah's relationship to 2 Kgs 14:25, which places Jonah ben Amittai in the reign of Jeroboam (see the discussion of Jonah's placement in the Twelve, page 270). Thus, while not disputing Bosshard's thesis that Jonah entered the Twelve later than the majority of the writings which exhibited awareness of Isaiah's structure, it is still possible to maintain that the existence of a prophetic narrative in Isaiah may have influenced Jonah's selection for the Twelve.

[2] Catchwords between Obad 10-14 and Jonah 1:11ff include: "cast lots" (Obad 11; Jonah 1:7); "his/this evil" (Obad 13; Jonah 1:8). Catchwords between Jonah 2:3ff and Mic 1:1-7 include: "your/his holy temple" (Jonah 2:5,8; Mic 1:2); "water" (Jonah 2:6; Mic 1:3); "mountains" (Jonah 2:7; Mic 1:4); "descend" (Jonah 2:7; Mic 1:3); "earth" (Jonah 2:7; Mic 1:2,3); "idols" (Jonah 2:9; Mic 1:7).

to a few sentences, but the manner in which the author tells this story marks it as one of the most artfully constructed works in the entire Old Testament. The narrative tells the story of a prophet who received a commission to preach against Nineveh, but who deliberately flees by ship in the opposite direction to avoid the task. YHWH, however, demonstrates that Jonah cannot escape, and by means of a great storm compels the sailors to cast Jonah into the sea. The results of this action are two-fold. The action results first in the pagan sailors' worship of YHWH (1:16), and second, in YHWH's appointment of a great fish to swallow Jonah, which — following a "prayer" in the current form of the book — deposits him impolitely back on the dry land after a suitably lengthy period. Once on land, Jonah receives a second commission to preach to Nineveh (3:1-3), which he wisely executes. Jonah's message has a miraculous effect upon the evil city, causing the entire city to repent in an effort to avoid punishment (3:4-10), including the king and the beasts. The final chapter reflects Jonah's angry confrontation with YHWH regarding YHWH's decision to relent concerning Nineveh's destruction. The narrative ends with an unanswered rhetorical question regarding YHWH's right to decide upon whom to bestow compassion.

The artistry of Jonah appears in the stylized manner in which the story is told, combining balanced structural elements with often witty portrayals of characters and situations deliberately designed to reverse stereotypical positions considered more orthodox. The narrative, in its current form, presents the story of Jonah in four self-contained, but inter-related scenes of action.[3] These four scenes present Jonah's commission and attempted flight; his prayer in the belly of the fish; the proclamation to Nineveh and its response; and Jonah's reaction to the "success" of that message. The literary form of the first two of these "scenes" needs brief treatment in order to evaluate the common words with Obad 11ff and Mic 1:1ff.

---

[3] See the discussion of Wolff, *BK* 14/3, 58-64, who considers the overarching unifying device in Jonah to be its "scenes." Wolff ties these to the form "novella." For the implications of this designation for the *Gattung* of Jonah, see the discussion below, beginning on page 262. The qualification "in its current form" reflects decisions on the question of the original unity of the second chapter. Evidence for these decisions is discussed in subsequent sections of this chapter (see below, page 252ff).

2. Literary Observations on Jonah 1-2

The first scene presents an almost perfectly symmetrical construction in which the alternation of speakers and the narrative elements play a central role:

Narrative introduction (1:1-3): Jonah goes from land to sea after hearing YHWH's command

A   Narrative and fear motif (1:4,5aa)
B   Prayer of sailors (5ab)
C   Narrative (5bc,6aa)
D   Speech of the captain (6ab,b)
E   Speech of the Sailors 1 (7a)
F   Narrative (7b)
G   Speech of the sailors 2 (8)
Ctr   Confession of Jonah and fear motif (9,10aa)
G'   Speech of the sailors 2 (10ab,b)
F'   Narrative (10c)
E'   Speech of the Sailors 1 (11)
D'   Speech of Jonah (12)
C'   Narrative (13)
B'   Prayer of the sailors (with text) (14)
A'   Narrative and fear motif (15,16)

Narrative transition (2:1f,11): Jonah goes from sea to land and hears YHWH's command

This diagram accentuates the chiastic elements of the structure.[4] This

---

[4]   The concentric structure of Jonah 1:4-16 was noted already by Norbert Lohfink, "Jona ging zur Stadt hinaus (Jona 4,5)," *BZ* NF 5 (1961): 185-203, especially 193-196, 200f. Rudolf Pesch, "Zur konzentrischen Struktur von Jona 1," *Biblica* 47 (1966): 577-581, builds upon and refines Lohfink's observations on 1:4-16. Their works undergird most recent discussions of the chapter: see for example, Jonathan Magonet, *Form and Meaning: Studies in Literary Techniques in the Book of Jonah*, Beiträge zur biblischen Exegese und Theologie 2 (Bern: Herbert Lang, 1976), 56f. Proponents of this structure have not dealt seriously with the question, as to why the structure is only present in 1:4-16, when it is difficult to argue that 1:4-16 is literarily independent. Already, this critique has been leveled by Raymond de Hoop, "The Book of Jonah as Poetry: An Analysis of Jonah 1:1-16," *Structural Analysis of Biblical and Canaanite Poetry*, JSOT Supplement Series 74, Willem van der Meer and Johannes C. de Moor, eds., (Sheffield: JSOT Press, 1988), 158f. However, no author subsequent to Pesch, including de Hoop, has sought to document this concentric structure beyond 1:4-16, possibly due to the fact that most who utilize these observations also want to prove the psalm in Jonah 2:3-10 belongs inherently to the narrative material. As noted in the diagram, the structural observations can easily be extended beyond 1:4-16, *provided one removes the psalm*

concentric structure contains some minor inconsistencies, but on the whole it evidences a deliberate compositional device by a single author.[5]

Additional internal elements, formal and contextual, also unify the narrative material. For example, the repeated motif of Jonah's "descent" commands considerable treatment in the commentaries. After being told to *rise up* and go to Nineveh (1:2), Jonah descends to Joppa (1:3), descends into the ship and further into the bottom of the ship (1:3,5). Jonah sinks even lower when he is thrown into the sea and swallowed by the fish. Then YHWH commands the fish to bring him up onto dry land (2:11), where he receives the second command to rise up and go to Nineveh. Likewise, the sailors are portrayed in a manner which progresses logically from the superstitious calling after their own god (אלהיו) in 1:5f, to their fear and sacrifice before YHWH in 1:16. Formally, several repeated motifs are phrased to produce an elevated movement. For example, the fear motif has an escalation which is built into the structure:[6]

A.	And the sailors feared	וייראו המלחים
Ctr.	And the men feared a great fear	וייראו האנשים יראה גדולה
A'	And the men feared YHWH	
	(with) a great fear.	וייראו האנשים יראה גדולה את־יהוה

In addition, the speeches of the sailors repeat a phrase with only slight variation:

E On whose account has this evil come upon us?
G On whose account has this evil come upon us?[7]

---

from consideration. This observation strengthens other arguments that the psalm is indeed a secondary addition to the work. See discussion below, beginning on page 252. Additionally, the inclusion of 1:1-3, and 2:1f,11 also increases emphasis on the center of the concentric structure. Jonah 1:9 emphasizes YHWH's authority over "the sea and dry land," which corresponds perfectly with the narrative portions on either end.

[5] Rudolph, *KAT* 14/2, 340, disagrees vehemently with this concentric model, in part, because of the inconsistencies. These inconsistencies include the fact that D and D' do not correspond exactly. The former is a speech of the captain and the latter is a speech of Jonah. The other "inconsistency" relates to Pesch's omission of 1:16b. However, 1:16b presents the sailors' sacrifices as a direct result of the fear motif, and in this regard it can be subsumed under the fear motif with 1:16a.

[6] See Pesch, *Biblica* 47 (1966): 578f. The letters to the left of these elements relate to the structural diagram above.

[7] The value of these observations is debated. Pesch argues the phrase in 1:8aa is not a secondary insertion because of this repetition pattern, while others discount this evidence. Contrast Wolff, *BK* 14/3, 83, and Rudolph, *KAT* 13/2, 340, who argue the

G' What is this you are doing?

E' What should we do to you?

Taken together, these elements yield an artfully constructed chapter.

Jonah **2:3-10** leaves the narrative style of the remainder of the writing, and offers a psalm of thanksgiving whose language is much more at home in the psalter than in a prophetic writing.[8] The psalm has long been treated with suspicion relative to its origin. A majority of scholars still hold to the view that the psalm is not germane to the narrative, but of independent origin.[9] The psalm consists of three parts (2:3f,5-8,9f), the first two of which are bound together by repeating motifs and catchwords. These motifs appear in chiastic order:[10]

---

phrase was a marginal note to explain the form בשלמי in 1:7, since the lot has already answered the question, and since the question is missing in several mss.

[8] The language of Jonah 2:3-10 exhibits a considerable number of phrases from the psalter. See the discussion in Magonet, *Form and Meaning*, 44-50, especially page 50.

[9] In recent years, a sizable minority has countered that the psalm closely relates to the surrounding context. However, much confusion reigns in these works regarding the use of terms such as "genuine" and "original" in relation to this psalm. These words are often inserted into discussions regarding how these verses *function* in the context, with the assumption being — sometimes explicitly stated — that since the hymn functions meaningfully, it must be "genuine." Fuller treatment of the arguments and counter-arguments regarding Jonah 2:3-10 is provided in a separate section. Here only the structure of the psalm is discussed. A typical example of this confusion may be noted in James S. Ackerman, "Satire and Symbolism in the Song of Jonah," in *Traditions in Transformation. Turning Points in Biblical Faith*, B. Halpern and J.D. Levenson, eds. (Winona Lake, Indiana: Eisenbrauns, 1981), 214f. He lists the counter-arguments to the view that the psalm is a later interpolation, but refers to these counter-arguments as signs of "literary artistry" relating the hymn to the narrative. This designation begs the question of whether the psalm existed independently, since it does not ask whether a pre-existing psalm was selected with the Jonah narrative in mind or whether this "literary artistry" derives from the author of the hymn. Ackerman lists the following counter-arguments: (1) The story has many incongruities. (2) Chapter two contains two prayers, a prayer for help (2:2) and a prayer of thanksgiving (2:3-10). (3) The fish plays a role of deliverance, and should not be treated as a monster. (4) The archaic language and the switch between second and third person indicate that the hymn was used in worship services at one time, but was inserted here by the *author* (not redactor) of the prose narrative. (5) The song does not indicate psychological inconsistency. (6) One might expect differences between the poem and the narrative, but the poem contains a surprising number of parallels demonstrating "that the prose narrative and the song of thanks are a well integrated unity." Neither Ackerman nor those whose views he summarizes, ever adequately clarify how one should understand the character of this "integrated unity" in light of diametrically opposed arguments numbered (4) and (6).

[10] See also Frank M. Cross, "Studies in the Structure of Hebrew Verse: The Prosody of

2:3a: The prayer in distress

	2:8: In distress the prayer reaches YHWH
2:3b: The depths of Sheol/underworld	2:7: The base of the mountains/bars of the earth/underworld
2:4: Cosmic waters	2:6: Cosmic waters

The second part of the hymn (2:5-8) contains catchwords tying the various parts together: reference to YHWH's holy temple appears twice (2:5,8), and both the cosmic waters and the underworld imagery are stated in terms that explicitly threaten the life (נפשי) of the speaker. The fact that 2:5-8 begins with a new quotation formula also marks it as a new section (cf 2:3).

The last two verses of the hymn (2:9f) do not participate in the preceding chiastic elements, nor do they take up other images from the psalm.[11] Rather, the verses offer a particular slant as to how the psalm should be understood in the context. These verses are not inappropriate to the thanksgiving hymn, since they do assume gratitude for deliverance, but the specific nature of that deliverance raises real questions for those who argue the psalm of Jonah as an original part of the narrative. The

the Psalm of Jonah," In *The Quest for the Kingdom of God: Studies in Honor of George E. Mendenhall*, H.B. Huffmon and others, eds, (Winona Lake, Indiana: Eisenbrauns, 1983), 159-167. Cross bases his observations on the meter and language, and only sees the chiasm through 2:7, thereby missing the similarities of 2:8 and 2:5. He ascribes 2:8-10 to a later hand than the original author to the psalm. By contrast, it is argued here that 2:8 continues the chiastic motifs of the first part, that it utilizes the catchword repetition of the second, and that it summarizes the entire poem to that point. Other evidence supports Cross in assigning Jonah 2:9f to a later hand. See also Jerome T. Walsh, "Jonah 2:3-10: A Rhetorical Critical Study." *Biblica* 63 (1982): 226f, whose rhetorical study concludes that 2:9f falls outside the spatial and thematic concerns of 2:3-8. Walsh sees the contrast of spatial movement in 2:3-8 in the verbs stressing distance by downward movement (verticality) and horizontal movement. Thematically, he notes concern in 2:3-8 for the question of the presence/absence of YHWH.

[11] These last two verses are often assigned to the original portion of the hymn on form-critical grounds, e.g., Terence E. Fretheim, *The Message of Jonah: A Theological Commentary* (Minneapolis, Minnesota: Augsburg Publishing House, 1977) 94f. He ties 2:8-10 to the song of thanksgiving simply as "the conclusion," whose parts function differently. These parts contain a recapitulation of the first three elements (2:8); the drawing of a lesson (2:9); a vow (2:10a); and a final statement of praise (2:10b). However, closer inspection reveals these elements are not entirely consistent with other thanksgiving hymns. This tension is particularly evident in the portion which Fretheim refers to as the "drawing of a lesson," which is not typical for thanksgiving hymns. Additionally, the "vow" in 10:a is more correctly categorized as anti-idol polemic in light of 2:9, also setting it apart from the thanksgiving form.

verses juxtapose two groups whose identity is not clear from the immediate context: the pious "I" (who by context must be understood as Jonah), and those sacrificing to false idols who forsake their faithfulness. The antagonists in the latter group must be understood as an inner-Israelite group, since their actions result in the loss of the *hesed* which YHWH had bestowed upon them.[12] This dichotomy of who truly constitutes "Israel" presents a certain tension regarding the narrative and the psalm, since Jonah is the only "Israelite" mentioned in either. Jonah 2:9f also contains no *direct* relationship to the narrative as some claim. On the one hand, the speaker's sacrifices with a voice of thanksgiving, an action which parallels the sailors' action on the boat in 1:16. On the other hand, the narrative portrays that sacrifice positively, while the psalm portrays the idol worship of the antagonists in 2:9 negatively. Jonah 2:9 presupposes a covenant relationship which they are in danger of losing. Thus, despite the parallel action of sacrifice, Jon 2:9f does not refer directly to the narrative, nor does it take up the images of 2:3-8.

Returning to the major portion of the psalm, 2:3-8, it has been noted that these verses impart a coherent structure and consistent images. Those considering the psalm an original part of the narrative often refer to its portrayal of distress as evidence.[13] They maintain that the references to the sea and the water presume the position in the narrative. However, these arguments either ignore or brush over the fact that, according to the narrative, Jonah has already been swallowed by a fish, and is not drowning in the sea. Likewise, the argument that the psalm was originally composed for Jonah, requires that its adherents explain away the fact that in the narrative, the sailors have cast Jonah into the sea (1:17), while in the psalm it is YHWH who has cast "Jonah" into the waters (2:4).[14] These major discrepancies argue strongly that the psalm was not originally composed for

---

[12] See Wolff, *BK* 14/3, 113. Note: the specific formulation that they "will forsake their faithfulness" (חסדם), implies "those keeping vain idols" must bear responsibility for the loss of this relationship.

[13] For example, Jonathan Magonet, *Form and Meaning*, 52; Jacque Ellul, *The Judgment of Jonah*, Geoffrey W. Bromiley, trans., (Grand Rapids: Eerdmans, 1971), 47f; George A.F. Knight, and Friedman W. Golka, *Revelation of God: The Song of Songs and Jonah*, International Theological Commentary (Grand Rapids: Eerdmans, 1988), 94. Raymond de Hoop, "The Book of Jonah as Poetry," 171, strongly implies the unity of the psalm, although his article treats only 1:4-16 in detail.

[14] For example, James S. Ackerman, "Satire and Symbolism in the Song of Jonah," 213-15, lists both objections against the originality of the psalm, but his discussion of responses to these objections, states only that other incongruities make one expect the unexpected.

the narrative. A second group of interpreters admits that the psalm existed before its incorporation into Jonah, but claim that the *author* of the narrative incorporated it as a suitable prayer in the mouth of Jonah. This position more readily accounts for the discrepancies of the psalm, but the claim that the author of the narrative was the one who incorporated the psalm is too simplistic. Not only does the narrative reads seamlessly if the psalm is removed, but as noted, it reveals an earlier structural relationship more in keeping with the remainder of 1:1ff. Thus, the argument that 1:1-2:2,11 existed in *literary* form prior to the psalm's incorporation outweighs the arguments that the same person who wrote the narrative also inserted the psalm.[15] However, even this last statement must be qualified, since the redaction history of the narrative itself poses considerable problems.[16]

The preceding literary observations on Jonah 1-2 present an interesting problem regarding the common words appearing between Jonah, Obadiah, and Micah. The narrative elements in Jonah 1-2 exhibit a very consistent structure, and are so artfully constructed that the assumption of a single author offers the best explanation for its existence. The psalm, on the other hand, presents a more complicated picture. It not only interrupts the narrative, indicating it has been inserted into a pre-existing literary context, it also manifests two distinct sections, which are not inherently bound (2:3-8,9f). Before attempting to synthesize these observations, the redaction history of Jonah and the much debated question of the *Gattung* of Jonah require decisions.

3. Theories on the Transmission and Redaction History of Jonah

Almost universal consensus argues that Jonah reflects the interests and conditions of post-exilic Judaism in its present form.[17] Nevertheless,

---

[15] See also Günter Bader, "Das Gebet Jonas. Eine Meditation." *ZTK* 70 (1973): 162-205.

[16] See the next section, "Theories on the Transmission and Redaction History of Jonah."

[17] Against this consensus, see Bezalel Porten, "Baalshamem and the Date of the Book of Jonah," in *De la Tôrah au Messie. Études d'exégèse et d'Herméneutique Bibliques Offertes à Henri CAZELLES pour se 25 années d'Enseignement á l'Institut Catholique de Paris (Octobre 1979)*, Maurice Carrez, et al, eds., (Paris: Desclée, 1981), 237-244. Porten argues Jonah is pre-exilic based on parallels of the style of Omride period legends, and Jonah's use of the term "God of heaven." His evidence, however, is unconvincing. Porten makes several misleading statements, and some of his categories are too vague. For example, Porten's contention that the post-exilic period "was not

the contention that the narrative relies upon older material has never entirely disappeared from the scene.[18] In the late 19th and early 20th centuries, several scholars argued that the book of Jonah was the product of several sources, but their views represent a minority position which is scarcely mentioned in recent commentaries.[19] While the majority opinion considers the psalm an independent unit, only later attached to the

---

noted for miracles," (240) is not true, particularly if one accepts a date for Jonah, which many do, after Greek influence began to grow in Palestine. Many of the stories inserted by the Chronicler certainly contain miraculous elements. Additionally, one of Porten's major arguments is open to critique. He argues that Jonah's use of the term "the god of heaven" is more in keeping with pre-exilic thoughts, and yet he admits that the phrase "God of heaven" appears more frequently in post-exilic texts: Ezra 1:2; 5:12; 6:9f; 7:12,21,23; Neh 1:4f; 2:4,20; Dan 2:18f,37,44; Jdt 5:8; 6:19; 11:11; Tob 10:11f. Porten's pre-eixilic claims rest on *extra-biblical* evidence of parallel terms.

[18] In addition to Porten, "The Date of the Book of Jonah," see also Otto Eissfeldt, "Amos und Jona in Volkstümlicher Überlieferung," in *Kleine Schriften*, vol 4, Rudolph Sellheim and Fritz Maass, eds., (Tübingen: Mohr, 1968), 137-142. Eissfeldt considers Jonah a midrash-like story based upon 2 Kgs 14:23-29. He acknowledges the current written form comes from the 4th century, but doubts very much if the story was created during that time. He is cautious about reconstructing the original form of the story, but thinks it dealt with the reduction of Jonah, the nationalistic prophet of the north, to a figure of the absurd. Eissfeldt believes the story originally stems from the salvation prophets of Judah, who would have opposed the aims of a man like Jonah, and thus created the story about the Northern prophet. This story, according to Eissfeldt, remained alive (presumably in oral form), but was modified during the intervening centuries. Eissfeldt admits he cannot explain how the motif of Jonah's flight westward in a ship entered the tradition, if the story goes back as early as he supposes.

[19] For a summary of various positions, see Ludwig Schmidt, *'De Deo'. Studien zur Literarkritik und Theologie des Buches Jona, des Gesprächs zwischen Abraham und Jahwe in Gen 18:22ff. und von Hi 1*, BZAW 143 (Berlin: DeGruyter, 1976), 12f; and George Adam Smith, *The Book of the Twelve Prophets*, vol. 2, 497f. Proponents of multiple sources include: Böhme, Procksch, and Schmidt. W. Böhme, "Die Composition des Buches Jona," *ZAW* 7 (1887): 224-284, argues for a Yahwistic core (1:1-2:1,11; 3:1-5; 4:1,5-11), expanded by an Elohistic version of chapters three and four (which added 3:6-10; 4:5b,11*). Later, according to Böhme, a redactor inserted the psalm in 2:2-10, several partial verses in chapter 1 and 4:2f. Otto Procksch, *Die kleinen prophetischen Schriften nach dem Exil*, (Stuttgart: Calwer, 1916), 88-97, maintains Jonah circulated via a primary source and a *Nebenquelle*, which used the name Elohim. The combination of these two sources, according to Procksch, resulted in the incorporation from the *Nebenquelle* of 1:4ab,5b,6,12b,8,9,11b,13f,15b,16,3b*,5a*; 3:3b-5,8ab,9f; 4:5,8,9. Hans Schmidt, "Die Komposition des Buches Jona," *ZAW* 25 (1905): 285-310, claims an editor added 2:3-10, 3:6-9, and wove the story of the prophet's flight in chapter one into a second legend very similar to the stilling of the storm in Mark 4:35-41. For a critique of the inadequacy of this parallel see L. Schmidt, *De Deo*, 51f.

narrative (either by the author or an editor), questions regarding the unity of the narrative received very little serious consideration for most of this century. However, three authors in the last twenty years, Kraeling, L. Schmidt, and Weimar, challenge this consensus so that a unified narrative can no longer be presumed without discussion.[20]

Kraeling depicts a gradual development, beginning in the Persian period, which incorporates various motifs.[21] He believes the oldest portion of the story appears in chapters 3-4, but even in these chapters, he finds evidence of editorial changes in at least seven different places in 3-4.[22] Unfortunately, while Kraeling makes interesting observations on these chapters which do raise serious questions about a unified composition, he does not effectively relate the various observations to one another, making it very difficult to construct his view of the order in which these changes occur.[23] Kraeling does clearly contend that chapters 1-2 were appended

---

[20] Emil G. Kraeling, "The Evolution of the Story of Jonah," in *Hommages à André Dupont-Sommer*, (Paris: Librairie d'Amérique et d'Orient Adrien Maisonneuve, 1971), 305-318; Ludwig Schmidt, *De Deo*, 4-130; and works by Peter Weimar, "Literarische Kritik und Literarkritik. Unzeitgemässe Beobachtungen zu Jon 1:4-16," in *Künder des Wortes. Beiträge zur Theologie der Propheten*, Festschrift für Josef Schreiner, L. Ruppert and others, eds., (Würzburg: Echter Verlag, 1982) 217-235; "Jon 4,5. Beobachtungen zur Entstehung der Jonaerzählung." *BN* 18 (1982): 86-109; "Jonapsalm und Jonaerzählung." *BZ* 28 (1984): 43-68.

[21] Emil G. Kraeling, "The Evolution of the Story of Jonah," 307f, argues the Persian period is the earliest time for a story which conceived of a mission to Nineveh. He argues that the story cannot represent historical events. In 7th century Nineveh, not only would the problem of language have been prohibitive, but any foreigner preaching subversion would have been summarily killed. Only the advent of the Persian system, which united the entire region politically, could have produced these images.

[22] Kraeling, "The Evolution of the Story of Jonah," 308-315. These seven alterations include: 1) the exaggeration of the size of Nineveh from one day's journey to three days journey; 2) the increase of the time allowed for repentance to the Ninevites from three days (so LXX) to forty days; 3) the interruption (3:5-4:4) of the plot in which Jonah prophecies (3:4) and immediately exits to await the events of judgment (4:5), in which the themes of fasting, God's repentance, and Jonah's anger were added; 4) the initial announcement of a fast (3:5) receives an expansion (3:6-9); 5) the incorporation of the folk-story of the gourd (4:6-10); 6) the change of the divine name from Elohim to YHWH; 7) 1:1f are the fragments of the original narrative, making 3:1f (not just "a second time" in 3:1) a later addition from the time of the incorporation of chapters 1-2.

[23] For example, Kraeling argues that the "three days" in 3:4 of the LXX represents the original *Vorlage*. If true, it would necessitate a deliberate change (using his arguments, 309) after the LXX translation. This change would thus post-date incorporation of 1-2, which he considers the final layer. Wolff, *BK* 14/3, 119, maintains the priority of MT.

to the story of 3-4 as the latest redactional layer.[24] Kraeling believes
chapter one incorporates biblical motifs by adapting a Hellenistic shipwreck
story. Parallels of the motifs of being thrown overboard and saved by a sea
monster, or being swallowed by a sea monster and later disgorged, appear
in other Hellenistic literature.[25] Kraeling believes the hymn was added at
the same time as the adaptation of the shipwreck story, but his rationale
are not convincing in light of the literary observations made above.[26]

Ludwig Schmidt presents a much less complicated picture in which he
portrays the *narrative* as the result of two layers of redactional activity: a
fundamental narrative component and an editorial layer. Schmidt argues
that the psalm was added to the edited version of the narrative. According
to Schmidt, the original narrative was composed as a didactic narrative.
The majority of its constituent parts appear in chapters 3-4, with only 1:2
belonging to this layer.[27] This didactic narrative discussed the universal
expansion of Deuteronomistic repentance theology on the basis of Jer 18:7f,
and, by extension, the corollary in 18:9-10. Jer 18:7-10 reads:

> At one moment I might speak concerning a nation or concerning a kingdom to
> uproot, to pull down, or to destroy. If that nation against which I have spoken turns
> from its evil, I will relent concerning the calamity I planned to bring on it. Or at
> another moment I might speak concerning a nation or concerning a kingdom to build
> up or to plant. If it does evil in my sight by not obeying my voice, then I will think
> better of the good with which I had promised to bless it.

The author of Jonah's didactic narrative concentrates upon 18:7f, addressing
question of the repentance a nation against whom judgment was spoken.[28]
The narrative affirms Jer 18:7ff, and implies the rationale that God as the

---

[24] Kraeling, "The Evolution of the Story of Jonah," 315.

[25] Kraeling, "The Evolution of the Story of Jonah," 315f. He discusses the motifs against
four Hellenistic stories: Arion, the minstrel thrown overboard by sailors to get his
treasure; Jason being disgorged by a fish before Athena (known only in non-literary
form from a Greek vase); Heracles and Hesione; and the Perseus-Andromeda story.

[26] Kraeling, "The Evolution of the Story of Jonah," 317, maintains, "It is the fashion
nowadays to consider the psalm a later editorial addition, but the mention of the three
days and nights (2:1) would be unmotivated without the prayer of Jonah." These
elements, however, appear frequently in Biblical traditions as temporal descriptions:
Gen 30:36; 40:13,18,19,21; Exod 3:18; 5:3; 8:23; 10:22, etc.

[27] L. Schmidt, *De Deo*, 124f, lists the following as part of the *Grundbestand*: 1:2; 3:3a
(without "according to the word of YHWH"), 3:3b-10; 4:1,5a,6aa (without YHWH),
4:6b-11.   The specific introduction of the early layer was replaced, but 1:2 was
presumably a part of that introduction.

[28] L. Schmidt, *De Deo*, 33,43-47.

creator and supporter has compassion on all creation, even to the point of reversing the announcement of judgment. Schmidt argues that the author of this narrative had a close relationship to wisdom circles.

The second stage of development, according to Schmidt, involved the expansion of the original narrative in order to eliminate any doubt that only YHWH has power over all creation.[29] This author expands the central motif of the narrative. In the first section (1:1-2:1,11), the author develops the theme of YHWH's universal power, and in the second section (4:2-4, 6ab) he reinforces the opinion of the propriety YHWH's grace.[30] Schmidt maintains that this expanding layer also stems from post-exilic wisdom circles interested in the universal recognition of YHWH.[31]

Schmidt sees the third and final layer of the text as the work of a redactor who inserted Jonah 2:2-10. The narrative of Jonah had already become a type of prophetic legend. This layer changes from the theological interest (YHWH's right to decide upon whom to display compassion) to an emphasis upon the person Jonah.[32] Jonah's experience in the belly of the fish, restores him to a trust in YHWH.

In three related articles, Weimar offers a third redactional hypothesis on Jonah.[33] He works from a highly literary-critical orientation and

---

[29]   This edition added 1:1,3-16 (without 1:8ab,10bb); 2:1,11; 3:3a* ("according to the word of YHWH"); 4:2-4,5b,6aa (YHWH),6ab, and replaced Elohim in 4:10 with YHWH.

[30]   Schmidt, *De Deo*, 125.

[31]   Schmidt, *De Deo*, 126, differentiates three streams of thought in post-exilic wisdom literature. All acknowledge god as creator and sustainer, but they differ in their designation for god, and over the question whether all humanity knows the one true god. The author of the original story in Jonah 3-4 presupposes that humanity knows a single god, Elohim. Other streams of wisdom literature presuppose humanity knows that this god is named YHWH (cf Job 1; Mal 1:11). The author of the expansion of the Jonah narrative, in contrast to the other streams, does not presuppose a general knowledge of god, but is presupposes the differences in religions. This author fundamentally distinguishes between Hebrews and heathens. Only the former knows the one true god as YHWH. Thus, the sailors call after their weak gods when the storm strikes. For this author, the core of true YHWH worship comes not from belonging to a specific holy place or a chosen people, but comes from the recognition of YHWH. Regarding the *date* of this layer, Schmidt maintains the story must have been reworked somewhere between 300 and 250. Hellenistic motifs points to a period after 300, but Sir 49:10 confirms that by 180 the Book of the Twelve included Jonah.

[32]   Schmidt, *De Deo*, 119.

[33]   Peter Weimar, "Literarische Kritik und Literarkritik. Unzeitgemässe Beobachtungen zu Jon 1:4-16," in *Künder des Wortes. Beiträge zur Theologie der Propheten*, Festschrift für Josef Schreiner, L. Ruppert and others, eds., (Würzburg: Echter Verlag, 1982) 217-235; "Jon 4,5. Beobachtungen zur Entstehung der Jonaerzählung." *BN* 18 (1982): 86-109;

concludes that Jonah reflects a three stage process, the original narrative and two redactional adaptations. Unlike Kraeling and Schmidt, Weimar does not consign the original narrative to chapters 3-4. He argues the story originally contained the motif of Jonah's flight to the sea, albeit in condensed form.[34] Weimar considers the original narrative as decidedly *non-theological*.[35] Weimar's second stage doubles the size of Jonah in a redactional overhaul which included an initial version of the psalm.[36] The

---

"Jonapsalm und Jonaerzählung." *BZ* 28 (1984): 43-68.

[34] Weimar, *BN* 18 (1982): 86-109, conceives a literary core so dramatically reduced that it only includes 1:1+2,3a*,3b*,4abb,5a,7,11a,12a,15a; 2:1,11; 3:3a,4b,5,10b; 4:5a,6aa,6b*, 7,8*,11a,11ba. Despite the rather intimidating list of verses and partial verses, one cannot criticize Weimar on the grounds that he leaves a fragmented narrative. Weimar's version of the narrative does indeed hang together as a consistent story, which reads as follows: And the word of YHWH came to Jonah son of Amittai saying, Arise and go to Nineveh the great city, and cry against it, for their wickedness has come up before me. But Jonah arose to flee, and he went down to Joppa and he found a ship going to Tarshish, and he paid its fare and he descended in it to go with them toward Tarshish. And then there was a great storm and the ship was about to break up, and the sailors became afraid, and they cast cargo which was in the ship into the sea to lighten it from upon them. And then each man said to his neighbor, come and let us cast lots so that we might learn on whose account this evil has come upon us. And they cast lots, and the lot fell upon Jonah. And they said to him, What should we do to you that the sea should be calm over us? And he said to them, throw me into the sea, and then the sea will become calm over you. And they lifted Jonah, and threw him into the sea. And then YHWH appointed a great fish to swallow Jonah, and Jonah was in the belly of the fish three days and three nights. And then YHWH told the fish to throw up Jonah to the dry land. And then Jonah went to Nineveh according to the word of YHWH, and he called out and said, Yet forty days and Nineveh will be overthrown. But the men of Nineveh believed on God, and they proclaimed a fast and clothed themselves with sackcloth, from the greatest of them to the least of them. And then God had compassion concerning the evil which he spoke to do to them, and he did not do it. And then Jonah went from the city and dwelt east of the city, and God appointed a plant and it went up over Jonah to be shade upon his head. And Jonah rejoiced about the plant. And then God appointed a worm when dawn came the next day, and it attacked the plant the next day, and it withered. And then the sun beat down on Jonah's head and he became faint, and he asked with all his soul to die, and he said better my dying than my living. (And then God said,) Should I not have compassion upon Nineveh the great city, when there is in her more than 120,000 persons?

[35] Weimar, "Literarische Kritik und Literarkritik," 230.

[36] Weimar is convinced that despite the fact that the psalm is a redactional insertion, that it is more integrally related to the narrative. Pulling together Weimar's observations from the various articles, it is possible to assign the following portions to the first redactional adaptation: 1:4aa,5a*,5b,6,8a,10,11b,13,14a,16;2:2+3aa*,3b,4a*,7b,3:1f,3b,6-10a,; 4:1-2a,3f,5b,6ab,b*,8aa,9f,11bb.

redactor of this layer created a theological treatise from the story. The early version of the psalm served as a complaint, as a contrast to 1:4-16, and as a parallel to the complaint in 4:2a+3-4.[37] Weimar believes the third and final stage includes the remainder of the psalm and occasional additions to the narrative. The expanded psalm changes from complaint to thanksgiving, and is adapted for use in a temple service.[38] Simultaneously, these additions portray Jonah more positively.[39]

These three redactional perspectives on the growth of Jonah differ considerably in details, agreeing only in the conviction that the narrative as it now stands does not stem from a single author. Nevertheless, comparison of the different views helps to shed some interesting light upon Jonah and its incorporation into the Book of the Twelve. Kraeling and Schmidt agree that the early portion of the narrative revolves around chapters three and four, with Hellenistic influence accounting for the sea episode.[40] Schmidt and Weimar concur that the psalm interrupts an earlier narrative.[41] All three agree that (at least) the majority of Jonah 2:3-10 entered the corpus as part of the latest redactional layer.

It is now possible to relate the arguments of Kraeling, Schmidt, and Weimar to the literary observations made on Jonah 1-2 in this work. Two remarks in particular should be made. First, the literary unity of Jonah 1:1-16; 2:1f,11 concurs with the observations of Kraeling and Schmidt that Jonah 3-4 contains the earliest literary portion of the work. The fact that 1:1-1:16; 2:1f,11 presupposes a continuation means that these verses did not

---

[37] Weimar, *BZ* 28 (1984): 64-66, does not believe the psalm at this stage was a song of thanksgiving. He argues the psalm contains typical elements of a complaint: the complaint (2:3aa,b), the portrayal of the situation (4a*), and the expression of confidence that YHWH would deliver (2:7b).

[38] Weimar, *BZ* 28 (1984): 67f, argues a new thematic/theological interest characterizes the expanded psalm, from which one can explain its more anthological character. Weimar's original psalm had only one quote from the psalter, while the expanded version is full of them. This expansion underscores the experience of the existential threat against Jonah by tripling the *Notschilderung* (2:4,6 + 7aa*, and 7*), and adding the mythically influenced death metaphors. This layer also adds the complaint and affirmation (2:5,8).

[39] These positive additions include 1:8b+9,14ab,b, and the confession in 4:2b.

[40] So also Wolff, *BK* 14/3, 86f, although his examples argue against simply assuming that Greek influence requires a time after Alexander.

[41] Weimar's arguments for two versions of this psalm, do not appear convincing. His contention that a psalm of thanksgiving was created out of a very short complaint psalm creates more questions than the literary tensions he finds in the text itself.

exist independently of chapters 3-4.[42] Simultaneously, the structure of the last 3-4 does not demonstrate the same tightly woven structure as 1-2. A related observation notes that the psalm in 2:3-10 interrupts the pre-existing literary context in 1:1-16; 2:1f,11 which was itself added to chapters 3-4. These observations thus concur that the psalm is the latest block to enter the corpus. These literary observations thus coincide readily with Schmidt's hypothesis.[43] Before looking at how the growth of Jonah relates to its incorporation into the Book of the Twelve, it is necessary to briefly discuss the question of the genre of Jonah.

4. Problems of Genre and Jonah

It is not possible in a short space, if at all, to resolve the thorny question of the literary genre of Jonah. Merely listing the possibilities offered in previous decades presents a monumental challenge since these chapters have been labeled midrash,[44] prophetic narrative,[45] parable,[46] legend,[47] novella,[48] satire,[49] didactic narrative,[50] literary drama,[51] and

---

[42] The fact that Jonah is delivered from the fish for a specific purpose presupposes knowledge of chapters 3-4. Note also how the structural elements build this deliverance into the concentric pattern in 1:1-3 and 2:1,11; 3:1.

[43] Schmidt presents the closest redactional model to the observations made here, while Kraeling and Weimar differ at significant points. Kraeling does not distinguish the psalm as a later addition to the narrative connection of chapters 1,3-4. Weimar, by contrast, admits the literary interruption caused by the psalm, but his incorporation of the flight to the sea motif into the original narrative is not convincing, because of the difference of style and motifs, and the structural coherence which it manifests.

[44] Otto Eissfeldt, "Amos und Jona in Volkstümlicher Überlieferung," In *Kleine Schriften*, vol 4, Rudolph Sellheim and Fritz Maass, eds. (Tübingen: Mohr, 1968), 137-142; Oswald Loretz, "Herkunft und Sinn der Jona-Erzählung," *BZ* NF 5 (1961): 27f.

[45] Weiser, *ATD* 25, 188.

[46] George M. Landes, "Jonah: A Māšāl?" *Israelite Wisdom: Theological and Literary Essays in Honor of Samuel Terrien*. J.G. Gammie, and others, eds. (Missoula, Montana: Scholars Press, 1978), 137-158.

[47] Alfred Jepsen, "Anmerkungen zum Buche Jona," in *Wort - Gebot - Glaube, Beiträge zur Theologie des Alten Testaments. Walther Eichrodt zum 80. Geburtstag*, J.J. Stamm and Ernst Jenni, eds. (Zürich: Zwingli Verlag, 1970), 297-305.

[48] Wolff, *BK* 14/3, 58-64.

[49] Numerous commentators lean toward this classification, especially those who still maintain that the psalm in 2:3-10 is an integral part of the narrative. Examples include, John C. Holbert, "'Deliverance Belongs to Yahweh!': Satire in the Book of Jonah,"

philosophical book.[52] Indeed, one wonders if such categories hold much value since many of the definitions used by various proponents overlap so much it becomes difficult to distinguish one term from another in regard to Jonah. Nevertheless, at least one genre-related question forces itself to the forefront, in light of the frequency with which it is used in recent literature. Is Jonah a satire, or does it even contain satiric elements? Several recent authors suggest that the entire writing should be read satirically, and they claim this satirical understanding accounts for the tension of the "prayer" of the second chapter.[53] Others do not recognize the validity of the satirical elements, treating even those portions of the narrative which portray Jonah with positive statements as later *corrections* to Jonah's negative image.[54] Should Jonah's prayer be read as a satirical elaboration on the plight of a hypocritical prophet? Should positive elements within the narrative be read as a redactor's attempt to paint Jonah in a better light? The answer in both cases is "no." Textually based observations argue that the author of the narrative of chapter one worked with a sense of satire when composing the work, while Jonah in chapter two should be categorized as a corrective insertion which was not motivated by this same sense of parody.

The narrative in chapter one displays several clues that the author writes satirically. The portrayal of Jonah deliberately inverts the typical expected obedience of a prophet. He is told to rise up and preach (typical language for a prophetic commission) to Nineveh in the east, but Jonah rises up to flee *westward*, beginning a series of *descents* in the process (1:3,5). The sailors appear as positive foils against the apathy of Jonah. The sailors pray (1:14), try to avoid throwing Jonah overboard (1:13), and chastise Jonah for attempting to disobey YHWH (1:10). The concentric

---

JSOT 21 (1981): 59-81; James S. Ackerman, "Satire and Symbolism in the Song of Jonah," 215; George A.F. Knight, and Friedman W. Golka. *Revelation of God: The Song of Songs and Jonah*, International Theological Commentary (Grand Rapids: Eerdmans, 1988), 92; Jonathan Magonet, *Form and Meaning: Studies in Literary Techniques in the Book of Jonah*, Beiträge zur biblischen Exegese und Theologie 2 (Bern: Herbert Lang, 1976), 51-53, similarly, prefers the term ironic.

50 Ronald E. Clements, "The Purpose of the Book of Jonah," *VT.S* 28 (1974): 17; Ludwig Schmidt, *De Deo*, see 125f (even though he does not use the term); Grace I. Emmerson, "Another Look at the Book of Jonah," *Expository Times* 88 (1976): 86-88; Terence E. Fretheim, "Jonah and Theodicy," *ZAW* 90 (1978): 227-37.

51 Watts, *Joel, etc.*, 72.

52 Etan Levine, "Jonah as a Philosophical Book," *ZAW* 96 (1984): 235-245.

53 See note 49 above.

54 So Weimar, *BZ* 28 (1984): 68; "Literarische Kritik und Literarkritik," 227f, treats 1:8-10 as secondary because Jonah's confession is surprising, while others take it satirically.

structure of the chapter centers around Jonah's profession in 1:9 that he worships YHWH, the creator of the heaven and earth, yet this profession does not portray Jonah positive since the sailors immediately confront him over the folly of his actions.[55] Thus, the most positive statement Jonah makes in the first chapter is turned against him as an indictment. The same hermeneutic operates in 4:2, with Jonah's citation of YHWH's compassion. The stereotypical phrase, by virtue of the context, does not function in a manner consistent with its content.[56] Rather, citing YHWH's compassion serves as Jonah's rationale for the call for YHWH to take Jonah's life. For these reasons, one may conclude that Jonah's positive statements in the narrative do not attempt to correct the picture of Jonah so much as they use traditional language to portray the absurdity of his behavior.

These same criteria cannot be applied to the psalm of chapter two. To be sure, this psalm presents numerous points of contact with the psalter, and this phenomenon could be argued as somewhat parallel to the use of stereotypical language in the narrative.[57] However, if one carefully notes how the psalm *functions* in the context, one may appreciate that the psalm has an entirely different function than the traditional language in the narrative. The psalm, unlike the narrative, uses the typical language in a manner which is consistent with the context, in terms of what it seeks to justify. Jonah "prays" a song of thanksgiving for deliverance in a distinct context, between the actions of the sailors throwing him into the sea and the action of YHWH's commanding the fish to regurgitate him onto the land. The order of events indicates a distinct intention. The sailors throw Jonah overboard (1:15). YHWH appoints a fish to swallow Jonah, and Jonah remains in the belly of the fish three days and three nights (2:1), before finally offering a prayer (2:2) and a psalm of thanksgiving.[58] The

---

[55] Contra Weimar, "Literarische Kritik und Literarkritik," 230, who considers all of 1:8-10 as later accretions to the story, and believes that these verses enter the story with two different redactional layers.

[56] Unlike Jonah 1:9, which functions integrally in the narrative's concentric structure, the confession of compassion in 4:2 can be removed without jeopardizing the narrative. Use of כי to introduce redactional insertions is well attested. Incorporation of the phrase heightens the hyperbole, however, and could well have been added to Jonah 3-4 at the time that the satire of chapter one was added to Jonah. Weimar may be correct in assigning this phrase to a redactional hand.

[57] So, for example, Magonet, *Form and Meaning*, 52, takes the psalm as similar to the "pious affirmations" elsewhere in the book.

[58] Whether Jonah 2:2 already formed part of the narrative when the psalm was added or whether 2:2 was composed as a narrative transition for the psalm at the point of its incorporation causes considerable debate. Those opting for the latter position see the

prayer and the psalm immediately precede YHWH's command to the fish. Jonah relates very typically and piously to YHWH in the psalm, but unlike Jonah's narrative statements about YHWH, the immediate context does not convert the psalm's piosity into an indictment against Jonah. Rather, the psalm's language serves as justification for YHWH's deliverance of Jonah. Thus, observing the manner in which Jonah's positive statements about YHWH function in their contexts, allows the conclusion that the narrative statements are indeed intended satirically, while those of the psalm seek to correct the image of Jonah produced by the narrative.

In summary, the preceding sections prepare the way for postulations regarding the impulses behind the insertion of the psalm into the writing of Jonah. Elimination of satirical readings for Jonah 2:3-10, and conclusions that the psalm was redactionally inserted, argue that the psalm corrects the negative image of Jonah. However, questions of the psalm's content allow these observations to be taken further. One may deduce how the redactors understood Jonah when inserting the psalm, and one may suppose that they incorporated the psalm when Jonah entered the Book of the Twelve.

5. Jonah 2:3-10 and the Book of the Twelve

Literary observations on Jonah 2:3-10 revealed a tightly constructed psalm in 2:3-8 with a two verse addendum (2:9f) which falls outside its compositional and linguistic frame. The psalm contains several superficial catchwords to the narrative, but tensions inherent in 2:3-8 *argue against* understanding the psalm as *composed specifically* for Jonah.[59] Likely, an

---

repetition of פלל in 2:2 as evidence of a deliberately created parallel to the actions of the sailors in 1:16. However, the arguments for 2:2 as part of the narrative prior to the inclusion of the psalm provide a more likely picture. Günter Bader, "Das Gebet Jonas. Eine Meditation," *ZTK* 70 (1973): 163f, summarizes these arguments. Importantly, he notes that the verb used in Jonah 2:2 (פלל) leads one to suspect a complaint, not a song of thanksgiving as in 2:3-10. This observation argues against the same hand incorporating 2:2 and 2:3-10. Note that the verb פלל does appear as an introduction to the complaint in Jonah 4:2. This parallel suggests the narrative element in 2:2 deliberately fashioned Jonah's belated response after Jonah's complaint to YHWH in 4:2 for showing compassion to Nineveh, and not as an introduction to the song of thanksgiving in 2:3ff. Note also that the duplicate introduction to 2:3 ("and he said ...") strengthens the understanding of 2:3ff as an addition to 2:2.

59   The most significant of these associations relates to the situation of distress from which the psalmist is "calling out" while drowning in the "sea" (2:3).

editor selected the psalm because of its general appropriateness to the narrative. Yet, if these few catchwords anchor 2:3-8 to the narrative, it is necessary to note that even more catchword associations tie the psalm, again superficially, with Mic 1:2-7. These catchwords occur primarily in the second half of the psalm (2:5-8).[60] Alone, these formal observations do not do justice to the psalm's content or to the driving hermeneutic behind its inclusion. These two elements require evaluating the psalm from the perspectives of the content of the distress and the addendum in 2:9f.

In the debate regarding the original relationship of Jonah 2:3-10 to the narrative, both sides presume that the psalm should be interpreted in light of the narrative.[61] It is suggested here that the function of the psalm can only be properly understood if this interpretive process is reversed. The psalm should not be harmonized with the narrative, rather, one should ask, "How does the psalm interpret the narrative?" If one takes this transposed perspective to the text, several interesting observations result. The psalm is placed in jonah's mouth, and it portrays his proper response to distress. Jonah finally turns to YHWH. The psalm's position preceding Jonah's deliverance implies that the redactor felt this attitude on the part of "Jonah" was required prior to his returning to dry land. Most significantly, however, the content of the distress in which "Jonah" finds himself affords a pathway into one perspective of the hermeneutic with which the redactor operates. In short, a discussion of this content reveals that, for the redactor, "Jonah" has become a symbol for Israel. For the redactor who inserted the psalm, the writing was not simply a story, and Jonah was not simply a prophet. Rather, Jonah represents Israel itself.

Because of the similarity of images to the narrative, much discussion centers around the fact that Jonah's distress relates to the ocean. Yet within the psalm, the (primordial) sea represents only one metaphorical image. The underworld imagery also depicts the distress metaphorically. While these images of distress take the reader into the realm of the mythological, the most concrete references in the entire psalm specifically relate to the distress of the redactor's "Jonah." Twice the psalm explicitly ties Jonah's distress to being cut off from the temple (2:5,8). In order to

---

[60] Jonah 2:5-8 contains the catchwords "your holy temple" (twice), "mountains," "descend," and "earth." Only the synonym for "idols" (2:9) appears outside 2:5-8.

[61] Compare those who argue the psalm is a satire (see above, note 49), with those, like Wolff and Rudolph, who argue the psalm is not germane to the context. Both groups relate the imagery of the psalm to the narrative, but do not give much consideration to the rationale behind its inclusion.

evaluate the extent to which this observation effects the interpretation of Jonah, one must remember that the psalm existed independently from the narrative. Recognition of this independence makes the expulsion from the temple even more dominant, and makes it very unlikely that the redactor overlooked this motif in selecting the psalm. Rather, the centrality of the motif in the independent psalm argues this depiction of distress played a major role in the selection of the psalm for inclusion into Jonah.

Recognizing that expulsion from the temple concretely manifests the distress in 2:3-8 provides the crux for the hermeneutic behind the psalm's insertion. It indicates the key to understanding the redactor's Jonah and his descent into the sea. Inserting this psalm equates Jonah's descent with temple expulsion. Hence, for the redactor, Jonah *represented* someone whom YHWH had expelled from the temple. Incorporation of this theme presumes the redactor interprets Jonah allegorically, or metaphorically, since the temple itself does not figure in the narrative. The "Jonah" of the psalm can only be Israel, and if one asks the nature of the expulsion from the temple, the most logical explanation suggests that the redactor intends the destruction of the temple in Jerusalem in 587 and the subsequent exile. There is thus good reason to suspect that the psalm has been inserted here to reflect a redactional interpretation which treated Jonah paradigmatically in light of Israel's history.

Based upon these observations, the general train of thought may be suggested, given that the psalm reflects a theological contemplation upon the exilic period. Jonah's disobedience of YHWH's word was directly responsible for his punishment. Jonah was punished by being hurled into the sea by pagan sailors, but the sailors were forced to this action. Jonah/ Israel nearly expires as a result of this punishment, and only when they remember YHWH are they miraculously delivered. Then they receive a new commission. Despite this new commission, questions remain regarding YHWH's compassion to Israel and the nations, but the "Jonah" of 2:3-10 offers a corrected image to the "Jonah" of the narrative. He now confesses that his own deliverance comes from YHWH.

In addition to the hermeneutic behind the incorporation of 2:3-10, one should not overlook the addendum to the psalm. These verses, sometimes mislabeled as a thanksgiving formula, change to a polemical statement regarding true worship as the source of YHWH's חסד.[62] Why does the end of the psalm suddenly introduce a thematic shift which falls outside the content and structure of the psalm itself? Were the verses simply part of

---

[62] See above, page 253.

the text added to the psalm prior to its incorporation into Jonah?[63] The verses make more sense as additions to the psalm for incorporation into the Book of the Twelve, particularly in light of two passages.

The sudden thematic shift reflects accusations against Samaria in Mic 1:7, where the city is condemned for wanton idolatry and cult prostitution: "All her *idols* will be burned with fire, and all of her images I will make desolate, for she collected them from a harlot's earning and to the earnings of a harlot they will return." Jonah 2:9 takes up these images in summary form: "those regarding vain idols forsake their faithfulness" (חסד). One should not too quickly deduce an anti-Samaritan polemic from the fact that Jonah 2:9 imports the theme from Mic 1:7.[64] Mic 1:2-9 utilizes YHWH's judgment against Samaria as a warning to Jerusalem and Judah. Mic 1:7 condemns Samaria while simultaneously threatening Jerusalem.

In addition to Mic 1:7, there are reasons to believe that Hosea affects the formulation of Jonah 2:9f. Most of Jonah 2:9f has affinity to Hoseanic language.[65] Most significant in this relationship is Hos 5:15; 6:1-6. Hos 5:15 announces YHWH's intention toward his people: "I will go away (and) return to my place until they acknowledge their guilt and seek my face; in their affliction they will earnestly seek me." The concept of YHWH's departure causing Israel distress suits the context of Jonah 2:3ff.[66] Hos 6:1-2 exhort the people to return to YHWH, who both wounds and heals (6:1). This act of punishment and healing is further elaborated in 6:2 in a manner which has obvious parallels to Jonah 2:1: "He will revive us after two days, on the third day, he will raise us up, that we may live before

---

[63] Cross,"The Prosody of the Psalm of Jonah," 167, despite arguing the verses are secondary, does not postulate at what level they entered the text.

[64] Some interpreters (e.g. Eissfeldt, "Amos und Jona in Volkstümlicher Überlieferung," 137-142) have seen Jonah as representative of Northern nationalistic prophecy since 2 Kgs 14:25 names him as a prophet in the court of Jeroboam. This correlation may have played a role in earlier layers of the writing (or oral transmission), but does not appear to be at issue in the insertion of the psalm.

[65] Compare the "worthless oaths" in Hos 10:4, and the combination of the worthlessness of Gilgal with and the false sacrifice of Gilead in 12:12. Compare Hos 8:13, which condemns Ephraim because they built temples and forgot their maker. Not directly related, but perhaps significant by way of association is Hos 7:11 describes Ephraim as a silly dove (יונה), forming a natural word-play on the name of the prophet Jonah. See Fretheim, *The Message of Jonah*, 39f.

[66] Compare especially Jonah 2:3 where Jonah calls out to YHWH from his distress. Hos 5:15 (צר) and Jonah 2:3 (צרה) use related nominal forms for "distress."

him."[67]   Jonah 2:3ff very clearly plays out this scene. On the third day
Jonah offers his "prayer." In Hos 6:4f, YHWH, unmoved by the people's
profession, describes them as fickle, their loyalty (חסד) having no more
substance than a morning cloud. This perspective has a certain affinity to
Jonah 3-4.[68]   Finally (Hos 6:6), YHWH announces, "I delight in loyalty
(חסד) rather than sacrifice, and in the knowledge of God rather than burnt
offerings." This combination of חסד and sacrifice (זבח) appears in Jonah
2:9f, where Jonah proclaims that those sacrificing to vain idols forfeit the
חסד given them by YHWH, whereas those truly repentant will sacrifice
with a voice of thanksgiving. Even the reference to the paying of vows in
Jonah 2:10 has a thematic counterpart in Hos 5:15-6:6. The people swear
to return to YHWH, but YHWH is dubious about their commitment (6:3f).
Jonah 2:10 thus reads like an affirmation from the mouth of Jonah/Israel:
"that which I have vowed, I will pay. Salvation comes from YHWH."[69]

The parallel between Hos 5:15-6:6 and Jonah 2:1-11 strengthens the
observation that the redactional insertion of the psalm hermeneutically
presumes Jonah as Israel. The psalm, with its addendum, accentuates
Israel's responsibility for its own distress, while simultaneously displaying the
conviction that deliverance comes from YHWH. Because the psalm is
placed within the narrative framework, it does not override the basic thrust
of the Jonah's story, namely that YHWH can and does deliver whom he
chooses, including the foreigners of chapter one, and the Ninevites in
chapter three. Inclusion of the psalm emphasizes that Israel's deliverance
rests not on an inherent position as YHWH's elect, but upon profession
that YHWH is god (cf Jonah 2:7f).

---

[67]   The idea of raising "Israel" after three days of punishment, may have brought the Hosea
passage to the mind of the redactor enough to effect the formulation of Jonah 2:9f.

[68]   Despite Jonah's prayer and affirmation in 2:3-10, he is angry that YHWH has
compassion on Nineveh. Jonah reverts anti-hero as in chapter one, with the exception
that flight and apathy are replaced by anger.

[69]   The precise formulation may incorporate Nah 2:1 which parallels Isa 52:7, but the
parallel in Nah 2:1 commands Judah to "pay your vows," because Assyria has been
destroyed. This command does not appear in Isa 52:7.

6. The Position, Function, and Date of Jonah

Wolff correctly observes that chronological reflections and content determine Jonah's position in the Book of the Twelve.[70] Chronologically, 2 Kgs 14:23-25 places Jonah in the reign of Jeroboam II which dictates that Jonah's placement falls between Amos and Micah (cf Hos 1:1; Amos 1:1; Mic 1:1). Since Micah lists only kings later than Uzziah (and Jeroboam by implication), Jonah logically precedes Micah. Wolff asks why it does not come nearer to Amos or Hosea. He suggests two possibilities: 1) Obadiah was considered older than Jonah by the collector, because he understood Obadiah as the chief servant of the earlier king Ahab.[71] 2) Jonah could logically follow Obadiah because Obad 1 mentions a messenger sent among the nations, and a collector could have considered Jonah as that messenger, especially since Jonah 1:1 begins the narrative with "*and* it happened."[72]

It is possible to build upon Wolff's observations. Despite the fact that no literary observations support an argument that the narrative of Jonah 1:1-17 was redactionally altered on the basis of Obadiah, the catchwords in Obad 11-14 could have influenced Jonah's position. In Obad 11, Edom as enemy is commanded not to "cast lots" over YHWH's people in Jerusalem when it is destroyed. In Jonah 1:7, sailors do "cast lots" over Jonah. While this possibility cannot be ruled out, neither does it seem very significant, even if it is true, since a clear train of thought does not present itself regarding a rationale for such a relationship.

Another observation illuminates the question why Jonah was selected for inclusion in the Book of the Twelve at all, especially in light of its uniqueness among prophetic writings. The most obvious reason is probably the best in this case. The narrative was selected as a contrast to the views of Nahum, whose bitter denunciation of Nineveh (within the context of cosmic judgment) leaves no room for YHWH's salvific action among the

---

[70] Wolff, *BK* 14/3, 53.

[71] See 1 Kgs 18:1-16. Wolff has a point since later traditions develop which relate Obadiah in Kings to the prophetic writing. See Louis Ginzberg, *Legends of the Jews*, vol. 4 (Philadelphia: The Jewish Publication Society of America, 1946-47), 240-242.

[72] This interpretation requires of course that one ignore the fact that Obad 1 portrays the messenger sent to rally the nations against Edom while Jonah is sent to preach against Nineveh. Such a harmonization is difficult for the modern mind, but in light of other places in the Ancient Near East where specific enemies, including Edom and Assyria, symbolize the evil of all nations, it is not improbable to assume that these thoughts played a role in Jonah's placement. See also Rudolph, *KAT* 13/2, 334-336, who relates the "and" in Jonah 1:1 to a deliberate continuation of 2Kgs 14:23-25.

nations. Even in the larger context of the Micah/Nahum connection, the nations are the tools of YHWH, but no real consideration is given to the possibility of their relationship to YHWH. Jonah goes well beyond the concepts in Nahum. It *presumes* the nations can have a salvific relationship with the God of Israel. Classifying Jonah as a contrast to Nahum is endemic to the narrative, and probably even played a role even in Jonah's compositional formulation.[73] Early traditions regarding Jonah and Nahum frequently brought the message of these two books into play with one another. The most common traditions claim Nineveh's repentance (Jonah) was temporary, while later actions result in their destruction (Nahum).[74] One cannot help but think that a redactor deliberately created this tension, particularly when one recognizes that both these dimensions appear in Jer 18:7-10, while Jonah only treats the question of the repentance of the nation (18:7f), not of the nation's return to evil actions (18:9f).[75]

If the arguments above are correct, however, and Jonah 2:3-10 entered the narrative with its incorporation into the Book of the Twelve, then one cannot limit the incorporation of Jonah solely to a counterpiece to Nahum. The psalm is not concerned with these questions, but reflects Israel's responsibility for its own judgment, and its need to return to YHWH. Thus, Jonah's inability to inescape from YHWH (1:1-16), and the punishment for disobedience presumed in chapter two (particularly when read with Hos 5:15-6:6), both coincide with motifs of the Amos/Obadiah connection. The Amos/Obadiah connection also places a heavy emphasis upon the fact that neither Israel (specifically, the Northern kingdom) nor Edom can escape YHWH's judgment.[76] Jonah 1:1-2:11 certainly offers a thematic parallel to this emphasis, making its redactional *placement*, and the addition of the psalm, even easier to understand. The narrative in 1:1-16 demonstrates the disobedience of Israel and its subsequent punishment

---

[73] See T.F. Glasson, "Nahum and Jonah," *Expository Times* 81 (1969/70): 54-55. Literary observations in this chapter center upon chapters 1-2 because of catchwords to Micah and Obadiah. Chapters 3-4 also contain touchstones to other portions of the Twelve which cannot be treated here. Alan Cooper, "In Praise of Divine Caprice: The Significance of the Book of Jonah," *Among the Prophets: Language, Image and Structure in the Prophetic Writings*, JSOT Supplement 144 (Sheffield: Sheffield Academic Press, 1993), 144-163. Cooper documents a number of passages in Jonah 3-4 which have redactional implications for Jonah and the Book of the Twelve.

[74] Ginzberg, *Legends of the Jews*, vol. 4, 252.

[75] See above discussion of the redaction theory of L. Schmidt, on page 258.

[76] Compare Amos 9:1-4 and Obad 1-5 and the discussion of their relationship in the chapter on the Amos—Obadiah connection.

according to the redactor who inserted the psalm. Only when "Jonah" remembers YHWH (2:8), do his fortunes change.

A sizable majority of scholars date Jonah simply as late post-exilic, with more than a handful suggesting it did not reach its final form until early in the third century.[77] None of the preceding arguments contradicts this opinion. Rather, most of the observations support the arguments of those arguing for a date after Alexander, although further precision is not possible. Jonah's insertion into a previously existing connection, which did not arise prior to the fourth century, adds to the arguments that Jonah's canonical form must be classified as one of the latest prophetic writings. Jonah is certainly included in the reference to "the Twelve" in Sir 49:12 (dated around 180), so one cannot go too far into the third century.

The narrative's openness to the inclusion of foreigners as YHWH fearers represents a theological perspective which finds its closest parallels in Trito-Isaiah, Zech 8:20-23, Mal 1:11-14, and Zech 14:16ff, even though the interrelationships of these texts are difficult to trace. Of these passages, Jonah demonstrates a more optimistic attitude toward the nations than Zech 14:16ff, whose context blunts the incorporation of the nations into the salvific picture with the special treatment of Egypt, and it presupposes a final battle prior to the pilgrimage of the remainder of those nations.[78] Jonah's positive outlook more closely parallels Zech 8:20-23, but that passage presumes the nations must come to Jerusalem to worship, which Jonah does not. The closest parallel in the Book of the Twelve is Mal 1:11-14, which presumes YHWH's name will be honored "among the nations" who will make offerings to YHWH in their land. Both Jonah and Mal 1:11-14 use the nations as examples to castigate particularists in Israel. However, one must approach the question of direct relationship cautiously since the situations presumed by the two writings differ considerably.[79]

---

[77] See discussion of the date of Jonah above, page 255.

[78] See discussion in the following chapter.

[79] The narrative in Jonah attacks particularist *attitudes* which allow no room for the nations' relationship to YHWH, which in many respects describes the group responsible for compiling the majority of the Book of the Twelve. The incorporation of the psalm of Jonah works with a hermeneutic of history which blames Israel itself for the loss of the temple. Mal 1:1-14 condemns specific cultic abuses, which provides certain affinities to the psalm's addendum (2:9f). Jonah does not, however, exhibit strong literary connections to Malachi. In addition, the observations on Zech 8:20-23 and Malachi (including 1:11-14) indicate that it was incorporated into the Book of the Twelve prior to Jonah's incorporation. In balancing all of the possibilities, one can only postulate currently that Jonah entered after Proto-Zechariah and Malachi were

The incorporation of Jonah 2:3-10, with its concern for the temple, brings a Jerusalem orientation to Jonah which would otherwise be lacking. This lack of *explicit* accentuation of Jerusalem differentiates the narrative from these other Book of the Twelve texts treating the nations positively. The remainder of these texts are heavily oriented toward the Jerusalem cult, but the addition of the psalm perhaps indicates how Jonah was adapted by the circle responsible for transmitting the larger corpus.

---

attached, and prior to or perhaps at the same time as Zech 14:1ff because of its interest in the cult. The most likely candidate, however, appears to be the corrective layer(s) of Zech 12:2-13:6. This layer portrays Jerusalem's repentance similarly to the psalm of Jonah, and it also contains an anti-prophet polemic (13:3-6) which coincides well with the narrative emphasis. Lacking further evidence, one may postulate cautiously that Jonah entered with this corrective material. Jonah's incorporation post-dated the Joel-related additions to the Book of the Twelve, despite the fact that Jonah uses Joel (cf Jonah 4:2; Joel 2:13; Nah 1:3). Note, however, that Jonah 4:2 uses the reference to Joel 2:13 satirically, indicating the two have entirely different interests. See also the discussion of Mic 7:19b, whose awareness of Jonah 2:4 post-dated the Micah-Nahum connection. One final note regarding significant parallels is also in order. In light of the relationship between Isa 66:16ff and Zech 14:1ff, it might be of some significance that there may be some historical similarity of circumstance hidden behind the veiled reference to the "those keeping vain idols" in Jonah 2:9 and the strange syncretistic practices described in Isa 66:17. It is not surprising, in light of recent studies on the latest redactional stages of Isaiah, to consider these two texts contemporaneous.

Summary

This study completes an evaluation begun in an earlier volume. Together, these works explore the implications of catchword connections at the beginning and end of the writings of the Book of the Twelve. The breadth of the investigation warrants a summary of both volumes, although it will emphasize the writings treated in this volume.

1. Pre-existing Multi-volume Corpora

Observations presented in the earlier work suggested the existence of two multi-volume corpora as literary precursors to the Book of the Twelve. The writings of these two corpora received adaptations at the beginning and end which demonstrated literary awareness of the larger corpus. One of these multi-volume works, the Haggai-Zechariah corpus, already commands scholarly support from previous studies which also concluded that Haggai and Zech 1-8 had been published in a single volume to document the prophetic impetus which led to the reconstruction of the temple.

The second pre-existing corpus, labeled as the Deuteronomistic corpus, contained the writings of Hosea, Amos, Micah, and Zephaniah. These four writings evidence common literary devices and theological paradigms which allow one to trace consistent emphases across the individual writings. These unifying elements include: superscriptive bracketing of historical eras, catchword connections between the beginnings and ends of these four writings, detectable conformation of the writings to a dominant (Deuteronomistic) pattern, and editorial expansions transversing these four writings. Hosea and Amos record God's prophetic word to the Northern Kingdom while Micah and Zephaniah functioned as Southern counterparts in this corpus. Broadly stated, Hosea alternates between YHWH's pronouncements of judgment and salvation for Israel. Amos presumes Israel's recalcitrance in Hosea, and announces judgment on Israel. Micah assumes Samaria's destruction from Amos as a warning to Judah of a similar fate if it does not change. As with Hosea, Micah's current form alternates between passages of hope and doom. Zephaniah centers its message on YHWH's judgment, like Amos, but that message is directed to Judah and Jerusalem. Prior to incorporation into what would become the Book of the Twelve, this Deuteronomisic corpus likely received editorial expansions which accented YHWH's positive intentions for a remnant (Hos 2:18ff; Amos 9:7-10,11-15*; Mic 2:12f; 4-5*; 7; Zeph 3:9-19*). Zephaniah, and perhaps Micah, received more extensive additions than Hosea and Amos at the point of incorporation into the larger corpus as part of the Joel-related layer (see below).[1]

Finally, a series of observations indicates that redactional glosses were added to the Deuteronomistic corpus and to the Haggai-Zechariah corpus when these writings were incorporated into the larger prophetic work now known as the Book of the Twelve. These connections used catchwords to juxtapose the situation in one writing with its literary neighbor. Moreover, they rely upon the vocabulary of Joel and Isaiah to fashion a compendium of YHWH's prophetic message.

2. The Joel-related Layer

Evidence from this study documents a similar process of adapting prophetic material for a larger corpus by creating significant touchstones with Joel and Isaiah. The majority of the editorial work related to the production of the Book of the Twelve occurs in this "Joel-related layer." This layer combined the Deuteronomistic corpus and the Haggai-Zechariah corpus, and it expanded upon the chronological framework supplied by these existing corpora by merging Joel, Obadiah, Nahum, Habakkuk, and Malachi into the two pre-existing corpora.

Nahum and Habakkuk existed as literary works with recognizable structures, but they were substantially expanded for this larger literary horizon. Editors prefixed a semi-acrostic theophany (1:2-8) to the front of Nahum, and wove a transition (1:9f,12b-13; 2:1-3) into the existing Nahum corpus. Slight modifications to the hymn disrupted the semi-acrostic poem, in part, to strengthen catchword connections to Mic 7:8ff, and, in part, to extend motifs from Joel and Isaiah across this new prophetic compendium. The end of Nahum received minor redactional glosses (3:15ac,16b) which interpreted Assyria as one of the "locusts" in Joel. Similarly, Habakkuk

---

[1] Evidence suggests that the vacillation between judgment and deliverance may reflect subsequent editorial expansions (probably still within the Deuteronomistic corpus) which accented the parallel functions of Hosea and Micah. If so, the earlier material of Mic 1-3+6 would have been more heavily oriented toward explanations for Jerusalem's destruction.

existed in literary form as a wisdom-oriented discussion concerning the prosperity of the wicked in Judah. This discussion was expanded by a Babylonian commentary (1:5-11,12*,15-17 and portions of the woe oracles in 2:5ff) and by affixing a cultically transmitted theophanic prayer (3:1ff) to the existing corpus. The commentary immitates formulations from Nah 3:1ff (with occasional allusions to Joel), but adapts Nahum's Assyrian predictions to Babylon. The theophanic prayer (3:1ff) receives slight modifications (3:16b-17) for the larger corpus which, similarly to Nah 1, interpret the theophany in light of the message of Joel.

This investigation suggests a strong probability that two writings, Joel and Obadiah, were first compiled, by adapting existing material, as part of the literary production of the Book of the Twelve. Joel serves as the literary anchor to the larger corpus. Chapters 1-2 combine images of locust plagues and drought to call Judah to repentance. Two existing poems (1:5ff; 2:1ff) are expanded in light of the literary context between Hosea and Amos. Similarly, Joel 4:1ff combines two existing pieces (4:4-8,9ff) into a coherent unit which resolves the situation of Joel 1-2 and eschatologizes the oracles against the nations in Amos. The resulting composition presents a paradigm of history which is "played out" literarily in the corpus. In Joel, "locust" plaugues, in the form of armies, devastate the land as a result of the guilt of the people. Redactional formulations in Nahum and Habakkuk interpret Assyria and Babylon as two of these locusts. In Joel's paradigm, when the people repent (2:18ff), YHWH will restore the land's agricultural bounty which the "locusts" devastated. Glosses in Haggai and Zech 1-8 interpret the temple reconstruction as beginning the restoration of YHWH's blessing in the form of agricultural restoration. Other glosses also draw upon these motifs (e.g. Hos 14:8; Amos 9:13; Hab 3:15b-16). In Joel, YWHH will judge the nations who took advantage of Israel while YHWH punished it. Obadiah and several theophanies (Nah 1:2ff, Hab 3:1ff, Mic 1:2ff, Zeph 1:2f) underscore these motifs. Despite Joel's efforts on behalf of the entire people (of Judah), the literary development illustrates only a remnant of YHWH's people will heed the message. By Malachi, not only does the land still suffer from the "drought" and the "devourers" (cf 3:10f), but only a portion will benefit from YHWH's message (cf 3:3,16-18).

Like Joel, Obadiah provides evidence that its current literary form results from a composition process which specifically combined independent oracles for The Twelve. Direct parallels between Obad 1-5 and Jer 49:9,14-16 demonstrate conclusively that Obad 1-5 has been adapted to immitate Amos 9:1ff. Less objectively, but still highly probable, Obad 15-21 suggests a pre-existing literary piece has been adapted for the literary position.

These adaptations parallel structural and thematic elements from Amos 9:11ff and they anticipate Mic 1:2ff. Interestingly, both ends of Obadiah thus go to considerable lengths to associate the fate of Edom with the fate of the Northern Kingdom. Obad 8-14 draws from Isaiah and Ezekiel in its formulations, providing evidence that Obadiah can be characterized as a mosaic of anti-Edom oracles compiled for the Book of the Twelve. Mal 1:2-5 literally confirms predictions of Edom's downfall.

A fifth writing, Malachi, also reflects substantial involvement with the Joel-related layer, although the character of that involvement requires further study. In addition to the current volume, recent works by Bosshard, Kratz, and Steck all associate Malachi with the formation of the Book of the Twelve, but the explanations of that relationship vary slightly.[2] This study presumed Malachi, like Nahum and Habakkuk, existed independently as a prophetic disputation. This disputation was selected for its affinity to the theological purpose of the editors who required a thematic counter to the hopeful message of Zech 7-8. As Malachi was incorporated, it was adapted for the Book of the Twelve by expansions which evidence this larger literary horizon (e.g. 1:2-5; 3:10f,16ff). Bosshard, Kratz, and Steck offer a plausible alternative model treating Malachi as a redactional continuation (*Fortschreibung*) of Zech 7-8 which never existed as an independent corpus. Their model offers advantages since it more easily explains the close association of Malachi to Zech 7-8, but isolating this continuation to the Haggai-Zechariah corpus does not adequately explain motifs related to Obadiah and Joel noted in this study. The superscription in Mal 1:1 indicates Malachi existed — or at least was considered — as a separate work adapted for the larger corpus, since its use of מלאכי creates a separate book, unlike the nearly identical formulations in Zech 9:1; 12:1. One question requiring further evaluation is the question of when this separation occurred. Bosshard, Kratz, and Steck argue these three superscriptions were added simultaneously during later redactional activity. This study has argued that Mal 1:1 already separated Malachi from Zech 7-8, and that Zech 9:1 and 12:1 imitated Mal 1:1.

This last argument derives, in part, from observations on other superscriptions in the Joel-related layer. The superscriptions in Joel, Obadiah, Nahum, Habakkuk, and Malachi demonstrate considerable inter-

---

2   Erich Bosshard and Reinhard Gregor Kratz, "Maleachi im Zwölfprophetenbuch," *BN* 52 (1990): 27-46; and Odil Hannes Steck, *Der Abschluβ der Prophetie im Alten Testament. Ein Versuch zur Frage der Vorgeschichte des Kanons*, Biblisch Theologische Studien 17 (Neukirchener Verlag, 1991).

play with their respective contexts in the Book of the Twelve. Joel's superscription (The word of YHWH came to Joel, son of Pethuel.) lacks only the royal cross-references as an immitation of Hos 1:1. Obadiah's superscription (The vision [חזון] of Obadiah) makes sense in light of the editorial desire to parallel Obadiah with the final vision of Amos (9:1ff). Both Nah 1:1 and Hab 1:1 contain משׂא and forms of חזה. Mal 1:1 takes superscriptive elements from the Deuteronomistic corpus (דבר יהוה), the Haggai-Zechariah corpus (ביד), and the Joel-related layer (משׂה). Zech 9:1 and 12:1 do not contain the element from the Haggai-Zechariah corpus even though they both begin identically to Mal 1:1. Zech 9:1 and 12:1 both exhibit literary tensions in the current blocks they introduce (9-11; 12-14), whereas Mal 1:1 demonstrates no such tensions.

3. Subsequent Additions

After the work of the Joel-related layer, two substantial text blocks entered the corpus to complete the Book of the Twelve: Jonah and Zech 9-14. Editors adapted Jonah for the Book of the Twelve by incorporating an existing hymn of thanksgiving (2:3-8) with an addendum (2:9f) that anticipates Micah. Evidence suggests that at least two rationale motivated Jonah's inclusion. First, Jonah provides a more positive orientation toward the fate of the nations in YHWH's plans than was contained in much of the corpus prior to that point. Thus, Jonah supposes deliverance for nations who recognize YHWH's sovereignty. Second, those incorporating the book understood "Jonah" as Israel. Both the addendum in 2:9f and Mic 7:19b, which aludes backward to Jonah, interpret the fate of Jonah in light of the fate of Israel.

Both the current study and recent works by Bosshard, Kratz, and Steck all conclude that Zech 9-14 interrupts the previous connection between Zech 8:9ff and Mal 1:1ff.[3] All agree that Zech 9-14 also reflects more than one layer of material, but variations in models explain literary tensions differently. This study concluded that editorial incorporation of independent blocks allowed one to suggest that two editorial movements could account for these chapters in their current context. The first compiled Zech 9-13* (by adapting existing blocks) to create a literary transition from the hopeful message of Zech 7-8 to the negative situation

---

[3]   See footnote 2 above.

presumed in Malachi. Some evidence suggests this editorial layer occurs simultaneously with the incorporation of Jonah. Zech 14:1ff (and Mal 3:22-24) supplies a redactional continuation of 9-13. It concluded the editorial work on the entire prophetic corpus (Josh-Mal). Steck, building on the work of Kratz and Bosshard, likewise associates these chapters with the deliberate conclusion of the prophetic corpus. He concludes, however, that these chapters (with additions to Malachi) reveal a succession of four redactional continuations reflecting historical developments in the century following Alexander's occupation (332-323) of Palestine. Together, these works argue that Zech 9-14 exhibits canonical awareness as a major element in its formulation. Variations in the details deserve further study.

4. Provenence for the Book of the Twelve

Any discussion of the date of the Book of the Twelve requires careful consideration of several elements: 1) the literary history of the individual writings; 2) the literary history of pre-existing blocks incorporated into those writings for the Book of the Twelve, 3) the possible transmission of more than one writing as part of a previous multi-volume corpus; and 4) the purpose of redactional expansions. Conclusions reached in this study attempt to do justice to all four of these factors.

Constitution of the Deuteronomistic corpus presumes the exile, implying Hosea, Amos, Micah and Zephaniah were combined on a single corpus following 587 to explain Jerusalem's destruction. Subsequent eschatological expansions provided hope to the remnant population that YHWH would reconstitute the kingdom. These expansions likely occurred in the early post-exilic period. The Haggai-Zechariah corpus documents prophetic activity surrounding the temple reconstruction, and several years thereafter (cf Zech 7:1).

The formative compilation of the larger corpus presupposes Joel as a literary corpus. Consistent redactional allusions to Joel's paradigm of history in most of the remainder of the writings demand this conclusion. Unfortunately, opinions on the date of Joel complicate decisions for the Book of the Twelve. For reasons cited in the discussion of Joel (the existence of the wall of Jerusalem in 2:7, the political alliance of the seaboard coalition in 4:4-8, and the advanced eschatological assumptions), this study sides with those who see Joel as a product of the first half of the fourth century (400-350). Certain reservations must be held open at this point since evidence suggest both 4:4-8 and and 2:7 were part of existing literary compositions used to shape the book of Joel. How long these blocks existed indpendently prior to the formation of Joel is not yet settled, but solid evidence implies Joel existed prior to Alexander's invasion. Zech 9-13 contains allusions to Alexander's campaign (9:13). Since it interrupts the connection between Zech 8 and Malachi, it appearss plausible that the formative work on this larger corpus took place in the latter portions of the Persian period, while the subsequent additions (Jonah, Zech 9-14) did not enter the corpus until after 332.[4]

The group(s) responsible for the Book of the Twelve were closely associated with those who transmitted the Isaiah corpus. Similar outlooks associate these two corpora extensively. Both Isaiah and the Twelve demonstrate that they inherited and incorporated Deuteronomistically-influenced texts as part of their transmission. The transmission history of pre-exisiting blocks (e.g. Nah 1:2-8; Hab 3:1ff; Jonah 2:3-8) also demonstrates this group had (ongoing) access to cultic texts which they could adapt to new prophetic contexts. The Joel-related layer exhibits knowledge of Jeremiah and Ezekiel (especially in Obadiah), but these writings do not substantively impact the shape of the larger corpus like Isaiah. Zech 9-14 manifests a stronger awareness of the prophetic canon, and of the function of the Twelve as the conclusion to that portion of the canon. It is not possible here to delve the implications of these characteristics for understanding post-exilic developments in Judah, but it adds evidence which should be considered when attempting to describe the complicated process of the formation of the prophetic canon.

---

[4]   See also Steck, *Der Abschluß der Prophetie.*

Works Cited

Ackerman, James S. "Satire and Symbolism in the Song of Jonah." In *Traditions in Transformation. Turning Points in Biblical Faith*. B. Halpern and J.D. Levenson, eds. 213-246. Winona Lake, Indiana: Eisenbrauns, 1981.

Ahlström, G.W. *Joel and the Temple cult of Jerusalem*. Supplements to Vetus Testamentum 21. Leiden: E.J. Brill, 1971.

Albright, William F. "The Land of Damascus 1850-1750 B.C." *BASOR* 83 (1941): 30-36.

Albright, William F. "The Psalm of Habakkuk." In *Studies in Old Testament Prophecy, Presented to Professor Theodore H. Robinson, by the Society for the Old Testament Study on his 65. Birthday August 9th, 1946*. H.H. Rowley, ed. 1-18. Edinburgh: T&T Clark, 1950.

Allen, Leslie C. *The Books of Joel, Obadiah, Jonah, and Micah*. New International Commentary. Grand Rapids: Eerdmans, 1976.

Allis, Oswald T. "Nahum, Niniveh, Elkoch." *Evangelical Quarterly* 27 (1955): 67-80.

Amsler, Samuel. "Amos." In *Osée. Joël, Abdias, Jonas. Amos.* Commentaire de l'Ancien Testament 11a. Neuchâtel: Delachaux & Niestlé, 1965.

Bader, Günter. "Das Gebet Jonas. Eine Meditation." *ZTK* 70 (1973): 162-205.

Baldwin, J.G. "Malachi 1:11 and the Worship of the Nations in the Old Testament." *Tyndale Bulletin* 23 (1972): 117-124.

Bartlett, John R. "The Brotherhood of Edom." *JSOT* 4 (Oct. 1977): 2-27.

Bartlett, John R. "The Rise and Fall of the Kingdom of Edom." *Palestine Exploration Quarterly* 104 (1972): 26-37.

Bartlett, John R. *Edom and the Edomites*. JSOTS 77. Sheffield: JOST, 1989.

Bergler, Siegfried. *Joel als Schriftinterpret*. Beiträge zur Erforschung des Alten Testaments und des antiken Judentums 16. Frankfurt: Peter Lang, 1988.

Beyerlin, Walter. *Der 52. Psalm. Studien zu seiner Ordnung*. BWANT 111. Stuttgart: Kohlhammer, 1980.

Bič, Miloš. "Zur Problematik des Buches Obadjah." In *Supplements to Vetus Testamentum*, Vol. 1 (1953): 11-25.

Bič, Miloš. *Das Buch Joel*. Berlin: Evangelische Verlagsanstalt, 1960.

Bič, Miloš. *Das Buch Sacharja*. Berlin: Evangelische Verlagsanstalt, 1962.

Biddle, Mark Edward. *A Redaction History of Jeremiah 2:1-4:2*. Abhandlungen zur Theologie des Alten und Neuen Testaments 77. Zürich: Theologischer Verlag, 1990.

Boadt, Lawrence. *Jeremiah 26-52, Habakkuk, Zephaniah, Nahum*. Old Testament Message 10. Wilmington, Delaware: Michael Glazier, 1982.

Boecker, Hans Jochen. "Bemerkungen zur formgeschichtlichen Terminologie des Buches Maleachi." *ZAW* 78 (1966): 78-80.

Böhme, W. "Die Composition des Buches Jona." *ZAW* 7 (1887): 224-284.

Bosshard, Erich, and Reinhard Gregor Kratz. "Maleachi im Zwölfprophetenbuch." *BN* 52 (1990): 27-46.

Bosshard, Erich. "Beobachtungen zum Zwölfprophetenbuch." *BN* 40 (1987): 30-62.

Botterweck, G. Johannes. "Jakob habe ich lieb." *Bibel und Leben* 1 (1960): 28-38.

Bourke, J. "Le Jour de Jahvé dans Joël." *Revue Biblique* 66 (1959): 5-31.

Braun, Roddy. *1 Chronicles*. Word Biblical Commentary 14. Waco, Texas: Word Books, 1986.

Brownlee, William H. *The Midrah Pesher of Habakkuk*. SBL Monograph Series 24. Missoula, Montana: Scholars Press, 1979.

Cannon, William W. "The Integrity of Habakkuk cc. 1.2." *ZAW* 43 (1925): 62-90.

Carroll, Robert P. "Eschatological Delay in the Prophetic Tradition?" *ZAW* 94 (1982): 47-58.

Carroll, Robert P. *Jeremiah: A Commentary*. Old Testament Library. LondonL SCM, 1986.

Cassuto, Umberto. "Chapter 3 of Habakkuk and the Ras Shamra Texts." In *Biblical and Oriental Studies*, vol. 2, p. 3-15. Bible and Ancient Oriental Texts. I. Abrahams, trans. Jerusalem: Magnes Press, 1975.

Chary, Théophane. *Les Prophètes et le Culte à Partir de l'Exil*. Paris: Desclée, 1955.

Childs, Brevard S. "The Canonical Shape of the Book of Jonah." In *Essays in Honor of William Sanford LaSor*, F.A. Tuttle, ed., 122-128. Grand Rapids: Eerdmans, 1978.

Childs, Brevard S. "The Enemy from the North and the Chaos Tradition." *JBL* 78 (1959): 187-198.

Childs, Brevard S. *Introduction to the Old Testament as Scripture*. Philadelphia: Fortress Press, 1979.

Christensen, Duane L. "The Acrostic of Nahum Reconsidered." *ZAW* 87 (1975): 17-30.

Christensen, Duane L. *Transformations of the War Oracle in Old Testament Prophecy: Studies in the Oracles Against the Nations*. Harvard Dissertations in Religion 3. Missoula, MT: Scholars Press, 1975.

Clements, Ronald E. "Patterns in the Prophetic Canon." In *Canon and Authority: Essays in Old Testament Religion and Theology*, 42-55. Philadelphia: Fortress, 1977.

Clements, Ronald E. "The Purpose of the Book of Jonah." *VT.S* 28 (1974): 16-28.

Coggins, Richard J. and S. Paul Re'emi. *Nahum, Obadiah, Esther*. International Theological Commentary. Grand Rapids: Eerdmans, 1985.

Coggins, Richard J. "An Alternative Prophetic Tradition?" In *Israel's Prophetic Tradition: Essays in Honour of Peter Ackroyd*, Richard Coggins, et al, eds. 77-94. London: Cambridge University Press, 1982.

Cohen, Simon. "Nabateans." *IDB*, vol. 3. 491-493.

Cooper, Alan. "In Praise of Divine Caprice: The Significance of the Book of Jonah. *Among the Prophets: Language, Image and Structure in the Prophetic Writings*. Philip R. Davies and David J.A. Clines, eds. JSOT Supp 144. Sheffield: JSOT Press, 1993, 144-163.

Cornelius, Izak. "Paradise Motifs in the 'Eschatology' of the Minor Prophets and the Iconography of the Ancient Near East. The Concepts of Fertility, Water, Trees, and 'Tierfrieden' and Gen 2-3." *JNSL* 14 (1988): 41-83.

Cross, Frank Moore. "אל." *ThWAT* 1, 278.

Cross, Frank Moore. "A Reconstruction of the Judean Restoration." *JBL* 94 (1975): 4-18.

Cross, Frank Moore. "Studies in the Structure of Hebrew Verse: The Prosody of the Psalm of Jonah." In *The Quest for the Kingdom of God: Studies in Honor of George E. Mendenhall*. H.B. Huffmon et al. (eds.). 159-167. Winona Lake, Indiana: Eisenbrauns, 1983.

Day, John. *God's Conflict with the Dragon and the Sea: Echoes of a Canaanite Myth in the Old Testament*. Cambridge: Cambridge University Press, 1985.

Delitzsch, Franz. "Wann weissagte Obadja." *ZThK* 12 (1851): 91-102.

Delitzsch, Franz. *Biblical Commentary on the Psalms*. 3 Vol. Francis Boulton (trans.). Grand Rapids: Eerdmans, 1949, orig. 1866.

Dillard, Raymond B. *2 Chronicles*. Word Biblical Commentary 15. Waco, Texas: Word Publishing Company, 1987.

Duhm, Bernhard. *Das Buch Habakuk: Text, Übersetzung und Erklärung*. Tübingen: J.C.B. Mohr, 1906.

Dumbrell, W.J. "Malachi and the Ezra-Nehemiah Reforms." *Reformed Theological Review* 35/2 (1976): 42-52.

Dykes, Donna S. *Diversity and Unity in Habakkuk*. Yale University Dissertation. Minneapolis: University Microfilm, 1976. Order no. 76-22.358.

Eaton, J.H. *Obadiah, Nahum, Habakkuk, and Zephaniah*. Torch Bible Commentary. London: SCM, 1961.

Eissfeldt, Otto. "Amos und Jona in Volkstümlicher Überlieferung." In *Kleine Schriften*, vol 4. Rudolph Sellheim and Fritz Maass, eds., 137-142. Tübingen: Mohr, 1968.

Eissfeldt, Otto. *The Old Testament: An Introduction: The History of the Formation of the Old Testament*. Peter Ackroyd (trans.). New York: Harper and Row, 1965.

Elliger, Karl. "Ein Zeugnis aus der jüdischen Gemeinde im Alexanderjahr 332 v Chr." *ZAW* 62 (1949/50): 63-115.

Elliger, Karl. *Das Buch der Zwölf Kleinen Propheten 2. Die Propheten Nahum, Habakuk, Zephanja, Haggai, Sacharja, Maleachi. Übersetzt u. erklärt*. ATD 25. Göttingen: Vandenhoeck & Ruprecht, 1950.

Ellul, Danielle. "Variations sur le thème de la guerre sainte dans le Deutéro-Zacharie." *Etudes Théologiques et Religieuses* 56 (1981): 55-71.

Ellul, Jacque. *The Judgment of Jonah*. Geoffrey W. Bromiley, trans. Grand Rapids: Eerdmans, 1971.

Emmerson, Grace I. "Another Look at the Book of Jonah." *Expository Times* 88 (1976): 86-88.

Ewald, Heinrich. *Die Propheten des Alten Bundes*. 3 vols. Göttingen: Vandenhoeck & Ruprecht, [2]1868.

Fishbane, Michael. *Biblical Interpretation in Ancient Israel*. Oxford: Clarendon Press, 1985.

Fohrer, Georg. *Einleitung in das Alte Testament*. Heidelberg: Quelle & Meyer, 1969.

Fohrer, Georg. "Die Sprüche Obadjas." In *Studien zu alttestamentlichen Texten und Themen* (1966-1972). BZAW 155. 69-80. Berlin: Gruyter, 1981.

Fohrer, Georg. *Die Propheten des Alten Testaments. Band 2: Die Propheten des 7. Jahrhunderts*. Gütersloh: Gerd Mohn, 1974.

Fretheim, Terence E. "Jonah and Theodicy." *ZAW* 90 (1978): 227-37.

Fretheim, Terence E. *The Message of Jonah: A Theological Commentary*. Minneapolis, Minnesota: Augsburg Publishing House, 1977.

Fritz, Volkmar. *Tempel und Zelt. Studien zum Tempelbau in Israel und zum Zeltheiligtum der Priesterschaft*. Neukirchen: Neukirchner Verlag, 1977.

Gerstenberger, Erhard S. *Psalms. Part I, with an Introduction to Cultic Poetry*. Forms of the Old Testament Literature 14. Grand Rapids: Eerdmans, 1988.

Gerstenberger, Erhard S. "The Woe Oracle of the Prophets." *JBL* 81 (1962): 249-263.

Ginzberg, Louis. *The Legends of the Jews*. 7 Vols. Philadelphia: The Jewish Publication Society of America, 1946-7.

Glasson, T.F. "Nahum and Jonah." *Expository Times* 81 (1969/70): 54-55.

Glazier-McDonald, Beth. *Malachi: The Divine Messenger*. SBL Dissertation Series. Atlanta: Scholars Press, 1987.

Gray, John. "The Diaspora of Israel and Judah in Obadiah v. 20." *ZAW* 65 (1953): 53-59.

Greenwood, David C. "On the Jewish Hope for a Restored Northern Kingdom." *ZAW* 88 (1976): 376-385.

Gruenthaler, M.J. "Chaldeans or Macedonians? A Recent Theory on the Prophecy of Habakkuk." *Biblica* 8 (1927): 129-160; 251-289.

Gunneweg, Antonius H.J. "Habakuk und das Problem des leidenden צדיק." *ZAW* 98 (1986): 400-415.

Gunneweg, Antonius H.J. *Geschichte Israels bis Bar Kochba*. 5th ed. Stuttgart: Kohlhammer, 1984.

Gyllenberg, R. "Die Bedeutung des Wortes Sela." *ZAW* 58 (1940/41): 153-156.

Habel, Norman C. *The Book of Job: A Commentray*. Old Testament Library. Philadelphia: Westminster Press, 1985.

Haldar, Alfred. *Studies in the Book of Nahum*. UUA 1946:7. Uppsala: Almquist & Wiksells Boktryckerei, 1947.

Hanson, Paul D. *Old Testament Apocalyptic*. Interpreting Biblical Texts. Nashville: Abingdon, 1987.

Hanson, Paul D. *The Dawn of Apocalyptic*. Philadelphia: Fortress Press, 1975.

Hiebert, Theodore. *God of My Victory: The Ancient Hymn in Habakkuk 3*. Harvard Semitic Monographs 38. Atlanta: Scholars Press, 1987.

Hitzig, Ferdinand. *Die zwölf kleinen Propheten*. Leipzig: Hirzel Verlag, [4]1881.

Holbert, John C. "'Deliverance Belongs to Yahweh!': Satire in the Book of Jonah." *JSOT* 21 (1981): 59-81.

Holladay, William. *Jeremiah 2: A Commentary on the Book of the Prophet Jeremiah Chapters 26-52*. Hermeneia. Minneapolis: Fortress Press, 1989.

Hoop, Raymond de. "The Book of Jonah as Poetry: An Analysis of Jonah 1:1-16." *Structural Analysis of Biblical and Canaanite Poetry*. JSOT Supplement Series 74. Willem van der Meer and Johannes C. de Moor, eds. 156-171. Sheffield: JSOT Press, 1988.

Hornung, Erik. *Grundzüge der ägyptischen Geschichte*. Darmstadt: Wissenschaftliche Buchgesellschaft, 1978.

Horst, F. *Nahum bis Maleachi*. Handbuch zum Alten Testament 14/2. Tübingen: J.C.B. Mohr, 1938.

House, Paul R. *The Unity of the Twelve*. JSOT 77. Sheffield: Sheffield Academic Press, 1990.

Humbert, Paul. "Essai d'Analyse de Nahoum 1:2-2:3." *ZAW* 44 (1926): 266-280.

Humbert, Paul. *Problèmes du Livre d'Habakkuk*. Neuchâtel: Secréteriat de l'Université, 1944.

Irwin, William A. "The Psalm of Habakkuk." *Journal of Near Eastern Studies* 1 (1942): 10-40.

Jepsen, Alfred. "Anmerkungen zum Buche Jona." In *Wort - Gebot - Glaube. Beiträge zur Theologie des Alten Testaments. Walther Eichrodt zum 80. Geburtstag*. J.J. Stamm and Ernst Jenni, eds. 297-305. Zürich: Zwingli Verlag, 1970.

Jeremias, Jörg. "Theophany in the Old Testament." *IDB Supplement*. 896-898.

Jeremias, Jörg. *Der Prophet Hosea. Übersetzt und erklärt*. Das Alte Testament Deutsch, Neues Göttinger Bibelwerk 24/1. Göttingen: Vandenhoeck & Ruprecht, 1983.

Jeremias, Jörg. *Kultprophetie und Gerichtsverkündigung in der späten Königszeit Israels.* Wissenschaftliche Monographien zum Alten und Neuen Testament 35. Neukirchen: Neukirchener Verlag, 1970.

Jeremias, Jörg. *Theophanie. Die Geschichte einer alttestamentlichen Gattung.* Neukirchen: Neukirchner Verlag, 1965.

Jöcken, Peter. "War Habakuk ein Kultprophet?" In *Bausteine biblischer Theologie. Festgabe für G. Johannes Botterweck zum 60. Gegurtstag dargebracht von seinen Schülern.* 319-332. Bonner Biblische Beiträge 50. Köln-Bonn: Peter Hanstein Verlag, 1977.

Jöcken, Peter. *Das Buch Habakuk. Darstellung der Geschichte seiner kritischen Erforschung mit einer eigenen Beurteilung.* Bonner biblische Beiträge 48. Köln-Bonn: Peter Hanstein, 1977.

Johnson, Marshall D. "The Paralysis of Torah in Habakkuk 1:4." *VT* 35 (1985): 257-266.

Junker, Hubert. *Die Zwölf kleinen Propheten.* Vol. 2: *Nahum, Habakuk, Sophonias, Aggäus, Zacharias, Malachias. Übersetzt und erklärt.* Die Heilige Schrift des A.T. 8. Bonn: Hanstein, 1938.

Kaiser, Otto. *Introduction to the Old Testament: A Presentation of Its Results and Problems.* John Sturdy, trans. Oxford: Basil Blackwell, 1984.

Kapelrud, Arvid S. *Joel Studies.* Uppsala Universitets Arsskrift 1948:4. Uppsala: Lundequistska, 1948.

Keel, Othmar. *The Symbolism of the Biblical World. Ancient Near Eastern Iconography and the Book of Psalms.* Timothy J. Hallet, trans. New York: Crossroad, 1985.

Keller, Carl A. and René Vuilleumier. *Michée, Nahoum, Habacuc, Sophonie.* CAT 11b. Neuchâtel: Delachaux & Niestlé, 1971.

Knight, George A.F. and Friedman W. Golka. *Revelation of God: The Song of Songs and Jonah.* International Theological Commentary. Grand Rapids: Eerdmans, 1988.

Kraeling, Emil G. "The Evolution of the Story of Jonah." In *Hommages à André Dupont-Sommer.* 305-318. Paris: Librairie d'Amérique et d'Orient Adrien Maisonneve, 1971.

Kraeling, Emil G. *The Brooklyn Museum Aramaic Papyri: New Documents of the Fifth Century B.C. from the Jewish Colony at Elephantine.* New Haven: Yale University Press, 1953.

Kutsch, Ernst. "Das Sog. »Bundesblut« in Ex 24:8 und Sach 9:11." *VT* 23 (1973): 25-30.

Lamarche, Paul. *Zacharie 9-14. Structure Littéraire et Messianisme.* Études Biblique. Paris: Gabalda, 1961.

Landes, George M. "Jonah: A Māšāl?" *Israelite Wisdom: Theological and Literary Essays in Honor of Samuel Terrien.* J.G. Gammie, and others, eds. 137-158. Missoula, Montana: Scholars Press, 1978.

Lehmann, Manfred R. "A New Interpretation of the term שדרמות." *VT* 3 (1953): 361-371.

Levine, Etan. "Jonah as a Philosophical Book." *ZAW* 96 (1984): 235-245.

Lindblom, Johannes. *Prophecy in Ancient Israel.* Oxford: Blackwell, 1962.

Lindsay, John. "The Babylonian Kings and Edom, 605-550 B.C." *Palestinian Exploration Quarterly* 108 (1976): 23-29.

Lohfink, Norbert. "Jona ging zur Stadt hinaus (Jona 4,5)," *BZ* NF 5 (1961): 185-203.

Loretz, Oswald. "Herkunft und Sinn der Jona-Erzählung." *Biblische Zeitschrift* NF 5 (1961): 18-29.

Lutz, Hanns-Martin. *Jahwe, Jerusalem und die Völker. Zur Vorgeschichte von Sach 12:1-8 und 14:1-5.* Wissenschaftliche Monographien zum Alten und Neuen Testament 27. Neukirchen: Neukirchener Verlag, 1968.

Magonet, Jonathan. *Form and Meaning: Studies in Literary Techniques in the Book of Jonah*. Beiträge zur biblischen Exegese und Theologie 2. Bern: Herbert Lang, 1976.

Maier, Walter A. *The Book of Nahum: A Commentary*. St. Louis, Mo.: Concordia, 1959.

March, W. Eugene. "Prophecy." In *Old Testament Form Criticism*. John H. Hayes, ed. 141-177. San Antonio, Texas: Trinity University Press, 1974.

Marti, Karl. *Das Dodekapropheton*. HCAT 13. Tübingen: Mohr, 1904.

Mason, Rex. "Some Examples of Inner Biblical Exegesis in Zech 9-14." *Studia Evangelica* 7 (Texte und Untersuchungen zur Geschichte der altchristlichen Literatur 126), 343-354. Berlin: Akademie-Verlag, 1982.

Mason, Rex. "The Purpose of the 'Editorial Framework' in the Book of Haggai." *VT* 27 (1977): 413-421.

Mason, Rex. *The Books of Haggai, Zechariah and Malachi*. Cambridge Bible Commentary. New York/London: Cambridge University Press, 1977.

Milgrom, J. and L. Harper. "משמרת." In *ThWAT*, vol 5, 75-85.

Miller, J. Maxwell and John H. Hayes. *A History of Ancient Israel and Judah*. London: SCM, 1986.

Mowinckel, Sigmund. *The Psalms in Israel's Worship*. 2 vols. Oxford: Basil Blackwell, 1962.

Muntingh, L.M. "Teman and Paran in the Prayer of Habakkuk." *Oud-Testamentiese Werkgemeenskap van Suid-Afrika* (1969): 64-70.

Myers, Jacob M. "Some Considerations Bearing on the Date of Joel." *ZAW* 74 (1962): 177-195.

Nestle, Eberhard. "Miscellen." *ZAW* 27 (1907): 111-121.

Nielsen, Eduard. "The Righteous and the Wicked in Habaqquq." *Studia Theologica* 6 (1952): 54-78.

Nogalski, James D. *Literary Precursors to the Book of the Twelve*. BZAW. Berlin: De Gruyter, 1993.

Nogalski, James D. *The Use of Stichwörter as a Redactional Unification Technique in the Book of the Twelve*. ThM Thesis. Rüschlikon, Switzerland: Baptist Theological Seminary, 1987.

Nowack, Wilhelm. *Die kleinen Propheten übersetzt und erklärt*. 3rd ed. Göttingen: Vandenhoeck & Ruprecht, 1922.

Ogden, Graham and Richard R. Deutsch. *A Promise of Hope — A Call to Obedience: Joel and Malachi*. International Theological Commentary. Grand Rapids: Eerdmans, 1987.

Ogden, Graham S. "Joel 4 and Prophetic Responses to National Laments." *JSOT* 26 (1983): 97-106.

Olávarri, Emilio. "Cronológia y Estructura Literaria del Oráculo de Abdias." *Estudios Biblicos* 22 (1963): 303-313.

Otto, Eckart. "Die Theologie des Buches Habakuk." *VT* 35 (1985): 274-295.

Otzen, Benedikt. *Studien über Deuterosacharja*. Acta Theologica Danica 6. Copenhagen: Munksgaard, 1964.

Peckham, Brian. "The Vision of Habakkuk." *CBQ* 48 (1986): 617-636.

Pesch, Rudolf. "Zur konzentrischen Struktur von Jona 1." *Biblica* 47 (1966): 577-581.

Petersen, David. *Late Israelite Prophecy: Studies in Deutero-Prophetic Literature and in Chronicles* SBLMS 23. Missoula, MT: Scholars Press, 1977.

Pfeiffer, Egon. "Die Disputationsworte im Buche Maleachi. Ein Beitrag zur formgeschichtlichen Struktur." *Evangelische Theologie* 19 (1959): 546-568.

Pierce, Ronald. "A Thematic Development of the Haggai-Zechariah-Malachi Corpus." *JETS* 27 (1984): 401-11.

Pierce, Ronald. "Literary Connectors and a Haggai-Zechariah-Malachi Corpus." *JETS* 27 (1984): 277-89.

Plöger, Otto. *Theocracy and Eschatology*. S. Rudman, trans. Original, 1959. Oxford: Blackwell, 1968.

Porten, Bezalel. "Baalshamem and the Date of the Book of Jonah." In *De la Tôrah au Messie. Études d'exégèse et d'Herméneutique Bibliques Offertes à Henri CAZELLES pour se 25 années d'Enseignement á l'Institut Catholique de Paris (Octobre 1979)*, Maurice Carrez, et al, eds. 237-244. Paris: Desclée, 1981.

Prinsloo, Willem. *The Theology of the Book of Joel*. BZAW 163. Berlin: Walter de Gruyter, 1985.

Pritchard, James, ed. *Ancient Near Eastern Texts Relating to the Old Testament*. 3rd ed. Princeton: Princeton University Press, 1969.

Procksch, Otto. *Die kleinen prophetischen Schriften nach dem Exil*. Stuttgart: Calwer, 1916.

Reicke, Bo. "Joel und seine Zeit." In *Wort - Gebot - Glaube. Beiträge zur Theologie des Alten Testaments. Walther Eichrodt zum 80. Geburtstag*. J.J. Stamm and Ernst Jenni, eds. 133-141. Zürich: Zwingli Verlag, 1970.

Roberts, J.J.M. "Job and the Israelite Religious Tradition." *ZAW* 89 (1977): 107-114.

Robertson, O. Palmer. *The Books of Nahum, Habakkuk, and Zephaniah*. The New International Commentary on the Old Testament. Grand Rapids: Eerdmans, 1990.

Robinson, Theodore and Friedrich Horst. *Die Zwölf Kleinen Propheten*. 2nd edition. Handbuch zum Alten Testament. Tübingen: Mohr, 1954.

Rudolph, Wilhelm. "Wann wirkte Joel." In *Das ferne und nahe Worte. Festschrift L. Rost*. F. Maass, ed., 193-198. BZAW 105. Berlin: Töpelmann, 1967.

Rudolph, Wilhelm. *Haggai - Sacharja 1-8 - Sacharja 9-14 - Maleachi*. KAT 13/4. Gütersloh: Gerd Mohn, 1976.

Rudolph, Wilhelm. *Hosea*. KAT 13/1. Gütersloh: Gerd Mohn, 1966.

Rudolph, Wilhelm. *Joel - Amos - Obadja - Jona*. KAT 13/2. Gütersloh: Gerd Mohn, 1971.

Rudolph, Wilhelm. *Micha - Nahum - Habakuk - Zephanja*. KAT 13/3. Gütersloh: Gerd Mohn, 1975.

Saebø, Magne. "Chronistische Theologie/Chronistisches Geschichtswerk." *Theologische Realenzyklopädie* 8 (Berlin: De Gruyter, 1981), 74-87.

Saebø, Magne. *Sacharja 9-14. Untersuchungen von Text und Form*. Wissenschaftliche Monographien zum Alten und Neuen Testament 34. Neukirchen: Neukirchener Verlag, 1969.

Saggs, H.W.F. "Nahum and the Fall of Nineveh." *JTS* 20 (1969): 220-225.

Saggs, H.W.F. *The Might that Was Assyria*. Sidgwick & Jackson Great Civilizations Series. London: Sidgwick & Jackson, 1984.

Schmidt, Hans. "Die Komposition des Buches Jona." *ZAW* 25 (1905): 285-310.

Schmidt, L. *'De Deo'. Studien zur Literarkritik und Theologie des Buches Jona, des Gesprächs zwischen Abraham und Jahwe in Gen 18:22ff. und von Hi 1*. BZAW 143. Berlin: DeGruyter, 1976.

Schneider, Dale Allen. *The Unity of the Book of the Twelve*. Yale University PhD Diss., 1979.

Schulz, H. *Das Buch Nahum. Eine redaktionskritische Untersuchung*. BZAW 129. Berlin: DeGruyter, 1973.

Sellin, E. *Das Zwölfprophetenbuch*. 1st ed. 1922. 2 vols. Leipzig: Deichert, vol. 1 1929; vol. 2 1930.

Seybold, Klaus. "Reverenz und Gebet: Erwägungen zu der Wendung hilla pan î m." *ZAW* 88 (1976): 2-16.

Seybold, Klaus. *Die Psalmen. Eine Einführung*. Urban-Taschenbücher. Stuttgart: Kohlhammer, 1986.

Seybold, Klaus. *Profane Prophetie. Studien zum Buch Nahum*. Stuttgarter Bibelstudien 135. Stuttgart: Verlag Katholisches Bibelwerk, 1989.

Seybold, Klaus. *Satirische Prophetie. Studien zum Buch Zefanja*. Stuttgarter Bibelstudien 120. Stuttgart: Verlag Katholisches Bibelwerk, 1985.

Skehan, P.W. and A.A. Di Lella. *The Wisdom of Ben Sirach*. Anchor Bible New York: Doubleday, 1987.

Smend, Rudolf. *Die Entstehung des Alten Testaments*. 3rd ed. Stuttgart: Kohlhammer, 1984.

Smith, George Adam. *The Book of the Twelve Prophets*. 2 vols. New York: Harper and Brothers, 1928.

Smith, Ralph L. *Micah - Malachi*. Word Biblical Commentary 32. Waco: Word Books, 1984.

Snaith, Norman H. "Selah." *VT* 2 (1952): 43-56.

Snyman, S.D. "Antithesis in Malachi 1:2-5." *ZAW* 98 (1986): 436-438.

Stade, Bernhard. "Deuterozacharja. Eine kritische Studie." *ZAW* 1 (1881): 1-96.

Stade, Bernhard. "Deuterozacharja. Eine kritische Studie." *ZAW* 2 (1882): 151-172, 275-309.

Staerk, W. "Zu Habakuk 1:5-11. Geschichte oder Mythos?" *ZAW* 51 (1933): 1-28.

Steck, Odil Hannes. *Der Abschluß der Prophetie im Alten Testament. Ein Versuch zur Frage der Vorgeschichte des Kanons*. Biblisch Theologische Studien 17. Neukirchener Verlag, 1991.

Steck, Odil Hannes. *Bereitete Heimkehr. Jesaja 35 als redaktionelle Brücke zwischen dem Ersten und dem Zweiten Jesaja*. Stuttgarter Bibelstudien 121. Stuttgart: Katholisches Bibelwerk, 1985.

Stephenson, F.R. "The Date of the Book of Joel." *VT* 19 (1969): 224-229.

Stolz, Fritz. *Strukturen und Figuren im Kult von Jerusalem. Studien zur altorientalischen vor- und frühisraelitischen Religion*. BZAW 118. Berlin: De Gruyter, 1970.

Stuart, Douglas. *Hosea - Jonah*. Word Biblical Commentary 31. Waco, Texas: Word, 1987.

Thompson, John A. "The Date of Joel." In *A New Light unto My Path. Old Testament Studies in Honor of Jacob M. Myers*. H.N. Bream, ed. 453-464. Philadelphia: Temple University Press, 1974.

Thompson, John A. "The Use of Repetition in the Prophecy of Joel." In *Festschrift für E.A. Nida*. M. Black, ed., 101-110. The Hague: Mouton, 1974.

Utzschneider, Helmut. *Künder oder Schreiber? Eine These zum Problem der »Schriftprophetie« auf Grund von Maleachi 1,6-2:9*. Beiträge zur Erforschung des Alten Testaments und des Antiken Judentums 19. Frankfurt: Peter Lang, 1989.

Verhoef, Pieter. *The Books of Haggai and Malachi*. New International Commentary. Grand Rapids: Eerdmans, 1987.

Vries, J. De. "The Acrostic of Nahum in the Jerusalem Liturgy. *VT* 16 (1966): 476-481.

Vuilleumier, René and C.A. Keller. *Michée, Nahoum, Habacuc, Sophonie*. Commentaire de l'Ancien Testament 11b. Neuchâtel: Delachaux et Niestlé, 1971.

Wallis, G. "Wesen und Struktur der Botschaft Maleachis." In *Das ferne und nahe Worte. Festschrift L. Rost*. F. Maass, ed., 229-237. BZAW 105. Berlin: Töpelmann, 1967.

Walsh, Jerome T. "Jonah 2:3-10: A Rhetorical Critical Study." *Biblica* 63 (1982): 219-229.

Warmuth, G. "נקה." In *ThWAT* vol 5, 592.

Watts, John D.W. *Obadiah: A Critical Exegetical Commentary.* Grand Rapids: Eerdmans, 1969.

Watts, John D.W. *The Books of Joel, Obadiah, Jonah, Nahum, Habakkuk and Zephaniah.* Cambridge Bible Commentary. London: Cambridge University Press, 1975.

Watts, John D.W. *Vision and Prophecy in Amos.* Leiden: E.J. Brill, 1958.

Wehrle, J. *Prophetie und Textanalyse der Komposition Obadja 1-21. Interpretiert auf der Basis textlinguistischer und semiotischer Konzeptionen.* Arbeiten zu Text und Sprache im Alten Testament 28. Müncher Universitätschriften: Philosophische Fakultät: Altertumskunde und Kulturwissenschaften. St Ottilien: EOS, 1987.

Weimar, Peter. "Jon 4,5. Beobachtungen zur Entstehung der Jonaerzählung." *BN* 18 (1982): 86-109.

Weimar, Peter. "Jonapsalm und Jonaerzählung." *BZ* 28 (1984): 43-68.

Weimar, Peter. "Literarische Kritik und Literarkritik. Unzeitgemässe Beobachtungen zu Jon 1:4-16." In *Künder des Wortes. Beiträge zur Theologie der Propheten. Josef Schreiner zum 60. Geburtstag.* L. Ruppert and Peter Weimar, eds., Würzburg: Echter Verlag, 1982.

Weimar, Peter. "Obadja. Eine redaktionskritische Analyse." *BN* 27 (1985): 35-99.

Weippert, H. "Pferd und Streitwagen." In *Biblisches Reallexikon.* Tübingen: Mohr, 1977.

Weiser, Artur. *Die Propheten Hosea, Joel, Amos, Obadja, Jona, Micha. Übersetzt und erklärt.* ATD 24. Göttingen: Vandenhoeck & Ruprecht, [3]1985.

Wellhausen, Julius. *Die kleinen Propheten übersetzt und erklärt.* Skizzen und Vorarbeiten 5. Berlin: Reimer, 1892.

Westermann, Claus. *Basic Forms of Prophetic Speech.* London: Lutterworth Press, 1967.

Willi-Plein, Ina. *Prophetie am Ende. Untersuchungen zu Sacharja 9-14.* Bonner biblische Beiträge 42. Köln: Hanstein, 1974.

Wilson, Gerald Henry. *The Editing of the Hebrew Psalter.* SBL Dissertation Series 76. Chico, California: Scholars Press, 1985.

Wilson, Robert R. *Prophecy and Society in Ancient Israel.* Philadelphia: Fortress, 1980.

Wolff, Hans-Walter. "Der Aufruf zur Volksklage." *ZAW* 76 (1964): 48-56.

Wolff, Hans-Walter. *Joel und Amos.* Biblischer Kommentar 14/2. Neukirchen: Neukirchener Verlag, 1969.

Wolff, Hans-Walter. *Micha.* Biblischer Kommentar 14/4. Neukirchen: Neukirchener Verlag, 1982.

Wolff, Hans-Walter. *Obadja und Jona.* Biblischer Kommentar 14/3. Neukirchen: Neukirchener Verlag, 1977.

Yadin, Yigael. *The Art of Warfare in Biblical Lands in the Light of Archaeological Study.* 2 vols. New York: McGraw-Hill, 1963.

Zimmerli, Walter. "Vom Prophetenwort zum Prophetenbuch." *ThLZ* 104 (1979): 481-496.

Zimmerli, Walter. *Ezekiel.* 2 vols. Biblischer Kommentar 13. Neukirchen: Neukirchner Verlag, 1969.

Appendix of Allusions and Citations Noted in this Volume

→ = "draws from";   ← = "is used by"

This appendix gathers together texts demonstrating intertextual awareness. The
appendix does not characterize the extent of that awareness, only the direction.
The reader should consult the discussion of the relevant text in the body of this
work for more detailed explanations.

Amos 1:2	← Joel 4:16		Jer 25:15ff	← Obad 16
Amos 1:2	← Nah 1:4		Jer 25:15	← Jer 49:12
Amos 1:3ff	← Joel 4:1ff		Jer 49:9	← Obad 5
Amos 9:1ff	← Obad 1-5		Jer 49:12	→ Jer 25:15
Amos 9:1ff	← Obad 1		Jer 49:14-16	← Obad 1-4
Amos 9:7ff	← Obad 8		Jer 51:58	← Hab 2:13
Amos 9:11-15	← Obad 15-21		Joel 1-3	← Mal 3:10
Amos 9:12	→ Obad 17		Joel 1-2	→ 1 Kgs 8:37-39
Amos 9:13	→ Joel 4:18		Joel 1-2	← Hab 3:17
2 Chr 20:1-30	← Joel 4:9-17		Joel 1-2	← Nah 2:1
Ezek 35:1ff	← Obad 10-15		Joel 1:1ff	← Hos 14:8
Ezek 37:15-28	← Zech 11:4-17		Joel 1:1ff	← Nah 2:3
Hab 1:4	← Zeph 3:4		Joel 1:2ff	→ Hos 14
Hab 1:5-17	→ Nah 3:1ff		Joel 1:2	→ Hos 14
Hab 1:9	→ Joel 2:6-9		Joel 1:4	← Mal 3:11
Hab 2:8	→ Mic 3:10		Joel 1:4	← Nah 3:15-16
Hab 2:12	→ Mic 3:10		Joel 1:4	← Nah 3:17
Hab 2:13	→ Jer 51:58		Joel 1:5	← Joel 4:18
Hab 2:15	→ Obad 15ff		Joel 1:7	← Nah 2:3
Hab 2:17	→ Nah 1:4		Joel 1:8	→ Hos 2:3ff
Hab 3:17	→ Joel 1-2		Joel 1:9	← Joel 4:18
Hos 1:9	← Zech 13:9		Joel 1:20	← Joel 4:18
Hos 14	← Joel 1:2ff		Joel 2:2	← Joel 4:20
Hos 14:8	→ Hos 2:18ff		Joel 2:3	← Joel 4:19
Hos 14:8	→ Joel 1		Joel 2:6-9	← Hab 1:9
Hos 2:3ff	← Joel 1:8		Joel 2:10	← Joel 4:15
Hos 2:18ff	← Hos 14:8		Joel 2:13	← Nah 1:3
Hos 2:25	← Zech 13:9		Joel 2:25	← Nah 3:15-16
Hos 5:15-6:6	← Jonah 2:9f		Joel 2:25	← Nah 3:17
Isa 2:2ff	← Zech 14:10		Joel 3:4	← Mal 3:23
Isa 2:2-4	← Mic 4:1-3		Joel 4:1ff	→ Amos 1:3ff
Isa 2:7	← Zech 14:20		Joel 4:1-3	→ Joel 4:4-21
Isa 10:6f	← Nah 1:9f		Joel 4:1	← Zeph 3:20
Isa 10:17ff	← Nah 1:9f		Joel 4:4-21	← Joel 4:1-3
Isa 33:9-14	← Nah 1:4		Joel 4:9-17	→ 2 Chr 20:1-30
Isa 52:7	← Nah 2:1		Joel 4:15	→ Joel 2:10
Isa 66:16ff	← Zech 14:16ff		Joel 4:16	→ Amos 1:2
Jer 18:7-10	← Jonah 1-4		Joel 4:18	← Amos 9:13

→ = "draws from";   ← = "is used by"

Joel 4:18	→ Joel 1:20		Nah 3:15-16	→ Joel 1:4
Joel 4:18	→ Joel 1:5		Nah 3:15-16	→ Joel 2:25
Joel 4:18	→ Joel 1:9		Nah 3:17	→ Joel 1:4
Joel 4:19	→ Joel 2:3		Nah 3:17	→ Joel 2:25
Joel 4:20	→ Joel 2:2		Nah 3:18f	→ Nah 1:14
Joel 4:21	← Nah 1:3		Obad 1-5	→ Amos 9:1ff
Jonah 1-4	→ Jer 18:7-10		Obad 1-4	→ Jer 49:14-16
Jonah 2:4	← Mic 7:19		Obad 1	→ Amos 9:1ff
Jonah 2:9f	→ Hos 5:15-6:6		Obad 3f	← Mal 1:2-5
Jonah 2:9f	→ Mic 1:7		Obad 5	→ Jer 49:9
Jonah 4:2	→ Nah 1:3		Obad 8	→ Amos 9:7ff
Josh 1:2,7	← Mal 3:22		Obad 10-15	→ Ezek 35:1ff
1 Kgs 8:37-39	← Joel 1-2		Obad 15-21	→ Amos 9:11-15
Mal 1:1-14	→ Zech 8:9ff		Obad 15-21	← Hab 2:15
Mal 1:1	← Zech 9:1		Obad 16	→ Jer 25:15ff
Mal 1:1	← Zech 12:1		Obad 17	← Amos 9:12
Mal 1:2-5	→ Obad 3f		Obad 19	→ Mic 1:6
Mal 3:2f	← Zech 13:9		Zech 8:9ff	← Mal 1:1-14
Mal 3:10	→ Joel 1-3		Zech 9:1-17	← Zech 12:1-10
Mal 3:11	→ Joel 1:4		Zech 9:1	→ Mal 1:1
Mal 3:22	→ Josh 1:2,7		Zech 11:4-17	→ Ezek 37:15-28
Mal 3:23	→ Joel 3:4		Zech 12:1-10	→ Zech 9:1-17
Mic 1:6	← Obad 19		Zech 12:1	→ Mal 1:1
Mic 1:7	← Jonah 2:9f		Zech 13:9	→ Hos 1:9
Mic 3:10	← Hab 2:8		Zech 13:9	→ Hos 2:25
Mic 3:10	← Hab 2:12		Zech 13:9	→ Mal 3:2f
Mic 4:1-3	→ Isa 2:2-4		Zech 14:10	→ Isa 2:2ff
Mic 7:18-20	← Nah 1:2-3		Zech 14:16ff	→ Isa 66:16ff
Mic 7:19	→ Jonah 2:4		Zech 14:20	→ Isa 2:7
Nah 1:2-3	→ Mic 7:18-20		Zeph 3:4	→ Hab 1:4
Nah 1:3	→ Joel 2:13		Zeph 3:20	→ Joel 4:1
Nah 1:3	→ Joel 4:21			
Nah 1:3	← Jonah 4:2			
Nah 1:4	→ Amos 1:2			
Nah 1:4	← Hab 2:17			
Nah 1:4	→ Isa 33:9-14			
Nah 1:9f	→ Isa 10:6f			
Nah 1:9f	→ Isa 10:17ff			
Nah 1:11-12	← Nah 3:15-17			
Nah 1:14	← Nah 3:18f			
Nah 2:1	→ Isa 52:7			
Nah 2:1	→ Joel 1-2			
Nah 2:3	→ Joel 1			
Nah 2:3	→ Joel 1:7			
Nah 3:1ff	← Hab 1:5-17			
Nah 3:15-17	→ Nah 1:11-12			

Alphabetical Index of Biblical and Extra-Biblical Citations

Amos
1:1-9:6 45
1:1 . . . . 83, 137, 240
1:2 . . 27, 37, 43-46, 108, 115,
                  160, 167
1:3-5 120
1:4f 120
1:11f 60, 76, 77
1:12 161
3:1 14
3:9 83
4:1 . . . . 14, 83
4:6ff 6
4:7 9
4:9 177
4:13 188
5:1 14
5:2 20
5:8f 188
5:18f 239
5:20 242
6:1 83
6:4 178
7:1 100
7:4 100
7:7 100
7:14 157
8:1ff 68
8:1 100
8:8f 239
8:14 83
9 . . . . 62, 67, 68
9:1ff . 59, 64, 67, 68, 75, 78,
          79, 91, 92, 276, 278
9:1-10 73
9:1-6 66
9:1-4 . . . . 62, 64, 271
9:1 100
9:2-4 65
9:2 64
9:5f 188
9:7-15 275
9:7-10 66
9:7-8 66
9:7 67
9:8-10 66
9:8 67
9:10 150
9:11-15 . . 64, 69, 71, 72, 82
9:11 . . . . 67, 72
9:12 . . . . 72, 73, 82, 161
9:13 . . 43-46, 48, 67, 71, 276
9:14f 68

1 Chronicles
1:5 54

1:7 54
1:32 163
1:43 87
1:46 . . . . 84, 163
2:1 87
6:49 87
8:8 84
11:4-6 221
13:6 72
18:10 237
27:1 87

2 Chronicles
5:2 87
5:10 87
6:11 87
6:26f 17
6:28-30 17
6:33 72
7:3 87
7:14 72
8:2 87
8:5 154
8:6 108
8:8 87
8:9 87
9:29 64
10:17 87
11:5 154
13:12 87
13:16 87
13:18 87
14:9-17 33
16:3 87
20:1-30 . . . . . 32, 35, 36, 54
20:1ff 37
20:7 82
20:11 82
20:22 31
21:16 163
25:13 82
25:18 108
28:3 82
28:8 87
30:6 87
30:21 87
31:1 87
31:5 87
31:6 87
32:32 64
33:2 . . . . 82, 87
33:9 87
34:13 158
34:33 87
35:17 87
37:9 82

37:11 82
37:22 82
37:29 82
37:34 82

Canticles
3:6 121
4:11 108
4:15 108
5:5 119
5:15 108
7:5 108

Daniel
2:18f 255
2:37 255
2:44 255
7:10 208
8:21 54
9:18f 72
10:20 54
11:2 54

Deuteronomy
1:5 139
1:7 108
3:25 108
4:8 139
4:10 16
4:11 239
4:32 16
4:33 16
4:44 139
5:23 239
6:4 242
11:24 108
15:20f 196
17:18 139
24:1 207
24:3 207
27:3 139
27:26 139
28:10 72
28:58 139
29:21 139
29:29 139
30:10 139
31:9 139
31:11-12 139
32:15 161
32:17 161
32:46 139
33:1ff 162
33:2 160-162
33:4 140
33:8-11 196
33:29 179
34:1-12 179

34:6f 106
Esther
6:1 . . . . 207, 209
Exodus
2:15-22 163
2:15 163
3:18 258
5:3 258
8:23 258
10:22 258
15:9 82
18:8 196
19:16 239
19:18 239
20:14 196
20:18 239
24:4-7 208
24:8 . . . . 223, 224
24:15 239
24:16 239
33:9 110
34:6 106
34:7 106
Ezekiel
2:3 88
4:2 154
4:13 88
11:23 242
16:1-63 224
17:3 108
17:4 121
17:17 57
22:2 131
24:6 131
24:9 131
26:1-28:19 219
27:3-24 121
27:5 108
27:13 54
27:19 54
27:22f 29
28 53
29:9 56
29:12 . . . . 53, 56
31:3 108
31:15f 108
31:15 9
34:27 177
35 . . . . 58, 60, 68, 77-79, 91
35:3 . . . . 56, 88
35:5-6 77
35:15 77
36:20-23 196
37:15-28 232
37:16 . . . . 87, 88
37:21 88
38:13 29

39:1-16 33
43:1-3 242
43:7 88
44:6f 196
44:9 88
44:15f 196
44:15 88
47:1ff 242
47:22 88
48:11 88
Ezra
1:2 255
5:12 255
6:9f 255
7:12 255
7:21 255
7:23 255
9:11 82
9:12 82
Genesis
8:22 . . . . 239, 242
10:2 54
10:4 54
14:7 84
15:3-8 82
17:9-14 223
19:27 110
22:17 82
24:60 82
25:4 163
28:4 82
29:31 119
30:22 119
30:36 258
32f 196
32:4 84
32:31 197
34:24 82
36:35 . . . . 84, 163
40:13 258
40:18 258
40:19 258
40:21 258
44:1 87
49:1 87
Habakkuk
1:1-2:5 135
1:1-17 118, 129, 146, 150, 151
1:1 . 100, 129, 136, 137, 139,
189, 278
1:2-2:5 . . . . 129, 146
1:2-4 . . . 129, 138-140, 142,
144-146, 149, 150
1:2 139
1:3 147
1:4 . . . . 135, 139, 152
1:5-12 276

1:5-11 . . 129, 130, 140-142,
144, 145, 149, 150, 151
1:5-10 142
1:5 . . 138, 140, 141, 147, 149
1:6 . . 134, 140, 142, 147, 149
1:7 121
1:8 147
1:9 . . . . 23, 147, 148
1:10 147-149
1:11 . . . . 132, 141, 145, 147,
148, 151, 170
1:12-17 . . . . 129, 142
1:12f 129
1:12 . 130, 141-146, 149, 150
1:13-14 . . . . 143, 150
1:13f 144-146, 151
1:13 . . . . 130, 147
1:14-17 . . . . 129, 130
1:14 . . . . . 145, 147, 148, 151
1:15-17 . . 141, 143-145, 149,
151, 276
1:15f 147, 148
1:17 . . . . 147, 149, 151
2:1ff 150, 151
2:1-5 . . . 129, 130, 136, 137,
142, 144-146
2:1 . . . . . 136, 153, 154, 174
2:2-5 174
2:5ff 276
2:6ff 144, 146, 150
2:6-20 130
2:6-19 129
2:6-9 130
2:6-8 130
2:9-11 131
2:9 131
2:12-14 . . . . 131, 132
2:13 136
2:15-17 132
2:18f 133
2:20 . . . . 129, 133
3 115
3:1ff 130, 151, 174, 276, 280
3:1-19 . . 133, 136, 150, 154,
156, 157, 159, 161, 176, 180
3:1f 156
3:1 . 129, 131, 133, 136, 137,
155-158, 180
3:2ff 136
3:2 . 138, 157, 159, 160, 170,
171, 173, 174
3:3ff 227, 230
3:3-17 138
3:3-15 . . 156, 167, 168, 171,
173, 174, 179
3:3-7 . . . 160, 164, 173, 179
3:3-6 . . . . 157, 159

3:3f 230
3:3 .   133, 155, 165, 174, 180,
               227
3:4 . . . . 161, 226, 227
3:5 162
3:6f 162, 168
3:6 . . . . 171, 179
3:7 .   100, 137, 159, 165, 169,
               175
3:8-15 . . 157, 159, 160, 164,
    165, 171, 173, 174, 175, 180
3:8-11 168
3:8 . . . . 165, 172
3:9-14 172
3:9 . . . . . 133, 155, 166, 180
3:10 . . . . 167, 175
3:11 . . . . 110, 166, 168
3:12 . . . . 171, 175
3:12-14 . . . . 168, 179
3:13-14 179
3:13 . . . . 133, 155, 169, 171,
             175, 180
3:14 . . . . 169, 171, 175
3:15-16 276
3:15 . . . . 165, 172
3:16-19 . 156, 157, 160, 164,
           171, 173, 174
3:16ff 170
3:16-17 . . . . . 180, 181, 276
3:16 . . . . 136, 142, 149, 159,
          174-176, 178
3:17 . . . . 159, 176-179
3:18f 138, 159, 175
3:18 177-179
3:19 . . . . 133, 151, 155, 158,
          179, 180
Haggai
1:1 . . . . 157, 188, 201
1:3-11 201
1:10 177
1:12-15 202
1:15 201
2:1-9 201
2:1 . . . . 188, 201
2:10-19 201
2:10 201
2:11 . . . . 139, 152
2:12 152
2:18f 205
2:19 177
2:20 201
2:20-23 . . . . . . 91, 201, 202
2:23 55
Hosea
1:1ff 245
1:1 278
1:4 245

1:6 245
1:9 . . . . 235, 245
2:1ff 5
2:1 245
2:2 245
2:3ff 13, 18-21
2:8-17 19
2:9ff 21
2:10f 18
2:10 19
2:14 . . . . 19, 177
2:15 19
2:17 21
2:18ff 275
2:18f 233
2:22f 18
2:24 18
2:25 . . . . 233, 235
4:1ff 13
4:9 14
4:11 18
5:1 14
5:15-6:6 . . . . 269, 271
5:15 268
6:1-6 268
7:1 83
7:11 268
7:12 65
7:14 18
8:1 222
8:5 83
8:6 83
8:13 268
9:2 177
9:10 177
9:13 84
9:15 222
10:1 177
10:4 268
10:5 83
10:7 83
10:11 84
10:12 . . . . 6, 22
11:1ff 191
11:8 84
12:4 191
12:12 268
13:1 84
13:8 84
14 4
14:1 83
14:2ff 5, 16, 22, 24, 25
14:2-9 22
14:5-10 25
14:5ff 13, 42
14:6 . . . . 108, 115, 177
14:7 . . . . 108, 177

14:8 . . 26, 42, 108, 115, 177,
            276
Isaiah
1:1 64
1:7-9 243
1:24ff 243
2:1-4 242
2:1ff 243
2:2ff 243
2:2-4 242
2:2 242
2:7 243
2:13 108
4:3 208
5:30 239
8:2 213
10:1ff 113
10:6f 112
10:11 112
10:12 112
10:16-18 112
10:17 112
10:23 112
11:9f 132
11:9 132
13:1 137
13:10 239
14:16ff 242
21:8 153
21:11f 74, 75
22:1-14 33
23:1-14 7
23:12 20
24:23 . . . . 74, 242
26:7ff 74
26:21 131
27:1 174
27:12 75
27:13 74
30:32 237
33 171
33:9 . . . . 97, 109
33:11 109
33:12 109
33:14 109
34:5ff 161
35:2 . . . . 115, 132
37:31f 46
37:35 231
38:6 231
40:4ff 242
40:5 132
42:6f 225
47:1-15 14
47:1 20
48:1-11 14
48:1 14

48:12-16 14
48:14 14
48:16 14
50:2 97
51:21 171
52:1 97
52:2 113
52:4 113
52:7 . . . . . 97, 113, 116, 269
52:15 87
53:7 178
53:8 178
54:6 21
54:11 171
60:1-3 132
60:5 163
60:6 163
60:19 242
61:1ff 225
61:7 225
63:10 237
63:19 72
65:9 82
65:25 222
66:1ff 243
66:1 222
66:6 222
66:16ff 242, 272
66:18-24 242
66:18 132
66:19 54
66:20 . . . . 242, 243

Jeremiah
1:5 157
2:1-4:2 20
2:13 242
2:32 20
3:3 9
3:5 106
3:12 106
3:21 88
4:23 239
7:10 72
7:11 72
7:14 72
7:30 72
7:34 19
11:2 14
11:6 14
14:1-15:9 6
14:9 72
14:17 20
15:16 72
18:1-3 201
18:7-10 271
18:7f 258
18:9-10 258

18:13 20
18:14 108
19:1 201
22:6 108
23:7 88
25:14-31:44 69
25 60
25:9 242
25:11 201
25:15-29 . . . . 69, 71
25:15-28 71
25:15-17 46
25:15ff . . . 61, 70, 71, 73, 75,
78, 80, 91
25:15f 70
25:15 . . . . 62, 71
25:17-26 70
25:17 71
25:29 72
25:30 45
27:3 51
29:10 201
30:11 106
31:4 20
31:21 20
31:38-40 242
32:6-15 201
32:34 72
34:15 72
34:21 57
37:5-11 57
43:28 242
46:2-28 69
46:10 68
46:11 20
46:26 68
47:1-7 69
47:4 68
48:11 110
48:41 68
48:47 68
49:1-6 . . . . 53, 67, 69
49:7ff . . . 46, 59, 61, 67-69,
73, 79
49:7-23 62
49:7-22 69
49:8 192
49:9 . . 59, 60, 62, 65, 66, 74,
80, 90, 192, 276
49:10 192
49:12-16 61
49:12 . 46, 61, 70, 71, 75, 78,
80
49:14-16 . 60, 62, 65, 80, 90,
192, 276
49:14 . . . . 63, 80
49:16 . . . . 59, 64, 192

49:17-19 63
49:22 68
49:23-27 69
49:23 67
49:26 68
49:28-33 69
49:34-39 69
49:39 68
50-51 69
50:4 68
50:17f 152
50:20 68
50:30 68
51:2 68
51:7 70
51:11 68
51:27 121
51:28 121
51:33 68
51:34 68
51:38 136
51:40 65
51:58 132

Job
1 259
3:4 167

Joel
1-2 176
1:1ff 6, 114, 212
1:1-14 . . . . 3, 7, 13
1:1 . . . . 1, 7, 189
1:2ff 27, 42
1:2-2:17 3
1:2-2:11 44
1:2-20 3
1:2-14 13
1:2-4 . . . . 7, 11, 14, 24
1:2 15
1:4ff 205
1:4 . . . . 23, 125, 205
1:5ff 116, 276
1:5-14 7
1:5-13 11
1:5-12 10
1:5-7 . . . . 3, 7
1:5 . . . . . . 6, 17, 18, 42, 116
1:6-8 10-12
1:6f 23, 176, 205
1:7 . . 23, 116, 121, 125, 177,
205
1:8-10 . . . . 3, 8
1:8 . . . . 18, 20
1:9-13 6
1:9 42
1:10 . . . . 18, 177
1:11-12 8
1:12 177

1:13-14 8
1:13f 3, 10
1:13 10
1:14-16 11
1:15ff 10
1:15-20 3
1:15 3
1:16-20 3
1:16f 205
1:16 177
1:17-20 . . . . 6, 11
1:18 178
1:20 42
2:1ff 8, 10, 37, 50, 276
2:1-17 3
2:1-11 . . . . . . 9, 10, 12, 43
2:1-10 7
2:1 . . . . 4, 8
2:2-10 126
2:2 . . . . 10, 42, 239
2:3 . . . . 42, 46, 120
2:6-9 3
2:7 279
2:9 . . . . 49, 50
2:10 . . . . 37, 43, 45
2:11 4
2:12-17 . . . . 4, 22
2:12-14 . . . . 6, 116
2:12 8
2:13 . . . . 106, 115, 272
2:17 26
2:18ff 276
2:18-3:5 3
2:18-27 . . . . 4, 27
2:18-20 3
2:18 . . . . 3, 4, 8, 209
2:19ff 6
2:20 . . . . 7, 43, 116
2:21-24 . . . . 6, 8
2:22 177
2:23-25 205
2:23 22
2:25 . . . . 11, 125, 205
2:27 27
3:1-4:21 . . . . 6, 43
3:1ff 27
3:1-5 . . . . 4, 6, 27
3:1f 11
3:3-5 26
3:3f 239
3:4 . . . . 46, 204
3:5 . . . . 8, 46
4:1-21 . . . 1, 4, 6, 23, 26, 27,
                            48, 181
4:1ff 13, 92, 276
4:1-3 . . . . . 5, 26-28, 38, 48
4:1 . . . . 27, 47

4:2 30
4:3 46
4:4-8 . 1, 4, 5, 26, 28, 29, 32,
                38, 45, 48, 50, 51, 56,
                            276, 279
4:4 46
4:6 . . . . 46, 226
4:7-17 118
4:7 46
4:8 . . . . 30, 46
4:9-17 . . . . . 26, 28, 30, 32,
                            35-38, 54
4:9ff 212, 240, 276
4:9 46
4:11 46
4:12 46
4:14-21 41
4:14-17 . . . . 41, 43
4:14 . . . . 38, 41, 46
4:15f 41
4:15 . . . . 43, 239
4:16 . . . . 27, 43, 45, 88, 167
4:17 . . . . 46, 49, 242
4:18-21 . . . 8, 26, 28, 32, 37,
                        38, 41-43, 55
4:18 . 30, 41, 43, 45, 46, 242
4:19-21 . . . . 38, 41
4:19f 45
4:19 . 17, 46, 53, 56, 116, 161
4:21 . . . . . . 29, 46, 106, 116

John
1:21 185
1:25 185

Jonah
1-2 261
1:1-2:11 271
1:1-2:2 255
1:1-2:1 . . . . 256, 259
1:1-17 270
1:1-16 271
1:1-3 250
1:1ff 256, 260
1:1f 257
1:1 . . . . 259, 270
1:2 . . . . 251, 258
1:3-16 259
1:3 . . . . 251, 263
1:4-16 . . 248, 250, 254, 261
1:5f 251
1:5 . . . . 251, 263
1:7 . . . . 248, 251
1:8-10 263
1:8 . . . . 248, 251
1:9 . . . . 250, 264
1:10 263
1:13 263
1:14 263

1:15 264
1:16 . . . . 249, 251, 254
1:17 254
2:1-11 269
2:1f 250
2:1 . . . . 258-260, 264
2:2-10 . . . . 256, 259
2:2 264
2:3-10 . . 248, 250, 252, 256,
                261, 262, 264, 265, 266,
                            267, 271
2:3-8 . . . 254, 255, 267, 278,
                                280
2:3ff 248, 268
2:4 272
2:5-8 253
2:5 . . . . 248, 261, 266
2:6 248
2:7 248
2:8 . . . . . . 248, 261, 266, 272
2:9f . 253, 255, 268, 272, 278
2:9 . . . . . . 248, 268, 272
2:11 . . . . 250, 251, 255, 256,
                            259, 260
3-4 261
3:1ff 256
3:1-5 256
3:1-3 249
3:1f 257
3:3ff 260
3:3-10 258
3:3 . . . . 258, 259
3:4-10 249
3:4 257
3:5-4:4 257
3:6-10 256
3:6-9 256
3:9 6
4:1 . . . . 256, 258
4:2-6 259
4:2-4 . . . . 259, 261
4:2f 256
4:2 . . . . 6, 106, 115, 264, 272
4:5ff 256, 260
4:5-11 256
4:5 256-258
4:6-11 258
4:6-10 257
4:6 258
4:10 259
4:11 256

Joshua
1:2 . . . . 185, 244, 245
1:4 108
1:7 . . . . 185, 244, 245
11:17 108
12:7 108

13:2f 50
13:5f 108
15:63 221
20:4 110
24:7 239

Judges
1:21 221
3:3 108
5:4f 160, 161
5:4 .... 84, 162
9:15 108
9:33 121
9:44 121
20:6 84
20:37 121

1 Kings
8:35-36 17
8:37-39 17
8:43 72
9:13 108
10:2 29
10:15 121
12:17 87
14:24 .... 82, 87
18:1-16 270
21:26 .... 82, 87

2 Kings
7:1 16
7:2 16
7:19 16
14:9 108
14:23-29 256
14:23-25 270
14:25 .... 248, 268
16:3 .... 82, 87
17:7-9 87
17:8 82
17:13 87
18:4 87
18:32 177
19:21 20
19:32f 46
19:34 231
20:6 231
21:2 .... 82, 87
21:9 87
23:8 236
24:2f 51
25:1ff 152
25:27-30 169

Lamentations
1:9 172
1:15 20
2:1 222
2:13 20

Leviticus
6:4 121

16:23 121
19:18 106
20:24 82
25:46 82

Luke
1:17 185

Malachi
1:1ff ... 198, 235, 246, 278
1:1-14 .. 182, 187, 189, 196,
        200, 203, 204, 272
1:1 .. 182, 183, 187-189, 217,
        244, 246, 277, 278
1:2ff 90
1:2-5 . 91, 161, 182-184, 186,
        187, 190, 192, 193, 194,
        196, 197, 277
1:2-4 .... 161, 211
1:2f 199
1:4 199
1:5ff 150
1:6ff 197, 235
1:6-2:9 ...... 182-184, 187,
        192-196, 211
1:6-2:3 191
1:6-14 195
1:6-10 195
1:6 ..... 190, 193, 194, 209
1:7 194
1:8-10 .... 194, 197
1:8 199
1:9 .... 197, 199
1:10 199
1:11-14 .. 27, 185, 194, 198,
        272
1:11 259
1:12 .... 177, 194
1:13 199
1:14 .... 182, 198
2:1-9 .... 194, 195
2:2 .... 194, 197
2:5 194
2:8 212
2:9 194
2:10-16 ...... 182-184, 193
2:10-12 182
2:10 183
2:11-13 186
2:14 21
2:17-3:5 ...... 182-184, 193
3:1 .... 186, 200
3:2f 235
3:3 276
3:6-12 ... 182-184, 191, 193
3:8f 205
3:8 205
3:9 205
3:10f ... 191, 205, 276, 277

3:10 205
3:11 .... 177, 205
3:12 205
3:13-21 .. 182-184, 193, 194
3:15 .... 193, 206
3:16ff 212, 277
3:16-24 211
3:16-21 206
3:16-18 . 206, 208, 209, 276
3:16 207
3:17 193
3:22-24 . 182, 183, 185, 187,
        189, 204, 206, 209, 212, 279
3:22-23 202
3:22 .... 185, 244-246
3:23f 185
3:23 204

Mark
4:35-41 256

Matthew
11:14 185
16:14 185
17:3ff 185
27:9f 213
27:47 185
27:49 185

Micah
1:1ff 249
1:1-7 .... 78, 83, 248
1:2ff 60, 69, 276, 277
1:2-9 268
1:2-7 .... 84, 115, 266
1:2 248
1:3 248
1:4 .... 167, 248
1:5 83
1:6 .... 82, 84, 91, 177
1:7 268
2:12f 178, 275
3:9 14
3:10 .... 131, 132
3:12 177
4-5 275
4:1ff 242, 243
4:1-4 242
4:1-3 242
4:6f 47
4:14 154
5:1-15 223
5:2ff 222
5:2 88
6:1 87
6:15 177
7 275
7:1ff 171
7:2 131
7:8 105

7:8-20 . . . . 8, 110
7:8ff   113, 115, 124, 142, 275
7:10 105
7:11-13 149
7:12f 150
7:12 223
7:13 111
7:14 . . . . 108, 115, 150, 166,
                   170, 178
7:18-20 107
7:18 105
7:19 . . . . 272, 278

Nahum

1:1 . . . . 64, 93, 99, 100, 111,
                   137, 189, 278
1:2ff 96, 276
1:2-2:3 103
1:2-8 . 93, 100-103, 105, 109,
         113, 115, 122, 124, 167,
                181, 275, 280
1:2-6 102
1:2-3 . . . . 103, 105-107
1:2 . . . . 95, 101
1:3-6 101
1:3 . . . . 115, 272
1:4 . . . 97, 101, 105-109, 115,
                   133, 177
1:5 . . . . 106, 110, 111
1:6 . . 95, 105, 106, 109, 110,
                   112
1:7-8 . . . . 101, 106
1:7 . . . 95, 101, 106, 110-112
1:8 . . . 99, 110, 112, 126, 167
1:9ff 100, 116
1:9-11   93, 109, 112, 113, 126
1:9-10 112
1:9 . . . 95, 101, 105, 109, 112
1:9f 100, 111, 115, 122,
                   124, 275
1:10 . . . . . 95, 109, 111, 116
1:11ff 123
1:11-14 122
1:11-12 114
1:11 . . . . . 96, 100, 111, 114
1:12ff 113
1:12-13 . . . . 114, 275
1:12f 8, 96, 109
1:12 . . 93, 101, 111, 113, 114,
                   124
1:13 113
1:14 . . 96, 111, 113, 114, 123
1:15 97
2:1-3 . . . . 113, 275
2:1 . . . . 93, 96, 97, 113, 116,
                118, 149, 269
2:2 . . . . 96, 126
2:3 . . . . 96, 116

2:4-14 . . . . 114, 116
2:4-13 . . . . 93, 96, 113, 123
2:4-8 123
2:7 99
2:9-11 123
2:9 100
2:12-3:6 95
2:12-13 123
2:12f 117
2:14 . . . . 96, 117, 123
3:1ff   . 23, 100, 142, 148, 276
3:1-19 . . 117, 142, 146-148,
               151, 152, 154
3:1-15 114
3:1-14 123
3:1-7 123
3:1-4 . . . . . . 117, 118, 127
3:1 . . . . 93, 96
3:2f 96
3:2 147
3:3 147
3:4-7 148
3:4 . . . . . 96, 118, 147, 149
3:5-7 . . . . 96, 117-119
3:5f 119
3:5 . . . . 100, 147, 149
3:6 128
3:7 . . . . 95, 100, 147
3:8-19 96
3:8-17 . . . . 117, 118
3:8-11 . . . . . 118, 123, 149
3:8f 147, 148
3:8 . . . . 85, 97, 98, 119, 147
3:9f 119
3:9 . . . . 147, 164
3:11 119
3:12-15 . . . . 119, 123
3:12 147
3:14-15 120
3:14 . . . . 147, 148
3:15-17   . 116, 120, 121, 125,
                   148
3:15-16 . . . . 124, 128, 275
3:15 23
3:16-17 . . . . 114, 123
3:16 147
3:17 23
3:18-19 . . . . 122, 123
3:18f   114, 117, 120, 148, 149
3:18 . . . . 147, 148
3:19 . . . . 128, 147, 149

Nehemiah

1:3 50
1:4f 255
2:4 255
2:11ff 50
2:20 255

3:31 121
4:7 49
6:15 50
9:15 82
9:17 106
9:22-25 82
9:32 196
13:14 208
13:20 121
13:23f 49

Numbers

12:1 163
14:18 106
21:20 84
25:10-13 196
25:15 163
31:1-11 163

Obadiah

1ff 59, 192
1-15 . . . . 89, 91
1-14 . . . . 58, 70, 72
1-9 . . . . 58, 73, 76
1-5   . 59-62, 80, 90, 91, 271,
                   276
1-4 . . . . 65, 67
1   46, 59, 63, 64, 80, 270, 278
2-4 . . . . 59, 65
2 . . . . 59, 64
3-4 191
3 . . . . 63, 91, 192
4 65
4f 192
5-6 74
5f 75
5 . . . . 63, 66, 67
7 . . . . 46, 192
8-21 . . . . 59, 68
8-14 277
8f 58, 67, 68
8 . . . . 59, 67, 68, 192
9 . . . . 46, 67, 76, 77, 161
10-14   58, 68, 75-77, 172, 248
10 . . . . 46, 192
11ff 249
11-14 . . . . 24, 270
11 . . . . 46, 248, 270
13 . . . . 76, 248
14 79
15ff 68, 133
15-21   . 58, 71, 73-75, 79, 89,
                   91, 276
15a,16-21 69
15   . . . 46, 60, 70, 76, 78, 79,
                   89, 91
16-21 78
16ff 70
16-17 89

16 . . . 46, 60, 64, 70-73, 80,
              89, 90, 106
17-21 . . 71-73, 79, 86, 90, 91
17-18 90
17 . . . . . 4, 46, 74, 77-79, 81
18 . . . 46, 59, 74, 77, 78, 80,
              81, 85, 91, 192
19-21 . . . . 81, 90
19f 59, 72, 74, 89
19 . . . . . . 46, 77, 83-85, 91
20 . . . . . . 46, 72, 77, 85-87
21 . . . 46, 59, 72, 74, 77, 79,
              88, 89

Proverbs
1:19 131
5:18 21
10:7 207
15:27 131

Psalms
3:3 160
4:1 158
6:1 158
7:1 158
18:1-12 239
18:8 167
18:32 161
18:34 179
44:2f 174
44:2 140
44:4 82
46:4 167
49:2 14
50:22 161
54:1 158
55:1 158
67:1 158
67:2 160
68:9 162
68:23 108
69:5 87
69:29 208
69:36 82
72:8 223
72:16 108
74:12-15 174
76:1 158
82:2 160
83:10 163
86:1 . . . . 156, 174
86:15 106
90:1 . . . . 156, 174
90:7 156
90:16 140
92:13 108
97:2 239
99:5 222
102:1 . . . . 156, 174

102:16-24 156
103:8 106
103:9 106
104:16 108
111:4 207
113f 196
114:7 161
139:16 208
139:19 161
140:4 156
140:6 156
142:1 . . . . 156, 174
143:6 156
145:8 106

Ruth
1:2 84
1:6 84

1 Samuel
6:1 84
16:3 87
19:24 121
23:27 121
27:7 84
27:8 121
27:10 121
27:11 84
30:1 121
30:14 121
30:15 65

2 Samuel
2:31 196
5:6f 221
6:2 72

Zechariah
1:1-6 202
1:1 . . . . 157, 201, 213
1:2-6 200-202
1:4 201
1:5f 201
1:6 . . . . 150, 201
1:7 201
1:8 100
1:9 202
1:12 201
1:18 100
1:19 202
1:21 202
2:1 100
2:2 202
2:4 202
2:10 201
2:11 202
2:12 202
2:17 201
3:1 100
3:2 202
3:6 201

3:7 201
3:10 177
3:13 201
4:2 . . . . 100, 202
4:5 202
4:7 202
4:13 202
5:1 100
5:2 202
5:3-4 201
5:5 100
5:6 202
5:10 202
6:1 100
6:4 202
6:9-15 202
6:15 201
7-8 277
7:1-8:23 197
7:1-14 201
7:1-3 198
7:1 . . . . 201, 202, 279
7:3 . . . . 197, 198
7:4 202
7:5-7 201
7:5 . . . . 197, 202
7:8 202
7:9-14 200
7:9 202
8:1-23 201
8:1 202
8:2 202
8:3 202
8:4 202
8:6 202
8:7 202
8:9ff . . . 187, 198, 235, 278
8:9-23 . . 189, 203, 204, 210
8:9-15 200
8:9-13 198
8:12 . . . . 177, 199
8:14-17 150
8:14 202
8:15 199
8:16 199
8:17 199
8:18f 198
8:18 202
8:19 202
8:20-23 . . 27, 198, 242, 272
8:20 202
8:21f 197
8:22f 242
8:23 202
9:1-17 . . 216, 227, 228, 233
9:1-10 216
9:1-8 . . . . 216, 230

9:1-7 ... 188, 218-221, 228, 230, 231
9:1 . 187, 188, 217, 221, 223, 226, 244, 246, 277, 278
9:2-4 230
9:2 220
9:3 .... 154, 219, 228
9:4 219
9:5 219
9:7 ..... 221, 223, 226, 228
9:8-10:12 218
9:8ff 228
9:8 . 221, 222, 226, 227, 230, 231
9:9-13 ...... 222, 226, 227, 229-232, 234, 236
9:9f 169, 221, 222, 231
9:9 222
9:10 .... 83, 223, 226
9:11-17 216
9:11-13 223
9:11 .... 222, 223, 225
9:12 225
9:13 .. 54, 83, 216, 219, 222, 225-227, 231, 280
9:14-17 .. 222, 226-228, 230
9:14 .... 227, 230
9:15 .... 227, 230, 231
9:16 .... 218, 223, 233
10:1-3 .... 216, 233
10:1f 233
10:2 .... 223, 229, 233, 235
10:3-11:3 216
10:7 83
11:1-17 218
11:2 7
11:4 .... 228, 229
11:4-17 . 188, 215, 216, 230, 232, 234, 245, 246
11:12f 213
11:13 201
11:14 .... 244, 245
11:17 .... 217, 234
12:1-13:9 216
12:1-13:6 .. 234, 236, 246
12:1-13:2 233
12:1-13:1 215
12:1-10 .... 231, 233
12:1-9 .... 215, 232
12:1 .... 187, 188, 217, 244, 246, 277, 278
12:2-13:6 272
12:2 238
12:3 218
12:4 218
12:6 .... 218, 231
12:7-13:1 222

12:8 .... 218, 231
12:9 218
12:10ff 233
12:11-13 233
12:11 218
12:12-14 .... 233, 234
13:1 .... 218, 233
13:2-6 .... 215, 233
13:2 .... 218, 233
13:3-6 233
13:3-5 233
13:4 218
13:7-9 .. 188, 215, 217, 233, 234, 244, 246
13:8f 242, 245
13:9 .... 235, 246
14:1ff 272, 279
14:1-21 . 214, 216, 230-232, 234, 236, 241, 243, 246, 247
14:1-15 232
14:1-5 .... 237, 239, 240
14:1 .... 218, 236
14:2 246
14:3 .... 236, 237
14:4 .... 218, 236
14:5 240
14:6f 239, 240
14:6 .... 218, 236
14:8-11 .... 237, 240
14:8 .... 218, 236
14:9 .... 218, 236, 240
14:10 ...... 236, 240, 242
14:11 237
14:12-15 237
14:12 .... 237, 238
14:13 ...... 218, 236, 238
14:14 .... 237, 238
14:15 243
14:16ff 242, 272
14:16 .... 237, 238
14:17-19 237
14:17 238
14:18f 237, 238
14:18 238
14:20-21 237
14:20f 242, 243
14:20 .... 218, 236
14:21 .... 218, 236
Zephaniah
1:1ff 155
1:2f 276
1:3 178
1:4 83
1:15 .... 176, 180, 239
2:3 169
2:8-11 53
2:12 164

3:4 139
3:9ff 171
3:9-19 275
3:10 164
3:11-12 169
3:12 171
3:14-20 8
3:18-20 .... 47, 48
3:20 .... 47, 48

Extra-Biblical Works

1 Enoch
82:1f 208
93:2 208
1 Maccabees
4:29 236
5:65 236
Jubilees
23:32 208
30:21 208
Judith
5:8 255
6:19 255
11:11 255
Sirach
49:10 ...... 209, 247, 259
49:12 272
Testament of Asher
2:10 208
Testament of Levi
5:4 208
Tobit
10:11f 255

BEIHEFTE ZUR ZEITSCHRIFT FÜR DIE ALTTESTAMENTLICHE WISSENSCHAFT

Groß-Oktav · Ganzleinen

HARALD-MARTIN WAHL

Der gerechte Schöpfer

Eine redaktions- und theologiegeschichtliche Untersuchung
der Elihureden — Hiob 32—37

XVI, 246 Seiten. 1993. ISBN 3-11-013637-6 (Band 207)

FRIEDRICH FECHTER

Bewältigung der Katastrophe

Untersuchungen zu ausgewählten
Fremdvölkersprüchen im Ezechielbuch

X, 350 Seiten. 1992. ISBN 3-11-013642-2 (Band 208)

RUDOLF MEYER

Beiträge zur Geschichte von Text und Sprache des Alten Testaments

Gesammelte Aufsätze

Herausgegeben von Waltraut Bernhardt

VIII, 259 Seiten. 1 Abbildung. 1993. ISBN 3-11-013695-3 (Band 209)

JEAN-MARIE HUSSER

Le songe et la parole

Étude sur le rêve et sa fonction dans l'ancien Israël

IX, 294 Seiten. 1994. ISBN 3-11-013719-4 (Band 210)

THEODOR LESCOW

Das Stufenschema

Untersuchungen zur Struktur alttestamentlicher Texte

X, 282 Seiten. 1992. ISBN 3-11-013768-2 (Band 211)

Walter de Gruyter Berlin · New York

BEIHEFTE ZUR ZEITSCHRIFT
FÜR DIE ALTTESTAMENTLICHE WISSENSCHAFT

Groß-Oktav · Ganzleinen

HANS-JÜRGEN ZOBEL

Altes Testament —
Literatursammlung und Heilige Schrift

Gesammelte Aufsätze zur Entstehung, Geschichte und Auslegung
des Alten Testaments

Herausgegeben von Julia Männchen und Ernst-Joachim Waschke

VIII, 306 Seiten. 1993. ISBN 3-11-013982-0 (Band 212)

BODO SEIDEL

Karl David Ilgen und die Pentateuchforschung
im Umkreis der sog. Älteren Urkundenhypothese

Studien zur Geschichte der exegetischen Hermeneutik
in der späten Aufklärung

XII, 363 Seiten. 1993. ISBN 3-11-013833-6 (Band 213)

LUDWIG SCHMIDT

Studien zur Priesterschrift

VIII, 281 Seiten. 1993. ISBN 3-11-013867-0 (Band 214)

UDO RÜTERSWÖRDEN

dominium terrae

Studien zur Genese einer alttestamentlichen Vorstellung

IX, 205 Seiten. 1993. ISBN 3-11-013948-0 (Band 215)

CAROLYN PRESSLER

The View of Women Found in the
Deuteronomic Family Laws

IX, 127 pages. 1993. ISBN 3-11-013743-7 (Volume 216)

Walter de Gruyter

Berlin · New York